Intergenerational
Relationships

Intergenerational Relationships

Edited by **Vjenka Garms-Homolová**
Freie Universität Berlin

Erika M. Hoerning
*Max Planck Institute for
Human Development and Education,
Berlin*

Doris Schaeffer
Freie Universität Berlin

1984

C. J. Hogrefe, Inc.

Lewiston, NY · Toronto

HQ
799.95
.I57
1984

Library of Congress Cataloging in Publication Data
Main entry under title:
Intergenerational relationships.
   Bibliography: p.
   1. Adulthood – Addresses, essays, lectures. 2. Age
groups – Addresses, essays, lectures. 3. Conflict of
generations – Addresses, essays, lectures. 4. Alienation
(Social sciences) – Addresses, essays, lectures. 5. Power
(Social sciences) – Addresses, essays, lectures.
I. Garms-Homolová, Vjenka, 1944–   . II. Hoerning,
Erika M., 1941–   . III. Schaeffer, Doris, 1953–

HQ799.95.I57 1984   305.2   84-6661
ISBN 0-88937-007-9

Canadian Cataloguing in Publication Data
Main entry under title:
Intergenerational relationships
Based on the International Symposium on Intergenerational Relationships
held in Berlin, Feb. 1983.
Bibliography: p.
ISBN 0-88937-007-9
1. Interpersonal relations – Congresses. 2. Conflict
of generations – Congresses. 3. Family – Congresses.
I. Garms-Homolová, Vjenka, 1944–   II. Hoerning,
Erika M., 1941–   III. Schaeffer, Doris, 1953–
IV. International Symposium on Intergenerational Relationships
(1983 : Berlin, Germany).

HM132.I58 1984   302.4   C84-098589-4

Copyright © 1984 by C. J. Hogrefe, Inc.

C. J. Hogrefe, Inc.
P. O. Box 51
Lewiston, NY 14092

Canadian Edition published by
C. J. Hogrefe, Inc.
525 Eglinton Avenue East
Toronto, Ontario M4P 1N5

Printed in Canada

ISBN 0 88937 007 9

Table of Contents

Preface

The idea of compiling a volume on intergenerational relationships arose in 1981. We were working at the time on stereotypes in everyday communication among members of different age groups. While studying the communication structure of interactions between students of medicine and the social sciences and older people, we observed certain schemata which indicated that a considerable distance, not to say alienation, existed between the life worlds of the two groups. Surprisingly, even those young people who had regular contacts with the elderly seemed to possess only a limited knowledge of their actual, everyday lives. The same was true for the aged — despite active contacts, they too had very little insight into the life world of their younger contemporaries. This was indicated by the analysis we made of the interpretation patterns used by each group.

Our attempts to discover the conditions that shape such patterns gave rise to a number of questions which far transcended our original inquiry. We began to wonder what consequences largely age-segregated environments of experience — young people's discos, bars, and "alternative culture" or the senior citizen world of the elderly — might have for the formation and continuance of the socio-cultural orientations and values of each group. What role do generational identity and specific generational consciousness play in this regard? What influence do they exert? Can belonging to a subculture superimpose upon the relevance of age group or even generational membership and, in the end, even work to counteract the progressed age differentiation of society? What significance does membership in a generation have in everyday life and interaction between different age groups?

These and many other questions led us to go more deeply into the problem of relationships among the generations. It soon became evident that in different spheres of society these relationships are given quite unequal attention. While public interest has continually grown over recent years, making intergenerational relationships a topic of ongoing discussion especially during periods when social and political problems are acute, the academic and scholarly world has devoted only sporadic attention to the subject.

In public life and through the media we are daily confronted with problems that result — seemingly or actually — from generational succession and from relationships between generations. The turbulence of those ostensibly generational conflicts of the late 1960s and early 1970s, when young people began dismantling established structures in all areas of life, has since subsided; yet muteness and estrangement still obviously reign between those who are firmly established in the framework of economic and political power and those on the verge of adulthood who are experimenting with new lifestyles in alternative communities or simply championing new fashions and new looks.

The sensitive spots of intergenerational relationships are also evident at their natural, "biologically determined" source — in the coexistence of familial lineage generations. The years gained as a result of increased life expectancy — as parents of grown-up children, as grandparents, great-grandparents, and even great-great-grandparents — bring numerous and historically unprecedented problems in their wake. The extent of contacts and of association or autonomy of the members of multi-generation families must be negotiated anew, since adequate patterns are not available. Ever since the preindustrial age the family has had to delegate many of its functions (e.g., certain areas of the education and socialization of offspring) to outside institutions, and now it is increasingly confronted with other tasks such as support of the elderly, often of two or three generations simultaneously. Such developments, imprecisely described in popular or pseudo-scientific media, have nourished a variety of myths, such as that of old people abandoned by their families, or of women who attempt to shift responsibility for their children and forbears to social institutions, or the myth of the past golden age of family life ...

Not only in multi-generation families have the mutual commitments of lineage generations changed. The growing proportion of the aged within the population has increased the burdens arising from the generational contract. The ghost of empty social security coffers and unbearably high social budgets is haunting the public and prompting experts to make pessimistic prognoses for the future. The danger of economically determined generational or age conflicts is being trumpeted on all hands, not lastly due to such structural problems as high youth unemployment. These concerns have spurred debate on redistribution of scarce jobs and restructuring of the lifetime working period.

Numerous other examples might be given to illustrate the scope of public interest in the subject of intergenerational relationships. This volume, however, is more than simply a reaction to the current political explosiveness of the issue. More central are the obvious deficits that exist in the scientific discussion. The fact that questions of intergenerational coexistence are usually considered more implicitly than explicitly, sporadically rather than systematically, and more within subdisciplines than from the complex perspective they deserve, creates the impression that discussion in this area has stagnated.

This statement holds true despite the considerable amount of data which has accumulated within various social scientific subdisciplines on selected problems in intergenerational relationships. Data of this kind, as we intend to show later, may well be adequate to form a picture of a socio-historic moment or to provide a description which moves within narrow limits. Examples from youth and family research show, however, that neither such data in themselves nor their ahistorical interpretation can help us to overcome ideological biases and contribute to an understanding of the dynamics of socio-cultural change, which traditionally has been closely associated with generational succession.

The foregoing statements elucidate the intention we have pursued in publishing this book: We wished to provide insight into those fields of research where the complex of intergenerational relationships is currently being probed. In this volume, various themes and a multitude of empirical findings have been brought together in an attempt to shed light on the nature of relations among the generations today and on the consequences of these relations for the community and its members. This, of course, implies presenting and discussing differing theoretical and methodological approaches in which more traditional lines of thought confront attempts at working out new conceptions. We have encouraged scholars of quite diverse backgrounds to air their views, a diversity that reflects their membership in a particular discipline or their adherence to a certain school of thought. The partially controversial analyses and standpoints in these contributions should provide incentives and motivation for a revival of scientific discussion on the problem of intergenerational relationships.

Intergenerational Relationships has been designed for a wide audience. It is intended to serve as a sourcebook to supplement and complement existing literature for researchers, practitioners, graduate and post-graduate students, as well as professionals and policymakers for youth, the elderly, and social security.

The aim of communicating both what we know and what we need to know about intergenerational relationships today and in the coming decades, characterizes the four chapters of this book. They are preceded by an introduction where we locate the theme within the context of scientific tradition, investigating theorems and also the less pregnant approaches for the perspectives they contain on the *relationships* among generations.

The first chapter comprises a retrospective of the development of intergenerational relationships from the pre- and early industrial age down to the present day. The significance of generations for the historical development of civilization, the process of societal age differentiation, and hence also the age-related distribution and transmission of such resources as power, property, etc. are discussed.

Chapter Two is dedicated to present-day forms of coexistence within the multigeneration family. Its first section deals with attempts to approach the problem of cohesion of familial generations via a solidarity model based on Durkheim's work. The second part of Chapter Two has a primarily descriptive character. Its subject is the functions which members of various lineage generations fulfill for one another. Here the contributions focus on families of several generations of adults, investigating the consequences of functional distribution within these families for the members of each lineage generation, and concentrating particularly on the burden which devolves upon women. Implications of the theme for social policy are touched upon, and methodological considerations are raised in almost every contribution to this chapter.

The title of Chapter Three, "Distance and Alienation of Life Worlds," indicates that here the authors attempt to shed light on the realms of experience of each of the age groups in our highly age-differentiated society. Youth subcultures, alternative movements and lifestyles, as well as the senior citizens' culture of the elderly which is apparently *in statu nascendi*, are investigated, particularly their linkage with what Karl Mannheim called "generation." Generational and age-related conflicts and interactional problems between members of different age groups are discussed here as one of the phenomena of polarization of life worlds.

The fourth and final chapter takes the reader back to the theoretical conceptions on which analyses of the character and relevance of intergenerational relationships are based. Though the term generation and the generation concept are the central issues here, an attempt is also made to distinguish this conception from other (related) ones such as cohorts, age groups, etc. Of significance here is a discourse on the theoretical scope and empirical usefulness of the generation concept, which, though alluded to in the foregoing chapters, is discussed here as the principal focus.

We would like to thank all of the authors who cooperated on this volume and who participated in the Symposium on Intergenerational Relationships (Berlin,

February 1983) which preceded this publication. Our particular gratitude is owed to those three institutions whose financial and technical support contributed substantially to the publication of this book: The Max Planck Institute for Human Development and Educational Research, Berlin; the Volkswagen Foundation, Hannover; and the Institute for Social Medicine at the Freie Universität Berlin. Our thanks go also to the many assistants and helpers who performed so well those countless workaday tasks without which no volume of this kind would ever appear.

The present volume is a cooperative production of its three editors. In numerous discussions we worked out the underlying conception and determined how each chapter was to contribute to the whole. We split up the editorial work on the individual contributions, while the Introduction, "Intergenerational Relationships — Approaches in Theory and Research," was a cooperative effort. The author of the introductions to Chapters One and Three is Doris Schaeffer. Vjenka Garms-Homolová wrote the introductory texts for both parts of the chapter on "The Multi-Generational Family," and Erika M. Hoerning prefaced Chapter Four, "The Generation Concept and Tendencies in Research." Translations of foreign-language contributions were provided by the authors themselves.

Berlin, 1984   Vjenka Garms-Homolová

X

Intergenerational Relationships: Approaches in Theory and Research

As a universal theme of human history, L. Feuer once characterized the relations among generations. For millennia generations and their succession have represented the continuity and development of societies and cultures. The generational relationship figures as an embodiment of the transmission of material and immaterial values, but also of those conflicts and breaches which spur change and innovation.

Much can be learned about the relations among generations from the plethora of material which has come down to us in the shape of the cultural and religious heritage of past societies. Yet these depictions of lineage and tribal development, of blood relation and the life cycle, are not so much authentic descriptions of generational coexistence but images of the dynamics and continuity of these societies. These depictions provide insights into social order, hierarchic structures, and rise and fall of earlier forms of human coexistence. The history of a respective past society is transmitted to us primarily in terms of a genealogical paradigm, with the vital succession of generations as a symbol of continuity. In the descriptions of this succession we can recognize the laws and rhythms which govern sociohistoric development.

The genealogical paradigm illustrates the power relationships which predominated in a particular era and the changes to which they were subject, changes in traditions and the replacement of existing *Weltanschauung* by new spiritual streams, as these appear in descriptions of tribal rivalries, conflicts between fathers and sons, or of the next generation's accession to the house, power, or land of their ancestors. In this context the term "generation" already takes on a meaning akin to that currently attached to it. It is an expression of participation in certain historic events and existing orientations, norms, and values. The individual was predestined for this participation by birth (entry into existence), together with others born at the same time. And this participation would seem to have relevance for the shaping of his generation and its specific consciousness, for upon it depended whether that generation would become a driving force in history, an actor in social change, a vehicle of cultural and intellectual development.

Generations – Traditional Perspectives

Yet despite this tradition and undisrupted interest in the relations among generations, scientific concern with the subject is of a relatively recent date. Not until the 19th century did "the generations" become an integral part of scientific research. This development is closely associated with the names of the positivists (August Comte, 1798–1857; Jean-Louis Giraud/Soulavie, 1753–1813; John Stuart Mill, 1806–1873) as well as with the work of Gustav Rümelin (1815–1889) on the term, duration, and historical significance of the generation. Rümelin, Leopold von Ranke (1795–1886) – with his thoughts on the role of generations in history – and Ottokar Lorenz (1832–1907) who attempted to provide a genealogical foundation for the generation theory: they all belong to the "German language tradition" of scientific work on the generation problem.

These "fathers" of generation research all shared an interest in the quantitative aspects of historical development: they searched for the laws underlying historical rhythms, and for an explanation of the pace of history and progress.

These scholars already dealt with a number of problems which have continued to arise in connection with the concept of generations and intergenerational relationships down to the present day:
- The problem of the duration and demarcation of a generation (Rümelin and Soulavie);
- the significance of life expectancy for the development and structure of society (Comte, Mill, Lorenz); and
- the mechanism of historical change through generational succession (Comte) and periodical appearance of innovative tendencies.

The attempts made at the time to solve these problems must be judged today against the background of two streams of scientific thought. To historicism, which reached its peak in the early 19th century, they owe the method of reconstructive comprehension based on discovered materials and reprocessed sources. The quantitative, descriptive procedure, however, had its inception in the natural sciences (e.g., statistics with Rümelin and biology with Lorenz), whose spell on the social sciences grew ever stronger in the course of the 19th century.

A new tradition of theorems on the problem of generations was founded by Wilhelm Dilthey, the historian and philosopher. In his work the influence of *Lebensphilosophie* is quite traceable: his attention concentrated on questions of experience, and on biography and autobiography as reconstructions of experiential contexts. What was new about Dilthey's generation concept – as Mannheim later noted – was its shift of emphasis from chronological simultaneity to the qualitative category of a historical situation experienced in common. Another new factor which was to exert great influence on future thinking was Dilthey's emphasis on youth, those "years of receptivity" during which the emerging generation acquired the "accumulated spiritual content" ("assets of intellectual culture"). At the same time, Dilthey reasoned, the young generation – able to absorb the cultural heritage – would come under the influence of present-day life and the current cultural situation, which he considered particularly crucial in forming a generation. The "dependence on the same great events and transformations" that appeared in "their age of receptivity" and which tied the generation into "a homogeneous whole" are found again in Karl Mannheim's concept and in successive work.

In the 19th century nearly all the essential aspects of modern theoretizing on generations were known, but no theory of generations was produced. Advanced theoretical constructs did not appear until the 20th century, particularly following World War I. These are bound up with the names of François Mentré in France, José Ortega y Gasset in Spain, and Karl Mannheim in Germany.

A "collective stage of mind embodied in a group of human beings" (Mentré) and "sharing as essential destiny" were thought to characterize generational unity. Yet this consciousness of unity and the generation itself were shaped less by historical or political events than by spiritual transformation (Mentré) and intellectual thought (Ortega). These are key concepts which Mannheim refined in his thinking.

Karl Mannheim formulated his socioscientific conception of generations in terms of the constitutive traits of generation location, generation as an actuality and generation unit. This was the quintessence of Mannheim's search for classes and other subgroups in a society caught up in rapid social change. Mannheim described the vital succession of generations in terms of a continual renewal of the participants in the cultural process. The respective generation takes on the character of a new participant in the cultural process as a consequence of its particular location in sociohistorical space. It is this factor, together with the phenomenon of varying stratification of experience, which distinguished the generations from one another.

The location of a particular generation in sociohistorical space is the precondition for the formation of generation as an actuality, which bears a similarity to class membership. A generation *unit*, however, develops only when a conscious bond between individuals arises. This unit does not exclude the possibility that polar interpretation schemes may exist within it.

The process of social transformation determines the qualitative differences between one generation and those that succeed it. The more rapid this process, the greater will be the potential of the respective generation to react to a changed situation by bringing forth new entelechies. Conveyor of new entelechies, according to Mannheim, is youth, the formative phase in a person's life. Adults and older members of society, he conceded, have only the possibility to modify sociocultural orientations and value systems, in order to bring new impulses into conformance with existing experiences.

The process of social and cultural change is also constitutive for the problem of intergenerational relationships since it determines the transmission of experiences, values, etc. to the succeeding generation. If this process is very rapid in pace, new experience patterns which differ from traditional ones will be formed with comparable swiftness (cf. also Dreitzel, this volume). And while these consolidate, new impulses arise for generational configurations.

With Mannheim's generation model, discussion on the problem of generations culminated. As early as the 1930s interest had already begun to decline. Thus the history of the reception of Mannheim's concept is, initially, a history of its *non*-reception (Kohli, 1978, 34). Though in the social sciences, interest has never flagged in the topic of generations, research into it has shifted increasingly to subdisciplines of sociology. No comprehensive theoretical scheme with universalist character of the type attempted by Comte, Mill, Dilthey, and Mannheim has since appeared, with the possible exception of Julian Marías' "universal mechanics of generational succession."

Essential Features in Current Research

The influences of "classical" generation theories are ubiquitous not only in the social sciences; psychology, pedagogy, and cultural history have all been affected even though the reference is not always explicit. Sociologists hark back to the tradition of classical concepts — particularly to Mannheim's concept — whenever the question as to the conveying of cultural and social change arises. Nevertheless, as Marshall, Berger, Hoerning, and also Hollstein in this volume show, no consensus has yet been reached in attempts to explain the formation and scope of a new collective consciousness. Above all the question remains unanswered as to whether collective consciousness and collective identity can come about at all, let alone be

3

identified, in a social aggregate such as a generation, in view of the structural inequalities (stratum or class differences) it contains. Controversy continues over the relevance of the youth phase in which significant sociocultural orientations and values are thought to take shape under the influence of basic historic events. Moreover, the problem of the constancy of these orientations over the course of a generation's further existence remains unsolved (Elder, 1979; Elder & Liker, 1982; Rosenmayr, 1983b; Hoerning, 1983; Rosenthal, 1983, to name only a few).

By the same token, numerous divergencies have become apparent in the discussion of possible ways to operationalize the generation concept and apply it in empirical research (Marshall, this volume; and Mayer, 1975; Müller, 1978; Kertzer, 1983). Especially in this context it is necessary to distinguish the generation concept from other, related ones, particularly the age stratification theory and cohort concept (Riley, 1971; Riley et al., 1972; Riley, 1976a, b; Ryder, 1965; Foner, 1976; Cain, 1967; Neugarten & Datan, 1976; Schaie, 1976; Streib, 1976; Maddox & Wiley, 1976, etc.).

More than other sociological subdisciplines, *youth sociology* has recourse to the tradition of earlier theoreticians. In this field, the generation concept serves, as a rule, to provide a basis for the detection and legitimation of "generation-specific" characteristics within a particular age group – that of youth. Such descriptions as "the sceptical generation" (Schelsky, 1957), "generation of candour" (Blücher, 1966), the "new" or the "shattered" generation (Jaide, 1961; Tartler, 1955, etc.), in addition to such newer labels as "the generation of no-sayers" or "give a shit generation," all point to the fact that here the term generation is being used as a synonym for youth. Youth's relation to "the others" (meaning other generations) is usually seen in terms of (generational) conflicts (cf., e.g., Feuer, 1969; Bettelheim, 1963; Elsler, 1974), or from a perspective of maintenance of social continuity by preparing youth to assume adult status and full membership in society (e.g., Heberle, 1951; Erikson, 1968; Braungart, 1974). In the first-named context of conflict and revolt, researchers are obviously concerned to come to terms with recent developments, relying on the way the problem is treated in the public and political discussion. These include, for example, an investigation of student movements (e.g., Feuer, 1969; Weinberg & Walker, 1969; Elsler, 1971; Braungart & Braungart, 1980); on the difficulty of integrating youth in the labor market and other social spheres (Hornstein, 1982; Shell-Studie Jugend '81, 1983, etc.); and on the troubles of young dropouts (Ibid., and Hollstein, 1979; 1983; Jaide, 1978).

In these approaches, youth is generally identified as a driving force of change, a motor of revolt and social movements, but the attempts to explain these phenomena rely on rather different bases. They either focus on social discontinuities and breakdowns in the structure of society (e.g., Eisenstadt, 1978) or on the character of youth as a quasi-homogeneous group without clearly defined roles (breathing space), but also lacking access to social resources which they have yet to attain (Parsons, 1963; Braungart, 1974; 1982). Correspondingly, the estimations differ on the significance of youth movements and revolts as regards profound political change and social transformation (cf. also Hollstein and Berger, this volume).

The view that youth is a special phase of development and life, a phase predestined for fragile relations to others (whether generations or age groups), marks the intersection between the approach of youth sociology and explanations based in psychology or psychoanalysis. Here, conflict-ridden relations are generally seen in terms of a search for identity, ego formation, detachment, social control (deficitary) socialization, estrangement and deviation, etc. (Freud, 1856–1939; Erikson, 1968; Stierlin, 1975; Elkind, 1980; Coleman, 1970; Becker, 1975; Brunner, 1982, etc.). Harmonious relations are traced back to the maturation process and the fulfilment of developmental tasks, to the acquisition of social competence and autonomy, to active adjustment and identification with positive models (White, 1974; Havighurst, 1972; Erikson, 1968; Haan, 1977; Hall, 1904; Spranger, 1926; Jaide, 1970, etc.).

Youth is given much attention in the *political sciences* as well, as the representative of that force which can bring about social change through new political attitudes or through conflict and revolt. Discussion centers on questions of the transmission of political attitudes among the generations, political socialization, and the education of adolescents (Lipset, 1967; Lipset et al., 1969; 1976; Flacks, 1971; Jennings & Niemi, 1975; Braungart, 1974; Loewenberg, 1974; Keniston, 1968). Numerous empirical findings in the field of opinion research and particularly research on voting behavior reveal differences in political orientation and behavior among age groups or cohorts. Interpretations of such findings are used implicitly to conclude how far the generation succession is relevant for changes in everyday policy-making practice as well as for longer term political developments (Hunt, 1982). This involves the problem of formation and stability of political attitudes in the life course of cohorts on the one hand, and the political behavior of different cohorts (age groups) during a given period on the other, that is, the question of progressiveness or conservatism (Agnello, 1973; Bengtson & Cutler, 1976; Fendrich, 1974; Glenn, 1974; Hudson & Binstock, 1976; Jennings & Niemi, 1981, etc.). Wherever the political mobilizability of social groups (as a rule, youth groups) is analyzed, Mannheim's generation concept usually comes into play again, particularly his construct of a generation unit. The simultaneous appearance of left-wing and right-wing groups within "the same youth," activists and pressure groups among otherwise passive and unpolitical adolescents, and potentially intragenerational conflicts, are explained in terms of that polarity which according to Mannheim may exist within any generation unit (Westby & Braungart, 1966; Braungart, 1982).

Now and then the same approach is favored by *subculture* researchers (insofar as they deal with adolescent subcultures), regardless of whether they are anchored more in youth sociology, cultural sociology, developmental psychology, or the political sciences (cf., e.g., Elsler, 1974; Brake, 1981; Braungart, 1982; and Berger, this volume). The marginal position of youth — a generation in statu nascendi — predestines it for the emergence of alienation and detachment from mainstream culture all the way to its negation (Elsler, 1971). Intercourse with like-minded people encourages the formation of partial cultures alongside the main culture (Tenbruck, 1965), or a peer-group culture characterized by the external segregation of an age-homogeneous group, or even of a counterculture that represents a counterweight to the overall culture of a society. However, the generation concept is no longer sufficient to adequately explain subcultural phenomena (Braungart, 1982), such as material and immaterial products of a subculture, or even to detect the "sources" of subcultural phenomena and their relevance for society (or culture) as a whole. Recent subculture research in particular — as is suggested in Chapter III — derives from quite diverse approaches to social reality. There is some evidence that conventional thought linked to a functionalist perspective is giving way to more phenomenologically-oriented approaches (Brake, 1981; Clarke et al., 1981; Diedrichsen et al., 1983, and the work of the Birmingham Center for Cultural Studies), or to approaches founded in the neo-psychoanalysis which, using the narcissism concept, investigate the dynamics of adolescents' "subjective self-structures" (Ziehe, 1981; Ziehe & Stubenrauch, 1982).

That translation problems arise between these different theoretical levels, is something that becomes obvious in the present volume as well. Thus the question remains open as to whether, in adolescent subcultures, an increasing politization of public behavior and simultaneous depolitization of their everyday lives can be made out (Ziehe, 1981; Ziehe & Stubenrauch, 1982) — a contradiction that could be explained in terms of Mannheim's polarity. Or is it that both developments have nothing in common? Maybe researchers identify one or the other depending on whether they focus more on the function of subcultures for societal change or on everyday reality and experience within a subculture. For a long time the marginality of adolescent status before the acquisition of full membership in society, and even a certain discrimination, figured as causes for the formation of specific subcultural expressions. Recently a different assumption has begun to find favor, namely that the offer of adult status has lost its binding force (Ibid.). This is to characterize subcultures as refuges in which their members can experience youthfulness with as little outside disturbance as possible. In this way and through the commercialization of subcultural products, the myth of youthfulness gets further nourishment, this myth which has long been a key characteristic of relationships among the different age groups.

As we shall indicate in Chapter II of this volume, *the family* represents a multifarious and manifold area of scientific involvement with the subject of intergenerational relationships. In this context, unlike its use in the fields mentioned above, the term generation describes lineage and succession, whereby such purely biological determinants as blood relation play a greater or lesser role depending on the particular cultural and sociohistoric conditions (Huber, 1979). In recent years the focus of scientific interest has shifted both as regards the subject itself and as regards approaches to it. Relatively new, for instance, is the interest of historians and historical demographers in researching the qualitative and quantitative links between lineage generations in the past (cf. Mitterauer & Sieder, 1977; Mitterauer, 1981; 1982; Imhof, 1981; Conrad, 1982; Hubbart, 1983; Duby, 1981, etc.). Based on the tradition of analyses of annals and collected source materials, investigation in this field concentrates on broad sectors of the population, frequently with the aim of reconstructing the everyday reality of past periods and the mentality of average people who lived through them. The manifold references of this topic to economics, politics, culture, and education have awakened the interest not only of historians but of sociologists, economists, and educators as well, which has precipitated, among other things, in new methods of analyzing comtemporary society and in new economic and social security models (Grohmann, 1980; 1981; Plaschke, 1983, etc.).

A reorientation is likewise evident in those approaches to intergenerational relationships within the family which are based on developmental psychology and socialization theory. Just a short time ago researchers concentrated on the influences of primary familial socialization on infants and children. They emphasized that many of the traditional tasks of the nuclear family were no longer required but at the same time they identified new functions of, for example, an emotional and social or cognitive and intellectual kind (Ainsworth et al., 1973; 1978; Carew, 1977; 1980; Lamb, 1977; Lehr, 1973; Papoušek & Papoušek, 1979; Rauh, 1976; White, 1970; Yarrow et al., 1979, etc.).

Moreover, developmental psychology has provided many fundamental results which contributed to an explanation of the idiosyncratic relations between adolescents and their parents. Yet as we have already indicated, interest focussed primarily on the consequences of these relations for youth, while in recent years the question has come to the fore as to the extent to which parents' development is influenced by the events associated with their childrens' growing up (cf., e.g., Kimmel, 1974; Alpert & Richardson, 1980).

If previously adolescence represented that point in life where most psychologists ceased to trace the development of the individual and his familial relationships, today more and more attention is being paid to the entire life-span and particularly to the "midlife transition," to a redefinition of developmental tasks and familial ties with their implications for psychopathology (Troll, 1975; Cytrynbaum et al., 1980). The multi-generational family found its true entrance into the research scene with work in the area of psychological and social gerontology, that is, when researchers began to take into account the demographic fact that the proportion of elderly and very old in the population had markedly increased. Particularly in the course of the discussion sparked by the publication of the disengagement theory (Cumming & Henry, 1961), research into the social relationships of older people, including their familial ties, experienced a great upswing. The need to find solutions for the problem of support for the very old also contributed to making the strength of intergenerational ties a subject of numerous empirical research studies. For an impressive overview of this field, see Bengtson et al. and Ursula Lehr, this volume.

All of this research points up the fact that the involvement of developmental psychologists with problems of intergenerational relationships within multi-generational families has been based mainly on concrete problems and conducted with an eye to applications. Examples of this are the economic and especially the sociopolitical implications of the subject mentioned above, a few aspects of the latter are discussed in this volume; further examples are studies on the occurrence of and coping with critical life events and life crises in the context of familial relationships (Filipp, 1981; 1982) and their significance for health, prevention of diseases, coping with the aging process, and life expectancy. Another important domain of application is family psychotherapy (Boszormenyi-Nagy & Spark, 1973; 1975; Boszormenyi-Nagy, 1975; Radebold & Schlesinger-Kipp, 1982, and many others). This complex of problems, like that of pedagogic and educative application of the theme of intergenerational relationships within families, has yet to be given a foundation in developmental psychology (Montada & Schmitt, 1982).

Problems that occur in sociology with the use of the term generation and with the examination of the theoretical and empirical impact of the generation concept, prove to be less relevant in connection with lineage generations. Instead, other conceptual divergencies dominate the discussion. This becomes apparent in this volume not lastly when the term and concept of "solidarity" is employed (Bengtson et al., Knipscheer, Rosenmayr). Efforts to link theoretical or developmental psychological studies on the multi-generational family to the ecological and environmental models are in the starting phase rather than in the stage of solution. No doubt exists, however, as to the fruitfulness of this connection (Bronfenbrenner, 1978; 1979; Parr, 1980; Garms-Homolová, 1982; 1983, and others).

Reference to time dimensions is the most striking feature of recent reorientations in the way scientists view vertical familial relationships. Initially, the historic time dimension is emphasized: the change of generational ties in the context of sociohistorical and sociocultural development (Elder, 1978a; Mitterauer & Sieder, 1977; Mitterauer, 1981; 1982; Imhof, 1981; Conrad, 1982; Hubbart, 1983).

The second time dimension considered is the lifetime of the individual which in the course of increasing emphasis on the entire life-span by developmental psychologists is fructifying research into intergenerational relationships within the family as well. The third time dimension — social time — which refers to the age-grade system of society (Neugarten & Datan, 1976) is "a middle-level approach to the study of family patterns, one that attends to both general structural trends and to the behavior of families in concrete settings; that investigates expressions of generalized institutional arrangements in particular settings and explicates processes of family change in this context which have implications for social development as a whole" (Elder, 1978a, 34).

Nascent research (cf. Elder, 1975; 1978a; 1981b; Hagestad and others, this volume) already suggests that this level will probably move to the center of both theoretical and empirical study of intergenerational relationships in the future. Since it represents the basis both for connecting the individual life-spans of family members and for the network of expectations, dependencies, contacts, and functions, this level forms the framework of relations among familial generations and of negotiations concerning these relationships namely their intensity and meaning. Analytically, this level is well-suited to identifying the types of courses of relationship patterns, and for corresponding trend prognosing. It could provide firmer foundations for application-oriented study of this subject. From the perspective of social time, the family represents a platform for encounter, exchange, and reciprocal influence of members of different cohorts and age groups (Mackensen, this volume). By means of the biographies of its members we can gain insights into the everyday nature of familial coexistence (Menne, 1981), and through family biographies, insights into important historical periods ("lived history," e.g., Mannzmann, 1981) and into individual and social processing of the guidelines offered by society and culture.

* * * * *

Thus far the stage at which the considerations underlying this volume begin. If traditional attempts to formulate a general theory of intergenerational relationships were characterized by all-too global claims, later and current efforts tend to draw the opposite criticism — that they limit themselves, often empiristically, to partial aspects of the problem and questions of detail. The reason for this, as may have become clear from the above, lies not lastly in the fact that only with difficulty can the existing theoretical constructs be applied in an empirical context. Bringing together the various perspectives and explanatory attempts, as we have done in this volume, in itself represents a first step towards a theoretical conception of intergenerational relationships. It should prepare the way for a perspective which is more complex than the research approaches now in currency.

Vjenka Garms-Homolová
Erika M. Hoerning
Doris Schaeffer

Chapter I: Intergenerational Relationships in the Process of Civilization

This chapter takes up a dimension of the subject that has often been neglected in generation research and particularly in the study of intergenerational relationships. It focusses on analysis and description of comparatively *long-term* transmission processes, both on the level of general social development and on that of everyday practice.

Though discussions of generations in historical terms are available (Marías, 1970; Spitzer, 1973; Jaeger, 1977, and others) and several intercultural comparisons have been made (Mead, 1970; Wieder & Zimmermann, 1974), many of these studies are devoted to more or less limited fields of inquiry, spotlighting as it were certain details of particular historic periods and special cultural circumstances. Most of them do not attempt systematic analysis from a broader perspective. And like the social sciences in general, discussion of generational problems is characterized by this predominant trend of a — usually empiricist — analysis of current developments. "Very little effort seems to be given any more ... to tracing the idiosyncracies of present-day societies with the aid of broad historical or ethnological knowledge and comparisons with other developmental stages of society, in order at last to get a theoretical grasp of this development itself" (Elias, 1983, 31). An effort of this kind, however, would imply that more far-reaching perspectives and observations made over longer historical time spans must be taken into account, focussing on the transformation of society, changes in social character (Riesman, 1958), and changes in human relationships. It would also mean incorporating the results of many different scientific disciplines, including the subdisciplines.

Why does an analysis and description of comparatively long-term transmission processes appear so important to us? It is not only the social contingency of current intergenerational relationships, their state of becoming, that must be elucidated by way of example and comparison and thus rendered amenable to systematic analysis. Rather, the fundamental dependency of one human being on the next has to be taken account of: the transformation of meaning for each individual life actually lived. Generation research is currently dominated by analysis of generational relations in an attempt to explain social and historic change. This attempt is legitimated by numerous theoretical constructs on the problem of generations, by concepts seeking to explain historical rhythms like that of Mentre, Rümelin, von Ranke, etc. as well as by the historically more recent and still very useful construct advanced by Mannheim in 1928. Inquiries into the vehicle of social transformation, on the role of generations, etc. are the main focus of this work. Yet the converse is rarely inquired, namely, what is the significance of continuity and dependency in human relationships, and of the changes that take place in them in the course of social developments — a question that is of equal explanatory value in analyzing the relationships among generations.

In generational succession this dependency becomes apparent not only with respect to the transmission of knowledge and the passing down of power and property — as investigated, for example, by Held in this chapter — but is manifests itself particularly in what people consider meaningful and fulfilling. "That the significance of everything a human being does, lies in what it means to others, and not only to those living now but to the yet unborn, thus making him dependent on the continuance of human society through the generations, certainly belongs to the fundamental dependencies of human beings on one another" – this is how Elias describes this dependency (1982b, 54). Individual life planning is significant only when it goes beyond one's own life and becomes meaningful for others, above all for future generations. Hence, the structuring of individual lives must be seen as contingent on the continuity of social development, predestined by the traditions of the past and shaped by hope in the future.

This perspective leads particularly to a consideration of the everyday life of past periods. Not only must human relationships and their dependency on historic change be investigated, but also changing attitudes to life and death and to the different phases and cycles of life, that is life planning and living as oriented to the lives of future generations. It moreover means studying past notions of careers or life courses and their phases, as well as the attitudes such notions imply concerning the relationships between different age groups. The contribution by Kondratowitz is devoted to these questions, and clearly indicates that the problem of generations is necessarily involved with the problem of life courses.

If here generational relationships are seen in connection with the development of Western civilization, we also look at the topic of continuity from another point of view. In contrast to the process of cultural development, this point of view stresses continuity as an ongoing process of "humanization of peoples" (Humboldt) or, as Max Weber called it, a universal process which through its formative tendencies "affects cultural aspiration and behaviour." Weber basically saw this process as a progressive intellectualization of the way people cope with existence. Elias, whose work may be considered the most significant in the field, emphasizes another aspect as the main characteristic of the civilization process – an increasing restraint of human affects and a raising of the embarrassment plateau (Elias, 1977).

Elias describes the process of civilization as a continual increase of external controls over all direct emotional and physical expressions, and an internalization of these controls by the individual. This process is linear and takes place in two phases. The first involves the formation and ritualization of norms, manifested, for example, in a widening dissemination of "etiquette literature," in changing educational concepts, etc. The second phase brings an internalization of norms via the socialization process. Self-control becomes the predominant character trait; external sanctions are replaced by such psychological reactions as shame, embarrassment, guilt feelings, etc. This is also the period in which the psychological sciences, including psychopathology, develop. According to Elias, this process filters through the class strata from top to bottom, beginning in the upper class and gradually extending down to the lower. A superb description of this processual aspect of the civilization process may be found in the work of Philippe Ariès (1975; 1980). He shows how the formation and institutionalization of the various age groups begins in the aristocratic, upper stratum while the lower social strata retain residues of older – and from the point of view of the history of civilization, outmoded – ideas.

In the context of our topic, however, another more comprehensive question initially arises, that as to the relationship of generations to historic social structures and to social evolution. What function can be attributed to generations and relationships among generations in the process of civilization, and for the maintenance of the civilized behavior of a society, and what forms did intergenerational relationships take on during the various phases of this development? The contributors to this chapter have approached this question from the perspective of diverse scientific disciplines. By the way, the point of view outlined in this preface merely represents a programmatic sketch for an analysis of the generation problem which the individual contributions to this chapter can approach only tentatively. Tentatively, because each contribution necessarily analyzes the topic from the perspective of a single discipline and can take broader points of view into account only sporadically.

Hans Peter Dreitzel, in his introductory contribution, points out one basic characteristic of current intergenerational relationships. Increasingly rapid technological and social change produce an increasing differentiation in the realms of experience (Schütz) of the different age groups and thus a growing distance between them, and concomitantly lead to ongoing conflicts between the various age and/or generational groups.

Dreitzel develops his thesis with reference to the work of Elias (1970), but opens up a broader perspective in his analysis. Central to Dreitzel's discussion is the present, third phase of the process of civilization, which is characterized by a de-ritualization and de-emotionalization of everyday life. Typically representative of this phase is the person who has a highly flexible social character but must also develop a high degree of stability in order to cope with a multiplicity of differing demands — skills which are certainly contradictory and which face him or her with paradoxical challenges. Another consequence of accelerating technological and social change is that each age group assumes the character of a generation with its own specific historical experiences.

Dreitzel attributes a great significance particularly to youth, the vehicle of civilization in this third phase of the de-ritualization of everyday life. In contrast to the first two phases of civilization, where the development works its way straight through the class strata, it now works through the age groups, from youth through the progressively older groups and finally to the elderly.

By producing new fashions, subcultures and social movements, youth take a stand against the existing value system and against current formalized and ritualized behavior, thus encouraging that growing informality of behavioral standards which characterizes the process of civilization. Accordingly, this process becomes the very issue of ongoing generational conflict — older people are shocked by new, increasingly informal dress, drinking, dancing, or speaking habits, altered sexual behavior, and not lastly by young people's refusal to participate in formalized ceremonies (particularly in the family context — family reunions, etc.). The manner in which this confrontation comes about, that is, through the establishment of new trends, sounds, and styles in the various youth subcultures, is the subject of D. Hebdige's analyses (cf. Hebdige, 1979 and Hebdige, this volume, Chapter IV).

In sum, Dreitzel gives a clear answer to the question as to the function of generational succession in the process of civilization, seeing conflict among the generations as decisive. He considers it — at least in the present phase — to be the driving force behind developments in the direction of increasing informality of everyday life.

Hans-Joachim von Kondratowitz brings us from youth to the elderly. With recourse to "new social history" (cf. Mitterauer & Sieder, 1982) and particularly to the history of ideas, he attempts to trace the formation and institutionalization of age. In his analysis of various dictionary and encyclopedia articles he inquires into the changing historic significance of the life phase of old age. This inquiry necessarily leads to considering the entire life course, as well as age group (or generation) specific behavior, in a historic context. Kondratowitz reconstructs the way in which mental images and the doctrines of scientific disciplines were perpetuated in reference articles and how these in turn affected social practice.

Point of departure for his analysis is the hypothesis that attitudes toward the elderly have changed, from devotion and respect to an identification of this phase with physical and mental decline. This change has its source in modernization, and parallels a processualization of the social organization of knowledge, which analogous to the process of civilization takes place in three phases: from naturalistic thinking to the evolutionary tradition and finally to what might be called a re-naturalization of thought. Typical of the first two phases is that the division of life into separate stages gives way to the notion of a life curve, which automatically implies a decline towards the end, in old age. Kondratowitz sees the negative attitude to old age as a consequence of this development. Nevertheless, most reference book articles are characterized by what he calls an "unresolved tension" between these two notions, as expressed in the use of certain concepts. The category "life cycle" serves to link the two streams of thought. Kondratowitz also sees this term as indicating a re-naturalization of the scientific view, which is expressed in a tendency to let both positive and negative evaluations of old age stand side by side or, more recently, to see it in primarily positive terms.

In tracing this development, Kondratowitz illustrates very clearly the way in which different age groups were expected to deal with each other in the past and what codes of morals and behavior underlay changing conceptions of old age. Doctrines adapted to each phase of social development fed back into social practice, being transformed into rules and orientation patterns for everyday behavior.

Thomas Held looks at the topic from the point of view of social history. Based on an example — co-residence in northwest European households during the pre-industrial age — he elucidates the structure of intergenerational relationships and attempts to describe their function in the process of social transformation.

During the period analyzed by Held, generational coexistence within the family also included non-family members. Members of households, whether young or old, were frequently not relatives, for instance those young adults who as servants or maids were exchanged among different households. Held emphasizes that "service" should not be seen so much as an occupation per se, but as a specific phase in the life cycle which generally preceded the establishment of a household of the servant's own. The relations among generations in these families were characterized by common housekeeping; power over the household in the sense of authority and possession was embodied by the householder who as a rule was a member of the middle generation.

Held points out that the problem of the dependent elderly was much less pressing than is generally assumed. Thus he sheds doubt on the myth of the "family of bygone days" in which dependent elderly people were ostensibly well treated and cared for.

Finally, Held discusses the question of household authority and the transmission of social values. Though co-residence implied generational transfer, that is the transmission of authority, property, and social values, generational power problems, arising from the possession of social or political power, were themselves determined by the social structure. They were overlaid with feudal and semi-feudal dependencies. When individuals were incorporated as citizens and legal persons in the modern, bourgeois state, authority shifted to the extrafamilial realm. With this development the significance of familial generational succession for the transfer of social values declined, shifting more and more into the extrafamilial realm, that is, with the establishment of national education.

Rainer Mackensen traces the constants in long-term developments from the demographic perspective. Beginning with a definition of the terms "generation," "age group," and "cohort" and their relevance in the demographic context, Mackensen then asks what influence the population development which accompanied modernization has had on intergenerational relationships. The demographic perspective outlined by Mackensen represents an invaluable precondition for understanding present-day forms of familial coexistence. Some of these forms are treated in the subsequent chapters, that is, under the motto of "years gained" (Imhof, 1981) and that of the "empty nest" (Lehr, this volume), to name only two.

Particularly in view of the fact that demographic transition in other societies (developing countries) takes place at a different rate than in Western industrialized societies, the demographic perspective will certainly be deserving of increased attention in future research.

Generational Conflict from the Point of View of Civilization Theory

Hans Peter Dreitzel

The study of intergenerational relations presents us with a complex set of conceptual and empirical problems. While numerous studies of the different lifestyles, attitudes, and behavioral modes of different generations exist and, of course, each of us has his or her own personal experiences with intergenerational conflicts and with the historical fate of one's own generation, there still seems to be a lack of a more general theoretical framework which could serve as an interpretative guideline for the many phenomena connected with this topic. It seems to me that the best use I could make of the privilege to present the first contribution to this book is to attempt to draw an outline of such a theoretical framework in order to put some orientational sign-posts in the vast landscape of our area of interest. Of course, as is so often the case in our endeavors, it is only by standing on the shoulder of giants that I am able to try my hand at this task. Among these are notably Phillipe Ariès, and more especially Norbert Elias, on whose great study of the "Civilizing Process" (Elias, 1978; 1982a) my own suggestions are based[1].

Let me start with a simple observation, namely that over the past hundred years industrialized Western societies have experienced a general shift from formal and ritualized standards of behavior to informal and de-ritualized ones, an observation on which there seems to be much agreement among scholars from rather different fields of research. One notable study of this process comes, for instance, from a literary critic — I mean Lionell Trilling's brilliant essay on "Sincerety and Authenticity" (Trilling, 1972). Before I begin to analyze this development more closely it is important to state that the protagonists of this process have been and still are overwhelmingly members of the young generations. The young, it is true, have always found their cultural heroes also among the older ones, but on the level of everyday interactions the informalization process has been the very issue of the generational conflicts. At least since the beginnings of the bourgeois youth movement a century ago each successive generation has succeeded in shocking the older ones by their more informal habits of dressing and undressing, of dancing and drinking, of their manners of speech as well as their manners of erotic behavior, and last but not least, by their rejection of formal ceremonies, especially those connected with family life and educational institutions. Of course, there are some phenomena which do not fit into this picture as, for instance, the formal dress of Teddy Boys or Mods and, more importantly, the fascist experience. I leave these for later consideration and concentrate for the moment on the informalization process.

For a better understanding of this process let me first draw your attention to the theory put forward by the English anthropologist Mary Douglas in her book on "Natural Symbols" (Douglas, 1973). Using comparative ethnological material together with an analysis of the present situation of Western society her argument is basically this: A valuable distinction can be made between two different but universally found types of society each of which shows a characteristic combination of elements. On the one hand we find societies in which a rigid control over all bodily functions, especially over all matters related to bodily excretions, is the expected norm. In these societies we will also find a highly ritualized everyday behavior, a high degree of role differentiation and symbolic representation in formal rules, a power structure represented by concrete known individuals, and a morally oriented religiosity. On the other hand, societies with little restrictions on physical and emotional expressions will also display much informality in everyday behavior. These societies will show a low degree of symbolic representation in roles and generally a more informal and flexible role structure. They would also be characterized by an abstract and complex power structure and a chiliastic religiosity oriented toward authentic experience. This is a highly suggestive thesis even though its anthropological value may be debated. I will leave these questions aside here and instead take a look at Mary Douglas' analysis of modern Western society. In order to understand her point of view here, it is important to remember that she sees a cyclical movement in the development of societies, a swinging pendulum between the two extremes of rigid formality and informal spontaneity. With her eyes set on the cultural movements of the Sixties she finds that since the Victorian era the pendulum has swung to the other extreme: We live now in a society characterized by informal roles and a de-ritualized everyday behavior, which puts little restriction on the free expression of physical and emotional needs. Correspondingly, we can observe today a tendency toward chiliastic movements and an emphasis on authentic religious experiences rather than moralistic attitudes on the one hand and a highly abstract power structure on the other hand. This is a compelling description which will hardly be contradicted. Each of us could give many examples for the weakening of moral standards, the increasing flexibility and informality of behavioral patterns and for the many ways in which personal authenticity is sought today. After all, this process has been the issue of many generational conflicts and the target of all conservative social criticism in the course of this century. The question is rather: How we can explain this shift from the formal to the informal and whether Mary Douglas' view of a cyclical movement can be substantiated by an historical analysis probing farther back than the Victorian era.

In answer to these questions Mary Douglas has little to offer and we have to look elsewhere. Only recently historians have begun to focus more closely on everyday behavior and in particular to study the modes of physical and emotional expression which − I think − are particularly pertinent to the study of intergenerational relations. What is now sometimes called Psycho-History is still a new and rather vague field of scholarly endeavor. The most promising and extensive study as yet advanced in this field is, as far as I can see, still Norbert Elias' great analysis of The Civilizing Process. Elias has studied biographies, court reports, books on good manners and the like over the course of 500 years of European history between 1300 and 1800, in order to study the changing habits of everyday life in regard to hygienic standards, sexual mores, table manners, and styles of aggressive behavior among others. All of his material deals with the standards of emotional and body control. At the first impression the reader begins to realize how rigid our seemingly liberated behavior today is when compared to medieval standards and attitudes.

From that time on what Elias describes as the civilizing process are the gradually increasing external controls over all direct expressions of physical and emotional needs and the eventual internalization of these controls. The picture he gives us on the basis of his material is that of a more or less linear process rather than of a cyclical movement. Even though Elias is not quite clear about this, two phases in this process may be distinguished: At first the norms of behavior become more and more rigid, formalized, and ritualized. Manners of everyday behavior become now formally prescribed and the question: How am I expected to behave in this or that situation gradually gains in importance and gives rise to new educational practices and a whole literature on good manners. The second phase is the internalization of these formal norms of behavior via early socialization procedures. Now self-control becomes semi-automatic, eventually a sign of "character." The external sanctions against rule-breaking behavior are replaced by psychic reactions like embarrassment, shame, and guilt feelings. The modern type of super-ego comes into existence which is soon assisted by the endless commentaries of the new sciences of psychology and psychopathology. The second phase of the civilizing process is the birth of what David Riesman has called the inner-directed social character.

Now, before I come to the question how the recent informalization process fits into this picture let me briefly emphasize one other point, namely that Elias sees the civilizing process as working its way through the class strata — always beginning with the economically leading classes and only slowly making an impact on the lower classes. Indeed his book carries the subtitle: "On the Behavior of the Upper Classes in Western Society." The formalization of behavior always begins with the aristocracy and the early bourgeois patricians in the economically leading centers, first the city states of Northern Italy, then the courts of Paris, London, and Vienna, finally the smaller German courts. Typically the process moves on to the economically leading bourgeois trading families before it reaches the landed gentry. The peak of the formalization process is reached during the Ancient Régime in the mannerisms developed at the court of Versailles. There is, however, a certain vagueness in Elias' presentation which leaves us in the dark in regard to the role of the bourgeoisie as opposed to the aristocracy. While Elias presents some material indicating that the two stages of the process are always to be found successively in each class, it seems to me that much points to a different picture, namely that the second stage, the internalization of more rigid standards, was rather the work of the early bourgeoisie which ran, with a somewhat later start, parallel to the formalization of aristocratic behavior. Of course, in both classes the two stages are experienced. But it was the aristocracy who carried the formalization to its peak and it was the bourgeoisie who brought puritanical attitudes to its extremes. In any case, however, the general idea of a differential class distribution of civilized standards of behavior has a striking similarity to what Michael Young and Peter Willmott in their marvellous study on "The Symmetrical Family" (Young & Willmott, 1973) have called the "Principle of Stratified Diffusion." I should like to quote from this book, because the authors have a well-formulated principle, which is also central to Elias' work, of which they seem to be ignorant. "The image we are trying to suggest," they say, "is that of a marching column with the people at the head usually being the first to wheel in a new direction. The last rank keeps its distance from the first, and the distance between them does not lessen. But as the column advances, the last rank does eventually reach and pass the point which the first rank had passed some time before. In other words, the egalitarian tendency works with a time lag ... The source of the momentum is not too obscure. Without industrialization the column would not be on the move." This latter remark needs some qualification: In Western society the column was on the move ever since the earliest beginnings of capitalism, but it has gained enormously in speed since the industrial revolution. Young and Willmott's observation is of special value here not only because they have given the "Principle of Stratified Diffusion" a handy name, but more so because their analysis shows the *Principle* at work over the past 150 years – a time span not included in Elias' research.

In other words, the *Principle* is still functioning. And in its light we may indeed begin to understand something about the present fate of the civilizing process. We know, for instance, from research findings that in spite of varied cultural backgrounds there are typical class differences in socialization patterns which can be interpreted as the two stages of the civilizing process co-existing simultaneously in the middle and the lower classes: Educational practices in the middle classes tend to operate within what Basil Bernstein has called the elaborated language code. Here explanations and reasons are given for rules which children have to obey. The major negative sanction applied is the withdrawal of love and affection. The result is an early internalization of value standards, and the development of feelings of shame and guilt as a reaction to a loss of physical and emotional control. The educational practices of the lower classes are confined to a restricted language code within which statements of fact rather than explanations are given and orders and commands prevail over persuading and convincing. External punishments including physical penalties are the standard negative sanction. The result is an orientation to external stimuli modified by fear of loss of security. From these data I would conclude that we are dealing here with the simultaneity of two historical stages of the same process.

This may explain some of the striking differences between proletarian and middle-class youth subcultures in our times, especially in regard to the expression of a aggressive behavior. But before we get the full picture we have to take into account the driving forces behind the civilizing process.

Elias emphasizes that the civilizing process works through a multitude of cultural orientations and social movements and in the long run always prevails as if indifferent to the conscious intentions of the people. The forces which function in this or that way through actions of concrete persons and which explain the civilizing process, are twofold: First the increasingly far-reaching economic exchange processes which demand more and more foresight, a rational planning of expedient behavior and eventually the deference of gratification as a behavioral pattern. This is, of course, the process which Max Weber has analyzed at length as the disenchantment of the modern world by its rationalization and bureaucratization, forcing people into the affective neutrality which now becomes the standard of "reasonable" behavior. And secondly it is the eventual monopolization of the legitimate use of violence by the state, which gives rise to a more and more complex bureaucracy. Indeed, compared with the common daily experience of violence in Europe in the past – a past at least in America not that long ago after all – we live in an era of pervasive safety. Not that crimes of violence are absent, that riots are unknown. Yet we travel safely across the country by day or night without fear of being attacked by armed bands, rioting hordes or roaming madmen. The point is not that these no longer exist, but that they are exceptional, that we do not take them into account when we plan any activity. The fact that there are still unsafe, unpacified areas like certain slum neighborhoods or city parks at night rather emphasizes the general state of pacification of increasingly large territories. If we remember also that in our daily life we do not have to fear the plague, death is almost never seen, childbirth rarely, disease is quickly isolated in hospitals, hunger has disappeared, meat is eaten but no urban person ever sees an animal slaughtered — we begin to see the extent to which the exclusion of natural violence is taken for granted and guaranteed by public institutions.

Reading the story Elias has to tell with the eyes of Marx and Weber in our heads we see that it is both the emergence of capitalism *and* the rise of the modern state which are responsible for the civilizing process. We can even go further and postulate that the institution of formal prescriptions for the control over the physical and emotional reactions and expressions in everyday behavior corresponds to what Marx has called the stage of original capital accumulation, while the second phase, the development of internalized shame and guilt barriers correspond to the industrialization process. This is true for the peak of these developments in the economically leading classes who have been quick in the attempt to force the new standards of behavior upon the newly emerging proletariat — an attempt which at least among the proletarian youth and during economic depressions has not been fully successful until this day.

Now, since neither capitalism nor state bureaucracy have vanished, since on the contrary the chains of economic interdependence have become world-wide by now and the state bureaucracies have more influence on the everyday life of the citizen than ever before including the constant threat to use the unprecedented military power under its control — we might expect that the civilizing process, the internalization of external controls, has by no means come to an end. That is, we would expect, that the internal pacification via external and, preferably, internalized control mechanism will continue to prevail over all attempts to loosen the tightly woven network of more repressive norms of behavior.

However, the situation seems to be more complicated. For what are we to make of the de-ritualization of everyday life which I have called the informalization process and which has always found its strongest expression in the values and lifestyles of the younger generation? How do we explain the various liberation movements and the actual changes which have led us from the highly formal, all physical and emotional spontaneity repressing Victorian age to our present standards of relaxed formality and new concerns with physical and emotional expression? The question here is, whether the younger generations are only from time to time, and without lasting effect, rebelling against an iron law of a world-wide social evolution towards ever more restrained and hence predictable modes of behavior or whether they are — as they often see themselves — the avant-garde of an entirely new phase in the civilizing process.

In answer to this question we have, first of all, to note that the civilizing process is concerned with our relationship toward nature — the internal nature of our corporal existence with its emotional expressions and the external nature of our immediate environment and, more generally, of our habitat on this planet. And this is exactly the concern of all youth movements too, but in the opposite direction than the civilizing process points to. This is even true of the enthusiasm with which many fractions of the youth movement have greeted the advent of fascism. For what they were looking for even there was a new relation to nature and the hope to find a legitimizing authority for their struggle against the constraints of civilization. Whenever our relationship to nature is reconsidered without a simultaneous reconsideration of power and violence in society as well as in nature, the result will be a tendency toward fascist attitudes.

Much of the relationship between the generations during this century has to do with the new politicization of natural categories like race and region, gender and sexual preferences and even (young and old) age per se. All of these have become political issues with an inbuilt ambivalence: As political categories, they can serve as vehicles of emancipation for the in-group as well as vehicles for the repression of out-groups.

Secondly, I should like to briefly review the evidence for the informalization process in regard to new attitudes towards nature: Over the past hundred years *sports* have become a mass phenomenon. Leaving aside, here, the show aspect of sports and the champions of public contests, the interest in active sport — and more recently in out-door life — certainly indicates a new concern with physical health. This is partly a reflex action to the general medicalization of society, partly a response to the alienating and unhealthy aspects of urbanized life. More generally, the same applies to the various ecological movements which are more recently emerging. In regard to *nudity* the shame barrier seems to be lower today than 50 years ago. The major event here was the revolution in fashion before and after the First World War. This was a genuine re-evaluation of the natural beauty of the human body and its feeling which cannot be explained with the greater practicality of short skirts or trousers for working women. The end of the mandatory stays was the beginning of the end of the mandatory bra. And men's dresses have become much less formal and more comfortable, too. Swimming in the nude became acceptable in the ghettos of the nudist movement and is today at least tolerated generally in some countries. So also at home: Today children have a better chance to more than catch a glance of their parent's nude bodies than even my generation had. Also for copulation, nudity seems to have become the general standard. Kinsey, by the way, still reports characteristic differences in the attitude toward nudity between the middle and the lower classes.

As to the *sexual mores*, I don't think that there is genuine reason to speak of a sexual revolution, but a weakening of puritanical standards can definitely be observed. In fact, puritanical sexual attitudes seem to be most characteristic for societies which pass through the period of original capital accumulation. Today this is easily illustrated by the example of such variant countries as China, Cuba, or Algeria. There are, however, three major changes in regard to sexuality which are characteristic for late capitalism: One is, of course, the change in the status of women, which is a precondition for the acceptance of premarital sex and divorce as normal occurrences. The second is the availability of oral contraceptives, which have taken the highest risks from pre-marital and extra-marital sex. And third, the acceptability of a kind of general voyeurism, which finds its strongest expression in pictural pornography and art, but is also a dimension in certain sexual activities like swinging. This latter trend is but a more recent expression of what Foucault has called the "discursivation" of sex, the endless interest in the description, cataloging, and mapping of all aspects of sexuality, which paradoxically begins at the same time as the puritanical repression of actual sexuality.

Our *table manners* have become slightly less formal than our grandparent's but under strict and matter-of-fact observance of hygienic standards and with the clear rule that all noises from the eating and digesting process have to be controlled – a fact worth mentioning only because at other times people took much pleasure in such expressions of their bodily feasts. Of more interest in this connection are the marked changes in the rules of hospitality and in the norms of language use – where informality has almost gained the status of a value per se. The use of informal, almost sloppy, and often slang-like language among the young is probably the strongest symbolic marker along the cultural boundaries between the generations today. Importantly this language is lacking in ceremonial formulas but rich in stereotyped referrals to the imagined authenticity of irrational experiences like in English "weird" and "far out" or in German "echt," "irre," or "unheimlich."

The study of *ordinary language* use reveals one other important point: In spite of its informality and its tendency toward the irrational, the language of the young generation today seems almost empty of any emotional content except aggressive ones. In this respect the younger generation with its ideal of staying "cool" under all circumstances shows even more self-constraint than the older ones. This can most clearly be seen in the language used for *positive* emotions like in courtship and pairing behavior: Here expressions are partly lacking, partly bureaucratized or even brutalized. It seems that in regard to emotional expressions the process of internalization of external controls has in spite of the informalization of everyday behavior neither reversed nor has it come to a stop. The attitudes towards aggressiveness may give the best evidence here, for the process of increasing control over the spontaneous expression of aggressiveness is definitely continuing today: Even verbal fights are feared and frowned upon and all manners of physical assault are considered criminal acts. While the stones thrown at police cars always have news value, the apparently considerable amount of violence contained in the nuclear family is dealt with like other emotional expressions, too: as private affairs. This situation must be seen in direct relation to the massive potential of violence reified in the military and bureaucratic machineries under state monopoly. Characteristically the boundary between proletarian and middle-class fractions of rebellious youth groups is usually defined in terms of one's attitude toward violence: It is easier to violently rebel against external controls than against internalized ones.

This brief outline of the more recent developments of the civilizing process shows that it is neither really reversed nor does it simply follow its old path. Instead, it seems that the civilizing process has reached a third phase in which the internalization of emotional controls functions as a *basis* for more informal behavior. The inconsistency of present attitudes toward body and emotions must be seen in connection with the typical modes of identity-formation and reality-construction in our society. For the body is not a monadic entity but part of an organism/environment field and the emotions are spontaneous bodily judgments on the actual situation between the self and its objects. Characteristic for the emerging social character, represented as yet mostly among the young, seems to be a new flexibility of attachment and detachment with individuals and groups and a corresponding ability for constantly changing identifications with new roles. Robert Jay Lifton has seen this capacity and its drawbacks as the Protean character of modern man (Lifton, 1968). Proteus was the man in Greek mythology who could slip into any identity he wished. Much like David Riesman's earlier suggestion of an other-directed social character Lifton sees modern Protean Man as passing with ease through many identities in the course of his life yet with a vague sense of guilt for his rootlessness. "What actually has disappeared," he writes, "is the classic super-ego, the internalization of clearly defined criteria of right and wrong ... Protean Man requires freedom from precisely that kind of super-ego — he requires a symbolic fatherlessness — in order to carry out his explorations. But rather than being free of guilt ... his guilt takes on a different form from that of his predecessors. He indeed suffers from it considerably, but often without awareness of what is causing his suffering. For his is a form of hidden guilt: a vague but persistent kind of self-condemnation related to ... a sense of having no outlet for his loyalties and no symbolic structure for his achievements." Indeed the symbolic structures of this society are like a broken mirror: Man sees himself reflected in his many identity-fragments, yet does not recognize himself as a whole. The fate of ego-identity can never be separated from concerns over the reality status of what is perceived as going on. Yet few social theorists have made this connection. Or else they are too much attached to the previous phase of the civilizing process for which the formation of stable inner-directed personalities was an essential function. Marcuse's critique of one-dimensional man, for instance, does not seem to do justice to the seriousness of many young people's search for some new and more creative modes to relate to our inner nature and to our natural environment. Or Habermas' theory of communicative competence suffers from a rationalistic bias which prevents him to perceive the impoverishment of the emotional dimensions of our life, suffocated under the pressure of internalized constraints. And even Goffman's sharp analysis of the constantly shifting reality levels in modern social experience, which corresponds so well to the idea of Protean Man, in the end only succeeds in cynically diminishing the new flexibility of identity formation to an increased potential of deception and fabrication.

So a third phase in the civilizing process consists of a de-ritualization as well as a de-emotionalization of everyday life. The combination of these two elements leads at its best to what is really *new* in today's culture, namely a reflexive use of the body, the emotions, and the natural environment, and more generally, the reality-constructing activities in interactions. This new attitude, emerging in some fractions of the middle classes especially among the younger generation makes use of the cultural availability of roles and emotions, identities, and realities as sources of potential experience, as possible paths of self-discovery. Late capitalism does not seem to depend on the formation of a stable super-ego. Indeed, with the exception of those who are in executive positions of all ranks within the corporate system, internalized moral guidelines and lifelong value orientations seem to become obsolete in our economy no less than in our culture. The development of highly bureaucratized welfare systems, the medicalization of social problems, the incongruity of any feasible individual response to the world-wide system of interlocking chains of political and economic action, and the impossibility to react emotionally to the various horrors and disasters collected from all over the world by the TV networks — all these contribute in the formation of the flexible social character. Young people today have to face a lifetime within a society which will be continuously restructured by an unprecedented rate of cultural, economic, and technological change. More and more they will have to find their identities outside the workshops and professions in changing cultural lifestyles and varying political involvements. I suggest that the essence of the new phase in the civilizing process, namely a reflexive attitude toward the nature of our corporality and our environment, is the common denominator of certain apparently different phenomena which find their most pronounced expression among the young of the middle classes, namely: the informal styles of everyday behavior, the changed attitudes toward nudity and sexuality, the new emphasis on the political meaning of natural categories such as race, region, gender, and sex, the spread of experiential therapies emphasizing emotional breakthroughs, the search for authentic religious experience, the experimental attitude toward psychotropic drugs, and more generally the availability of different world-views and situational experiences of different reality status.

In conclusion, I should like to emphasize two points which are easily overlooked in discussions about the civilizing process. The first is that the different phases of this process all co-exist simultaneously in different social classes and generations at any given time. Today then, we would find the first phase still prevailing in the lower classes, while the second phase is the prevailing mode in the middle classes. With the emergence of the third phase it is more complicated: It certainly begins within the economically leading middle-class groups but is carried out and expressed most strongly by the young generation. The reason for this is given in the outline of a contribution by Ariès (1983): The main factor is the gradually increasing school enrollment which eventually alienates the young from their families and leads to the emergence of the peer group culture. To quote Ariès: "The peer group is isolated from society, made marginal to it, and in this respect it has nothing in common with the age classes of our traditional society; it is an entirely new phenomenon" (Ariès, 1983). However, not so new either for we can observe the peer group culture emerging as early as the beginning of the bourgeois youth movement during the Nineties of the last century. What happens during the third phase of the civilizing process is that the "Principle of Stratified Diffusion" now begins to work not only through the class stratification system but also through the age groups, always beginning with the young. New modes of identity formation and social adaptation are tried out and experimented with in the socially isolated peer groups who yet have, via their parents, a connection to the economic and bureaucratic power structure of the society. Many of the new modes are eventually given up, but some of them eventually filter through the older age groups as well as to the lower classes and the provinces. At the same time during this century the rate of political and technological change has become so quick that each age group emerges as a generation with its own specific historical experiences, especially in connection with the two World Wars. This adds to the tendency that today the civilizing process prevails through the conflict between the generations.

The second point, with which I should like to finish now, concerns modern individualism. In Western societies very gradually a concept of the individual as a self-responsible unity separate if not independent of its social ties has been developed which by now is deeply internalized in all its members. At the same time the civilizing process, pushed forward by increasing economic dependencies as well as by the increasing power accumulation of the state, has made the individual more and more dependent on abstract systems of power and exchange. Much could be said about the dialectical relation of these two contradictory processes. What may concern us here is that it may also explain some of the behavior of the young. For the paradoxical demand to develop a unique identity or personality of your own and at the same time to remain adaptable to the political and economical interdependencies beyond your reach must be most severely experienced by those who are still in search of their own identities. To be sure, the relatively isolated social position of those who still live within the peer group culture of the educational institutions keeps off the most immediate demands of political and economic life. Yet these are experienced in often slightly paranoic anticipation by them and lead to all kinds of bizarre reactions, be this political or cultural radicalism or no-future attitudes and drug addiction. To develop stability *and* flexibility at the same time is not an easy task and often it may appear to them as if the proletarian youth cultures with their more open expression of aggressiveness lead to a healthier life. Today the task seems to be to *live* with the civilizing process rather than to *follow* it. To learn this we need *all* the space for social experimentation there is.

Footnote

1 For more extensive elaboration see my essay on "The Socialization of Nature – Western Attitudes toward Body and Emotions," in: Heelas, P., & A. Lock (eds.), Indigenious Psychologies. London 1981.

Long-Term Changes in Attitudes Toward "Old Age"

Hans-Joachim von Kondratowitz

1. The problem of changes in attitudes toward old age immediately brings to mind numerous public statements made by gerontologists as well as social policy administrators. These commentators point to supposedly negative stereotypes of old age which are common today, and the need to undermine them. These negative stereotypes are presumably widely held and are, to a certain degree, reinforced by the institutionalization and segregation of old age. Consequently, how such attitudes have changed is of interest not only to the aged population itself, those who suffer from these negative judgements — but these changes are also a general social problem of the utmost importance. Possibilities for transforming them are now emerging through the application of learning models as well as in proposals for alternative experiences for the older population — for instance, by the aged taking over new responsibilities, redefining their needs by participating in self-determined groups, and in other ways. Because the mutual processes of social definition, acceptance, and imitation have created negative attitudes toward old age, it seems plausible to design models of learning in order to reshape behavior patterns. And therefore, step by step, one can try to break a "vicious circle" — the self-fulfilling prophecy of decreasing performance capacity in old age.

Out of these various developments the idea that attitudes toward old age are predominantly negative has been increasingly questioned in recent times; these developments point to the simultaneous existence of negative aspects with more positive attitudes, and they emphasize the individual variability and learning capacity still present in old age. By arguing in that vein, future societal developments of attitudes toward old age, in self-interpretation as well as in the interpretations by other and younger generations, seem to be more and more characterized by these dual attitudes. Whether we may look at these potential developments as the first signs of a fundamental change of values around old age remains to be seen. But regardless of this particular possibility, its very existence reveals an important fact. It implicitly demonstrates that attitudes toward old age have been historically transitory. Consequently, it implicates negative attitudes — even if they are still prevalent — as products of long-term but mutable developmental processes. And this raises the question of when and why these predominantly negative attitudes first emerged.

2. Numerous sociological and political science textbooks which discuss the aging of populations suggest that explaining changes in attitudes toward old age is simple. These textbooks usually tell the story of modernization. American historian David H. Fischer, drawing on the work of Donald Cowgill, convincingly summarized this perspective:

"Nearly to our own time, the story goes, western society remained nonliterate in its culture, agrarian in its economy, extended in its family structure, and rural in its residence. The old were few in number, but their authority was very great. Within the extended family the aged monopolized power; within an agrarian economy they controlled the land. A traditional culture surrounded them with an almost magical mystique of knowledge and authority.

But since 1900 (or 1850) a revolutionary process called modernization shattered this traditional society, and transformed the status of the aged in four ways at once. First, the development of modern health technology multiplied the numbers of the elderly, and contributed to the aging of the population and its work force. That situation, in turn, created pressures toward retirement, forced people out of the most valued and highly regarded roles, deprived them of utility, curtailed their income, and lowered their status. Second, modern economic technology created new occupations and transformed most of the old ones, which also meant loss of jobs, incomes, and status by the aged. Third, urbanization attracted the young to the cities, thus breaking down the extended family in favor of the nuclear conjugal unit. Finally, the growth of mass education and literacy meant that 'there can be no mystique of age' and no reverence for the aged on account of their superiority of knowledge and wisdom" (Fischer, 1978, 20 f.).

The implicit message here is that a very definite change in attitudes occurred, a movement from respect and reference towards the aged to predominantly negative stereotypes about them. Furthermore, this perspective describes that change as a consequence of modernization, and it traces the transformation back to the turn of the 20th century.

But empirical evidence completely fails to back this hypothesis, and Fischer (1978) was the first to point this out. He found eight major indications of change in the U.S. experience:

1. In the early American churches and meeting houses, people were seated by age, and the seats of highest honor went to the oldest rather than the richest citizens. That practice ended between 1775 and 1836, and it was replaced by putting the seats up for auction to the highest bidder.
2. Mandatory retirement for officials began (e.g., for judges, beginning in 1777 in New York), and the practice intensified up to 1818; it continued throughout the entire 19th century.
3. By using local census data from the New England states, a distortion in age statistics called "age-heaping" occurs which shows that men tended to overstate their ages in the 18th century, but to understate them in the 19th.
4. In dress, a definite shift from an age-oriented fashion in the 18th century (powdered wigs, long coats) to a youth-oriented fashion (natural hair, tight-fitting waistcoats) took place.
5. In the 19th century new expressions for ridicule of the old developed. Old words of respect disappeared, and once neutral words grew more negative.
6. In paintings, specifically in family portraits of the 18th century, the construction was hierarchical in age composition; the *pater familias* was enthroned above the family. In the 19th century he sat on the same plane as the rest of the family, a more egalitarian arrangement.
7. A change in legal procedures took place around 1775; partible (divisible) inheritance replaced impartibility in the legal codes of most states.
8. A change in naming practices occurred. The proportion of children named after their grandparents declined.

While these transformations admittedly had a limited applicability — specific to the "better classes" of society — a shift toward a predominantly negative image of old age occurred. Yet surprisingly, it took place almost 100 years before modernization theory accounts argue it did. Lawrence Stone, a harsh critic of Fischer's opinions, states the consequences quite bluntly:

"If true, this proposition would put a final nail in the coffin of modernization theory, since it would make all these fundamental transformations precede instead of follow industrialization and urbanization. The chain of causation would be stood on its head" (Stone, 1977a, 11).

28

However, Fischer's analysis proceeds in far greater detail, and it carefully side-steps over-generalizations. Sketching out the overall development, he writes,

"... The history of age relationships in America first ran through a period of involutionary change in which the exaltation of age became more elaborately developed; then through a period of revolutionary change, which occurred during the era of the French Revolution; and then through a period of evolutionary change in which status of old age steadily declined" (Fischer, 1978, 101).

Yet according to Lawrence Stone, Fischer misreads inherently ambiguous evidence because he has mistaken "a small part of the picture for the whole." Using a "magnifying and distorting lens," Fischer has detected a radical change which did not happen, and he "attributed that change to a cause, a shift to a more gerontophobic attitude, which also did not happen."

What actually happened? In Stone's opinion, American and English society at the turn of the 18th century experienced

"... a widespread shift toward a democratization of all human relations and institutions. There was a steady growth of egalitarianism and individualism that affected all personal behavior, including relations within the family. The trouble is that much of [Fischer's] evidence for changing attitudes toward the old is far more convincing as evidence of a different and broader kind of change, from deference to democracy, or from family patriarchy to greater intra-familial equality" (Stone, 1977b, 48).

Stone therefore argues that individualization established a new frame of reference in which attitudes toward old age acquired a new meaning and displayed new functions. But in Stone's opinion, attitudes toward "old age" remained invariably the same from ancient Greece and Rome up to now. Without going into further details of this debate, it clearly leaves much unresolved; furthermore, it calls upon readers to side with one of these irreconcilable positions. Indeed, the situation is exactly as Fischer himself pointed out:

"The result is as if I saw a red wagon and said, 'I see a red wagon.' My critic replies, 'Nonsense, you see red'" (Fischer, 1977, 47).

3. In order to avoid these extreme choices and still in search for our "red wagon," we need more information about these attitudes and processes in other socio-cultural contexts. To test Fischer's hypothesis through German experiences, this article analyzes key words and entries from 37 encyclopedias, handbooks, and dictionaries appearing between 1721 and 1914. Such an analysis helps to gauge the extent to which these words and definitions suggest deep attitudinal changes toward old age, and how this compares with Fischer's findings.

What kind of evidence can this source offer about mentality changes in this period? It would be an illusion to assume that we can find "every-day attitudes" about widespread social practices in these key words; these words were often chosen and written by leading scientists of the time, or by highly educated and learned essayists from the middle class, who were writing for an "educated public" or the "educated classes." However, to interpret these encyclopedia entries as "elitist" and only relevant for a small part of society would be too hasty a reaction. If the encyclopedia contributors were to understand fully key words, their construction had to link up scientific developments with everyday conceptions of life. Therefore, they had to reflect not only the lived experience of a bourgeois "life-world," but had to keep up with new information and revelations as well; they needed to offer the opportunity for reapplying and reconnecting these words and their meanings to immediate experience, and thereby shape patterns of perception.

Because science, specifically medical science, played such an important role in constructing these key words, it is useful to scrutinize the dynamics of contemporary scientific development. Using recent French studies in the history of science (e.g., by Canguilhem or Foucault), we can see a fundamental change in scientific approaches in medicine in the past. This change could be described as a transition from the natural history model, which uses hierarchical devices of classification — to the developmental history model, which uses a deliberately "temporalized" approach with "fluid" boundaries[1]. On the one hand, we can detect this "denaturalization" in the changing range of objects in different disciplines, in the principles operating in the construction of theories, and in the organizational structure of these disciplines. This tendency also generated new disciplines which, for instance, the rise of psychology demonstrates. On the other hand, this history of science tells us that this process of generating these new dimensions could also be reversed; often a "renaturalization" of previously "temporalized" branches of knowledge occurred. As we shall see, these renaturalizations were nevertheless intensely "enriched" by developmental thinking and they never constituted a mere "return" to former classifications (cf. Lepenies, 1976, 18–20, 78–96).

3.1   In the definition and description of the key word *"Alter"* in Jablonski's *Allgemeines Lexikon der Künste und Wissenschaften (General Encyclopedia of Arts and Sciences)* of 1721, we find evidence for a perception of natural history. The encyclopedia described the word as,

"Generally, the natural duration of a thing. In such understanding it is used of human beings; in this sense it is used for human beings, animals, trees — as well as inanimate things" (Jablonski, 1721, 29; same in Jablonski & Schwaben, 1767, 65; Zedler, 1732, Col. 699)[2].

In comparison, the definition appearing in Adelung was, "The natural duration of each thing, especially of a human being" (Adelung, 1793, Col. 238). The increasing significance of *human* age already indicates a shift away from natural history. For instance, the dominant opinion in 18th century medicine was that only one medicine existed, referring equally to human beings and animals (Lepenies, 1976, 92). Human life was divided into seven stages, "childhood, youth, growing youth, young manhood, male (!) age, and decrepit age" (Jablonski, 1721, 29). Apart from the mythological seven-year intervals, which represented the ancient doctrine of equivalence between cosmological and biological phenomena, childhood and youth were clearly subdivided into more intervals than a human's later years. This probably reflected the "discovery" of childhood in the 18th century. Another way of constructing stages of life was even more revealing:

"Other people let the ages of life rise from age ten in ten-year intervals up to one hundred, according to the well-known proverb: ten years, a child; twenty, a young man; thirty, a grown man; forty, well done; fifty, standing still; sixty, old age begins; seventy, a gray man; eighty, does not know anything anymore; ninety, ridiculed by children; one hundred, pray to God" (Jablonski, 1721, 29 f.; Zedler, 1732, Col. 1552).

By referring to the age of 100 years, demographically unlikely at that time, it becomes obvious that these stages were far from realistic descriptions. Rather, they

represented more independent unities, each one with its own special qualities. Looking at age in this light, we see a "path of life" (not course!) arranged horizontally, or like the ascent and descent of a staircase, a series of stages. A "certain physical condition of the body," and a "difference in morals," of "a tendency governing the soul," characterizes each stage. Consequently, Zedler tell us,

"With human age, one may furthermore take up physical and moral considerations – not looking on age as such, which is nothing more than the duration of a thing up to a certain objective, and is generally the case in only one way, that one point in existence simply follows the other; however, one ought to consider the natural and moral condition of a human being, as far as they are situated in this or that interval of their duration, and to assume that one always understands something like a moral universality ..." (Zedler, 1732, Col. 1554).

Let us look more closely at how these conditions influenced the image of old age.

Zedler's work offered a physical and specifically medical evaluation of the intervals through the framework of the prolongation of life, a wide-discussed topic at that time. The work recommended exercising abstinence from abundance and also recommended maintaining orderly behavior. But more important were the moral considerations surrounding age that the work offered, brought out by a discussion of the *Ars Poetica* of Horaz and its 18th-century meaning. Here a clear distinction between "male age" and "old age" arose. "Male age," 30 to 50 years, was characterized by "a sedate disposition," the irresponsibility of youth is given up, and "whilst in this interval the heat is gone, one says in the proverb, he has stopped romping, stopped raging" (Zedler, 1732, Cols. 1556–1557). Thus, male age was characterized as the best period in the life for a bourgeois man, the time when he has a full consciousness of his strength and power, during which he has to use his time economically and carefully regulate his social relations – and it is his last opportunity to acquire wealth for his family. Because the middle-aged man "has come to his senses, he looks deliberately for patrons and friends who could be useful later on." And in his outward appearance, the middle-aged man looks at

"his prestige and reputation, lives an outwardly honest life, and according to the rules of respectability, because he knows how important that is, if he wants to succeed in the world" (ibid.).

In contrast to that fairly positive image stands the concept of "mature age" (50 to 70 years). Here the encyclopedia began by bluntly stating that "old people are often avaricious," and that the less time they have to live, the more they tend frantically to scrape together their things. They seem to complain chronically about the present and tend to idealize their own youth. Nevertheless, the encyclopedia insisted that old people are honored at all times, and another contemporary encyclopedia mentioned that old people belong at the top of the social order (Jablonski, 1721, 31). The ambivalence in attitudes toward "mature age" is obvious.

Finally comes *decrepita aetas* (decrepit age). Here are "people completely worn out, having lost all power of body and soul" (Zedler, 1732, Col. 1553). Curiously, to get more information about these "worn-out people," we have to leave the key words "age," "stages of life," etc. behind, and turn to entries about the "Poor Law," "institutions for the poor," and others. Because the German word *arm* not only implies "being without money and wealth," but also means "being miserable," we find that the definition for *armselig* (miserable) encompasses "not only the poor, but widows, orphans, the old decrepit people, and those wasted by illness" (Jablonski, 1721, 100). Pity is therefore the most favorable attitude offered in the encyclopedia about "decrepit age"; more often, however, we can garner attitudes of indifference and sometimes even disgust from these texts. "Decrepit age" was, in the least, being ridiculed in daily life. It also usually meant being institutionalized, hidden away. And in institutions, "decrepit age" has meant daily life being brought under extremely strict regulation. But most important in this forced withdrawal was the attribute of infirmity of bodily functions in this age. This infirmity entailed needing help to walk, to move about, and also being forced by these circumstances to admit this helplessness in public. This condition was obviously enough to set into motion a process of dividing off the "decrepit age." The predominant way of evaluating the state of mind of people — specifically older people — in relation to the public visibility of physical weakness is important, because in that evaluation we find a broad societal definition of the ability or inability to contribute to society. Therefore, as long as the aged were thought to be capable of rendering services and making contributions to society, the attitudes emerging from contemporary texts showed ambivalence; these attitudes wavered between ostentatious veneration and hints of underlying distrust and mockery about the strange habits of older people. Furthermore, for those of "decrepit age," they seemed to turn into open disdain and a pressure toward segregation into institutionalized zones of society.

3.2   In the course of the 18th century, expectations of the future — previously grounded in the limitations of past experiences — were replaced by a conception in which the "future" meant endlessly rising possibilities. This new outlook served to envision and create programs which articulated the ideal of a "never-been-before" (cf. Gumbrecht, 1981, 46; Koselleck, 1979, 349—375). The concept of an irreversible "progress" served as the means to fuse the solitary quality of "history" and "future" into one term; therefore, the term reflected the new situation in which there was no longer a way sufficiently to derive expectations from former experiences.

By taking up the word "generation," we can evaluate the impact of that change on the relations between different age groups. Intrigued by this change, the German publisher and journalist Friedrich Perthes summed up its impact at the beginning of the century. He saw a dividing up of the political-social world of experiences, which up to that point had been bound to a line of consecutive generations. He remarked that the direction of change in social development formerly stretched out for centuries,

"but now our present time has united something completely incompatible in three generations living simultaneously. The extreme differences in experience of the years 1750, 1789, and 1815 lack all transitions and do not appear successively following each other, but as a side-by-side existence in the now-living people, depending on whether they are grandfathers, fathers, or grandsons" (Perthes, in: Koselleck, 1979, 367)[5].

A dynamic of multi-layered time-structures grew out of one period, and these operated at the same time.

"What 'progress' transformed into one single concept, the clashes between 'Old' and 'New,' in science and art, from country to country, from class to class, had become an everyday experience since the French Revolution. Indeed, the generations still lived in a common 'experiential space,' but this space was to be broken down into different perspectives, according to political generation and social position" (ibid.).

Under those circumstances, the opposite poles between "old" and "new" began to merge with the opposites "old" and "young." Furthermore, we can find the basis for this transformation toward a lasting association of "youth" and "future" in the concept of "progress." "Progress" then began to convey a new meaning for the middle class, for it allowed unbounded optimism to replace familiar experiential knowledge, opening the door to a new era of history (cf. Reulecke, 1983).

"Temporalization of concepts" was another consequence of a growing and widening process of societal "acceleration" of experiential backgrounds. Looking at the transition from natural history to developmental history, the change away from classificatory systems to developmental reasoning is also apparent in the key words of A. F. Macklot's dictionary (1816) and especially of Ersch & Gruber's encyclopedia (1819). This transition first becomes clear in definitions of age:

"Age: generally a certain number of years. Human life from birth to death passes through different epochs, called stages of life (Lebensalter) which all possess peculiarities in body and mind" (Macklot, 1816, 157).

The "peculiarities in mind" were later described as "psychic peculiarities." Ersch & Gruber's definition was even more striking:

"Age denotes ... each space of time in human life, distinguishable by perceivable changes in the activity of the forces of body and mind" (Ersch & Gruber, 1819, 242). And human life is described "as a constantly lasting series of developments, starting with procreation and ending with the destruction of organic individuality" (ibid.).

In a radical developmental perspective, any division of human life into separate stages must be considered a problematic task, for it implies a certain degree of standardization of individual and quite diverse characteristics. In that respect, the ideas put forward in Ersch & Gruber were quite well thought out:

"Each interval in life, essentially characterized by either the emergence of new activities (evolution) or the relapsing or dying away of former activities, constitutes a distinct stage of life (Lebensalter)." In addition, a vitalist perspective emerged which claimed "that there must be a point in time in the life of human beings at which they approach, as closely as possible, the idea which nature wanted to realize in them." This proposed a model of a "curve of life," with an age of heightened potentialities – a peak of life and a decline, although the criteria employed here were exclusively biological-physiological ones.

In contrast to that quite variegated conception, Macklot's way of distinguishing stages of life was more conventional. Macklot accepted a division of four stages, but added further subdivisions for up to eight stages. Childhood and youth comprised five stages, male age – three, and the Greisenalter – age of old men (60 years and up) – constituted another single interval. Compared with classifications of the 18th century, the existence of an old man was kept relatively separate. However, the stage formerly described as "mature age," then bearing relatively positive connotations, was included in the division of "male age." But no one homogeneous solution emerged in all the encyclopedias. In Ersch & Gruber, for instance, "childhood" and "youth" comprised five stages, while "male age" stood without further division, and "high age" kept the two already well-known subdivisions. But here lay a noteworthy difference which might be attributed to the acceleration of life-course as emphasized in the developmental perspective. First, Ersch & Gruber put much emphasis on the process of aging. In the first period, "the cause of the good state of the body shows hardly any remarkable decrease of strength, although it is gradually getting more obvious."

In the second period, the decrepit age, still "possible for only a small number of old men," one witnesses "the emergence of all bodily and psychic signs of old age to a greater degree." External and internal senses are

"fading more and more ... memory and imaginative power are vanishing, as well as the power of judgement, and the old man often becomes childish."

One biological function after another is lost, and finally life expires "in natural death out of *Altersschwäche* [decrepitude because of old age]" (Ersch & Gruber, 1819, 214). The same author responsible for the stages of life descriptions in Ersch & Gruber later stated his point even more precisely, and therefore revealed how this conception differed from today's concept of "multimorbidity":

"The second period, or the decrepit age, can only be experienced by a few old men, even if it represents the natural transition from life to death, occurring *without illness*" (Henke, 1841, 100, emphasis added).

But at the same time the writer did not see psychic and bodily functions and capacities as necessarily going into decline simultaneously. Rather, he emphasized that quite often their development — at least in "mature age" — might move in opposite directions. "As the body declines, the mind rises to an even higher level; reason is revealed in its purest light" (Brockhaus, 1819, 182).

Ersch & Gruber's key word "age" consists of several parts stemming from different origins, and this merits further comment. Apart from an extensive introduction on the subject, the encyclopedia's entry included a discussion of "determination of age" from the perspective of forensic medicine, a legal section written by an historian of law, a section on dietetics by a professor of medicine, and finally, a discussion of animal life by a veterinarian. The inclusion of these disciplines in the discussion of age is quite striking, particularly because the orientation point of all of them is the exercise of some kind of control. These disciplines focused on either control of living conditions through the police and total institutions such as prison, or control through regulations on the legal status of bourgeois individuals, or through the expectation of an internalized self-control — as in the case of dietetics. This illustrated that institutional contexts had already influenced the social defining of old age to a certain extent.

Dietetics are, in general, the art of constructing a balanced manner of living; they are not a new phenomenon, but have their origins in antiquity. In his contribution on age to the Ersch & Gruber encyclopedia, a reknowned professor of medicine, K. F. Burdach, made an interesting connection between developmental thinking and a dietetic approach. His advice was based on an already familiar idea:

"If in the duration of our bodily existence we want to achieve the most possible for human beings, the individuality of our organization has to come as close as possible to that ideal of human existence. But we do not give that individuality to ourselves; instead, it is given to us by the circumstances under which the individual comes into existence and develops further [*sich bildet*]" (Ersch & Gruber, 1819, 245).

These statements do not imply any model of "social causation" of aging. Rather, Burdach saw the word "circumstances" as the "organic forces" of the parents and resulting from them, and their "spiritual forces" at the time of their child's birth. If these forces were in a state of equilibrium, this resulted in a "harmony of the conditions of life." This would in turn lead to an "ideal life span" with biological and social forces existing in an equilibrium. However, biological processes would have primacy, in that they would determine the variability of the "circumstances." In this anthropologically-oriented viewpoint, harmony and due proportion in all daily activities represented the determining factor in dietetics, instead of the former search for recipes guaranteeing longevity.

"One ought relatively to diminish exertions; however, one should not suddenly move from a busy life into a completely idle one, because this sudden ceasing of the usual strain results in a weakening, as though a limb were taken [from an organism], and this quite often causes early death. Instead, work ought to become easier and to be lessened gradually." Likewise, Burdach's piece counselled, one should no longer engage in "completely unfamiliar and intricate business relations and work; instead, one ought to proceed along the path one is used to and where one was able to achieve before." Furthermore, "frequent contacts with younger, optimistic people, especially by being occupied with children," ought to guarantee the necessary vigor for life (Ersch & Gruber, 1819, 245 f.).

Of course these recommendations are somewhat noteworthy. And we should not overlook the fact that they were quite socially-specific. Apart from the obvious fact that Burdach's recommendations could only be applied to the well-off — for instance, wealthy craftsmen, lawyers, economically-secure military pensioners, or rentiers — they were also gender-specific. K. F. Burdach's writings confirm this impression, for they convey his infamous conception of the polarization of "gender characters" as based on natural inequalities between man and woman (cf. Hausen, 1976, 363–375). In 1837 he wrote a widely-read book, *Anthropology for the Educated Public* in this vein:

"In the female organism, the connection with reproduction, with preserving the species is prevalent; in the male organism, the *individuality* and its preservation is prevalent" (Burdach, 1837, 433).

This "individuality," which supposedly "ought to come close to the ideal of human existence" therefore implicitly appeared to exclude women — at least as long as they could not approach male gender. According to this conception of the polarization of character by gender, such a process of "approaching" took place increasingly in the higher female ages. The "age limit" of the female was seen in the menopause. "By losing her generative power, her character of gender is obscured to a certain extent, and therefore approaches male gender." He described this as the biological transition to a certain sturdiness, and wrote,

"... the character of the woman becomes more firm and steadfast, her whole way of acting becomes more decisive, more independent, bolder; individuality is altogether more apparent" (Burdach, 1837, 584 f.).

Another key word which appeared in an 1840 encyclopedia demonstrated what a powerful idea Burdach's words articulated. The structure of that key word was an oddity to which I will return later, in a different connection. It read:

"Female sex: 3 1/2 years, indication of female nature; 7 years, fully developed child, maiden; 10 1/2, presentiment of female fecundity; 17 1/2, presentiment of motherhood; 21, time of true love, in contrast to former fickleness; 24 1/2, zenith of womanhood; 28, best years of a woman as wife and mother; 31 1/2, experienced and understanding woman, still pleasant; 35, last perfect time in the life of a female, spinsterhood; 38 1/2, women getting older, dignity instead of former beauty; 42, respect and wealth as a substitute for the lost advantages of youth; 45 1/2, transition of female character into male; 49, female senium, crisis over waning womanhood, joy about son-in-laws and grandchildren" (Pierer, 1840, 273).

In addition to the recurrence of the concept of the approaching male gender character in this 1840 description, the view that women obviously seem to age sooner, and therefore reach old age at a comparatively earlier point than men is significant.

What conclusions can we draw from these developments? Very contradictory trends appeared to be having an effect simultaneously. There can be no question that in the movement towards developmental thinking, the key words increasingly looked at old age as a learning process, respectively as a growing possibility of a discontinuity between bodily decline and intellectual abilities, therefore allowing for more individual diversity. Accordingly, the images about old age conveyed in Macklot's, Ersch & Gruber's, and Brockhaus' key words definitely transmit a more positive than negative message. However, pointing to a general historical shift towards a more positive image of old age needs to be more specific. First, clear differences in the evaluation of "middle age" (or "male age") and "old age" still existed. The encyclopedias only offered unhesitatingly positive remarks about the "middle age" groups, although they lacked the orientation around everyday life and the naivety of pragmatic prescriptions appearing in the 18th century. Instead, we can observe a trend toward idealization and the creation of distinct types of situations, and therefore, a higher degree of generalization of life experiences emerged. On one hand, male age became

"... a period of fruits, reflection replaces frivolity, equanimity displaces inconstancy, prudence replaces thoughtlessness." Likewise, "the mind will be refined, the power of judgement is growing and it is going to be freed of former sensuousnesses" (Macklot, 1816, 160). On the other hand, these descriptions viewed old age in a more ambivalent way: "In that age, the expressions of the capacities of the soul decline in the same degree to which the machine (!) loses its ability, although without forcing reason itself to descend from its height. To the contrary, in an old man, sound in body and mind, reason seems to purify itself of its wordly sentiments and seems to become more independent of the daily preoccupations of life." But indeed, moral infirmities of old men also emerge to a greater extent: "Especially the ambition to be honored and stinginess, envy of the advantages and joy of youth; censoriousness, garrulity, clinging to preconceived opinions, caviling, and moody behavior are prevalent" (ibid.).

However, referring to "an old man, sound in body and mind" again implies a view separating "mature age" and "decrepit age." The attitudes expressed concerning this last stage of life oscillated between pity and indifference — although the presence of ridicule was clearly subdued, their connotations less distinctly negative; this pointed to a slightly more positive or at least neutral evaluation of this life stage.

4. Can this be described as a triumph of developmental thinking as reflected in the key words? This is an initial impression, reinforced by the fact that the first edition of the subsequent, and most widely distributed contemporary German encyclopedia, that of Brockhaus, took over the key word *"Alter"* (and its description) from Macklot's 1816 edition. Brockhaus reprinted Macklot's description from 1820 up to 1833 almost without changes. But already in the 1833 edition, and

finally from 1840 onwards, distinct signs of a "renaturalization" of the key words appeared. These showed a "narrowing down" of their meaning, and a reduction to exclusively negative attitudes toward old age. From then on, up to the end of the 19th century, these clearly remained dominant.

In the Brockhaus encyclopedia of 1833, trends toward renaturalization are basically visible in the insistence on a change to a seven-stage life-span (instead of the former four-stage span). Reference to a book by K. F. Burdach, *About the Chronology of Human Life*, also proves very instructive. Burdach surprisingly divided

"... the development of the human being into ten periods, each with seven years, thirty-one weeks, and six days ... three of them comprise the age of immaturity, the rest of them the time of maturity, and old age is one period among them" (Brockhaus, 1833 – *Alter*, 215). These obvious revisions of developmental history reached a peak in the developmentally-enriched classification already presented, in connection with the earlier "old age" of women. In this we find a division by use of *Stufenjahre* – that is, periods of four and a half, respectively nine years, and each interval was characterized by specific attributes (Pierer, 1840 – *Lebensalter*, 273). This remarkable rupture with developmental history was nevertheless preserved up to the 1867 edition, until finally, in 1880, an entirely new version of the key word was written. While this kind of almost rigid classificatory scheme undoubtedly constituted a special case, symptoms of a general renaturalization can be garnered from other 19th century encyclopedias as well. (As in: Reichenbach, 1840; Wigand, 1846; Manz, 1848; Kleiner Brockhaus, 1854; Brockhaus, since 1864; Spamer, 1881; Pierer, since 1888.) Only one encyclopedia retained a radical developmental perspective (Meyer, 1841 – *Alter*, 280). As a rule, from 1840 onwards, most key words for age underwent a more or less visible process of renaturalization, with unresolved tensions between developmental thinking and natural history traditions continuing.

Generally speaking, in this process of renaturalization, the temporal structure of reasoning in a developmental vein was usually maintained. However, up through certain linguistic phrases, it was schematized and standardized, respectively, later it was reduced almost exclusively to merely biological processes, so that it is tempting to speak of a "freeze" on developmental dynamics. In any case, this ironically meant that the developmental approach itself had the tendency to stiffen into a type of static classificatory system again.

This oscillation between natural and developmental history became specifically visible with the first appearance of the term "life cycle." It seems to have been introduced into the encyclopedias for the first time in the first edition of Manz' 1848 encyclopedia (Manz, 1848 – *Lebensalter*, 622). Use of this term was no coincidence. It had a special meaning, as brought out in cultural history research into the genesis and relevance of the term "cycle" and in the earlier fascination with a connection between meteorology and medicine (Pomian, 1979; Lepenies, 1976, 88–96). In that historical context, it embodied the specific quality of keeping movement stabilized by insisting that a periodicity repeated itself. Therefore, in transferring this term to the life history of individuals during that phase of a growing renaturalization appeared as a kind of "compromise" between natural and developmental history.

This process of renaturalization had an impact on the evaluation of the later stages of the life cycle as well. Examination of discontinuous, and sometimes apparently contradictory lines of variety in the process of human aging – present in earlier developmental thinking – were later narrowed down and standardized. The openness and richness in evaluation of the stages of life "shrank" more or less simultaneously. The ambivalence present in this earlier thinking, which leaned toward positive evaluations of old age, was generally reduced more and more to a negative perspective. Therefore, even if the entire process was much more uneven,

37

long-term trends in the German case strongly support D. H. Fischer's analysis. Inquiry into the complex and manifold underlying causes of this process should be the next step of analysis.

Footnotes

1 For a discussion of the concept of "temporalization" (*Verzeitlichung*) see Koselleck, 1979.
2 All the key word quotations that follow are my own translations. Unfortunately, the peculiarities of these quotations (such as rhyming endings or old German colloquial words) cannot be captured by this translation.
3 The dates given in the quotation refer to – 1750, type of experiences of "ancient règime" in German states; 1789, French Revolution; 1815, foundation of the German nationalistic and radical-liberal youth movement, the *Burschenschaft*.

Listing of all Key Words

German	English
Aetas, Senium, Seniorat	–
Alter	age
Lebensalter	ages of life
Lebensdauer	duration of life
Greis	old man
Greisenalter	old age
Mann, Frau	man, woman
Altersversorgung	provisions for old age
Altersunterstützungskassen	chest/fund for support in old age
Altersversicherung	old age pension
arm	poor
Armenwesen	poor relief
Armenanstalten	institutions for the poor

Listing of all Dictionaries and Encyclopedias

Dictionaries

1. Steinbach, Christoph Ernst:
Vollständiges Deutsches Wörter-Buch.
Breslau 1734.
2. Adelung, Johann Christoph:
Grammatisch-kritisches Wörterbuch der Hochdeutschen Mundart.
Leipzig 1793.
3. Heyse, Johann Christoph August:
Handwörterbuch der Deutschen Sprache.
Magdeburg 1833.
4. Heinsius, Theodor:
Vollständiges Wörterbuch der Deutschen Sprache.
Wien 1840.
5. Grimm, Jacob and Wilhelm:
Deutsches Wörterbuch.
Leipzig 1854.
6. Heyne, Moritz:
Deutsches Wörterbuch.
Leipzig 1905.

Encyclopedias

1. Jablonski, Johann Theodor:
Allgemeines Lexikon der Künste und Wissenschaften.
Leipzig 1721.
2. Jablonski, Johann Theodor:
Allgemeines Lexikon der Künste und Wissenschaften.
Verbessert und vermehret von Johann Joachim Schwaben.
Königsberg, Leipzig 1767.
3. Zedler, Johann Heinrich (ed.):
Großes vollständiges Universal-Lexikon aller Wissenschaften und Künste.
Halle, Leipzig 1732.
4. Krünitz, Johann Georg:
Oekonomische Encyclopaedie oder Allgemeines System der Staats-, Stadt-, Haus- und
Landwirtschaft.
Berlin 1773 (2nd ed. 1782).
5. Harl, Johann Paul (ed.):
Allgemeines alphabetisches Repertorium ...
Erlangen 1818.
6. Macklot, A. F.:
Conversations-Lexikon oder encyclopädisches Handwörterbuch für gebildete Stände.
Stuttgart 1816.
7. Real-Encyclopädie oder Conversations-Lexikon, Brockhaus.
Leipzig 1819.
8. Ersch, J. S. & Gruber, J. G. (eds.):
Allgemeine Encyclopädie der Wissenschaften und Künste in alphabetischer Folge.
Leipzig 1819.
9. Allgemeine deutsche Realencyclopädie (Conversations-Lexikon), Brockhaus.
Leipzig 1820, 5th ed.
10. Binzer, A. & Pierer, H. A. (eds.):
Encyclopädisches Wörterbuch der Wissenschaften, Künste und Gewerbe.
Altenburg 1822.
11. Allgemeine deutsche Realencyclopädie für die gebildeten Stände (Conversations-Lexikon),
Brockhaus.
Leipzig 1833, 8th ed.

12. Rotteck, Carl v. & Welcker, Carl (eds.):
Staats-Lexikon oder Encyclopädie der Staatswissenschaften.
Altona 1834.
13. Gebr. Reichenbach
Allgemeines deutsches Conversations-Lexikon für Gebildete eines jeden Standes.
Leipzig 1840.
14. Pierers Universal-Lexikon.
Altenburg 1840.
15. Meyers Conversations-Lexikon.
Hildburghausen 1841, 1st ed.
16. Wigands Conversations-Lexikon.
Leipzig 1846.
17. Allgemeines deutsches Volks-Conversations-Lexikon für Jedermann, Tramburgs Erb.
Hamburg 1845.
18. Allgemeine Realencyclopädie (Manzsche Encyclopädie).
Regensburg 1848, 1st ed.
19. Herders Conversations-Lexikon.
Freiburg 1854.
20. Kleineres Brockhaussches Conversations-Lexikon (in 4 volumes).
Leipzig 1854.
21. Meyers Neues Conversations-Lexikon.
Hildburghausen, New York 1857.
22. Bluntschli, J. C. & Brater, K.:
Deutsches Staats-Wörterbuch.
Stuttgart, Leipzig 1857.
23. Wagener, Hermann (ed.):
Neues Conversations-Lexikon; Staats- und Gesellschaftslexikon.
Berlin 1859.
24. Pierers Universal-Lexikon.
Altenburg 1862, 4th ed.
25. Allgemeine deutsche Realencyclopädie (Conversations-Lexikon), Brockhaus.
Leipzig 1864, 10th ed.
26. Allgemeine Realencyclopädie (Manz).
Regensburg 1865, 3rd ed.
27. Pierers Universal-Lexikon.
Altenburg 1867, 5th ed.
28. Meyers Konversations-Lexikon.
Hildburghausen, New York 1869, 2nd ed.
29. Meyers Konversations-Lexikon.
Leipzig 1874, 3rd ed.
30. Brockhaus Conversations-Lexikon.
Leipzig 1875, 12th ed.
31. Allgemeine Realencyclopädie (Manz).
Regensburg 1880, 4th ed.
32. Spamers Illustriertes Konversations-Lexikon.
Leipzig, Berlin 1881.
33. Pierers Konversations-Lexikon (ed. J. Kürschner).
Stuttgart 1888, 7th ed.
34. Meyers Konversations-Lexikon.
Leipzig, Wien 1890, 4th ed.
35. Brockhaus Konversations-Lexikon.
Leipzig 1892, 14th ed.
36. Brockhaus Konversations-Lexikon.
Leipzig 1893/4, 15th ed.
37. Habbels Konversations-Lexikon.
Regensburg 1912.

Generational Co-Residence and the Transfer of Authority: Some Illustrations from Austrian Household Listings

Thomas Held

The question whether and where, in pre-industrial times, adults of two or more generations lived together in a household has attracted sociologists and social historians since the late 19th century. Even the "new" social history of the family was dominated in its beginnings by the famous debate on the importance of the stem-family (Laslett, 1972; Berkner, 1972; 1975). It is now a well-established fact that in most of Western Europe, family households were predominantly nuclear at least since the early 17th and quite likely the 16th century. The quantitative irrelevance of households with three or four generations and, in particular, of the stem-family has been documented by a large body of local or regional studies. Moreover, computer simulation of various household formation rules has demonstrated that nuclear family households were frequent even under demographic assumptions most beneficial to the occurrence of generationally extended or complex families (Wachter, 1978).

Generational Co-Residence with Authority Transfer: The Retirement Arrangement

The consensus about the predominance of the nuclear family in the modern history of Western Europe does not imply a uniform family map for all of Europe. Differences in the patterns of generational co-residence and authority transfer are especially obvious between East and West, but also between North and Southern Europe where relatively high proportions of multiple-family households can be found (e.g., Kertzer, 1977). In Eastern and South-Eastern Europe, joint-family households with three or more generations living together were not uncommon (Hammel, 1972; Plakans, 1975; Czap, 1982; Mitterauer & Kagan, 1982). Here, household authority was not transferred inter-vivos, and not necessarily from father to son but rather within a patrilineal kinship system (Wheaton, 1975). Accordingly, marriage was not linked to headship status. In the West, especially in England (and also in colonial America and the U.S.A.), household formation followed a neolocal pattern and generational co-residence was generally infrequent. The elderly tended to live alone or as lodgers with unrelated persons. When adults of two generations lived together, it was the result of parents, typically a widowed mother, moving in with a child rather than of children staying in the household of their parents (Laslett, 1977, 208–213; Smith, 1979). This way, households with two generations of adults were established long after the children had left the parents' home.

Neither under the Eastern nor under the Western ideal type of household formation rule do generational co-residence and household authority seem to be in conflict. Although access to headship is tied to marriage, there is no institutionalized conflict over household authority within the neolocal formation pattern in Western Europe, and generational co-residence, if it occurs, is not formally linked to property transfer and inheritance. In the East, authority is not transferred until the death of the head of household, but access to marriage is not linked to headship status. Thus, under the patriarchal rule, generational co-residence does not constitute a challenge to household authority.

In Central Europe, and parts of North-Western Europe, however, a seemingly conflictive institutional combination of generational co-residence and transfer of household authority can be found. Here, as under the North-West European household formation pattern, marriage is closely linked to the entry into headship status. But this status — property and authority — is conferred to the younger generation only in exchange for retirement provisions. The result is a generationally extended or multiple-family household in which authority is located within the younger generation — in contrast to the classical stem-family of the Le-Play type (Mitterauer & Sieder, 1982; Gaunt, 1983; Held, 1982). In terms of ideal types of household formation rules, access to headship and marriage in the West is allocated through markets, while in Eastern Europe, marriage is not subject to property requirements, and access to headship follows a fixed seniority rule within the patriline (Wheaton, 1975; Mitterauer & Kagan, 1982). Within this latter pattern, the village community (i.e., the collective of elderly heads of household) or the landlord who deals with the village as a corporate unit take care of the re-allocation of property to household units. Under both "Western" and "Eastern" household formation rules, however, individual fathers are not extremely crucial in determining the timing of the son's marriage and his entry into household headship.

Under what could be called a "Central" European rule, this is clearly different. Here, the decision of the individual father to "retire" shapes the life chances of both the designated heir as well as the non-inheriting siblings. The structural base of generational co-residence in a stem-family of the retirement type is the strict impartiability of the farm property, guaranteed and enforced by the landlord and later by the absolutist state (Rebel, 1978). The historical roots of this specific form of inter-vivos inheritance are seen in relatively dependent and restricted forms of tenure growing out of the Medieval villication economy (Mitterauer & Sieder, 1982, 33 f.). Under these forms of tenure, the landlord could replace the holder of a farm at any time (Leibstiftrecht). Although these limited forms of tenure later gave way to inheritable, "emphiteutic" concepts of tenantship (Rebel, 1978)[1], it has been argued that retirement type households were most frequent in areas with a rather strong influence of the landlord (Mitterauer, 1976). In the territories which were colonized in the late Middle Ages, and in mountainous, remote areas in general (as some parts of the Alps), the greater autonomy of the peasants resulted in a near absence of retirement arrangements (Netting, 1979).

It is difficult, however, to establish a clear relationship between the influence of the manorial lord and the relative frequency of retirement type stem-households (Held, 1982). The rather broad distinction between different forms of tenure is blurred and often reversed by factors at the local level, such as the type of agriculture, the stratification of the village, and the inheritance practices (occasional forms of partible inheritance and differences between ultimogeniture and primogeniture

42

within the impartible regime). The close link between property transfer and the establishment of a retirement type stem-family means that in most cases only the holders of a full-size farm could afford to retire while small holders, cottagers, and day-laborers (more often than not the majority of the village population) only occasionally were able to benefit from a retirement arrangement (Mitterauer, 1983; Held, 1982).

Generational Co-Residence and Household Labor Organization

The retirement type stem-family is not the only household type that involves generational co-residence and problems of household authority. Hajnal (1982) has recently pointed to the crucial importance of servants within the North-Western European household pattern. The flux of unmarried persons between households guarantees the allocation of labor to fixed amounts of land. Servanthood is seen, under this perspective, as a stage in the life cycle, a *generational* rather than a *social* status. Although it is generally assumed that servants were substituted for children and vice-versa in the course of the family life cycle (Mitterauer & Sieder, 1979), households consisting of widowed elderly persons and unrelated (adult) servants are quite frequent in the Austrian villages. Generational co-residence is here implied in the master-servant relationship. By far more important in quantitative terms, however, are households with lodgers and inmates. The latter often constitute sub-families of their own. In elaborating on earlier arguments by Laslett (1972), Hajnal (1982) takes these groups as more or less independent nuclear households, equivalent to households in apartments in urban areas. The Austrian sources analyzed here do not seem to warrant such a categorization. Even if groups of inmates had separate quarters or a separate kitchen, they were socially and legally dependent upon the head of household, and in most cases they were also involved in the farm economy to some extent. It is not clear, however, whether the inmates or the inmate group belonged to "generation" (in terms of cohort membership) other than that of the head of household.

The problems of generational co-residence and household authority can be illustrated by looking at household structures or at the household statuses of individuals over the life cycle. Based on census type household lists from Austrian parishes and communities, this paper gives examples for both perspectives. Since the frequency and determinants of retirement type stem-families have been discussed elsewhere (Held, 1982), the change in household status over the life cycle will be emphasized.

Empirical Illustration I: Retirement Type Stem-Families

The data analyzed here cover a time period from 1632 to 1909. The household listings are based on "soul books" (Liber Status Animarum) which were established by the Catholic Church as a measure of the Counter-Reformation after the Council of Trent[2] (see Table 1).

The analysis of households shows that retirement arrangements were relatively infrequent. Only a small fraction of the households were retirement type stem-families, and only a minority of the population at risk (i.e., 60 years and older) lived as retirees. While the inheritance regime does not seem to affect the proportion of retirement households to a large extent, this household type is clearly more frequent in areas with a mixed agriculture (grain and milk production) than under subsistence conditions (extensive agriculture, cattle) or in small market towns with a high proportion of crafts and trade[3]. More remarkable in Table 1 is the increase of generationally extended households from the 18th to the 19th century[4]. This increase is not the result of changes in the age distribution or of a higher life expectancy. More "developed," central, or urban communities have a lower frequency of retirement arrangements. The highest frequency of retirement arrangement households can be found in relatively remote but wealthy parishes with scattered settlements and a mixed agriculture. Apparently, the retirement institution became more popular in those areas that benefited most from the expansion of cash crop production in the second half of the 19th century (Ehrmann, 1976). At the same time, the setting up of a retirement type stem-family seems to function as an alternative to remarriage for male heads of household. This is demonstrated by the strong increase in the relationship between the proportion of widowers and the relative frequency of households with members of the retired generation (Held, 1982, 250).

Empirical Illustration II: Household Roles and Age Groups

Figures 1a and 1b show the proportions of persons in main household roles over age groups as average over-all village censuses[5]. The age-specific proportions of household roles are interpreted here as individual trajectories, that is, cohort effects are neglected. The curves illustrate clearly the main features of Hajnal's North-West European household formation pattern. There is, first, a marked period of service for both men and women. The highest proportions of maids and servants can be found in the age group 25–34. Thus, servanthood in another than the parent's household did not universally begin in childhood. In the age group 15–24, some two-thirds of men and women are still listed as sons and daughters, and the reports on very young servants (e.g., in England) are not substantiated by the Austrian data. This is remarkable since sons and daughters past a certain age usually figure in the "soul books" as servants even if they continue to live in the parental household (see Figures 1a and 1b).

Figure 1a also shows a relative late entry into headship status for both men and women. Not more than 70 percent of the men and 65 percent of the women ever became heads of household. The elderly (age group 65–74) suffer from a loss of headship status but for women the drop is much steeper than for men. In accordance with the predominance of nuclear families, the proportions of relatives are small in all age groups but the last one. Here the retirement arrangements mentioned above are reflected by a decrease in the head-of-household category and a corresponding increase of relatives. For women, these transitions are more frequent than for men. In addition, the shrinking percentage of female heads is paralleled by a marked increase of females living as lodgers or inmates. The proportion of persons living as dependents in someone else's household is remarkably high over all age groups. This points to a stratification rather than a life course dimension. Nevertheless, the proportions of lodgers is increasing in the population 54 years and older (see Figures 2a and 2b, 3a and 3b).

The comparison of parish censuses taken before and after 1780 does not reveal very clear shifts in the institutionalized age-role-trajectories (Figure 2). In the second period, men enter household headship at a somewhat younger age but, at the same time, seem to retire from the headship position earlier in life and in greater numbers. The inmate or lodger status is less age-dependent in the second than in the first period, and in the center group of adults (45–54 years of age), the proportion of female inmates is lower. If we compare the type of economy (Figures 3a and 3b), the small-town parishes stand out with regard to the proportion of male and female heads. Also, women seem to benefit more from the opportunity structure of a local economy dominated by crafts and trade. This is demonstrated by the relatively low increase of female inmates for the older age categories. For men, on the other hand, it also matters whether the local economy is dominated by a subsistence type, extensive agriculture (cattle, lumber) or by a mixed, more intensive rural economy (grain and milk). In the second case, we find the lowest proportion of heads in the age group 64–75, whereas under subsistence conditions the proportion of male inmates among the elderly is highest.

The proportion of heads (both male and female) in the older age groups (55–64), on the other hand, is negatively associated with all types of extended family households (with Stem: $r = -.38, p < .001$; with lateral extension: $r = -.39$, $p < .001$) and also negatively with the percentage of servants ($r = -.53, p < .000$) and lodgers ($r = -.42, p < .000$) in the population. The underlying factor here is a settlement or occupational structure which supports the formation of independent household in general, making the elderly more likely to remain in headship position and reducing the dependent fluctuating population, that is, servants and inmates. In the Austrian data, the rural towns with a relatively high proportion of crafts and trade (including activities associated with mining) are an example for the latter situation.

Household Formation Patterns and Intergenerational Relations in Society

The empirical illustrations from rural Austria present a somewhat ambiguous picture. On one hand, authority position in the household is, at least for a major part of the population, clearly related to generational status. Young adults most likely lived as servants for an extended period of their life, and at the age of 40, only about half of the male adult population were heads of a household (or, in the case of women, married to a head). Similarly, headship status was of limited duration: The decline in the proportion of household heads or wives started for women around the age of 55, for men around the age of 65. Since all this took place in the absence of almost any form of institutionalized age care, these persons continued their lives either as parents under some form of retirement arrangement, or as inmates and lodgers in someone else's household. Retirement arrangements, however, were limited to areas and segments of the peasantry who could afford to support persons who, at least formally, were not, or only marginally, part of the farm labor force.

45

How then can the political and ideological importance of the idea of generational co-residence be explained? The persistence of this myth is amply documented by the current social security debates in most highly industrialized countries where conservative forces aim explicitly or implicitly at a so-called "re-privatization" of parts of social security transfers, especially old age benefits or pensions. Given the enormous amount of information to the contrary which family historians and historical demographers have assembled over the past 15 years, the persistence of the imagery of generational co-residence is startling. Conservative and fundamentalist propaganda alone cannot account for the widespread inclination to invoke the formula of the generationally extended household as a remedy for every social problem.

An alternative explanation for the importance of the myth of generational co-residence could focus not on the frequency and occurrence of retirement arrangements or the stem-families but on the fact that under the Central European household formation rule, the father had a pivotal position in determining the life chances of children. In the Central European situation, the key generational problem is *succession* rather than *emancipation*. In a very speculative manner, other features of the generational culture could be linked to differences in the household formation rules. Gillis (1981) has pointed to the strong fraternal or lateral elements in the youth culture of England, illustrated by the importance of self-rule bodies in schools, brotherhoods, etc. In these organizations, the master of the guild or profession functions, and is seen as, a brother rather than a father. The relative importance of a fraternal (lateral) over a paternal (or generational) control system may also relate to major differences in the demographic development between England and Central Europe. In England, secular and short-run changes in the standard of living were followed by corresponding changes in nuptiality and, with a larger time lag, in fertility. When times grew harder, fewer married and they waited longer to do so (Schofield & Wrigley, 1982, 254 ff.). With regard to generational relations, it is important that this control mechanism did not operate through fathers who delayed or limited access to headship position. Rather, marriages and births were delayed because the labor market did not allow for an accumulation of the means that were thought necessary for setting up a family. The operation of such a norm of a minimal family living standard requires, in turn, some kind of peer-group culture, that is, a culture with lateral rather than lineal orientation.

Smith (1981) has suggested that the household structure of the past still influences, to a certain extent, the forms of generational co-residence today. It remains an entirely speculative question whether and how the generational "regimes" as reflected by various household formation rules have shaped or are still shaping the wider societal and political frame of a culture. The importance of succession in a system of original impartiability may result not only in conflicts between parents and children but also in a cleavage between heirs and non-heirs. This intrafamilial class distinction which has both inter- and intragenerational elements has been illustrated in Rebel's (1978) description of the "highlife" of "retired" peasant who rather sold than just passed the estate to the son. This generational element of stratification may lower the subjective relevance of economic and occupational status hierarchies. In the West, however, particularly in Anglo-Saxon culture, differences between families, that is, social class differences, may have been more relevant[6].

It would certainly go too far to interpret cultural differences in the intensity and forms of generational conflicts of today by looking at household structures and co-residence rules of the 18th and 19th century. The way such conflicts are publicly perceived and the way they shape the individual mapping of society, however, should be analyzed with the history of households and families in mind. It remains for further studies to substantiate the impression that in Central Europe, society is more often interpreted in terms of generational membership, whereas in the "West" — as an ideal type of society — generations are looked at as one interest group among others and age constitutes just one but not necessarily the most important social dimension.

Footnotes

1 It follows from the emphyteutic nature of the tenantship that "the tenant could enjoy the lord's farm, and dispose of its substance as if it were his own, provided he did not lessen its value in any way. (...) If, at the death of the tenant or his spouse, the inventory showed liens in excess of the total value of all the assets, the estate authorities ... declared the tenancy bankrupt, and expropriated the incumbent tenant family" (Rebel, 1978, 281 f.).

2 Data are available for a total of 76 censuses from 32 communities or parishes. The listings cover a time period from 1632 to 1896. The major part of the listings was taken from "soul books," an ecclesiastical recording procedure established by the Church after the Council of Trent as a measure of the Counter-Reformation. The soul books have been supplemented by some listings from the Maria-Theresia conscription and the first Austrian census in 1857. The listings which have been described elsewhere in greater detail (Mitterauer & Sieder, 1979; Schmidtbauer, 1983), were collected between 1976 and 1978 by Michael Mitterauer and his group at the University of Vienna. The records usually give information on the (functional) position of an individual in the household, age, marital status, sex, and relationship to the head of household.

3 The weak relationship between inheritance rule and the relative frequency of retirement arrangements can be explained by the concentration of observations with primogeniture inheritance in the time period before 1780, that is, when retirement arrangements were less frequent. The negative influence of ultimogeniture (or exceptional forms of partible inheritance) is thus offset by the historical trend.

4 The distinction between censuses taken before 1780 and listings dating from the period after that year is, to a certain extent, determined by the distribution of the observations over time. On the other hand, the beginning of the reign of Joseph II also brought many determined attempts at agricultural reforms and improvements in the property and/or tenantship rights of peasants.

5 The age categories were chosen with the decades as centers (i.e., 5–14, 15–24, etc.) in order to correct for the substantial overcounting of the full decades and the undercounting of the ages just above and below these ages.

6 The coincidence of peasant autonomy (especially in juridical and political matters) and the absence of retirement arrangements (as, e.g., in some Alpine areas in Switzerland and Tyrol) provides another example of how the household regime may be related to the wider polity. The absence of a strong outside authority (landlord, central state) results in a political culture characterized by both community democracy and elements of gerontocracy.

Table 1: Retirement Type Stem-Families[a]

a) Frequency of Retirement Stem-Family Households and Proportion of Retirees among the Elderly

	Households with Retirement Arrangements (%)	Retirees in Age Group 51–70 (%)
All observations	10.9 (44)	7.8 (35)
– before 1780	7.4 (19)	4.5 (14)
– after 1780	13.6 (25)	10.0 (21)
F-test for comparison	6.85*	5.70*

b) Frequency of Retirement Stem-Families by Characteristics of Parishes

	Households with Retirement Arrangements (%)		
Parishes by:	All Observations	Before 1780	After 1780
Crafts, Trade			
– low, not important	13.6 (23)	9.0 (10)	17.2 (13)
– high, important	8.0 (21)	5.7 (9)	9.7 (12)
F-test for comparison	5.68*	1.97	4.81*
Inheritance Rule			
– primogeniture	9.5 (17)	9.0 (13)	11.1 (4)
– ultimogeniture[b]	13.4 (16)	2.6 (2)	14.9 (14)
F-test for comparison	1.94	2.76	.51
Agricultural Development			
– subsistence	10.7 (17)	8.7 (10)	13.6 (7)
– mixed (grain and milk)	17.4 (13)	11.8 (3)	19.1 (10)
– rural town	5.2 (14)	3.1 (6)	6.7 (8)
F-test for comparison	10.78***	4.09*	5.53**

48

c) Pearson Correlations (r) Between Proportion of Retirement Stem-Families
and Proportions of Heads, Males, and Widowed among the Elderly

	Households with Retirement Arrangements (%)		
	All Observations	Before 1780	After 1780
% Heads of household in age group 51–70	−.60*** (35)	−.52* (13)	−.71** (22)
% Widowers in age group 51–70	.40** (35)	.07 (13)	.46* (22)
% Males in age group 51–70	.21 (35)	−.33 (13)	.47** (22)

Notes:
(n) Number of observations.
*   p<.10.
**   p<.01.
*** p<.001.

a   From Held (1982, 239, 242, 244). The figures in this table are based on the same set of 32 parishes as the exhibits (only the town Salzburg has been substituted for Thalgau, a large agricultural parish close to Salzburg). However, of the 76 observations (due to multiple censuses for several villages), only 47 have been used here.
b   Including some wine producing parishes with partible inheritance.

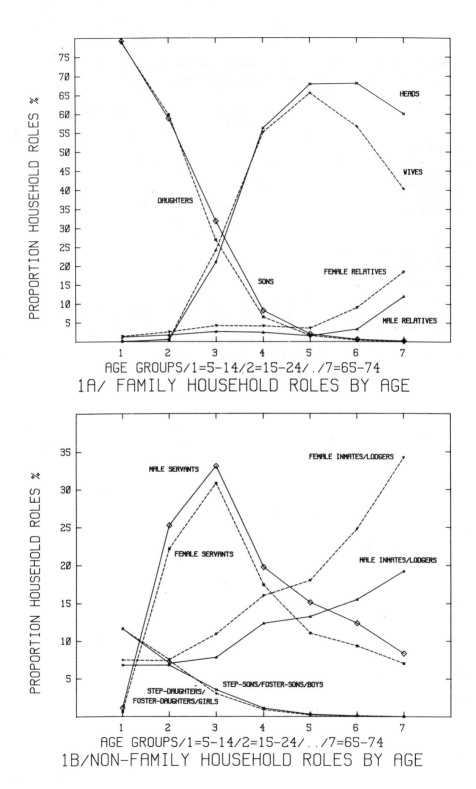

PROPORTION HOUSEHOLD ROLES %

75
70
65
60
55
50
45
40
35
30
25
20
15
10
5

HEADS
WIVES
DAUGHTERS
SONS
FEMALE RELATIVES
MALE RELATIVES

1   2   3   4   5   6   7
AGE GROUPS/1=5-14/2=15-24/../7=65-74
1A/ FAMILY HOUSEHOLD ROLES BY AGE

PROPORTION HOUSEHOLD ROLES %

35
30
25
20
15
10
5

MALE SERVANTS
FEMALE SERVANTS
FEMALE INMATES/LODGERS
MALE INMATES/LODGERS
STEP-SONS/FOSTER-SONS/BOYS
STEP-DAUGHTERS/
FOSTER-DAUGHTERS/GIRLS

1   2   3   4   5   6   7
AGE GROUPS/1=5-14/2=15-24/../7=65-74
1B/NON-FAMILY HOUSEHOLD ROLES BY AGE

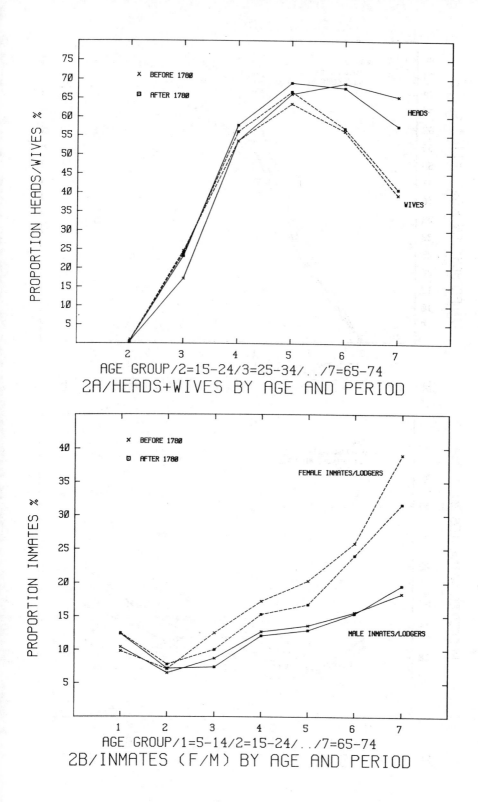

AGE GROUP/2=15-24/3=25-34/../7=65-74
2A/HEADS+WIVES BY AGE AND PERIOD

AGE GROUP/1=5-14/2=15-24/../7=65-74
2B/INMATES (F/M) BY AGE AND PERIOD

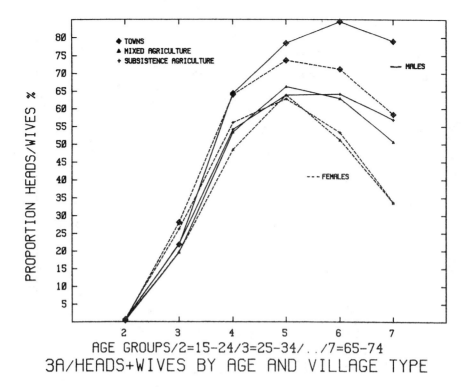

3A/HEADS+WIVES BY AGE AND VILLAGE TYPE

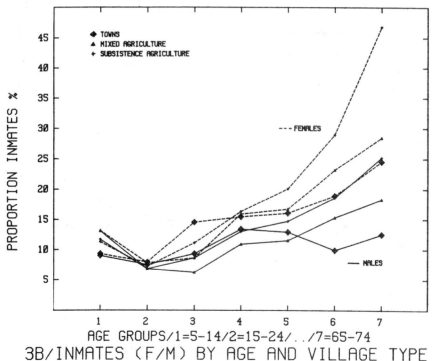

3B/INMATES (F/M) BY AGE AND VILLAGE TYPE

Changes in Demographic Potential and Intergenerational Relationships

1. Introductory Remarks

Intergenerational relations is not a conventional topic in either population research or demographic analysis. The concepts and materials employed in these fields, however, do allow us to deduce conditions which influence these relationships and the changes which take place in them over shorter and longer periods. To do so it will be necessary to complement quantitative data with a number of qualitative hypotheses drawn from general and family sociology.

One general hypothesis underlying the following discussion is that the relative size of coexisting generations has consequences for the mode and content of relationships among them. It is assumed that the composition and size — and changes in relative size — of succeeding generations influence the behavioral and emotional characteristics of the relations between the members of the generations.

Changes in the age structure of populations will be discussed here in light of this general hypothesis. Such changes occur over long periods as a result of demographic developments in society, mainly in such factors as mortality and fertility, but they may also result from such historical events as plagues and wars, or arise from oscillations in the mortality, fertility, etc. Before embarking on a discussion of these changes, it may be helpful to clarify the impact of age structure on the structure of generations, and to operationalize the conceptual terms used in this paper.

2. Notes on the Concepts of Generation and Cohort from the Standpoint of Social Demography

In family research, the term "generation" usually refers to the categories of parents and children, and to ancestors (grandparents, great-grandparents, etc.). The family role aspect dominates in this definition of generations. In family research, little attention has been paid to the fact that *members of one generational category may belong to different age groups,* or that conversely members of different generations may well be of the same age.

Indeed, this aspect has only slowly emerged over the past 200 years, and only in recent decades such a variety of implications emerged as to be regarded significant. It is quite unprecedented that children of one age group may have parents anywhere from 20 to 40 years of age and grandparents of 40, 60, or even 80. We now find parents and grandparents in different families who belong to the same age group, and families of four and even five generations are no longer nearly as rare as they were 200 years ago. Increased longevity and decreased age distance are the

53

macro-level causes behind this change on the family level. When we say that members of the same familial generation may belong to different age groups and vice versa, we imply that two different role definitions meet in their social position — that ascribed to membership in a generation, and that ascribed to their particular age group. While these two characteristics used generally to overlap in earlier periods, they now frequently tend to diverge. This makes for a new variety of behavioral patterns which also effect the relationships among generations.

Social relationships between each two of a possible four or five generations within a family will definitely be a function, among other things, of age distance.

Yet there is still a third demographic characteristic that further increases the variety, namely the *historical context* in which a group of people grows up and performs its generational and age-group roles. Demographers have introduced the term "cohort" to signify this dimension. A cohort is defined as a group of people born about the same calendar year, who will tend to have similar experiences, expectations, and roles at about the same age and *historical time*. The role of a mother, for example, is redefined to some extent even from decade to decade, and the same holds true of the roles of men and women at the age, say, of 60. Hence the relationships among generations will also be influenced by the type of cohort to which the members of each belong.

Members of different family generations (in different families) may belong to the same birth cohort; conversely, members of the same birth cohort may have different positions in the family life cycle.

The *concept of cohorts* adds a historical aspect to the socio-demographic analysis, by introducing a background of historical events and broad social transformation that might otherwise enter the picture only indirectly via changing demographic factors. Yet though they are identical at a certain point in time, age groups and cohorts nevertheless cannot be equated. Take the notion of the typical life tasks or stages in development of a particular age group. The 13- to 17-year-olds, for example, may face special problems in their relation to their parents — whether in 1940, 1960, or 1980. But since the members of this age group belong to different cohorts (born around 1925, 1945, and 1965, respectively), they will very likely have experienced typical adolescent problems in quite different ways.

Thus far we have explained the terms "generation" and "cohort" in the general sense in which they are currently used in socio-demographic analysis. As soon as the discussion becomes more specific or technical, however, we note that the terms have not always been employed in the same sense, and that even now, variations exist in their conceptualization and operationalization.

In earlier cohort analyses, there was a tendency to equate cohorts with generations (Dorn, 1959, 451). At that time, the term "generation" was used to designate the life history of people born in the same calendar year — which is now the established understanding of the term "birth cohort." "Cohort," as employed in the field of population analysis, was introduced to mean a group of birth cohorts united by a similar life history (Whelpton, 1954). In this meaning, a *cohort* can consist of more or fewer birth cohorts depending on the similarity of situations and events in a respective group of calendar years (e.g., years of peace or years of war). Similarly, *age groups* can be composed of varying numbers of years of age, which in qualitative analysis is a well-established procedure.

A consensus exists among population analysts that cohort data are the most reliable when studying individual life histories and family development. But such data are rarely available and at best cumbersome to establish, since the original statistics have usually been assembled by calendar year. There are many obstacles to transforming calendar year ("period") statistics into cohort data, which means that in many cases it is necessary to substitute the first for the second.

In the context of the present paper the term "generation" will also have to be operationalized mainly in this way, by equating it with *"period" age group*. This operationalization may be justified by institutionalized ascription of positions and roles. In other words, the use of age groups to represent generations is based on the probability that each such age group will consist primarily either of "children," "parents," or "grandparents." In this definition the age group of grandparents will also include great-grandparents and single persons without familial relatives in the direct descending order. Age groups of "parents" will correspondingly include *persons* without children, the proportion being around 20 percent.

3. Secular Trends in Demographic Potential

We have advanced the hypothesis that relations between generations depend to a relevant degree on the *quantitative size* of the generations concerned. These aspects have changed considerably over the past 200 years as a consequence of trends in demographic factors — mortality, marriage, and fertility. Changes in these trends are themselves induced by social change, and they have additional social change as a result. The causes, while mainly of an economic and political nature, are manifold, and they are discussed in other contributions to this chapter.

The combined trends in mortality, marriage, and fertility are responsible for altering the relative size of sequential generations. The general tendency towards marriage at a younger age, and towards marriage of almost everyone who comes of age, has led to diminished intergenerational distances.

Demographic change during the period of industrialization is generally conceived in terms of a transition from preindustrial to industrial demographic regimes. This conception is equivalent, in demographic language, to that of social modernization. The preindustrial demographic regime is characterized by high birth and death rates and low marriage rates, which together imply a slow population increase. Transition, in this view, comes about with decreasing mortality, and increasing life expectancy, a development due mainly to a lowered risk of infant and child mortality.

Empirical evidence in most countries during early and high industrialization (with the exception of France) has indicated that fertility declines with a certain time lag after mortality. In the theory of demographic transition, this observation is explained as an adaptation of the structure of the family to the decreased mortality risk of children and mothers, and to a broader chance of family formation. The process is thus understood to be one form of "rationalization," which, following Max Weber and others, is the driving force behind "modernization" (Schmid, 1976, 65 ff.; Ungern-Sternberg, 1931).

It is the time lag in the drop of the fertility curve against that of the mortality curve that results in a considerable increase in population during the industrialization period (Mackensen, 1968). The transition process leads, in theory, to a new demographic regime with modest increase due to low fertility and mortality rates.

This conception represents quite adequately the recent demographic history of most of the industrialized countries, despite variations in time and acceleration, and disregarding periodical oscillations and the influence of special historical events (e.g., wars). In France prior to 1820, the birth rate began to fall at about the same time as the death rate; consequently, there was little population growth in that country.

Incorporating the extrapolation of observed trends is the main fallacy of the model. This extrapolation rests on the old idea that population numbers cannot grow forever, and therefore, develop in a logistic rather than an exponential curve (Verhulst, 1838; Pearl & Reed, 1920). Hence the final state of transition is purely hypothetical. Around 1970 a new type of period emerged, a period of population decrease with fertility levels lower than mortality. This could not have been expected based on the formal argumentation of demographic transition theory or the theory of social modernization. Nevertheless, from an economic and sociological point of view, this development was quite logical, as several investigators have shown (Mackenroth, 1953, 482 ff.; Linde, 1978). Children, rather than being an economic advantage, have become a burden; the wage system rests not on family requirements but on individual performance, making a large family a hindrance to its members. The bearing and raising of children begins to compete with professional ambitions; and finally, the family has become a private affair, as distinguished from a responsibility to guarantee the continuance of society.

4. Recent and Future Changes

My discussion of them has taken recent changes into account, since the current situation cannot altogether be explained by long-term development tendencies alone. As I mentioned above, there is a controversy in the literature on whether such low birth rates as those of the last decade are a logical consequence of trends in industrial development since 1870, or are due to recent reactions against economic and technological changes of a different, more "modern" order, including an awareness of the limits of the earth. Particularly the changes observed in marriage and divorce behavior are difficult to explain in terms of secular trends — unless the altered family laws are themselves considered part of the secular process of civilization. Much recent change in family structure is being attributed to female employment, which definitely, in its present form, is a recent phenomenon, though it can also be interpreted as a logical consequence of social advance.

It is difficult to say whether secular tendencies in cultural and social change are major or only secondary determinants of the present conditions and of most of the demographic changes that have occurred over the past two decades. Nor will present conditions necessarily continue unaltered into the future.

Nevertheless, there is wide agreement among population sociologists that changes in family structure and demographic development present a persisting process. We may then have even fewer children and more elderly people in the population than now.

One of the recent developments that can be projected into the future is the changes and differentiation in age structure determined by components we know of already. The dramatic increase in life expectancy is a unique historical event: It is very unlikely that life expectancy will ever climb beyond 80. Not much more can be achieved by further declines in infant mortality, by improved workplaces, and traffic accident prevention. Even progress in the struggle against major causes of death leads mainly to a decreased mortality risk between the ages of 50 and 70.

We may also conclude that the margin of five-generation families can hardly be transcended: The total life-span cannot be expected to extend very much, and the intergenerational distance cannot shrink much more (in five-generation families it is already at or even below 20 years).

The main unknowns in the model, of course, are marriage behavior and the structure of the family life cycle. But even dramatic changes would take decades to lead to sizeable differences in population, structure, and development.

Chapter II: Multi-Generational Family

Part I: Concepts of Solidarity

Anyone who consults literature in the social sciences and particularly in psychology under the heading "Intergenerational Relationships" will be confronted at first sight with a plethora of publications on the family and familial coexistence. The use of the term "generation" in this context of descent and primarily biologically determined succession is not only rooted in idiomatic speech; it also dominates various scientific disciplines such as anthropology, developmental psychology, and demography.

The statement that the market of scientific and popular publications on familial problems continues to expand, is generally followed by an expression of regret about how limited our knowledge really is (cf. e.g., Orbach, 1983; Hubbart, 1983). A high degree of uncertainty reigns with regard to the question concerning the character of relations between present-day familial lineage generations, particularly in families that comprise four or five generations. Over long periods, research has concentrated on the mother-child constellation. Relations to middle-aged and elderly family members have been seen as destroyed in the course of the development from the pre-industrial to the industrial age.

Until about 15 years ago, many family sociologists held the opinion that the extended family, united in a common household and participating in common production and consumption, was the predominant family form of the pre-industrial period. Authority, stability, and solidarity were thought to be the characteristic traits of relationships between familial generations. The foundations of multi-generational cohesion were undermined by the transition from agrarian to industrial production, by urbanization tendencies, and by the growth of the service sector. When younger family members were compelled to offer their labor to industrial manufacturing, a profound division began between the "private" (familial) and "public" spheres. The dissolution of the familial production community and the geographic and social mobility associated with it, the argument went, also resulted in a dissolution of intergenerational ties, a process in which a devaluation of older people's experience and a loss of authority played a role. This went hand in hand with a shift of important "intergenerational functions" from the familial to the extrafamilial sphere — first, those of raising and education of offspring, and then much later (in Germany, with the introduction of social security in 1881) the function of economic support for elderly family members. The relations within the nuclear family, now largely isolated from the extended family, began to be emotionalized. The nuclear family thus became a refuge, a "space of retreat from the aggressiveness of an industrial society in unbridled expansion" (Ariès, 1979, 47). Since that period, it is widely held, solidarity among generations belongs irretrievably to the past, to the "world we have lost" (Laslett, 1965).

Recent studies by social historians have done much to demolish the hypothesis of a "linear transition from the traditional extended family to the modern, small, or nuclear family" (Hubbart, 1983, 12) as well as the myth of a "past golden age" of intergenerational relationships (Nydegger, 1983, 26).

Many assumptions of long standing are no longer scientifically defensible. The hypotheses of the generally widespread extended family and particularly of the multi-generational family have been disproved (Mitterauer, 1981; 1982; Ehmer, 1982; Imhof, 1981; Conrad, 1982; and Held, in the first chapter of this volume). The relations among lineage generations were determined primarily by economic interests and corresponding arrangements (Mitterauer, 1981; 1982; Dahlin, 1980; Held, this volume) and by no means were "naturally" harmonious and unproblematic. It would even appear that "our so strongly emotional and affective personal relationships within the family today may be quite a recent historic phenomenon" (Mitterauer, 1981, 45). Even "natural respect" for the elderly, so often considered the basis of the cohesion of the multi-generational group, was by no means the rule in the past, nor is it the rule today in certain other ethnic communities (Nydegger, 1983). The ritual esteem or respect which always and everywhere has been granted to only a handful of powerful elders, has been confused, due to tradition, with everyday practice.

Mobility of younger family members — currently often cited as one cause of the family's inability to support its older members properly — already existed to a certain extent during the pre-industrial period, since in those days children also left home to hire out as maids or servants (Held, this volume), or as soldiers, journeymen, or sailors (Nydegger, 1983).

Findings of this kind provided by sociohistoric analyses are a clear warning against idealizing the past. The past cannot be taken as a standard for the solidity of familial ties simply because the coexistence of several lineage generations within the family played no great role, quantitatively speaking, right down into the 19th century (cf. Imhof, 1981, and the remarks by Mackensen & Held in Chapter One, this volume). Anyone who speaks today of intergenerational relationships in a familial context must take into account the simultaneity of at least three lineage generations, as well as the fact that every individual experiences very different forms of familial constellation within his lifetime and, by the time he enters the middle phase of life at the latest, must fulfill two and perhaps even three "generation roles."

If we feel uncertainty with regard to intergenerational coexistence within the family in everyday life because traditional patterns apparently no longer suffice to guide us, a related uncertainty is all the more obvious in the scientific attempts to explain the "true nature" of intergenerational relationships. Can the traditional theoretical conceptions be applied to the current situation? Neither Freud nor Erikson took account of three or four or even five generations in their work; their perspective is determined by two generations. "Too often," writes Harold L. Orbach (1983, 24), "we seek to delineate the 'real' or 'true' character of the family and construct universal patterns of family relations as they should be — that is, as we might wish them to be."

This circumstance doubtlessly results from the fact that a great number of the statements of relevant disciplines on the problem of intergenerational relationships within today's family were shaped by the pragmatic need to solve burning sociopolitical problems. Thus, a great deal of attention continues to be given to the question concerning the frequency of contacts between the "middle" generation and old members of the family, in an attempt to determine whether conditions exist for the support of the elderly in today's families. The quality of these contacts is seen in connection with the mental well-being and health of the elderly. A similarly pragmatic approach also characterizes many studies on mutual expectations and support among adult family members, and marks a number of investigations on related problems (cf. the remarks by Troll, 1980, 436 ff.).

The contributions to this chapter stand in contrast to an everyday empiricism which apparently can do without theoretical concepts. Three approaches to intergenerational interaction are presented here. The first, a contribution by Vern Bengtson, Pierre Landry, and David Mangen, is a functionalistic concept of solidarity in multi-generational families. This concept is based on Durkheim's (1858–1917) explanation of solidarity in terms of collective consciousness within simple, differentiated social formations which results "naturally" from common characteristics (mechanical solidarity) or from a division of labor (organic solidarity). Drawing on Durkheim's theory, the authors discuss principal problems of interaction within three- (or multi-) generational families: First, the question as to the key issues of this interaction; secondly, that concerning the explanatory relevance of empirical variables for grasping the dimensions of intergenerational behavior; and finally, the question as to the general patterns of intergenerational relationships. Bengtson et al. give an impressive review of the results of numerous American studies and their own empirical findings, arranging them along the six dimensions of their solidarity concept and pointing the way for further empirical investigations. The authors emphasize the temporal variability of the solidarity dimensions, not only in the context of the individual development of family members but also in relation to the "aging" of the involved cohorts and with respect to the development of the social formation "multi-generational family." Seen in this light, solidarity is a dynamic and processual quality, if for no other reason than that it is the result of a neverending process of negotiation among the lineage generations.

The dynamic character of intergenerational solidarity is likewise the focus of the second contribution to this chapter. For Hilde Rosenmayr, not only changes in intergenerational relationships along the life course of families are worthy of special scrutiny, but above all sociohistoric change in that normative context which significantly determines the nature of familial solidarity from epoch to epoch. Looking back into the past, she discusses those conditions of familial cohesion which though they left little leeway for the individual, assured survival in a world of extreme existential pressure and social inequality. That was the basis of what Durkheim called "mechanical solidarity." The consequence of inequity in the division of labor, as the author explains following Durkheim's thoughts on the nature of organic solidarity, was a consciousness of shared necessity — a higher form of personal autonomy. Today, when sheer survival is no longer clearly dependent on family integration, life in the family is characterized by the need for distance, and personal fulfillment is connected with factors outside the family sphere. Thus, Rosenmayr sheds light on the ambivalence of intergenerational relationships which results from conflicts between responsibility among family members and their subjective, individual aspirations.

In her attempt to focus on the predominance of conflict in intergenerational relations, the author follows that dialectic tradition (Riegel, 1976) which sees tension and conflict in social relations not as "undesirable and worthy of elimination" but as "constructive and important events, where the discord created by contradictory forces may be a valuable source of further development" (Gergen & Morawski, 1980, 333).

In his contribution, the third in this chapter, Kees Knipscheer likewise discusses the ambivalence and ambiguity of relations among the generations. He too identifies a relation of tension between a desire for individuality on the one hand and solidarity on the other, and refers to Zena Blau's statement (1973) that grown-up children certainly do fulfill their material responsibilities vis-à-vis their parents in old age and remain in contact with them, but that differing everyday interests, experiences, and separate residences effectively lead to an alienation of the life worlds of lineage generations.

Knipscheer is highly critical of the behavioral models of intergenerational relationships, assuming that such models are not adequate to elucidate their qualitative dimensions and in particular the ambiguity and ambivalence of these relationships. His own empirical approach emphasizes the construct of "social support." Based on House's (1981) classification of supportive acts and particularly on the interconnection and mutual overlap of these types of support, the author drafts a method for future research which may well be suited to capture the qualitative aspects of intergenerational relationships within families.

The Multi-Generation Family: Concepts and Findings

Vern L. Bengtson, David J. Mangen, and Pierre H. Landry, Jr.

This paper outlines a conceptual scheme for assessing intergenerational solidarity within families, and reviews findings from some American surveys. The concept of solidarity addresses cohesion or integration, as well as implications for potential or actual social support between generations. Six components or dimensions of intergenerational solidarity are defined following Durkheim and Homans: (a) structure; (b) association; (c) affect; (d) consensus; (e) exchange; (f) norms.

The empirical literature on each of these six dimensions is reviewed, with a focus on the aging family. First, findings about structure suggest that middle-aged children do constitute a potential resource for most aged family members, though increasingly fewer generations share the same household. Second, adult generation members are in frequent contact with one another, despite geographic dispersal. Third, the available analysis suggests high degrees of satisfaction regarding contact, and a high level of positive affect — perceived closeness — between adult generations. Fourth, consensus appears high in some areas of values and socio-political attitudes, while differences are apparent in other topics. Fifth, there appears to be a high level of exchange — what may be termed "functional solidarity" — between generations, and not only in non-reciprocal forms of assistance (such as during the illness or incapacity of the older generation members). Finally, norms of filial responsibility appear quite strong, though most elderly parents maintain a reluctance to ask for assistance from their middle-aged children.

The assessment of intergenerational solidarity appears to be an important research agenda for the 1980s with implications for social policy and practice as well as for theory and research.

"One generation passeth away, and another generation cometh ..." (Ecclesiastes 11, 2). This phrase from one of the oldest books of the Old Testament summarizes the central problem of generations: continuity, is the context of change. How does the continuous succession of age groups — through birth, maturity, aging, and death — contribute to alteration patterns in social organization and behavior manifest in groups over time? What changes, and what remains the same; how does generational succession and aging affect the nature of the collective?

Generational succession is a normal and expectable attribute of any aggregate studied through time. Families, work groups, nations, and even civilizations evidence change through time, and many such alterations in structure or process appear causally related to the unending addition and removal of members through generational replacement. Our concern in this paper is the family, perhaps the most obvious group in which generational succession is evident. Our focus will be on three-generation families, especially the patterns of interaction that characterize relationships among elderly parents, and their middle-aged children, that can be summarized from gerontological research.

We will address several questions concerning family interaction in the context of several generations. First, what are the key issues and conceptual tools for examining multi-generational interaction? What dimensions of behavior, and what variables, are the most useful to address in empirical analysis? Second, what does existing research suggest about these dimensions of multi-generational family life? What are the patterns of parent-child relations in a middle and old age, seen in the context of what may be termed "intergenerational family solidarity"?

I. Solidarity: Dimensions of Family Intergenerational Relations

Relations between parents and children are obviously complex; to characterize them requires specification of focus, particularly when we take a truly developmental or life-span perspective on the relationship (see Troll & Bengtson, 1979; Elder, 1978c; 1981; Hagestad, 1981; 1982a). Most research concerning intergenerational relations has focused on children or youth and their interaction with parents who are themselves in their early to middle stages of adulthood. However, characterization of intergenerational relations takes on a somewhat different focus when we consider the later phases of family life. For example, much has been written lately about "family support systems" and aging (see, e.g., Brody, 1981; Dunkel-Schetter & Wortman, 1981; Robinson & Thurnher, 1979; Kahn & Antonucci, 1981). Such assessments focus on welfare and psychological well-being as a function of intergenerational interaction. They must be included in any discussion of parent-child interaction in times of crises involving an older family member. But implicit in any discussion of parent-child interaction, even in the later years, are other issues, reflecting aspects of family structure, negotiation, consensus, and power (Bengtson & deTerre, 1980).

To begin with, our research group examined the literature on family support systems and aging, as well as more general discussions of family interaction, to identify recurrent questions which appear germane to a comprehensive focus on intergenerational relations across the course of family life (Bengtson, Cutler, Mangen, & Marshall, in press). Practitioners are interested in identifying the potential family support system of an older person "at risk." Researchers attempt to understand the structure and dynamics of intergenerational relations in old age. We pursued both perspectives, and found that the following issues recur again and again:

1. The who, what, and where of *structure*: Who is available as a resource for the older individual? What is the relationship? Where do the family members live? Who lives with whom?

2. How much *contact* is there between the older individual and his/her family? What do they do together, and how often?

3. What is the *quality* of the interaction? How does the older individual feel about the relationship with specific members of the family? Are these sentiments perceived as being reciprocated?

4. How much *consensus* is there among members of the family? Does each indi-

64

vidual think there is conflict or agreement about opinions and values? How does this square with each generation's stated positions?

5. How much *assistance* or help does the older person say is received from the potential support system of his/her family? How much do they say they give? How about the other direction? What is the balance of power that is reflected by such exchange?

6. What norms or *expectations* do the older person or the middle-aged adult have concerning his/her family as a social system? How much filial obligation is perceived, by the elder parent and by the middle-aged child?

Studies of social aspects of aging almost always include some information concerning the relations of aged parents and their adult children, usually focusing on one or two of the above issues (Bengtson & deTerre, 1980). Unfortunately, such data are usually treated as descriptive only; conceptual bases for examining parent-child relations in old age appeared to be underdeveloped, especially with regard to any cohesion of issues based on theory-informed considerations.

Concepts: Finally, we went back to our research team's earlier attempts to encapsulate intergenerational relations within a broader sociological tradition. We had begun with Durkheim's (1893) discussion of "solidarity" as a crucial property of social groups, elaborated more comprehensively by Homans' (1950) analysis of similarity, agreement, and liking as a recurrent process within diverse human groups. These dimensions had been applied to analyses of family interaction among adolescents by Bowerman & Elder (see Elder, 1981a) and appeared congruent with the suggestion of Nye & Rushing (1966).

Our earlier formulation (Bengtson, Olander, & Haddad, 1976) focused on three dimensions: affectual solidarity (the positive or negative sentiment between family generation members), associational solidarity (the nature and frequency of intergenerational interaction), and consensual solidarity (their agreement or disagreement on values and opinions, with implications for conflict). But it seemed to us useful to expand these dimensions of solidarity, following the six questions or issues raised above, to include the structural context, the actual exchange of assistance or support, and the normative context of intergenerational support. Thus we developed six dimensions, reflecting the six questions listed above: (1) Family Structure; (2) Associational Solidarity; (3) Affectual Solidarity; (4) Consensual Solidarity; (5) Functional Solidarity or exchange of assistance and support; and (6) Normative Solidarity. The operational measurement of these dimensions is discussed elsewhere (Mangen et al., 1982). Theoretical constructs reflecting the above questions, as well as possible operationalizations in empirical research, are indicated in Table 1.

We present these six dimensions of intergenerational solidarity as a means of organizing the growing literature on parent-child interaction across the life-span. In addition, the typology represents a changing of empirical agendas for research to describe each, and to suggest their linkages and consequences.

II. Findings: Empirical Evidence Concerning Parent-Child Relations in Old Age

What does existing research suggest concerning intergenerational solidarity between middle-aged children and their aged parents? Specifically, what do existing surveys suggest is the degree of contact, affection, exchange, and consensus between generations in families with an aged individual?

To address these questions we will draw primarily from two American national-probability surveys (Shanas et al., 1968; and Shanas, 1978), and from some emerging data from our own study of three-generation families. This latter study (USC study) analyzes responses to a lengthy self-administered questionnaire collected for an earlier study in 1973 (see Mangen et al., 1982, for a more complete description of the sample and procedures). Respondents are 516 grandparents ("G1"), 701 middle-aged parents ("G2"), and 827 of their children ("G3"), sampled from membership lists of a large (840,000) prepaid medical care organization. Our selection procedure yielded 2,044 members of three-generation families who are almost exclusively Anglo-Caucasian, and who also have incomes a bit higher than census figures would lead us to expect.

Our purpose in presentation is not only to summarize findings from several American surveys, but also to suggest a framework which may be useful to other researchers in other national settings. This goal has, in fact, been successfully accomplished in empirical investigations in several nations: the Netherlands (Knipscheer & Bevers, 1981); Canada (Rosenthal, Marshall, & Sygne, 1981); and Japan (Morioka, 1982). Such cross-national elaboration already suggests the utility of a conceptual focus on "solidarity" as applied to family intergenerational relations.

Family structure: Structure refers to the descriptive characteristics of the lineage being examined. Characteristics of family structure are important to include in any analysis of lineage generations since they provide important information about the *potential* for mobilizing the family as a social support system in old age. Three types of characteristics appear most relevant for understanding the structure of families: (1) the *number* of living grandparents, children, and grandchildren; (2) the *geographic proximity* of these lineage members; and (3) the *composition* of the households containing these members (e.g., is three-generational co-residence characteristic of the lineage?).

The substantive findings from national surveys clearly suggest that, regarding family structure, intergenerational relationships are present for most aged family members as a potential source of support. Over 90 percent of the elderly have been married at least once (U.S. Bureau of the Census, 1973; Shanas, 1978) and approximately 80 percent of those over age 65 have one or more living children (Shanas, 1980). Furthermore, national survey data indicate that a majority of older persons are members of three- (38%) or four- (36%) generation families (Shanas, 1978), even though co-residence is rare. In a 1965 survey of the intergenerational family structure in Denmark, Britain, and the United States, the majority of respondents in each nation reported three generations of living family members (56%, 51%, and 44% respectively). Shanas (1978) reports data from a U.S.A. follow-up indicating change over time in this aspect of family structure. From 1962 to 1975, the percentage of older people who reported only three-generation families decreased (44 to 38%), while the percentage of four-generation families increased (from 29 to

31%). There was also an increase in over 15 years in the percentage of one-generation families, usually consisting of unmarried (widowed, divorced, or never-married) persons (18 to 21%) (see Table 2).

The Southern California sample contains, of course, only people in three-generation families. In terms of Shanas' categories, three-generation families whose parents (in G1) had "more than one child (in G2), with grandchildren (in G3)" stand a greater chance of being in the sample. This increased probability is reflected in the skewed distribution relative to Shanas' natural data: the G1 members have larger numbers of G2 children and G3 grandchildren (Table 3).

Moreover, it should be emphasized that rarely do the generations share living quarters; rather, "intimacy at a distance" (Rosenmayr & Köckeis, 1963, 89) appears to predominate. Only 17 percent of the unmarried elderly and 12 percent of the married lived with a child in the 1975 nation-wide American survey of Shanas (1978). For those relatively few elderly who do live with one of their offspring, most live with an unmarried child (Shanas, 1978). Despite the high rate of geographic mobility in American society, most older people are not physically isolated from their children. Approximately 75 percent of the elderly live within one-half hour of one of their children (Shanas, 1979b). These patterns clearly suggest that the elderly are *not* without families, at least on the level of family structure.

Family structure describes the resource context of the family for the older person; as such, it is a crucial aspect of a family support system. However, the presence of children and grandchildren only indicates the existence of these family role relationships; it does nothing to describe the nature of the relationship. It is here that the conceptual advantages of "solidarity" as a construct of intergenerational family life expands our understanding.

Association: This refers to the degree to which members of a lineage are in contact with one another, engage in shared behaviors, and interact in common activities (Bengtson & Schrader, 1982). Associational solidarity can be measured by several indices, including the overall *frequency* of intergenerational contact as well as the *type* of interaction. Contact which is *formal and ritualistic* (such as family reunions and ceremonies) versus *informal* interaction (brief visits or discussions) may have qualitatively different effects upon lineage members. A third distinction of associational solidarity may be seen in the *mode* of contact. Contact between generations may be "face-to-face," or indirect communication (e.g., via telephone or letters) may be the primary vehicle for maintaining social ties. In a highly mobile industrial society, those family members who are not geographically close may still maintain relatively close contact through the use of indirect contact mechanisms (Wilkening, Gurrero, & Ginsberg, 1972).

A substantial amount of research has looked at the associational solidarity of aged parents and their offspring. On the whole, adult generation members are in frequent contact with one another. Shanas (1973) found that about 80 percent of American elderly were in contact with at least one of their children on a regular basis. Approximately one-half of all old people with children saw one of those children on the day of the interview, or the day immediately prior to the interview. If the time-frame for contact is expanded to one week before the interview, three-quarters of the elderly parents had been in contact with one of their children. In general, the finding that older persons are *not* isolated from their children is well supported in the existing literature (e.g., Shanas et al., 1968; Shanas, 1978; 1979b; Litwak, 1960; Adams, 1968; Rosow, 1967; Rosenberg, 1970; N.C.O.A., 1975; Brown, 1960; see also Riley et al., 1968; Streib & Beck, 1980; Troll, 1971, and Troll, Miller, & Atchley, 1979, for summary reviews of the literature).

Using the Southern California data, we can look directly at the distinctions in associational solidarity mentioned above. With respect to the overall frequency of intergenerational contact, Table 4 displays the mean response for each dyad member's perception of the frequency of nine types of interaction. Between elderly parents (G1) and their middle-aged children (G2), each pair of estimates is very close, and when the nine items are taken as a summated scale, the difference between the G1 mean and the G2 mean is not statistically significant (p < .08) (see Table 4).

The reports of G2–G3 association are higher than for G1–G2 for all types of interaction except letters and phone calls, but the separate estimates are not as close. The middle-aged parents (G2) tend to report greater frequencies for each type of interaction than their young adult children (G3), and the difference of means on the summated scale naturally reflects that the exchange of letters is the only type of intergenerational contact not evidencing a statistically significant difference between G2 and G3, abetted no doubt by the "floor" affect due to low values.

When comparing ritualistic and informal types of contact, the above patterns hold: the G1–G2 estimates agree; G2 reports more of both kinds of contact with G3 than G3 reports; and the G2–G3 dyad reports more of each kind of interaction than G1–G2. Both dyads report more informal interaction than ritualistic.

A similar analysis of face-to-face versus indirect communication has a surprising difference. Once again the G2–G3 dyad is marked by higher G2 estimates, and higher means than the G1–G2 dyad. However, for G1–G2, not only are the G1 and G2 estimates again very close to each other for each kind of interaction; the estimates are also virtually the same for both face-to-face contact and indirect contact.

In short, there is greater agreement in perceptions of interaction within the G1–G2 dyad than the G2–G3 dyad, but reported frequencies for the latter tend to be higher. Nonetheless, the older members of the Southern California three-generation sample do not appear to be isolated from their families, and this reaffirms what others have reported about American elderly in general.

Affect: While the frequency of intergenerational quantity is indeed an important dimension of solidarity, contact cannot be equated with quality. Affectual solidarity refers to the degree of positive sentiment present in the intergenerational relationship. Relatively little research has focused on the quality of the intergenerational relationship. In general it may be said that both aged parents and their adult children express high levels of regard for one another (Bengtson & Black, 1973; Brown, 1960); this appears to be a continuation of lifelong patterns of positive affect (Lowenthal et al., 1975). Complete satisfaction regarding the amount of contact was expressed by over two-thirds of the cross-ethnic Los Angeles sample reported by Bengtson, Burton, & Mangen (1981), though whites were less likely (56%) to respond this way. Interestingly, some researchers have found little relationship between the frequency of intergenerational contact and the quality of the relationship (Adams, 1968; Angres, 1975).

Our USC study used a summated scale of the affect between parents and children, and our abbreviated five-item scale was used for G1—G3 comparisons. Table 5 shows a positive skew for all the distributions, but they were found to be uncontaminated by any tendencies to give socially-desired responses. In each dyadic comparison, the older generation perceived more positive family affect. When perceptions of relations with children are compared, the grandparent generation (G1) reports more positive affect with their children (G2) than their children (G2) do with *their* children (G3). Likewise for perceptions of relations with parents: G2 has higher scores than G3.

Consensus: A fourth aspect of solidarity in lineage relationships concerns the degree of consensus or conflict in beliefs or orientations external to the family. Political issues, religious practices or ideologies, global value orientations — these may be the topics of family traditions, on the one hand, or of protracted disagreements and conflict on the other.

While many studies have focused on the real or attributed contrasts between cohorts in opinions and orientations, few analyses have addressed the issue of lineage or parent-child continuities in the face of cohort contrasts (for exceptions, see Connell, 1972; Bengtson, 1975; Jennings & Niemi, 1975). Fewer still have focused on differences between the elderly and their descendants (for exceptions, see Bengtson, 1975; Fengler & Wood, 1972; Hill et al., 1970; Kalish & Johnson, 1972; Streib, 1965). On some issues the similarities between the two generations predominate — for example, values regarding fatalism and optimism (Hill et al., 1970) and general value orientations concerning materialism versus humanism (Bengtson, 1975). Such findings suggest the existence of strong consensus within families. For other variables, however, parent-child contrasts were marked — for example, values regarding childrearing (Hill et al., 1970) and general value orientations toward collectivism versus individualism (Bengtson, 1975). In these areas, the findings suggest substantial differences between parents and children.

Some of our current work at USC examines intrafamily consensus on sociopolitical issues. From a series of attitude and opinion items, we developed a "social conservatism" scale, one for marriage norms, and a third concerned with the legitimacy of Black's demands. Examining lineage dyadic correlations, we can compare the amount of similarity between generations on each of these scales (see Table 6).

In Table 6, we see that our sample is characterized overall by low-to-moderate positive relationships between the opinions of parents and their children. The strengths of the relationships vary somewhat by gender. Most notable are the weak correlations between sons and both of their parents regarding the legitimacy of Black's demands for social change, and between sons and their fathers on the social conservatism scale.

As for the eldest generation having a greater "stake" (Bengtson & Kuypers, 1971) in intergenerational consensus, we see the remarkable differences displayed in Table 7. The correlations between parent and child on self-report scale scores, representing objective consensus, are much lower across the board then the consensus that the parent perceives. This latter is measured by the correlation of the parent's self-reported position with the position the parent attributed to the child. In sum, the aged-parent generation seems to perceive much agreement where in fact there may be little (see Acock & Bengtson, 1980).

Functional solidarity: A fifth dimension of family solidarity refers to the degree

69

to which financial assistance and service exchanges occur among family members. It is within this context that much of the recent concern for family support systems (Brody, 1981; Lopata, 1979; Zarit, Reever, & Bach-Peterson, 1980; Fengler & Goodrich, 1979; Crossman, London, & Barry, 1981) is found. Mutual aid and assistance is an important aspect of the modified extended family structure; aged parents will turn to their children for assistance before they will ask for help from their siblings (Sussman & Burchinal, 1962; Shanas, 1978).

A number of different studies have examined the exchange aspect of intergenerational relationships. Contrary to the belief of asymmetric pattern of exchanges between the generations, the available evidence indicates that assistance is given and received by both aged parents and their adult offspring (Hill et al., 1970; Lopata, 1979; Shanas, 1979b; Streib, 1965; Shanas et al., 1968; Schorr, 1960; Sussman, 1965; Troll, 1971; Adams, 1968). Table 6, presenting data over 13 years from national surveys of the aged (Shanas, 1978) suggests that family assistance to the elderly in times of health-related crisis is especially important. Immediate family members, especially the spouse (if present) and children, provide "the major social support of the elderly in time of illness" (Shanas, 1979b, 173).

Assistance between the generations is not restricted to times of crisis, however. Table 8 documents change from 1962 to 1975 in patterns of exchange evident in Shanas' (1978) surveys. While 60 percent of the 1962 aged assisted their children, by 1975 this figure had increased to over 70 percent. An even greater increase is noted with help to grandchildren. The kinds of help given by older people to their children most frequently consist of gifts (69%), help with grandchildren (36%), and housekeeping (28%) (Shanas, 1978; higher estimates presented by N.C.O.A., 1975, 74 f.). During this 13-year interval, however, virtually no change in the overall receipt of assistance by older persons is noted, and reports of financial assistance to the elderly has substantially declined (Shanas, 1978).

The USC three-generation families were asked about intergenerational exchanges (see Table 9).

In terms of helping each other out, the G2–G3 dyad has more frequent exchanges; G1 seems neither to give or to receive aid from their children more than a few times a year. As for financial assistance, the youthfulness of G3 (16–26 years) may account for the flow of money from G2–G3. Elsewhere, there does not appear to be much financial support in this 1973 group of three-generation families.

Normative solidarity: A sixth dimension of intergenerational family solidarity addresses the *norms of familism* held by members of the family. To what extent are children *expected* to live proximal to, and provide support and assistance to their aged parents? In a similar vein, to what extent do aged parents expect this of their children? Much of the early work addressing this dimension focused on the nature of extended kin relations in a modern industrialized society (e.g., Litwak, 1960), with the conclusion that American society is characterized by a modified-extended family with expectations of assistance, but not the expectation of geographic proximity (see, e.g., Kerckhoff, 1966a, b). Blenkner (1965) discussed *filial maturity*, a characteristic hypothesized to develop during middle age which permits the middle-aged child to see his/her parents as legitimate recipients of assistance.

Within a lineage perspective, the Southern California sample displayed a declining adherence to familism norms as we go down the generations (Tables 10 and 11).

The differences in expectations is further highlighted when we look at correlations among members of the same lineage (Table 11).

In examining the area of normative solidarity, two observations are germane. As Lozier & Althouse (1974) illustrate, norms may be adhered to for a variety of reasons, including an adversion to the negative community opinion which could obtain from violations of the normative content. Thus the issue of *sanctions* which are used to enforce the norms of familism are important to consider (Hagestad, 1981; 1982b; Emerson, 1981). The techniques of norm enforcement await further examination in the gerontological literature.

Second, in a manner analagous to the discussion of consensual solidarity above, research must distinguish between the *normative content*, that is, what are the expected behaviors in an intergenerational relationship, and the *consensus* regarding the normative content. A child who adheres to strong norms of familism while his/ her aged parent seeks autonomy will likely provide little emotional comfort to the parent.

Third, there may be important within-cohort (subcultural) variations regarding norms about filial obligations in old age. For example, in the Los Angeles survey of three ethnic groups (Bengtson, Burton, & Mangen, 1981) almost 70 percent of Mexican-Americans agreed with the statement, "It is the obligation of adult children to care for their parents." By contrast, only 2.3 percent of the blacks and 27 percent of the white respondents indicated agreement.

The entire area of normative solidarity deserves greater attention in the gerontological literature. Typically, research has *assumed* that intergenerational interaction was obligatory. This assumption is questionable, however, in light of evidence which suggests that the normative expectations tend to be greater for daughters than sons (Hagestad, 1977).

III. Implications: Suggestions for Future Research

In this paper we have outlined some perspectives which may be useful in the micro-sociological approach to generational relations as examined within the family. Our first concern was to describe six issues or questions which face both practitioners and researchers as they address problems of intergenerational relations in the later years of family life. These reflect differing theoretical dimensions of "solidarity" in groups, as suggested by Durkheim & Homans in discussing various aspects of interaction within human groups; our concern was with the adequate definition and measurement of these dimensions to identify issues which have not been examined adequately in charting the course of family interaction in the later stages of the life-course.

Second, we examined existing studies for evidence of micro-social interaction in later life. First defined following Durkheim & Homans: (a) structure; (b) association; (c) affect; (d) consensus; (e) exchange; (f) norms.

We examined the empirical literature on each of these six dimensions reviewed, with a focus on the aging family. First, findings about structure suggest that middle-aged children do constitute a potential resource for most aged family members, though increasingly fewer generations share the same household. Second, adult gen-

71

eration members are in frequent contact with one another, despite geographic dispersal. Third, the available analysis suggests high degrees of satisfaction regarding contact, and a high level of positive affect — perceived closeness — between adult generations. Fourth, consensus appears high in some areas of values and socio-political attitudes, while differences are apparent in other topics. Fifth, there appears to be a high level of exchange — what may be termed "functional solidarity" — between generations, and not only in non-reciprocal forms of assistance (such as during the illness or incapacity of the older generation members). Finally, norms of filial responsibility appear quite strong, though most elderly parents maintain a reluctance to ask for assistance from their middle-aged children.

In conclusion, we suggest eight questions that relate both to our presentation of solidarity as a dimension and to future research concerning relations between generations within the family. These suggest important agendas for researchers, with implications for social policy and practice; many are, in fact, our own research team's charting of tasks for the coming year.

One set of questions is primarily methodological and conceptual. They represent important issues that too seldom have been addressed in setting the empirical foundations of research.

First, are these the right questions? Have we adequately identified issues in the vast and growing literature concerning aging, families, and generations?

Second, are the dimensions of solidarity we have outlined the correct ones? The areas that most adequately reflect the micro-sociology of generational relations? Are there other parameters or planes along which the aging family may be viewed: power, for example, or conflict, or exchange — are these adequately reflected in the portrait of family generational solidarity we have presented?

Third, are these dimensions of solidarity adequately measured? Of the questions asked in previous surveys concerning association, for example, which are the most reliable and valid indicators? For future surveys, which operationalizations are most likely to allow the most error-free predictors of intergenerational family life? How can our measures be improved?

A second set of questions are more substantive and of more immediate theoretical and practical significance.

First, what are the interrelations among the various dimensions of solidarity? Is there covariation, as Homans (1950) suggested, within families as there is postulated for other social groups, in the degree of association, affect, and agreement? Is there a direct and linear relationship — the higher the affect, the higher the agreement, as suggested by some writers; or is the relationship perhaps curvilinear: intermediate levels of association resulting in higher affect than either low or very high association? These questions are important to address, for various aspects of cohesion or solidarity are obviously related; but how, and with what curve of convergence, have not yet been explored.

Second, what are the relevant predictors of affect, association, and agreement? Which factors seem to be antecedents of high or low levels of each? Given variable levels of affect, for example, exhibited within families and between families, what conditions appear to be associated with the high levels? Is it true that lower-class families exhibit higher associational solidarity than upper-middle class families; if so, what do sex and generational placement have to do with it? These theoretically crucial questions were first asked by some of the earliest family sociologists. Answers have been proffered by Hill and his associates (1970) as well as Adams (1968) and Aldous (1978); but much more careful explication can be made, especially given some recent methodological advances in the social sciences that permit rigorous examinations of proposed causal systems.

Third, what might be some consequences of high or low intergenerational solidarity? Are there any demonstrable relationships, for example, between indicators of mental health, and affectual solidarity? If there is a positive and linear relationship observed in one part of the model — for example, the higher the affect the higher the mental health — would the introduction of other dimensions — for example, association — increase the degree of prediction? Alternately, is there a curvilinear relationship between affectual solidarity and mental health, which has something to do with association or consensus? And what is the balance between intergenerational agreement and mental health: or perhaps there is no relationship? Each of these substantive questions is important for current family theory; each has implications, to a lesser extent, for family policy and practice.

A fourth question concerns between-family contrasts. How can using the family lineage approach (Hagestad, 1982a) allow us more adequately to assess reasons for the obvious differences between generations? What types of "generational stations" (Hagestad, 1982b) create differences or similarities between generations? And what are the consequences for other members?

Other issues can be addressed profitably in the context of constructs such as solidarity; so the challenge is to articulate concepts and defensible measures with authentic family problems.

The assessment of intergenerational solidarity appears to be an important research agenda for the 1980s with implications for social policy and practice as well as for theory and research.

Table 1: Critical Constructs in the Analysis of Family Intergenerational Relations and Variables Reflecting their Measurement

Construct	Operationalizations

A. Family structure across generations: parameters of social unions	A−1. Number of living family lineage members of the subject
	   a. Children
	   b. Parents
	   c. Grandchildren
	   d. Lineal relatives by marriage (children-in-law, parents-in-law)
	   e. Siblings and siblings' lineal relations
	A−2. Sex-lineage type (male-male; male-female; female-female; female-male)
	A−3. Number and type of lineal "fictive kin"
	A−4. Geographical proximity of each of the above to the subject
	A−5. Household composition of the subject

B. Associational solidarity or integration	B−1. Frequency of interaction between subject and lineage members in common activities B−2. Type of common activities shared
C. Affectional solidarity or integration	C−1. Perceived quality of interaction: sentiments of warmth, closeness, trust, understanding, communication, respect toward the other C−2. Perceived reciprocity of interaction: sentiments from the other
D. Consensual solidarity or integration	D−1. Degree of similarity or conflict in general values D−2. Degree of similarity or conflict in specific opinions (socio-political or religious orientations) D−3. Perception of similarity or contrast and/or conflict
E. Functional solidarity or integration	E−1. Degree of exchange of services or assistance between lineage members E−2. Perception of potential support or assistance between lineage members
F. Normative solidarity or integration	F−1. Instances of norms enacted concerning associational, affectional, consensual, or functional solidarity F−2. Perceptions of norms potentially enacted

Source: Bengtson & Schrader (1982), 116−117.

Table 2: Number of Generations in the Family and Presence of Near Relatives,
Persons Aged 65 and Over: 1962 and 1975
(Percentage Distribution)

Number of Generations in Family and Presence of Near Relatives	1962	1975
One	18 %	21 %
Childless, unmarried, no siblings	3	3
Childless, unmarried, with siblings	8	10
Childless, married, no siblings	2	2
Childless, married, with siblings	5	6
Two	6%	4%
One son only, no grandchildren	2	2
One daughter only, no grandchildren	2	2
More than one child, no grandchildren	2	1
Three	44 %	38 %
One son only, with grandchildren	4	5
One daughter only, with grandchildren	6	7
More than one child, with grandchildren	35	27
Four	32 %	36 %
One child only, with grandchildren and great-grandchildren	3	5
More than one child, with grandchildren and great-grandchildren	29	31
Total	100 %	100 %
Number of cases*	(2436)	(5728)

*   The number of cases for 1962 is unweighted; the number of cases for 1975 is weighted.
Source: Shanas, 1978, Table 5–2A.

Table 3: Percentage Distributions for Presence of Near Relatives for Grandparents
in Three-Generation Families

	All G1 Couples	65 or Older
One son only, with grandchildren	7.0%	8.1%
One daughter only, with grandchildren	11.5	14.5
More than one child, with grandchildren	81.5	77.4
Total	(244)	(175)

Table 4: Intergenerational Association in the Southern California Sample. Differences of Means Between Reports by Parents and their Children

Scale Items: Types of Association (Range: 1–8)	Elderly Parent and Middle-Aged Child					Middle-Aged Parent and Young Adult Child				
	Parent's Report Mean (sd)	Child's Report Mean (sd)	n	Difference of Means	p(t)	Parent's Report Mean (sd)	Child's Report Mean (sd)	n	Difference of Means	p(t)
1. Recreation	2.35 (1.25)	2.20 (1.75)	477	0.15	.018	3.33 (1.45)	3.02 (1.61)	520	0.31	.000
2. Brief Visits	4.07 (2.00)	4.10 (1.97)	471	−0.03	.678	5.90 (2.10)	5.59 (2.17)	521	0.31	.001
3. Large Family Gatherings	2.73 (1.06)	2.70 (1.08)	488	0.03	.471	3.22 (1.19)	2.67 (1.09)	521	0.55	.000
4. Small Family Gatherings	2.75 (1.05)	2.79 (1.16)	464	−0.04	.481	3.37 (1.17)	3.04 (1.10)	521	0.33	.000
5. Talking	3.52 (1.92)	3.20 (1.99)	470	0.32	.002	5.01 (2.07)	4.36 (2.26)	520	0.65	.000
6. Religious Activities	1.78 (1.34)	1.64 (1.25)	467	0.14	.024	2.46 (2.00)	2.22 (1.92)	520	0.24	.000
7. Letters	2.77 (1.94)	2.77 (1.97)	456	0.00	.999	2.05 (1.89)	1.92 (1.69)	521	0.13	.112
8. Phone Calls	4.70 (1.92)	4.84 (1.83)	499	−0.14	.074	4.23 (2.42)	3.84 (2.43)	521	0.39	.002
9. Dine Together	3.22 (1.57)	3.36 (1.63)	482	−0.14	.056	6.00 (2.30)	5.49 (2.50)	521	0.51	.000
Summated Scale	27.47 (8.56)	26.84 (8.16)	386	0.63	.088	35.58 (8.72)	32.13 (8.61)	519	3.45	.000
Ritualistic (3, 4, 6)	7.27 (2.69)	7.10 (2.68)	448	0.17	.134	9.06 (2.74)	7.92 (2.93)	520	1.14	.000
Informal (1, 2, 5)	9.98 (4.29)	9.54 (4.06)	440	0.44	.016	14.24 (4.55)	12.97 (4.74)	519	1.27	.000
Face-to-Face (2, 5)	7.61 (3.52)	7.34 (3.44)	449	0.27	.071	10.91 (3.76)	9.95 (3.85)	520	0.96	.000
Indirect (7, 8)	7.39 (2.57)	7.52 (2.38)	452	−0.13	.341	6.27 (3.36)	5.75 (3.18)	521	0.52	.001

Table 5: Perceptions of Parent-Child Affect in the Southern California Three-Generation Sample. Differences of Means Between Reports by Parents and their Children

| | Report of Elder Dyad Member | | Report of Younger Dyad Member | | | | |
	Mean	(sd)	Mean	(sd)	n	Difference of Means	p(t)
G1–G2	52.62	(6.77)	49.81	(7.35)	511	2.81	.000
G2–G3	48.25	(7.40)	46.88	(8.43)	522	1.37	.000
G1–G3*	21.76	(5.12)	18.65	(6.23)	522	3.11	.000

* The affect between the older members and their grandchildren is measured with a five-item scale (range: 5–30). Contiguous-dyad relationships are measured with a ten-item scale (range: 10–60).

Table 6: Correlations of Self-Report Scores on Three Socio-Political Opinion Scales, for Members of Three-Generation Lineages, by Gender

| (C) Social Conservatism (M) Marriage Norms (B) Legitimacy of Black's Demands | | Parents | | | |
| | | Father | | Mother | |
		r	n	r	n
G2 son	C	.17	80	.29*	84
	M	.32*	85	.36*	86
	B	−.07	85	.08	86
G2 daughter	C	.37*	158	.25*	150
	M	.15	163	.19*	157
	B	.27*	158	.25*	154

* p < .05.

Table 7: Correlations of G1 Parents' Self-Reported Opinion Scale Scores with the Scores they Attribute to their Offspring, by Gender

(C) Social Conservatism (M) Marriage Norms (B) Legitimacy of Black's Demands		G2 Son				G2 Daughter			
		n	Att.	SR	Diff.	n	Att.	SR	Diff.
G1 father	C	77	.66	.18*	.48	160	.69	.37	.32
	M	82	.55	.28	.27	166	.58	.18	.40
	B	83	.72	−.03*	.75	163	.53	.21	.32
G1 mother	C	86	.56	.23	.33	158	.60	.26	.34
	M	87	.51	.38	.13	163	.53	.16	.37
	B	87	.55	.08*	.47	162	.60	.21	.39

* p > .05.

Table 8: Percentage of Persons Aged 65 and Over who Give Help to Children, Grandchildren, and Great-Grandchildren, and Receive Help from Children, by Sex

Help Patterns		1962			1975	
	Men	Women	All	Men	Women	All
Gives help to children	59	60	60	72	69	71
(Number of cases[a])	(901)	(1111)	(2012)	(1850)	(2701)	(4551)
Gives help to grandchildren	50	49	50	73	69	71
(Number of cases[a])	(826)	(1025)	(1851)	(1734)	(2603)	(4337)
Gives help to great- grandchildren	—[c]	–	–	40	50	46
(Number of cases[a])	—[c]	–	–	(678)	(1413)	(2091)
Receives help from children[b]	61	75	69	62	72	68
Regular money help	1	7	4	2	4	3
Occasional money gifts	25	43	35	10	16	14
Makes medical payments	—[c]	–	–	*	2	2
(Number of cases[a])	—[c]	–	–	(1847)	(2703)	(4549)

* Less than 1 percent after rounding.

a The number of cases for 1962 is unweighted; the number of cases for 1975 is weighted.
b Includes help from relatives in 1962.
c Data not reported in 1962.

Source: Shanas, 1978, Table 7–17A.

Table 9: Percentage Distributions for Intergenerational Exchanges: Parents
Responding about Relations with their Children

	Exchange Gifts		Give Help		Get Help	
	G1	G2	G1	G2	G1	G2
1. Almost never	4%	2%	59%	16%	52%	13%
2. About once/year	26	15	9	5	8	6
3. Several times/year	65	77	22	20	28	19
4. Every other month	4	4	3	6	2	5
5. About once/month	1	2	2	8	4	8
6. About once/week	0	0	3	15	3	15
7. Several times/week	0	0	1	20	2	20
8. Almost every day	0	0	1	10	1	14
(n)	(510)	(566)	(463)	(564)	(468)	(565)

	Give Financial Aid		Get Financial Aid	
	G1	G2	G1	G2
1. Not at all	79%	18%	98%	93%
2. Infrequently	19	17	2	6
3. Partial support	2	14	0	1
4. Most of support	0	51	0	0
(n)	(518)	(563)	(516)	(560)

Table 10: Mean Scores on Familism Norm Scales (Range: 5–20), for Three
Generations, by Gender

	Male			Female		
	n	Mean	sd	n	Mean	sd
G1	190	15.6	2.44	179	15.5	2.75
G2	88	14.0	2.33	155	13.7	2.74
G3	114	12.5	2.69	127	13.2	2.54

Table 11: Correlations Between Parents' and their Children's Scores on the Familism Norm Scale, by Gender

| | Parents | | | | |
| | Father | | Mother | | |
	r	n	r	n	
G2 Son	.274	60	.035	62	
G2 Daughter	.275*	123	.188*	110	
G3 Son	−.004	33	.125	78	
G3 Daughter	.281	50	−.106	72	

* p < .05.

Norms and Solidarity

Hilde Rosenmayr

The concept of solidarity encompasses such dimensions as common values, interdependence, reciprocity, exchange, and mutuality. We assume that relationships between generations are based to a certain extent on reciprocal relations, such as dependency and dependability. Expectations must be paired with the readiness to fulfill them — even in the face of various obstacles.

The way in which solidarity is expressed may be studied at a number of levels: availability, scope, functionality, degree of personal involvement, outcome of the effects of direct socialization and of countervailing influences (consensus on values and/or tolerance of dissent). All of these dimensions, which parallel those listed by Bengtson & Schrader (1982), have been regulated by norms and by their counterpart, namely feelings of obligation.

The role played by norms in influencing the exchange between generations has undergone considerable change, and is presently changing perhaps more than the other dimensions mentioned, although some of them have undergone considerable change as well. This paper attempts to provide a description of this normative change as it has developed historically.

At the same time we must acknowledge that there is also a change in intergenerational relationships during the life course of families. Thus family cohesion is broken up and different types of cohesion or relationships develop as the family passes from one life stage to another, or rather, from one cluster of life stages to the next one. For example, child rearing has become only one episode in a couple's life and is itself infringed upon by a multitude of factors other than the intergenerational context. However, relationships between generations continue and may — or rather must — take on different forms, which should be a continuous process. We know, however, that only rarely does development occur along these lines; there are many obstacles along the way. One of them is that one individual's perception of a relationship is by no means identical with the perceptions of the other individuals involved. Once relationships are subjected to deep and personalized reflection, they emerge as very complex since they become rooted in different consciousnesses. Finding a way back to a workable mutual consciousness of relationship may be very difficult.

Once More the Dream of the Multi-Generational Family of the Past

In pre-industrial times, the domain of the household in Europe was almost equivalent to that of what we now call the individual family. The household was the material and social unit of daily life; its cohesion was based on common production

81

and common consumption. Relations between members of a household, whether intergenerational or not, coincided strongly with the economic necessities of this joint production and consumption. Relationships existed largely within the matrix of daily duties. Mutual trust was expressed in common activities necessary to obtain the basic requirements of life. Sieder & Mitterauer (1983) point out that phases in the family life course relate directly to changes in the distribution of functions within the household, the most important one being succession in the headship of the household. In their study of household lists of four rural communities in different districts of Lower and Upper Austria they were also able to discover other than strictly familial ties which had general and specific economic implications for the development of the households, such as kin, neighborhood, and village relationships.

Sieder & Mitterauer stress that one important function among others of this household system was to ensure that a balance was kept between producers and non-producers (Sieder & Mitterauer, 1983, 341). Also in cases of personal crisis, this system provided a haven, for example, for unmarried mothers and their illegitimate children (Sieder & Mitterauer, 1983, 336).

This more complex view of the traditional family system breaks through idealizing pictures of "natural" harmony. According to Hagestad (1981) the concept of the ideal of the nuclear family of our times is being shattered. Hence, relationships must be studied in a total life context, recognizing

"that people's coping abilities and available supports are influenced not only by a constellation of events, but also by a family constellation of events, affecting individuals and their significant others ..." (Hagestad, 1981, 35).

It is generally assumed that under the conditions of a system where the family was geared to providing necessities, strictly enforced boundaries, rules, and norms were required to guarantee that the system of relationships could function. Intergenerational profiles were not very explicit – children did not really count, they were regarded as minors as long as they could not work and participate fully in the household. Youth groups assembled to serve community purposes; thus there remained the adults of both sexes and the (few) old people. Still there were fundamental conflicts going on within these generations: like the ancient myths and Greek tragedies, household stories are full of hatred, envy, jealousy, murder, revenge, and untruthfulness – but also of ways of coping with these destructive tendencies.

There was, however, a conviction derived from experience that harmony was a basis for the continuous functioning of daily life. And functioning of daily life was almost an equivalent to survival under conditions of ever-present danger, which had to be met by very hard labor – the "labor improbus" which the poet Vergil, himself a son of peasants, praises. Harmony was thought to be a goal which could be reached if one followed certain norms; if apparently insoluble problems arose, a "deus ex machina" appeared, as in many Greek tragedies, to provide a solution to the conflict by introducing norms of a higher level.

It was this form of solidarity which Durkheim meant when he spoke of social constraint and mechanical solidarity under conditions of social inequality. Decisions were made according to the exigencies of daily necessity, which did not leave open a wide range for choice. Motives for action were labeled in a dichotomy of either good or bad. Common practices cristallized into rites, and firm convictions had a power of integrative solidarity, which resisted questioning by private sensitivities. As the general consciousness drew its strength from a collective interpretation of life, individuals were obliged to conform to these expectations (Durkheim, 1893).

The Emergence of Individualized Sensitivity

We have come to understand the "modern family" as that form of family life, which originated in the bourgeois middle classes of Western European cities, and which gradually spread to other social classes until it has become the "norm" for all of Western society until the threshold of our present days. The general conditions of life have changed: the place of work is different from the place of habitation, there are fewer children, economic support is derived from one or two incomes and not from primary production, the necessities of life are procured through the market, which is ever expanding, there is a widening area of consumption beyond what is necessary to satisfy basic needs. To bolster up this system powerful economic, administrative, educational, and recreational institutions have expanded tremendously and begun to pervade almost all segments of private life.

In the traditional system of intergenerational relations, children had been an element of continuity. Now the child is regarded as an individual person, whose growing up and whose care and education is considered a special task. Childhood is viewed as an important phase in its own right, not just as the time spent between helplessness and being a performing adult.

Following the introduction of general schooling, another life phase was more generally recognized as a part of social reality, namely adolescence. A prolonged learning phase does not just mean that more knowledge and more culture can be accumulated, but also that the adolescent is able to gain an independent standing within society.

The autonomy of the individual was expanded by granting him or her a certain privacy with regard to intimate concerns. This included such developments as sleeping in one's own bed or room, improved hygiene and cleanliness, covering nudity and sexuality (Rosenmayr & Rosenmayr, 1978). All this had the effect of shielding the individual from direct proximity to and interaction with his or her physical and social surroundings. At the same time, this caused a form of alienation from direct communication with things and with other persons; we may regard it as parallel to the kind of alienation Marx described in the world of industrial production.

A certain kind of solidarity reached its peak between mother and child. If we follow Badinter's description of motherhood in the 18th and 19th century, mothers were led to believe in the primordial task of happily sacrificing their lives to provide for their children's well-being, health, happiness, and development. Badinter's book (1980) does not give the original reasons for the fact that the child became the "unquestioned sovereign in the family" (this Ariès [1960] has shown in his monumental work). That author rather pursues the idea that this supreme love of the child did not so much follow the natural inclinations of women as it served the dialectical power game between husbands and wives. Mothers gained a better position in the family by caring exclusively for the precious child; fathers gladly agreed to this intrafamilial supremacy of mothers because this occupation impeded females in the pursuit of extrafamilial involvements and thus in their questioning of ultimate male authority in the outside world.

The enforcement of this norm of mothers' concern with the child was very strict, as we can read in many passages in Badinter's study. It is hard to decide whether the love of mothers was a sort of "staged" norm, or how much real fulfillment – or rather: chances for development and fulfillment – it gave both to mothers and their children. It seems that some origins of future developments can be found here: children searching for greater autonomy, and the increasing questioning of norms in the course of the 20th century.

We do not have much conclusive knowledge about relationships between middle and older generations, about the "quality of relationships," as we term it today. Certainly there was a growing awareness of the possibility of differing attitudes towards old age. It does not seem, however, that intimate relationships developed between middle and older generations in the same sense as they had been constructed between mother and child, although it is likely that in one way or the other they took on color from this "supreme value." There is ample and diverse literature on aging in the 19th century (Cole, 1980), but it cannot be pursued here.

Rousseau (1755) explicitly states that bonds between parents and children cease to exist in a natural sense when children reach independence; they may decide to renew these bonds in a sort of contract on the basis of mutual attraction and freedom.

We are reminded of Durkheim's concept of organic solidarity, which is likely to emerge under conditions of the division of labor. Transcending Marx's idea of class solidarity based on solidarization with the aim of revolution, Durkheim expects a higher form of solidarity based on both: on the one hand the diversified yield of human labor founded on technical development, and on the other hand the spontaneously used higher margin of personal freedom from sheer necessity. Cooperation under conditions of inequality must be compensated by intentional relationships to others. Technological differentiation evokes differentiation of needs and their fulfillment. This, however, is not to lead to more isolation of individuals, but to a higher form of social justice and freedom based on interaction.

This concept of solidarity transcends mere contractual thinking. In order to make a social universe based on contracts not just livable but also expanding it is not sufficient for it to be based on freedom alone or on what individuals with a higher degree of consciousness decide to risk for a common goal. This kind of solidarity must come about by means of more personal investment than would be sufficient for sheer exchange; the idea is that in order to create equality the "free" individual may be expected to stake more than the balance missing from zero. Relational qualities are clearly envisaged in this game of accepting solidarity as a higher form of social existence.

Conflictual Solidarity

It may look as if the autonomy of the individual brought about by the efforts of the family in the past two-and-a-half centuries is now turning against the family and against intergenerational relations at large. Schulz (1982) reports varying outcomes of studies on people's primary concerns. A survey taken in the Federal Republic of Germany in 1973 showed that the family by far still headed the list of interests; the results of another study of 1979, the instruments of which were, however, more sensitized to a widened frame of aspirations, indicated, that still about 75 percent of those surveyed believed in the necessity to have a family and that the domain of family life is the most important factor in personal satisfaction. At the same time it was shown, however, that subjective aspirations of happiness are linked to factors outside the familial sphere, such as experiences of independence and freedom and to the realization of personal fulfillment in life based on feelings of intensiveness and erotic spontaneity.

With regard to the area of mutual protection, there is a tendency to demand more and more consideration for a distance for the individual. We can almost say, that we have families "à la carte" (Rosenmayr, 1982), meaning thereby that every member of the family wants to pick out what he or she finds palatable and that the search for common standpoints and for coordination of common interests may run against insurmountable obstacles.

It is even questionable whether one can support the contention — which is in itself pessimistic — that what remains of the family is the care of the old, which as gerontological textbooks have stated for decades, functions admirably in quantitative terms. Such declarations are usually followed by lamenting the heavy burden borne by the "women in the middle" caught between obligations towards children, parents, grandparents, great-grandparents, husbands, job, and their own emancipation.

It is a fact, that for some time the care of aged parents may hold the family together — but there may also be the concomitant effect that dependent parents, especially if they are clinging or even exploitative, prevent their children's further individual development or impede the solution of conflicts among the members of the younger generations. Under this pressure, the recognition of special individual needs, which remain unfulfilled in the constricting framework of the nuclearized family, often reach a critical potential of energy, which demands an opening up of channels to the outside (Richter, 1974, 70). Richter considers that this can be made feasible by entering larger groups, which would, however, have to be accompanied by careful therapy.

As soon as relations between different parties in a tight social framework lose their character of personal and object-related mutuality, the system is in danger of losing its balance. There is no use in denying the fact that care of ailing parents *is* a burden which is in our present society counterbalanced by little expectation of reward. Merely "moral" reward for "meeting an obligation," the character of which is more or less undefined, may be too weak an incentive if general values are geared towards individual happiness. It is difficult to appeal to a sense of responsibility for others, if responsibility is seen as primarily subjectively determined.

Moreover we observe growing uncertainty with regard to the family as a haven of mutual protection. The father-mother-child triangle, when probed by therapists, revealed characteristics that were proved to endanger mental health. Parents' expectations of their children can be viewed from two essentially different angles. The salient point is that, contradictory as they are, both of them are very often experienced at the same time, overlapping each other, thus giving rise to all-pervading attitudes of existential insecurity within the family. One standpoint is to concede to parents the honest wish that their children should become what they themselves would like to have been. The other standpoint interprets the parents' behavior as the hidden fear that the children would turn out as badly as they themselves feel they have but are afraid to admit. Richter (1974, 117) points out the heavy burden laid on children growing up under the mixed claims of both standpoints in combination.

The preponderance of conflicts and ambivalences in relationships entered the highly sensitized state of individualized consciousnesses, thus sharpening their impact. It is not just like eating the cake, and still wanting to have it; it is rather like a constant underlying accusation of having been told that cake is just the dessert after necessary proteins and vitamins, and of having been given too much cake with no proteins and vegetables provided. The available tools for remedying such conflictual constellations are usually too weak and not far-reaching enough to pursue the plethora of consequences. Intergenerational behavior has been regarded for too long as a "system governed by norms and thereby promising harmony"; now we feel we have to question the meaning of every word within the quotation marks for its validity. We still expect a "deus ex machina"; but we are admonished to look for him within our own selves in order to find solutions based on more fantasy (Strotzka, 1983).

There is general agreement, that also in intergenerational relationships the perception of reality may differ among significant interactors. There may be a variety of notions of what the governing principles of the individuals are and in what sense they are norm-adherent. There is no recent study on patterns of help and assistance between middle and older generations which does not explicitly distinguish between what old people think they give or receive and what members of the middle generations think they give or receive. Usually the difference is quite considerable; what is actually being given and received is still another matter.

The fulfillment of the obligation to care for the older generation in time of need may turn out to be quite different from what we expect. Usually normative notions, the feeling of necessary recompensation, of what we "owe" to our parents, will not be enough to really alleviate the misery of their loneliness, their distress about physical and mental deterioration, their deep experience of physical and spiritual deprivation accumulated during the course of a lifetime. We must indeed be grateful for the public solidarity of the welfare system existing in most Western countries; however, it does not altogether suffice to keep old people clean and fed and to make it possible for them to maintain a somewhat "decent" life. We must recognize, that if as sons and daughters we do no more than that we may not speak of "qualitatively good" intergenerational relationships.

To be useful a "model" of good intergenerational relationships must recognize the existence of conflicts and allow for means of solution. Otherwise qualitative development of relations between individuals will not be possible. Johnson (1983, 94) describes such a model in Italian-American families; this author refers to conditions of interdependence as

"... the sources of integration which create intimacy, need satisfaction, and group allegiance. It refers to a reciprocal, ongoing quid pro quo in family relationships. In contrast to dependence, interdependence connotes a gratification of need which is not accompanied by guilt or resentment, on one hand, or inordinate passivity or regression, on the other" (Johnson, 1983, 94).

In this example authority and power in the family as exercised by the old over the young and by males over the females is counterbalanced by

"... affect and emotions expansively expressed (which) tend to act as an escape valve to balance out the costs imposed by the authority structure. These feeling states function as oppositional forces ..." (Johnson, 1983, 94).

This model is taken from a social background where traditional norms still play an important role. Explicit external norms, however, reflect just one possible construction of reality. Understanding the reality of human relationships, the great issue of our present time, must not find its satisfaction in premature conclusions. A. and E. Mitscherlich (1967) rightly state that moral norms start as intuitive and purpose-oriented inventions of patterns of behavior, that come to be obeyed continuously in the course of time. It may then happen that automatization takes over and acts as a form of constraint on the important decisions individuals have to make under conditions which no longer correspond to the original situations. Nonetheless, it may also be destructive to do away with norms altogether as they may be based on a recognition of underlying truths which are obscured by what are only apparently totally new situations. After all, norms are meant to protect the needs and claims of those whom the individual actor may not perceive with the same clarity in which he or she may be aware of his or her own aspirations. This regulating social power of norms must not be obscured as well.

Concerning intergenerational solidarity we should recognize, however, the validity of the experience that doing more than just "repay" what our parents have given to us will imply heavy burdens, especially when it conflicts with our aspirations of subjective personal fulfillment. Our ability to bear ambivalent situations seems to be limited. It is difficult to arrive at a realization of a concept of overbalancing, of more than compensating (Rosenmayr, 1978, 59 ff.), which means, that we have to extend solidarity beyond ambivalence, to learn to forgive our parents what they have done to us − just as we must seek forgiveness for what we have done to them and to our own children. A sense of mutual shortcomings within our intergenerational relationships will certainly make us aware of large gaps, but there must be constant efforts to fill these gaps by mutual tolerance relying on deeply rooted trust in each other as well as in ourselves. The real task may well be to find out more about the nature of this margin we have to leave open for the solution of intergenerational conflicts, and in what direction the subjectivities of all persons concerned are to be activated.

Contact and exchange within a social unit that has a multitude of problems to master, such as the family, must certainly include motivations for the elderly to take part in constructive activities and contacts outside the family. Then the family may better serve as a support system to fall back upon; it will develop more ability to cope with or to solve conflicts and may even help to activate individuals' own strengths. But these strengths must be stimulated from inside as well as from outside. More often than not restriction to exclusively familial relations (which sometimes are termed intensive, but in reality may be just clinging ones and emotional exploitation) diminishes the capacity to solve problems with fairness. Hörl (1983) points out that persons who are able to develop a variety of formal or informal affective relationships with other persons besides (not instead of!) familial relationships, have a better capacity to develop their problem-solving capacities in old age than those who concentrate exclusively on "intensive" family contacts. On the other hand, he states, a sheer negation of the importance of family interaction also impairs the capacity to solve conflicts and problems; rather, the additional security a person may obtain from informal and formal extrafamilial relations may enable him to cope better with problems both with the family and with his own situation. This is in keeping with Lehr's statement, that

"... we might say that quality of life in old age is dependent rather on moderate intra-familial interaction (with high quality) than on intensive intra-familial interaction (with low quality) ..." (Lehr, 1982h, 15).

We must realize that what old age is and means is a consequence of a person's experiences during a lifetime and his ability to continue his own life. The way societies treat the elderly will largely depend on how individuals within their given social, economic, and political conditions have previously managed their lives, their relationships, and the crucial decisions they had to make, and how they continue to make them. An ideal of life-fulfillment in old age is meaningless if it does not include continuing development, which means working on one's own past for the sake of a more meaningful future.

Thus many problems which occur in the phase of old age are from the outset not really problems of old age, but had been problems during a person's entire lifetime. Their poignancy in old age depends on the fact that they accumulate and become aggravated as the individual's capacities diminish and he or she is less able to deal with them without outside help. In such situations the effectiveness of help will depend on the readiness both to give and to receive it. We may not expect a general willingness of a younger generation to give care, and an ability on the part of the older generation of receiving help without serious guilt feelings, if an attitude of giving and receiving help has not been a lifelong condition between the generations, and if − which is just as important − we do not allow for unexpected development beyond these conditions.

It is even possible that on the basis of such an attitude new forms of solidarity may emerge and new social aggregations may be devised. Streib (1982) for example, considers joint housing and living arrangements for the increasing number of divorced women with children following the model of old age joint housing, which would help to alleviate some of their economic, occupational, and educational problems.

The discussion of the need for intimacy (Kieffer, 1977) shows that there is a deep longing for mutual trust and understanding, and for a shared consciousness as well. We still need to find mutually understandable means of expressing solidarity. In this connection we may quote (as does Watzlawick, 1981) what Erwin Schrödinger (1958, 52) wrote about the perception of reality: that we must bear in mind that our sensitive, perceptive, and reflective Ego is nowhere to be found explicitly in such a vision; because it is an integral part of it and cannot be distilled from it.

On such grounds we may share perceptions of reality, even if we disagree on some aspects of them. We will not, however, be able to develop understanding, trust, and a sense of hope, which means belief in a development beyond what can already be seen within human relationships (Strotzka, 1983, 140), if we insist that reality can be nothing but the mirror of an uncontrolled uniqueness. The danger of regarding it as such lies both in the standpoint of desperate norm-enforcement, as well as in that of unrevised subjectivity. Taking steps beyond these standpoints is the crucial thing: inaction must be replaced by patient efforts of revision and the will to make intergenerational relationships fruitful.

The Quality of the Relationship Between Elderly People and Their Adult Children

Kees Knipscheer

1. Introduction

The research into intergenerational relationships between elderly people and their children is very extensive. A number of hypotheses on the atrophy of this relationship have been put forward and the need for research on qualitative aspects of these relations has been stressed.

After a brief review of the developments in this field some results of two studies are discussed which shed light on some qualitative characteristics of the elderly parent-child relationship. Next some suggestions are developed in connection with recent ideas in research and theory centered around social support. For further research into the qualitative aspects of this parent-child relationship we may find fruitful cues here.

2. Existing Research into the Elderly-Offspring Relationship

For approximately 30 years we have seen in family sociology, in social gerontology, and in social psychology a continuous stream of research into aspects of the relationship between elderly people and their children (Troll, 1971; Lee, 1980; Streib, 1980; Knipscheer, 1980). The research topics studied show a gradual development along the following lines:
- structural change in nuclear and extended family (Parsons, 1943),
- survival of the extended family (Sussman, 1959; 1965; Litwak, 1965),
- children's role in helping elderly parents (Shanas et al., 1968; Rosenmayr & Köckeis, 1965; Rosenmayr, 1973),
- intergenerational relationships, generation gap, and family solidarity (Bengtson et al., 1976; Troll & Bengtson, 1979),
- quality of parent-child relationships and its contribution to parental well-being (Kerckhoff, 1966c; Rosow, 1967; Wood & Robertson, 1978).

Beside these developments in the questions posed for research there has been at the same time some ideological conflict. On the one hand there are the optimists, the researchers who vigorously dispute Parsons' theory, the researchers who minimize the generation gap within the family and who tend to evaluate the relations between old people and their grown-up children in a very positive way. On the other hand there are the pessimists, those researchers who stress the disintegration of the family system, and/or speak of mutual alienation based on the cultural gap between elderly people and their children, and who see the family threatened by the tensions between individuality and solidarity. Sometimes it looks as though historical sociological research has been assigned a crucial role in this, on the one hand by showing that the family ties in the past have been far less positive than has been presumed for quite some time and on the other hand by showing that in spite of this the succeeding generations were dominated by strong tendencies of continuity. It is of course risky to separate researchers in this field into two opposite sides and I should certainly not want to deny them any scientific objectivity. However, I shall give a few examples. In a recent article Shanas concluded, based on research data over a period of 20 years in the U.S.A. and in Western European countries:

"What the data do show is that older parents see adult children often. The second hypothesis that because of the alienation of older parents from their children, most older parents rarely see their children, must also be rejected" (Shanas, 1979a).

Blau wondered what the meaning of these contacts between elderly parents and their children was:

"Adult children as a rule, fulfill their material obligations and dutifully maintain some contact with aging parents, but their separate existence, interests, and daily experiences lessen intimacy between the generations, and estrangement, carefully hidden on both sides, begins" (Blau, 1973, 51).

However, it may be that the research that has been done has confirmed that in most cases frequent contacts exist between elderly parents and their middle-aged children, that there is a regular exchange of help (from both sides), that the gap between the generations within the family system is narrower than many have presumed, and that the majority of the elderly people are reasonably content with the relationship with their children. At the same time, it has been found that an almost exclusive orientation of the elderly parents to their children does not contribute to a positive morale and/or to more "life satisfaction" (Kerckhoff, 1966c; Messer, 1968; Lehr, 1982a, g). Ursula Lehr summarizes it as follows:

"When the quantity of the contacts within the family exists at the cost of the quality of these contacts and at the cost of the contacts outside the family they become more of a disadvantage than of advantage for the elderly people" (Lehr, 1982a).

3. The Content of the Parent-Child Relationship and Self-Evaluation

Research findings that have been taken from a longitudinal relocation study enable us to test and differentiate this statement. In this relocation study in Nijmegen (n = 455 in first observation, of which 346 respondents were with children) I examined what activities occurred between the respondents (198 men and 257 women, mean age 72 years) and each of their children. Four relational contents were differentiated; namely with regard to birthday visiting, leisure activities, helping activities, and confidential activities[1]. Based on the content of the relationships of the respondent with each of his/her children, indices for each relational content were computed. These indices showed which percentage of the relationships between the elderly parent and his/her children was devoted to birthday visiting, leisure activities, helping activities, and confidential activities. In the analysis of the first observation no correlation was found between the indices on the content of the parent-child relationships and the score on a self-evaluation scale validated by

Coleman (1974). The variance explained by the four indices was 3.6 percent (n = 346). To test this result further we selected a group of 95 respondents on whom we made yearly observations, over a period of five years and using the same scales. Regression analyses of the data of each of these observations gave almost identical results (see Table 1).

Controlling for sex, marital status, and two specific research groups showed only very small differences.

This research did not show a linear correlation between the elderly parents' score on the self-evaluation scale and the percentage of the parent-child relationships within a family which had a certain content. It is notable, for instance, that it obviously does not make any difference whether the relationship with *each* child is of a confidential nature, or whether there is such a relationship *with half of the* children or *with none of the* children.

The self-evaluation scale which was used in this research comprised six items each of which consisted of two opposite statements. After the respondent had chosen one of the statements, he or she was asked why he or she had chosen that possibility. In a large number of cases respondents referred to family ties to justify their choice — mostly the ties with their children —. The references to family ties were most marked for the item that consisted of the statements "I don't count any more (socially)" and "I do count (socially)."

I tried to select a sample of statements for this item that pertain to the importance of the relationship with the children.

These statements are shown in Table 2. On the left are examples that warrant the choice for the positive part of the item and on the right the examples that warrant the choice for the negative side. In the left column the responses have been arranged so as to put those statements that are most positive at the top. Those of the lower part hardly warrant a positive choice. It is remarkable how uncertain the parents are about the extent to which "they count" with their children, and how much they think material benefits play a role for the children. Another remarkable fact is that the parents — rather easily — excuse their children for what the parents experience as a lack of attention and recognition. Each of these examples demonstrates to me, again, that assessment of the relationships between elderly people and their children is an enormously complex affair. It does make the earlier mentioned results of the analysis, the absence of a linear correlation between the self-evaluation score and the behavioral content of the relationship with the children, more understandable. What is going on within these relationships is one point, how this is perceived and experienced is another. Many parents are uncertain about how to interpret the children's behavior. They have their own guesses as to the motivation of the children's behavior and can easily find an excuse when their children disappoint them. The interpretations that occur as a matter of course in the relationships leave maximal space for subjective meanings on both sides. The boundaries of mutual expectations are vague and unstable. Possibly this might be called the ambiguity of the parent-child relationship in old age and explains what Rosenmayr calls the ambivalence of the relationship (pers. comm., 1981). That is also why the reasons given by the parents in Table 2 are so often cautiously phrased. In this respect there are of course large differences between the respondents, on the one hand connected with personality traits and developmental psychological factors (vulnerability, emotional dependency) and on the other hand situational factors like presence of stress, cultural views on parent-child relationships, and social-economical circumstances. The asymmetrical parent-child relationship mentioned elsewhere (Bengtson & Kuypers, 1971; Bengtson & Cutler, 1976; Knipscheer & Bevers, 1981) plays an important role here. Earlier research has shown that elderly people who have no other social contacts besides those with their children have a more negative morale. One may wonder how this relates to the ambiguity that is so often present in the relationship between elderly people and their children. The A-type that Lehr distinguishes in the analysis of the Bonner Longitudinal Study seems to correspond to a certain degree with this (Lehr, 1982g).

In the relocation study I also investigated who the respondents wanted to ask for help in case they should need care: family (mostly children) or professional assistance. The scores of the five items used to measure this attitude showed that there is wide variation in the answer to this question. The results of the analysis showed that there was no relationship between the extent of parent-child interaction and indicating that the family would be appealed to in the case of need for care. Therefore an intensive level of interaction between parents and their children does not heighten the chance that one counts on the children for care. The question is: Will the attitude towards care giving also be strongly influenced by the earlier mentioned ambiguity in the parent-child relationship or is it rather a matter of cultural views, or ought to or ought not to, and therefore independent of the extent of mutual interaction? Before coming to more general conclusions, I want to point to some results of another study.

4. Perceptions and Attitudes of Both Partners in the Parent-Child Relationship

A second study I should like to point to concerns 74 randomly sampled people of middle age (40–49 years old, 39 men and 35 women) and one of their parents who are living independently (26 men and 48 women). Starting with the middle-aged children, the partly structured interviews narrowed themselves to behavior and attitudes concerning matters that are important in the relationship between older parents and their children. Topics of the interviews included, for example, frequency and direction of visits, political and religious beliefs, the upbringing of the (grand)children, the way money was spent, and mutual dependence and independence. These interviews with parents and children yielded a colorful array of statements. These were selected and analyzed for their information on the asymmetrical character of the relations between the generations. Not all statements were noted down as they were given during the interview. The criterion was: To what extent did the answer of the parent or child include a typical characteristic of the relationship. An answer of a parent on, for example, a question on their housing situation like "I want to move because the roof of my house is leaking" was not of interest for this project, but the more than once heard reaction "I want to move because I like to live nearer to my children" was.

From these typical reactions of the parents and children on the questions posed to them, the difference in self-imposed behavioral codes and the connecting asymmetry in feelings of dependency are most marked. To start with the first, few relationships are so controlled by unwritten rules and norms as those between elderly people and their children. While for the children the formula "Thou shalt ... (visit, aid, respect the parents)" counts, parents abide more by the rule "Thou shalt not ... (interfere with the children, ask for something, bother)". Of course the parent-child relationship is not based on "dos" and "don'ts" but it is typical for these relations that children during the interviews stress prescriptions and parents are more attached to proscriptions. This difference showed, for instance, in a subject like care (assistance).

Generally children showed a great willingness to help. There are *more* children than parents who feel that children can help parents best when this is necessary (60 children think so and 43 parents). According to the children, parents should feel free to ask for this, they think it self-evident that children should be the obvious people to help. Some children do discern that their parents have great trouble in asking for help. A large number of parents felt little inclination to call upon their children for help, sometimes even when the children do think that they would be the obvious choice for help (see Table 3). This caution on the parents' side contrasts in a large number of cases with the willingness on the part of the children. Both parties participate in the relationship in a distinct way. It is of course hard to say how willing the children would be if they were really called on to help. In the parent-child dyads in these interviews this question was not yet a current issue. On the question whether parents needed a lot or little help there was much agreement. In 59 of the 74 dyads both parties answered that little help was required. Illustrative were again the amplifications that were given with these answers (see Table 4).

The caution on the part of the parents to ask for help is mostly clearly discerned by the children. It is here that we find another element in the relation between elderly people and their children. So far the questions and answers have been mostly concerned with practical help. With the last statements in Table 4 the emphasis shifts to the emotional side of the relationship. Here we find another important asymmetrical characteristic of the relationship between the generations within the family context: the emotional commitment. Characteristic of the way children talk about such subjects as visit, understanding, the relationship with their parents as such is the ability to maintain emotional distance, while the parents emphasize the emotional dependency and need for contact. Parents are generally more positive about visits than their children. Remarks like "we do it mostly for our parents" and "It doesn't mean very much to me" are typical for the children.

In those cases in which there is an asymmetry in the meaning and worth that the parties attach to visit, the party for whom it is most important is in a more dependent position and the other party will sooner feel obliged to go visit. Almost all parents affirm that they like to go visit their children (fact is they are the ones mostly visited), although some do add some objections, for instance, to the travelling, business. Characteristic of parents, too, is that they sometimes wonder if their visits are still appreciated, a thought that occurred with none of the children. The fact that parents, compared to their children, feel themselves more emotionally dependent on others does not mean that parents care more about their children than children care about their parents. This asymmetry should primarily be understood in a qualitative way and not in terms of more or less.

The interviews with the parents showed that they agree with the standard that one should fall back as little as possible on the children: Be independent and leave the children their freedom, that is the rule/norm. At the same time, parents are aware of the fact that the emotional need for contact does make them dependent on their children. Parents that feel themselves depending on their children in an emotional way were generally aware of the vulnerability of their position. Contrary to forms of dependency on the material or functional level, this emotional dependency is not always experienced as a negative one.

Relationships that rest almost exclusively on emotional ties are vulnerable. Almost all families know their typical situations that require careful and tactful handling. In this respect too, differences between parents and children are evident. Though both parties will try in situations like these to spare one another – not to hurt, worry, or distress –. For the parents there is the added fact that they want to secure the relationship as such. Parents are, if we speak in terms of power – which mostly is not a well-chosen terminology to characterize family relations – in the weaker position because they feel dependent on their children in an emotional way. They have to invest most in the relationship; but the person who invests most, also runs the greatest risk of losing most.

5. New Research Directions, Social Support as a Qualitative Construction

What can we learn from these findings of the relationships between elderly people and their children? It has already been repeated that there should be more attention paid to the quality of this relationship, but progress in this direction is, as far as I know, still rather limited. Based on our own results and in association with the recent support literature some guidelines for such research may be formulated. It has been found that there is a connection between "stressful life situations" and health/well-being. An important matter in this research is the effect of social support in this connection. Since Caplan elaborated his conception of social support (1974) a stream of research and theory has been started. House has tried to assess the results of this (House, 1981) and Thoits recently formulated a number of methodological questions (Thoits, 1982).

The first point that is of importance here is the definition of social support. After a content analysis of supportive acts and evaluating earlier definitions House distinguishes four classes or types of supportive acts, namely emotional support, evaluative support, informative support, and instrumental support (see Scheme 1). Thoits (1982) points to the fact that many researchers did not define the content of support only and measure the availability of support only by the availability of persons or relationships. She defines social support as:

"The degree to which a person's basic social needs are gratified through interaction with others. Basic social needs include affection, esteem, or approval, belonging, identity, and security. These needs may be met by either the provision of socio-emotional aid or the provision of instrumental aid."

In the research into the relationship between elderly people and their children the differentiation in functions and contents of the relationship has also not been amplified enough. The four types of social support that House distinguishes form

95

— in their interconnection and (mutual) overlap — the essential content of a qualitatively good relationship.

In a relation like this these four functions of mutual interaction should be in a certain balance. It seems very important to me for several reasons, especially in connection with the relation between elderly people and their children, to stress strongly the contents of these four types and the balance between them.

One reason is the generally negative views of elderly people. The social breakdown syndrome (Kuypers & Bengtson, 1973) makes them vulnerable, especially in connection with socio-emotional support. It therefore seems very useful to me that House (1981) distinguished between problem-oriented support and general support (see Scheme 1). This need for socio-emotional support does not originate with the onset of incapacities of the elderly but with the diminishing respect for the elderly. "General support" is vitally important to elderly people. In the second place, the balance between the four types of support is very important because a one-sided/unilateral emphasis on instrumental support endangers emotional and evaluative support. Especially where physical deterioration appears, and, therefore, gives rise to the need for instrumental support, the socio-emotional support should form a counterweight. When the need to take care of oneself as long as possible cannot be realized anymore, the physical dependence forms a threat to the feelings of self-respect and self-preservation. The very strong caution/reluctance of elderly people to call upon their children seems to be a telltale sign in this connection.

In the third place, the most important reason to plead for a balance between the four types of support lies in the supposed reciprocity of the support. At the moment that this reciprocity is impaired, a situation of one-sided dependency arises and this forms a direct threat to the quality of the relation. In this context it should be noted that parents and their children interpret/perceive certain support activities in a completely different way. This can also be seen in the earlier examples.

The extent to which the relations between elderly people and their children are characterized by the four types of support, both in general as well as in connection with certain problems should be empirically investigated. Special attention should be paid to the connection among these four types of support. The indication of a certain asymmetry and ambivalence in this relation does give rise to the presumption that there are limits to the quality of the relation between elderly people and their children. These limits make it possible to explain why elderly people who are almost exclusively orientated to their children have less positive morales. To be aware of limits to the quality of the parent-child relationship at advanced age obviously does not detract from the many forms of instrumental support that are exchanged between both parties. These, however, are supposed to be more founded on mutual involvement (Adams, 1968), durability of the relationship, and mutual responsibility rather than being based on the quality of the relation as such.

6. Concluding Remarks

Until now the research in the elderly-offspring relationship focused on the behavioral level. The need for research in the quality of this relationship is often stressed but did not get systematic attention. It is shown on the basis of qualitative data that this field of research will be complicated and deserves more attention in the future.

One of the possibilities for developing this research is indicated in the suggestion to start from four types of social support. A certain amount of these four types of support and a balance between them seems to say something about the quality of a relationship. It's evident that we exceed the behavioral level in this way.

Footnote:

1 Four types of activities: 1. Birthday visit
                                                2. Leisure activities
                                                3. Helping activities
                                                4. Intimacy

The questions regarding the four types of activities were as follows:
Ad 1. − Which of these persons visits you on your birthday?
Ad 2. − With which of these persons do you play cards (or any other game) occasionally?
          − With which of these persons do you go out for a day?
          − With which of these persons do you go for a walk or go shopping?
Ad 3. − Which of these persons helps you in the household?
          − Which of these persons goes shopping for you?
          − Which of these persons does some small jobs (carpentry, gardening) for you?
Ad 4. − With which of these persons can you talk confidentially?
          − Which of these persons talks to you about his problems?
          − With which of these persons do you talk about your problems?

The procedure was to present these questions to the respondent along with a list of the primary relationships he had identified. An activity was scored as present in a relationship when at least one of the questions in that category was answered positively.

Table 1: Percentages of Explained Variances in Self-Evaluation by Regression Analysis with Four Indices of Parent-Child Relationship Content as Independent Variables (n = 95)*

		Percent explained variances	Standard regression coefficient in last equation
1st observation:	birthday visit	3.75	−.19
self-evaluation	helping activities	4.00	−.06
mean : 7.73	leisure activities	4.19	.05
st. dev. : 1.72	intimacy	4.21	−.01
2nd observation:	intimacy	1.24	−.08
self-evaluation	leisure activities	1.88	−.08
mean : 7.87	birthday visit	1.92	−.02
st. dev. : 1.82			
3rd observation:	intimacy	3.68	−.28
self-evaluation	helping activities	5.62	.13
mean : 7.81	leisure activities	6.24	.08
st. dev. : 1.73	birthday visit	6.28	−.02
4th observation:	intimacy	2.40	−.12
self-evaluation	birthday visit	3.32	−.10
mean : 7.86	helping activities	3.61	−.06
st. dev. : 1.67	leisure activities	3.65	.02
5th observation:	helping activities	3.39	.22
self-evaluation	intimacy	4.66	−.09
mean : 7.88	leisure activities	4.94	−.06
st. dev. : 1.92	birthday visit	5.06	−.03

* Nie, N.H. et al., S.P.S.S., (1975, 2nd ed.), Standard Regression Method.

Table 2: Sample of Justifications for the Choice of one of the Opposite Statements of an Item of the Self-Evaluation Scale

I do count (socially)	I do not count anymore (socially)
1. Positive	2. Negative
– To talk with the children and give them a home.	– I do count a little bit to my son and grandchildren.
– There is nothing that happens that they do not involve me in.	– Not even to the children, they do phone every week, but I do not count to them either anymore.
– You notice that in your relations with children, you can feel that.	– At first the children attended you much more than now.
– Children still cannot miss me.	– Otherwise my children would come occasionally.
– Daughter still asks advice.	– No, the children do not come and I cannot do anything anymore.
– I can still talk with the children.	– The children do not give a damn about you.
– (Act) as a wailing-wall for the children.	– They do not care if I live or die.
– Sometimes the children are really not nice, but I do still really count.	
– Oh well, perhaps a little bit to the children, I think.	
– Yes, my children are all really sweet, but well they do all have their jobs and their family and then they cannot make a fuss over their granny/grandma.	
– As to my children, I do not ask them so I do not know.	
– I still have my money, and that makes a lot of difference, my children laugh at me, I am far too frugal.	
– To my grandchildren I do, but to my children I do not. Just when I am going then they know how to find me.	
– I still do anything to please the children.	
– Yes, to my friends I do, not to my children.	

Table 3: Examples of Comment on the Parents' Choice for Children or Others in Case of Need

Parents who think that *their own children* can help them best (n = 48)

– For one hour, because I do not want to be a bother to them.

– In small matters, because I do not want to be dependent on them.

– First the children and if that is not possible anymore then someone else will have to do it.

Parents who think that *others* can help them best (n = 26)

– Children have their own family. I would rather ask my niece for help.

– I cannot expect anything from my children.

– I would rather have paid help but my children do not want that.

– We want no help from the children, if it becomes necessary we want to move to a residential (care) home.

– They live too far away and have their own family.

Table 4: Examples of Comments Why Parents Think they Need Little Help and Why Children Think Their Parents Need Little Help

Children think that their parents need little help from the children.

- They are very independent, they want to stay independent for as long as possible.
- If it depends on them, they do need very little help.
- Father would like to have more help (e.g., transportation) but would not ask for it.
- They do not need help, but do need a lot of attention from their children.
- Not help but need for company.

Parents think that they need little help from the children.

- I do not easily ask for help.
- I can manage.
- It may come to be that I do need help.
- We help the children more than the other way around.
- When I need it they will help me.
- They cannot help much, they have to work hard themselves all day.
- I do expect understanding from my children, moral support.

Scheme 1: Types or Classes of Supportive Acts, Based on House (1981)

	general support	problem-oriented support
emotional support	intimacy, trust, love	love, empathy, trust, caring
appraisal support	acceptance, interrelational activities	promoting positive self-evaluation, positive feedback
informational support	helps people to help themselves	helps people to appeal for social assistance
		to find a job
instrumental support	exchange of practical help	effective practical help that meets a certain need

Part II: Socialization, Support, and Strain — Consequences for the Individual and for Intergenerational Relationships

It is no accident that our discussion on the problem of intergenerational relationships within the family is prefaced by sociohistoric considerations. Not only did we wish to point out the significance of historic development and sociocultural transformation, but also to emphasize the fact that it has been primarily work in the fields of social history and historical sociology which has made current family researchers and theoreticians more sensible to the complexity of the problem (Elder, 1981b; Mitterauer & Sieder, 1977). This complexity is evident, on the one hand, in the broad variety of questions which emerge in connection with the relations among lineage generations in a respective social context. On the other hand, it is represented by a multiplicity of analytical perspectives and theoretical levels which have developed within individual disciplines and which (depending on broader social trends [cf. e.g., Moscovici, 1972; 1976; Gergen & Morawski, 1980, and others]) have come to be preferred in each discipline.

The *thematic variety* becomes apparent in the contributions to the second part of the chapter "Multi-Generational Family," despite the fact that particular questions have been stressed. One of them is the analysis of *socialization* and socialization functions in the multi-generation family unit. This is the central theme of Gunhild Hagestad's paper. In her eyes, socialization represents much more than the preparation of children and adolescents to assume adult status, a narrow conception which still dominated the social sciences until about two decades ago (cf. Goslin, 1969). Nor does Hagestad conceive socialization in terms of a one-sided influencing of the older by the younger who have an information advantage, a process which some authors (e.g., Buchhofer, Friedrichs, & Lüdtke, 1970) saw as increasingly significant in dynamic societies. Hagestad defines socialization as a never-ending, mutual influence characterizing the relationship between lineage generations. Empirical support of this view is also expressed in the contribution by Ursula Lehr and the data gathered on the five-generation family by Andreas Kruse.

The second area of emphasis is the *role of women* in multi-generation families. Gunhild Hagestad is the first to take up this theme. In her exploration of some key aspects of vertical family ties and especially of intergenerational patterns of support she attempts to discern sex-specific differences.

Ursula Lehr begins her paper with a critical look at the ideology of family and motherhood which dominates current family and social policy, but which also can be identified in research in developmental psychology. Using a life history approach and numerous empirical data from longitudinal studies, she pinpoints some of the consequences that arise for women in the course of (frequently involuntary) disengagement from society in favor of family committment. The author emphasizes the negative effects of a strong family-centeredness in coping with the empty-nest situation and the way women deal with their own aging process. This problem has been largely disregarded by research up to now (as Alpert & Richardson 1980 expressly indicate).

Carol Hagemann-White analyzes the differentiation of responsibilities between the sexes which has developed within the family in the course of socio-economic transition. She thus provides a bridge to the first chapter of the volume. Sociohistorical change serves the author as a framework to investigate the current distribution of responsibility and the increasing psychologization of sex differences. Another aspect of psychologization is touched upon by Marianne Meinhold – that tendency of welfare institutions and helping professions to look for explanations and solutions of every kind of family problem in the interpersonal relations of its members. In Meinhold's contribution as well, woman – the mother – is the focus of concern. The author graphically illustrates that social intervention which sees its key function in behavior modification without taking the settings of intergenerational coexistence into account, can lead to only sporadic success and is more likely to have negative consequences – for example, the imputation of guilt to women or their self-inculpation.

Hence the contributions of Lehr, Hagemann-White, & Meinhold lead us to a further point of emphasis in this chapter: an *exposure of ideologically biased interpretations* in scientific findings and a questioning of "common sense" opinions current in sociopolitical practice. In his paper, "A Critique of Family Ideologies from a Historic Point of View," Michael Mitterauer (1981) has fundamentally analyzed why the theme of relations among familial generations is especially open to an ideological coloring. Observations on current politics (Binstock, 1983; Naegele, 1983, and others) show that the "ideology of subsidiarism" (Mitterauer, 1981, 48 ff.) in particular is again gaining ground in day-to-day political practice. The contributions by Lehr and Meinhold are particularly valuable in this connection, the first because it seeks ways "to yield understanding rather than bind people to existing forms of social reality" (Gergen & Morawski, 1980, 335), and the second because it elucidates how problematic it is to "transpose" scientific insights into practical action.

In the first part of this chapter, emphasis was already placed on the significance of the time dimension in shaping intergenerational relationships within the family. This was done with respect to *historic time* (Elder, 1981b) and the role of sociocultural transformation, and also with regard to the *family life course*, that process of social construction and reconstruction (Elder, 1975) during which both the constellation of family members and their mutual relationships continually change.

These two time dimensions, together with a third – that of *individual development age*, which marks the individual's position in the developmental process (Elder, 1975) – are emphasized to a differing extent from contribution to contribution. Thus, Hagemann-White, for example, chooses a long-term social development as the framework of her discussion, while Lehr and Hagestad consistently attempt to see individual development in the context of that of the family. Hagestad in particular never loses sight of the entire set of interwoven vertical family ties, emphasizing that the individual approach (like investigations of only one lineage generation) is not adequate to throw light on complex interaction patterns. The conclusions reached by Andreas Kruse in his pilot study point in the same direction.

An orientation based on the life course of families is seen as the adequate approach to the interweave of ties among lineage generations. This approach also offers an opportunity to investigate reciprocal relationships among simultaneous roles. Hagestad does this in regard to dual role occupants, women who in the three-generation family occupy both the role of mother and daughter. Discussions by Ursula Lehr and Andreas Kruse lead to the conclusion that this problem of simultaneous occupancy of several roles is worthy of more future attention, particularly in light of the increase in four- and five-generation families. This is also indicated by the results of investigations on the mental and psychosomatic health of women in multi-generational families as well as by experiences gained in psychotherapeutic practice (Bruder, 1982; Bruder et al., 1981; Radebold et al., 1982).

The majority of the authors present empirical findings here: data (Hagestad & Lehr), qualitative statements (Kruse) and case examples (Meinhold). This material is interesting per se as a description of generational coexistence and provides many insights into the multi-generational family. Moreover, the possibility of a comparison arises between differing methodological procedures. Like Bengtson et al. and Knipscheer in the first part of the chapter, these authors are concerned to at least partially answer the question as to adequate methodological and methodic approaches to the topic.

The focus of Hagestad's methodological considerations is the choice of an adequate level of analysis which would enable us to deal with families as actors in structured situations. Bengtson et al. have suggested treating the family as a social group, and Hagestad holds the same view and follows it up consistently in her discussion. To her way of thinking, families are units, and to approach them via the individual level and/or via a statistical aggregation of a group (family, generation) is not an appropriate way to analyze intergenerational relationships. Yet already in the next contribution, that of Andreas Kruse, certain "technical" difficulties become visible in connection with the application of this rule as soon as the researcher is confronted with four- or five-generation families and hence with a multiplicity of scattered family members.

Meinhold brings up methodological questions as well, in the search for an approach that besides data collecting and "knowledge production" simultaneously implies their reproduction and application. With reference to Bronfenbrenner (1978; 1979), who confronted the artificiality of conventional, experimental developmental psychology with an attempt to merge experimental elements with more naturalistic ones on an ecological basis, Meinhold attempts to develop a "situation-analytical approach." This procedure combines self-reports of family members with expert evaluation of interactive situations and contextual factors.

Although only a few methodological aspects are explicitly treated and several others implicitly touched upon in this chapter, it nonetheless reveals that the methodological side of research into intergenerational relationships does not play a subordinate role. New thematic stresses (e.g., the "everyday secularity" of family life [Menne, 1981]), and above all the shift in analytic perspectives within the social sciences which Elder (1981b) interprets as a turn away from structuralist models, urgently call for a revision of common methodological procedures.

Multi-Generational Families: Socialization, Support, and Strain

Gunhild O. Hagestad

Introduction: Studying Multi-Generational Families

Intergenerational relations in the family can be visualized as a set of interlocking, vertical ties, which weave together interdependent relationships and interconnected lives. The key linkage in such vertical connections is the parent-child dyad. Within a given linear unit, the oldest generation, *the Omega* (Hagestad, 1982b) has members who occupy the role of parent, but not that of child. At the opposite end of the generational spectrum are the newest members of the unit – *the Alpha* generation. Family members in this position occupy the role of child, but not that of parent. Between these two locations in a vertical, interlocked chain, there may be up to four generations who simultaneously occupy the role of parent and the role of child. Such individuals are "generational bridges" (Hill et al., 1970) who connect the young and the old. Because of their pivotal position in a set of vertical ties, they are key figures in the negotiation of continuity and change and in the allocation of family resources through intergenerational exchanges. Because of these functions, they are also the most likely to reflect the strains of multi-generational living. The study of such middle generations is critical to our understanding of multi-generational families.

This paper presents some research illustrations from families with three generations of adults. With a focus on the middle generation's relations with the young and the old, it explores some key aspects of vertical family ties. First, it discusses processes of socialization and influence across the generations. Second, it focuses on intergenerational patterns of support, particularly emotional support. Sources of strain and conflict are considered under both these topics. Finally, contrasts between men and women are addressed throughout the discussion.

In this brief discussion of middle generation men and women's involvement in intergenerational patterns of socialization, support, and conflict, I seek to illustrate two major points. First, because of the complex web of interconnections among lives and relationships across generations in the family, it is essential to take a truly multi-generational perspective, using family lineages as our units. Even if our particular research interest centers on one generation or one particular intergenerational dyad, we need to take into account the *wider* generational context. For example, our findings on how middle-aged individuals relate to aged parents will be incomplete at best, and quite possibly misleading, if we disregard the fact that the former are typically also parents of young adults. Our understanding of grandparent-grandchild relations will be fragmented and limited if we do not take into consideration how both these generations relate to the middle generation, who mediate between young and old (Robertson, 1977).

My second point is a methodological one. When we study relationships in two or more generations, we are dealing with units of analysis which should push us to try new strategies in research design and treatment of data. If we seek to understand such phenomena as socialization and support in multi-generational families, we have to move beyond individuals, or even dyads, as units. This may seem like an obvious and simplistic point, but a quick review of past intergenerational research would soon demonstrate to the reader that most work in this area has seldom maintained an *intrafamily* focus. Most commonly, "grandparents," "parents," and "grandchildren" have been treated as statistical aggregates or groups. For example, reports on how the middle-aged relate to the old are compared to how the middle-aged relate to the young, but such reports are not linked *within families*, to see how patterns of relating combine across two or more generations.

Because commonly used statistical techniques typically involve aggregating data on individuals, it is quite easy for the family to get lost in the computer, even though the researcher has data on multiple family members and their mutual relationships. Throughout my discussion, I will try to give some simple examples to illustrate this point. In a section on needed future work, I touch on some potential approaches to describing families as units.

Relations Between Three Generations of Adults: Some Research Illustrations

My discussion of socialization, support, and strain in intergenerational relations will pull from two pieces of research: a study of influence patterns in three generations of Chicago area families, and a study of divorce among middle-aged couples.

The Chicago Study
In the late 1970s, I was part of a team which studied members of three generations in 148 Chicago area families. From each family, we conducted separate interviews with one young adult grandchild, both the middle-aged mother and father, and one aged grandparent.

The basic research design was a dyadic one. Across intergenerational pairs, we asked both members to discuss each other and their relationship. We therefore had reciprocal data, reflecting the two individuals' views of their relationship. The only exception was that the grandparents were not asked to discuss their child-in-law.

A major section of the interview dealt with what family members talked about. A set of 11 "topic cards," each with a list of subtopics, were shown to the respondents. They were then asked, "Do you and ... talk about any of these?" If the answer was positive, the interviewers were trained to ask follow-up questions and record whether any influence attempts were related by the respondents. In cases where influence was reported, codes were made for whether the respondent recalled "sending" or "receiving" it. Thus, across these 11 domains, a summary score of influence sent and received was developed for each respondent's discussion of the other family members interviewed. The interview also included a number of open-ended questions about the relationships under discussion.

The Study of Midlife Divorce
During the academic year 1979–1980, M. Smyer and I (Hagestad, Smyer, & Stierman, 1983) conducted a study on middle-age divorce in a metropolitan area. Working from court records, we contacted and interviewed 93 men and women who had been divorced for about one year. The respondents had a mean age of 50. Prior to the divorce, they had been married an average of 25 years. All of them had children, the majority of them young adults. Sixty percent of the respondents also had at least one living parent, ranging in age from the early sixties to the upper eighties. The in-depth interviews concentrated on the divorce process, but obtained considerable information about relationships with the other two generations: maturing children and aging parents.

In subsequent sections, my examples of intergenerational patterns of socialization will be taken from the Chicago study, while my discussion of support will pull mainly from the divorce study.

Socialization and Influence
The late 1960s produced some major reconceptualizations of socialization. Increasingly, it was being discussed as a life-long reciprocal process. Some authors saw shifts over the life-span in the direction of influence between young and old, arguing that as parents age, "reversed socialization" occurs, with the children becoming the most powerful socializers (e.g., Brim, 1968). Others saw the shift as necessitated by historical change, that is, generational phenomena in the wider society. The best-known exponent of this latter view was Mead's *Culture and Commitment* (1970), in which she discussed older generations as "immigrants in time" who must rely on the young for needed knowledge and skills.

In my view, there are three aspects of intergenerational socialization which require our attention. First, there is an ongoing process of negotiating expectations regarding family relationships. Second, family members help one another face and understand a changing world. Third, there is the creation of family continuity. Let me comment on each of these in a bit more detail.

Several authors have argued that demographic and cultural changes have produced intergenerational roles and relationships which are not clearly defined or structured by societal norms (e.g., Hess & Waring, 1978). People in such relationships have to negotiate a common base for relating through the course of their interaction. Thus, in this view, the process of socialization does not involve the *transmission* of expectations, but the *creation* of them (Bengtson & Black, 1973). Such expectations need to accommodate the range of personal capabilities and outlooks which result from the different phases of development and historical experiences represented by generations in the family.

Family members also use one another as socialization resources in dealing with the world *outside* the family. This function of family socialization was the major topic of classic social science discussions. The emphasis was on how parents prepare children for life as adults in society. Increasingly, we have recognized that in a social context characterized by high rates of change, such preparation cannot be done "once and for all," but is a continuous, life-long process. I would agree with Margaret Mead that in today's society, we are likely to observe a good deal of influence from young to old in the family. Young members often serve as "cohort bridges" to the older generations, by mediating, interpreting, and making human sense of technological and cultural change. A current example from American middle-class families would be young children teaching their parents and grandparents how to use home computers.

A third type of socialization process involves a search for intergenerational continuity, in face of relationships which have no clear normative guidelines, a rapidly changing society, and the entry of new generations. Families strive to maintain a sense of communality and similarity – a set of "family ways" or "family themes" which transcend generational boundaries and endures generational turnover. In my view, this process is one of intergenerational transmission from old to young, because it is a question of what is to be passed on to future generations. The more I study families, the more impressed I become by the amount of effort they expand on maintaining a sense of continuity, and by the variability in what they choose as the core of such continuity. In some families, the emphasis is on ways and styles of relating. In others, the focus is on aspects of the outside world, such as orientations to work, ways of dealing with money, or political orientations. I also believe men and women differ in where they concentrate efforts to create and maintain continuity. I return to these points later in my discussion.

My presentation of data from the Chicago study will touch on the following questions: How did middle-aged men and women see their position in the flow of influence between generations? Did they report equal numbers of influence efforts "up" to aging parents and "down" to young adult children, or did they concentrate more on their children? How did they talk about themselves as the recipients of influence from the two other generations? Did more come from "above," their parents, or "below," from their children? What *types* of influence efforts were directed "down" and "up"?

If we look at average number of influence attempts reported by members of the middle generation and compare the figure for influence aimed at parents or parents-in-law to that for children, there appears to be a clear trend for the middle generation to concentrate more influence efforts on the young (X = 5.1) than on the old (X = 3.0). However, here is an example of how examining aggregate group figures does not allow us to tell a story about influence in families. If we use intrafamily comparisons and examine how individual middle-aged respondents spoke of influence up to their parent or parent-in-law, and down to their child, we find that about 30 percent reported roughly equal (within one point) number of influence attempts to old and young and 10 percent said they sent more "up" than "down." Thus, 40 percent of the sample did not conform to the pattern observed on a group level. Cases in which more influence was aimed at the aging parent than the young adult child most commonly were in families where a grandmother was interviewed. When we examined how the middle-aged respondents discussed attempts on behalf of others to influence *them*, nearly one-half reported equal numbers of such attempts from the child and the parent. Only about 15 percent said the child made more efforts to influence them than did the parent. Thus, a simple conclusion seems to be that parents never give up trying!

The one area of influence which cut across all the relationships we examined in the study was *health*. Family members in all three generations reported that they struggled to keep the others healthy by trying to get them to watch their diets, stop smoking, see the doctor, and take their medicines. Beyond that, we found considerable variation by generation and gender.

"Up" to their parent, middle-aged respondents concentrated on practical advice on everyday living, household management, dress and grooming, money, and the uses of time. It was pretty clear that a number of them served as consultants on money management for widowed mothers and mothers-in-law.

"Down" to their child, the middle generation concentrated most of their influence attempts on behaviors and outlooks related to the transition into adulthood: work, education, money management, and personal lifestyle, such as dress and grooming.

When we examined how the middle-aged saw the older generation's attempts to influence *them*, we found that parent-child relations were frequently mentioned, but also various aspects of personal lifestyle, such as dress and grooming and religious observance. Grandfathers were seen as concentrating on a more narrow range of issues than were grandmothers. Typically, it was reported that grandfathers concentrated on activities bridging family and the outside world, such as work, finances, and leisure activities. Grandmothers, in addition to such issues, would attempt to shape relationships *within* the family.

From their young adult child, the middle-aged men and women most commonly recognize influence attempts regarding leisure activities (e.g., vacation and travel) and current social issues. Fathers typically mentioned political issues, while mothers reported influence on questions related to sex roles.

Some interesting discrepancies emerged when we compared the two persons' reports across intergenerational dyads. In both parent-child linkages which we examined (grandparent-parent and parent-grandchild), the children tended to see the parents as more influential than the parents saw themselves. This was particularly true of influence efforts related to interpersonal issues, such as parent-child relations and ways to deal with family and friends.

When we examined influence in the other direction, from child to parent, these were exactly the domains in which we saw the opposite kind of discrepancy: the parents reported fewer influence efforts from children than the children did. In other words, some such messages appeared to fall on deaf ears. This was particularly the case with grandmothers and mothers. In relations with grandfathers, messages regarding social and political issues also seemed to be ignored by the recipient in the older generation.

Further light was shed on these discrepancies when we explored issues which created conflict and strain between generations. We asked our respondents if there were topics which "made things difficult" between them and the other family members they were discussing. In discussions of grandmothers and mothers, the clear trouble spots were topics dealing with interpersonal issues, particularly in the family realm. The most frequent mention of such touchy subjects was found among mothers discussing grandmothers, but they also were commonly identified in middle generation fathers' discussions of grandmothers, and by both sets of partners in mother-grandchild pairs. When grandfathers were discussed, views on social issues were by far the most commonly mentioned. Among the 40 families where a grandfather was interviewed, nearly all of them had at least one family member who said that such questions created difficulties with grandpa. Race relations, social policy, and sex roles were social issues which frequently came up. Some close qualitative analyses provided further insights into the relative salience of issues *within* the family and relations with the world *outside* the family to men and women in intergenerational relations.

We identified the families which had all male or all female lineage connections. The all-male lineage subgroup had a paternal grandfather, a father, and a grandson interviewed. There were 10 such families. The all-female lineage subgroup had a maternal grandmother, a mother, and a granddaughter interviewed. Twenty-four families fell in this pattern. In these 34 families, we again focused on "the straight line" and did not read the middle-generation parents who did not have their own parents interviewed. In close reading of entire family sets of interview protocols, we have concentrated on identifying *themes* (Troll & Bengtson, 1979). In order to be counted as a theme, the same issue had to be brought up by at least two of the three people and indirectly involve all three family members.

We grouped the themes into five main categories: (1) views on social issues; (2) work, education, and money; (3) health and personal appearance; (4) daily living at home (e.g., household maintenance); and (5) interpersonal relations. There were some striking differences in what men and women paid attention to and talked about in their relationships across generations. For men, themes fell into domains of instrumental concerns (work, education, and money) and social issues in society at large. For women, they were typically focused on interpersonal relations, mostly within the family.

During the qualitative analyses of the data, I have become increasingly impressed by the great variability in what issues engage attention, time, and energy in families. I have come to think that in seeking a common ground for relating across generations, the critical question may not be *how* to think on certain issues, but *what to think about* at all. Families vary a great deal in what they consider worthy of attention; what they think should be taken seriously.

The Chicago data also point to differences between men and women in what they emphasize in their search for "common ground" across generations. Contrasts between the sexes fell along the lines of Parsons & Bales' (1955) distinction between "instrumental" and "emotional-expressive" leadership. Grandfathers and fathers chose relationships with the wider society through work, education, and finances as their focus of attention. Particularly for grandfathers in the study (most of them born around the turn of the century), cohort changes in the rest of society appeared to present potential threats to a common family base. Women, on the other hand, concentrated attention on relationships *within* the family. The mothers and grandmothers in the study appeared to think of themselves as "ministers of the interior," specialists on interior family dynamics. The two older generations of Chicago women did not appear too open to advice from younger members on how to handle family affairs. Between middle-generation women and their mothers or mother-in-law, there appeared to be some tension between two "specialists," two "kin-keepers." On the other hand, women may be more likely than men to receive influence regarding the social context, such as views on changing sex roles, involvement in work and education, and changing styles of dress and grooming.

Patterns of Support

Much of my recent work as explored how members of different generations serve as interpersonal resources for one another. Above, I touched on how children may serve as "cohort bridges," softening the impact of social change in the wider society. Now, let me comment on emotional support. A sizable research literature has explored patterns of exchange across the generations. Repeatedly, it has been shown that even though modern society does not have an extended family structure, there is an impressive exchange of gifts and services between older people and their children. However, little work has explored the flow of support and concern "up" and "down" generational lines on an *intrafamily*, rather than on an aggregate group level. Again, members of a middle generation are an interesting research target.

In earlier research I was struck by questionnaire responses from nearly 800 undergraduate students who were asked about their relationships with their parents. The majority of both male and female students said their mother was more likely than their father to discuss personal problems and worries with them. Recent work on primary relationships in later adulthood has found that women, significantly more than men, use children as confidants (e.g., Babchuk, 1978). Our study of divorce in middle age (Hagestad, Smyer, & Stierman, 1983) found similar trends.

Two findings stood out from his study. First, during the divorce process, women utilized their "vertical connections" to parents and children more than men did. Women more frequently turned to the two other generations to discuss marital problems and to seek emotional and material support. Second, when family supports were relied on during the divorce process, children were both turned to more and seen as more helpful than parents, especially by women. Two-thirds of the women, compared to one-fourth of the men, said they had discussed their marital problems with their children. When the respondents were asked to identify the person who was the most helpful during the worst part of the divorce process, nearly one-fourth of the women named a child. Five percent of the men did so. Our data suggest that women, more than men, approached children as adult equals, to whom they could turn for advice and support. Parents were also turned to by a number of our respondents. Three-fourths of the women and half of the men who had surviving parents said they had discussed marital problems with them. However, only *one* respondent in the sample mentioned a parent as most helpful during the crisis of marital break-up. The tendency for these middle-aged individuals, particularly women, to rely more on help from grown children than from aging parents made me curious if this in part reflected negative attitudes towards divorce on behalf of the parent. In some recent pilot interviews with middle-aged women we asked them: "If you had a personal problem or worry, would you discuss it with your parent or your (oldest) child, do you think?" More than half of them (54%) said the child, less than a fourth (21%) said the parent.

So far, I have concentrated on members of the middle generation as *recipients* of support from parents and children. Several of the contributors in this volume address the middle-aged as *providers* of support and concern. There is no doubt that members of middle generations, particularly women, will often feel a "generational squeeze" between the needs of the old and the young. In a recent exploratory survey of state laws in the United States, I found that so-called "relative responsibility laws," indeed state legal responsibilities of adults to care for children, go beyond the age of majority *and* needy parents. Since most of these laws were modeled on Elizabethan poor laws, they are aimed at taking responsibility and pressure off the public sector, shifting them to the family. In times of a strained national economy, such pressures will intensify. In the United States, it is becoming clear that the state of the economy, as well as mounting divorce rates among young adults, are putting new strains on families. A growing number of mature offspring are now turning to their parents for shelter and emotional and financial support. However, again it is important to look both "up" and "down" generational lines, and to consider the total generational picture in a given lineal unit. The likelihood of the middle generations experiencing a "squeeze" is influenced by the needs and resources of several generations. Valerie Oppenheimer (1981) has given an excellent discussion of how patterns of timing of parenthood in three or more generations will influence the total intergenerational constellation of financial resources, including the probability that the middle generation will experience financial "overload." A similar multi-generational view is necessary if we consider other strains of "kin-keeping."

A student whose thesis I helped supervise (Smith, 1983) found that when middle-aged women experienced a sense of overload in caring for aged parents, they tended to have young adult children who were "off track" in *their* life course development. For example, one woman had a son in his late twenties, still without a job; another had a daughter whose marriage had failed and who had moved back into her old room. This study points to the importance of considering support patterns, as well as expectations across more than one parent-child link.

Future Work

We have barely scratched the surface in our efforts to understand relationships in multi-generational families, and researchers face a rich variety of challenges in this field of inquiry. I would like to briefly mention two sets of issues which need attention. First, we must attempt to bridge micro- and macro-levels in our explorations of intergenerational relations. Second, in seeking answers to new questions, we need to explore new avenues of research design, measurement, and data analysis.

Bridging Micro- and Macro-Levels
The above discussion of multi-generational families has taken a social-psychological perspective, conceptualizing generation as ranked descent in family lineages. (See Marshall's paper in this book for a conceptual overview.) However, in work on such lineal units, we cannot disregard macro-concepts of generation, particularly cohort membership. We also need to consider the effects of social context, both proximal and distal, on intergenerational relations in the family.

Developing Family Parameters
Families represent unique meeting grounds for individuals with different historical backgrounds. Through cross-generational interaction, cohort contrasts in the wider society are softened and modified, and historical changes are seen and interpreted through family lenses. However, as I have stated in an earlier paper

112

(Hagestad, 1981), it is important not to overlook the fact that *people do not file into generation by cohort*. We often forget that people from different families who are grouped in the same generational category such as "parent" or "grandparent," may represent quite different cohorts. Each family creates its own combinations of age and cohort memberships, reflecting the timing of births in several generations. Past research has shown that if we select families with three generations of adults, we are likely to end up with considerable age/cohort overlap between the two older generations. In three U.S. surveys of three-generational families — one in California (Bengtson et al., 1975), one in Minnesota (Hill et al., 1970), and one in Chicago (described above) — age ranges *within* the two older generations are 30 years or more, and a substantial age overlap exists *across* these two groups. For example, we find both "grandparents" and "parents" in their sixties. To many important research questions, this represents a serious shortcoming. We know extremely little about how families are distributed in patterns of age/cohort combinations. Those of us who have done research on three-generational families are often questioned about the representativeness of our samples. The answer is that we do not know, because we have no baseline knowledge about family constellations across more than two generations. For all societies represented in this symposium, census material uses individuals or households as units of analysis, which leaves us with no parameter estimates for families beyond the young nuclear family. For example, we do not really know how common four- and five-generation families are, and how many of them have members of all generations living in the same community. We know the proportion of a given cohort who remained childless. What we do *not* know, is how often these individuals had siblings or other members of their generation who had similar life patterns. For questions regarding support systems in old age, that is important information.

For a number of purposes, we could use demographic data on families, not individuals or households (Hagestad & Dixon, 1980). We need information on family age structures and dependency ratios. Such descriptive data could serve a diversity of research functions. For the planning of social policy and family-related services, they would have immediate application. For social researchers, they would form the basis for further work. Once basic descriptive data were available on family lineages and their constellations of ages and life careers, new research avenues could be pursued. For some purposes, carefully stratified samples would be drawn, matching respondents on age, family career phase, and generational status. One area of inquiry where such sampling would be appropriate, is in exploring the relative impact of family lineage and cohort memberships in shaping life course patterns and attitudes. This brings me to the issue of the social context of intergenerational relations.

Multi-Generational Families and Social Context
Both in the study of socialization, support, and conflict, we need to pay attention to the social fabric in which intergenerational relations are embedded. For example, one could hypothesize that the creation of family continuity is more problematic in a society characterized by rapid social change than in a fairly stable society. Furthermore, it would seem that a homogeneous social milieu would

113

aid the maintenance of continuity, because boundaries between family and community would be permeable. Thus, families would have community support in maintaining intergenerational continuity. We also need to explore the relative importance of the immediate social environment (the community) versus the larger social context (the wider society) in such considerations.

Similar issues need to be addressed in work on support patterns. In this book we have contributions from countries with sharply different national policies with regard to support of both the young and the old. The extent to which such social-structural differences have direct impact on family relations needs to be addressed in comparative work. Such research also needs to consider the relative impact of community characteristics and national policy in shaping patterns of intergenerational support, as well as the amount of strain experienced by different family generations.

Studying Family Units: New Strategies

In our attempts to understand multi-generational family units, we need to explore new research strategies. As a survey researcher, I find myself increasingly impatient with the limitations of verbal reports and have started to explore possible ways to observe intergenerational interaction directly, preferably in a naturalistic setting. It is rather amazing that research on adults and their parents has seldom or never used direct observation of the type which is so common in work on young children and their parents. In a multi-generational view of families, we inevitably move beyond the dyad and face the problem of finding ways to describe *families* as units, including the statistical headaches it presents. For those of us whose main research tool is the social survey, there are complex issues of dependence of measures, since a major way in which we can create variables to characterize dyads and larger units is to combine individual verbal reports into secondary, derived variables. Observational techniques offer the possibility of describing family units more directly, for instance in frequencies or ratios between certain types of interactions.

Finally, I think researchers in the 1980s can move beyond the limitations of cross-sectional research and begin to explore families over time. To my knowledge, this has not been done in intergenerational research. For example, it should be possible to construct longitudinal data sets by building on earlier research. Some of the work done on families in the 1950s and 1960s should allow for possibilities to restudy the same individuals in different phases of individual and family development. Such work should also allow us to study the effects of generational turnover — a much neglected topic in family research.

The sharp increase in the number of multi-generational families presents policy-makers and researchers with new challenges.

If we recognize families as unique social groups, in which lives and relationships are shaped through a complex web of interdependence, we need to focus a great deal of research attention on family lineages as social units. Families with three or more generations of adults should be key research targets for social scientists in the later part of the 20th century.

114

The Five-Generation Family – A Pilot Study[1]

Andreas Kruse

I. Theoretical Background and Assumptions which Gave Rise to our Studies

We were breaking new ground with our work on five-generation families, and so were not able to rely on prior studies in the field. Our purpose, therefore, was to ask questions and to establish assumptions which would help us comprehend the intergenerational contact among five-generation families in a differentiated way, using a multitude of existing literature on the "multi-generational family" (which is based either on the three-generation family and/or uses it as the background to its arguments).

The following deals with the first three generations of a five-generation family (the generation of the great-great-grandparents, the fifth generation; the generation of the great-grandparents, the fourth generation; and the generation of the grandparents, the third generation) using specific "topical aspects" which are the result of theoretical considerations.

(a) The Fifth Generation (The Great-Great-Grandparents)

Will the family be able to support its very old members during their process of aging, in a way that will concede them both autonomy and responsibility?

Background to the Question
As the questionnaires used for a survey by Hirschfield & Dennis (1979) show, "aging parents" not only aim at achieving "independence" in their relationship with their children ("autonomy") but also "responsibility," that is, they refuse one-sided dependency upon their children and advocate "reciprocity." Statements given by the participants show that such "reciprocity" is reflected in a variety of assignments which are fulfilled by the "aging parents" within the family.

Proceeding from this survey as well as from other papers concerning the "multi-generational family" which were able to prove the "symmetry" of help and care exchange between the "aging parents" and the "adult children" (Adams, 1968; Shanas et al., 1968; Hill et al., 1970; Troll, 1971), we established the following assumption: The family can encourage the great-great-grandparents during their aging process by allowing them to take responsibility, that is, exerting functions and fulfilling assignments. We assume that "responsibility" creates in the aged person a sense of "capability" and "acceptance" ("competence") (Kuypers & Bengtson, 1973; Bengtson et al., 1981), thus having favorable effects on his/her aging process.

115

(b) The Fourth Generation (The Great-Grandparents)

In what way will the life of the members of the fourth generation, who are "aging parents" themselves, be influenced by the fact that they still have parents?

Background to the Question
It is the fourth generation within a five-generation family that deserves our attention. In reading about "three-generation families" the care of the "aging parents" is a major topic with the "adult children" of intermediate age (Lehr, 1961; 1966; Lieberman, 1978; Neugarten, 1979), which justifies the assumption that in a five-generation family much more of the time of the members of the fourth generation – "aging parents" themselves – is taken up in the care of their elderly parents (the fifth generation) than is the case with the "sandwich generation" in a three-generation family.

For this reason my paper on five-generation families reconsiders also the notion of "filial maturity" (Blenker, 1965). The original meaning of "filial maturity" includes the willingness of "adult children" to take responsibility for and care of their "aging parents" (i.e., to relinquish receiving care in favor of granting care). Extended to the five-generation family this means that dependents, who are themselves aged, must take on this responsibility. Above all, the "adult children" within a five-generation family care for parents who – following Neugarten's terminology (1971) – belong in the groupings "old" or "old-old," and who thus are in need of a quite different kind of care than those "aging parents" that Blenker refers to.

Thus Brody's suggestion that "responsibility" in its real sense must include the knowledge of what is possible ("... when the needs of the very old exceed the diminished capacities of their aging children, successful negotiation of this stage involves the parents' acceptance as well as the children's acceptance of what those adult children can not do" [Brody, 1979, 279]) can be applied to a great extent to the two oldest generations within a five-generation family. And it is necessary to question *who supports* the "caring community" in its function of looking after the great-great-grandparents. On the one hand, we assume this is done by the third generation, who are the children of the fourth generation. On the other hand, when caring for their aged dependents, the family is in need of aid from public institutions. This aspect has been noted by numerous authors and is why Lehr (1982) and Bengtson & Treas (1980) emphasize the fact that the strength of the dependents would not be sufficient if it were the family's task alone to care for the old, especially should they be in need of extensive care.

(c) The Third Generation (Generation of the Grandparents)

The third generation, which forms the "sandwich generation" within the five-generation family, is confronted equally by demands from the two upper and the two lower generations. How do the multitude and diversity of family tasks influence the life of the members of the "sandwich generation"?

Background to the Question

In studies of three-generation families the *"accumulation* of tasks" (familial and occupational) became evident in the middle generation. The family tasks include the care of the "aging parents" and responsibility for the children. Above all, the middle generation has to promote contact between the upper and lower generations (Lehr, 1961; Neugarten, 1979; Brody, 1979; Shanas, 1979a, b). This task is characterized by Treas (1977) as the function of "kin-keeping" and by Hill et al. (1970) as the function of the "lineage bridge." Since the responsibility for the family is delegated to the wife in most cases, it is she particularly who is confronted with the above mentioned accumulation of tasks (Troll et al., 1979; Bengtson & Treas, 1980). She has to integrate both the demands of her profession and those of her family. A problem becomes apparent when one considers the fact that more than half the women aged 45–54 years work (Treas, 1979) (in 1978, 52% of women in the Federal Republic of Germany, according to the Statistisches Jahrbuch, 1979), and that two-fifths of the women who care for their parents, give as much time to them as to a full-time profession (Newman, 1976). Due to the increase in employment for women, support for the older people is no longer guaranteed within the family circle. That is why the function of care-giving has increasingly to be referred to public institutions (Shanas & Hauser, 1974; Shanas & Sussman, 1977; Rosenmayr, 1977; Morgan, 1981).

According to Thomae's proposal (1959; 1960; 1968) any psychological study of the aging process has to start with a concrete study of the roles and tasks with which a person must cope during his life-span. With this in mind we can see that middle-aged adult members in *five-generation families* have to cope with a greater number of family tasks than do the second generation in three-generation families due to the additional roles of the grandparents and the grandchildren. It follows that the middle-aged members of five-generation families are not only confronted with maintaining contact with aging parents and with perceiving and satisfying their needs, but – and this is our assumption – the middle-aged family members supply their "aging parents" with the support they need in order to be able to care for their own elderly parents (the great-great-grandparents). Thus the demands made on the middle-aged adults in a five-generation family are broadened and extended.

II. Tested Aspects of the Intergenerational Contact

The empirical part of our study is based on an investigation of family members over several hours. According to the psycho-physical well-being of the participants and their willingness to cooperate, the discussions extended from a minimum of three to a maximum of eight hours. During the discussions we tried to identify – apart from important biographical events and the "history of the family" ("sociography") – various components of the "objective solidarity" (quantitative aspects of interaction, the exchange of help and care existing among the generations, and the communal activities of the dependents) and components of the "subjective solidarity" (affection, confidence, and conflict).

The intergenerational exchange of help and care was *analyzed* according to those areas that Hill and his collaborators (1970) included in their paper on three-generation families (emotional area, economical area, area of household management, area of sickness). For all the family members taken together, the pattern of help and care indicated *cooperation* within the family. The analysis of the quantitative components of the *interaction* involved statements about the frequency of visits, contacts by letter and by telephone, and types of communal activities. In this connection, we also tried to determine which family members initiated the communal activities.

The qualitative components of the interaction, that is, the "subjective solidarity," was considered from the following points of view: How great is the confidence (a), understanding (b), sympathy (c), affection (d), that the family member in question offers his relatives? What degree of involvement does he show in his dealings with other family members (e)? To what extent does he seek contact with his relatives (f)? The results of this analysis show, among other things, the "subjective family networks" (Lowenthal & Robinson, 1976) or "family sociograms" (as suggested by Lehr in personal discussion). To establish such "subjective family networks" and "family sociograms" it was also necessary to make statements about the extent to which the relationship among family members is conflict-prone and around which "topics" these conflicts are grouped (*conflict*) (g).

Finally, we tried to set up a "topical analysis" based on our investigations, as did Lehr (1961; 1966; 1969), Thomae (1951; 1959; 1960; 1968), and Lehr & Thomae (1958; 1965) in a different context.

Through this "topical analysis" we attempted to come to grips with the respective individual's inner confrontation with his own existence. We asked the family member which subjects his experience centered around, and what degree of spiritual energy this confrontation required. To do this, we began with a *variety* of potential "topics," including "personal biography," "family," "profession," "social responsibility," "participation in various social organizations," and "creation and pursuit of friendships." We classified the answers according to "intensity," "tendency," and "aspects" of the particular topic. "Intensity" refers to the degree of the predominance of the topic. "Tendency" refers to the degree of "requirement" or "relief" deriving from the topic. "Aspects" refer to those facets of the topic which stand out in the foreground for the individual experience.

This procedure aims at ascertaining the extent to which "family" is a topic of inner confrontation. Is the topic "family" foremost in the experience of the individual or are other topics more important. *How* does he see the "family"? Is he aware of it as demanding (in the sense of requiring) or as giving (in the sense of relieving and enriching)? Finally, we can explain which aspects of family are important to the member: Is it care for the aged parents that predominates in the life of the fourth generation? Do the members of the third generation feel more stressed in their role as parents or grandparents or in their role as children or grandchildren? Statements of this kind touch on the aspect of the experience of the questioned family member. Our aim is to determine which generation is the "center" of the family, and which generation is more and which is less affected by the family and their demands.

In order to get a differentiated catalog of statements concerning the intergenerational contact, we performed a "content-analysis," using the categories outlined above.

III. The Sample

Five five-generation families participated. *The fifth generation* consisted of five women, great-great-grandmothers aged between 81 and 95 years, who had been widowed for a long time, some more than 25 years.

The fourth generation consisted of two widowed great-grandmothers and three great-grandcouples. The youngest great-grandmother was 58, the oldest 74 years of age. It is questionable whether the members of this generation do indeed belong to the same generation; if we define "generations" as "cohorts," then they do not.

Since we were particularly interested in the mode of cooperation among the members of the "caring community" we included *the brothers and sisters* of the great-grandparents (in total 15 persons) in our sample. In addition, five grandparents (*third generation*) and five parents (*second generation*) took part, making a total of 48 participants. Therefore, a statistical analysis was not performed.

IV. Results

We observed different patterns of intergenerational contact in the five-generation families, which underlines the necessity for differentiated considerations of the intrafamilial interactions. By comparing three of the families we will attempt to identify these differential aspects, which differ above all by the degree of "social competence" and "activity" of the great-great-grandmother.

(a) High "Social Competence" of the Great-Great-Grandmother

The 95-year-old great-great-grandmother Frau Bader[2] showed not only a high degree of "social competence" (e.g., she has a household of her own, looks after a handicapped daughter, her extrafamilial activity is high) but also an "autonomous" and "responsible" position within the family, shown by the exchange of help and support between herself and her children (Diagram 1).

This high *degree of exchange* reflects Frau Bader's integration within the family. *The balance between giving and receiving* in relationship to three of her daughters, and above all, her position as "giver" in her relations with her youngest daughter, indicates a high degree of autonomy and responsibility for the great-great-grandmother within the family. It is significant that the help given and received embraces *all areas* and is not concentrated in any one particular area. In conversations with Frau Bader it became obvious that she connects her "satisfaction in life" (which we define as satisfaction with the achievements of the past and with the possibilities for the future) with the tasks she fulfills within the family. Thus, we can confirm our assumption that the autonomous and responsible position within the family has positively influenced Frau Bader's aging process.

It is true that the high "social competence" of Frau Bader relieves her children of the task of caring for her. However, the successful aging of this great-great-grandmother makes it more difficult for her children to come to terms with their own aging problems.

The conflict in the Elsässer family also centers around this *subject* (Diagram 2).

In this family the problems are intensified as the competent great-great-grand-mother (who heads a three-generation household) has developed a high degree of intrafamilial activity but only limited extrafamilial activity. Consequently, the children in this family, and especially the one who belongs to the three-generation household, see their autonomy as threatened and the care given by the great-great-grandmother as interference in their lives.

Summary

If we want to summarize this first "pattern" of interaction between the fifth and the fourth generations, we could say that the demands the great-great-grandmother makes on her children are slight, due to her high "social competence." But for the children, her "successful aging" becomes a problem because it complicates the con-frontation with their own age. This is particularly true when the great-great-grandmother leads a family-centered lifestyle.

(b) Low "Social Competence" of the Great-Great-Grandmother

In the Schumann family there is quite a different pattern of intergenerational con-tact. Because of the bad health and low "social competence" of the great-great-grandmother, the exchange of help and support between her and her children is not mutually based. In this family, the children are in a giving position and the great-great-grandmother in the receiving position.

From the analysis of the intergenerational contact in the Schumann family, we can draw conclusions as to how the members of the "caring community" work to-gether. The great-grandparents (Herr and Frau Wiedenhofer), in whose household the great-great-grandmother lives, form the "inner caring community." There is *one child* who, with the support of his spouse, takes on most of the responsibility for the great-great-grandmother. However, the "inner caring community" is sup-ported by brothers and sisters. This support consists of regular visits, taking over re-sponsibility from time to time, giving advice to the "inner caring community," and financial support.

These "external" aspects of family support became apparent during explorations with members of the "caring community." Additionally, the children of the great-great-grandmother felt *internally* very much concerned with their mother. Above all, they expressed worry about the approaching necessity to move the great-great-grandmother to a nursing home. The anticipation of this "critical life event" was as-sociated with feelings of sorrow and uncertainty, as well as with feelings of help-lessness. The forthcoming placement was regarded more as an event which had to be accepted contrary to one's own will, rather than as an opportunity to live a life more free from responsibilities.

It is worth mentioning that in the Schumann family, the members of the "sand-wich generation" were not so concerned with the tasks the fifth generation set the fourth generation as we had expected them to be. Entirely different aspects of life are of paramount importance to Herr and Frau Eschenbach (third generation) (Dia-gram 3).

In exploration with Frau Eschenbach familial tasks stayed in the background and made room for a detailed description of her life up to the present (topic 1). She then reported in detail about her everyday routine at work, which she sees as an enrichment to her life and as an opportunity for autonomy within her family (topic 2). In the hierarchical order of "topics," the topic "family" occupies only third position for Frau Eschenbach, and she associates "family" less with the demands of her parents but with those of her children (see "aspects" of the topic).

The exploration with Herr Eschenbach was dominated by uncertainty about life after his retirement (as a member of the German Army, he retires at age 53). Additionally, he described extensively his professional routine, which he also saw as enriching his life. As illustrated in the above diagram, the topic "family" occupies an inferior position compared to the topic "profession." As does his wife, Herr Eschenbach feels mainly responsible for his children and grandchildren and less responsible for his parents-in-law or for his grandmother-in-law.

Herr and Frau Eschenbach's answer to the question of how far the relationship between the fifth and the fourth generation influences their own life, is the same. They are aware of the fact that their parents (parents-in-law) are heavily involved in caring for the great-great-grandmother. On the one hand, they want to respect their parents' wish to be independent in caring for the great-great-grandmother, and on the other hand, the responsibility for their own children prevents them from assuming responsibilities for other members of the family. Conversely, the members of the fourth generation emphasize that they do not demand support from their children. They still feel like "parents," and for them the parental role implies duties *towards* their children rather than the demand of support *from* their children.

Summary

The second "pattern" of intergenerational contact shows the tasks which the fourth generation in a five-generation family has to fulfill if the fifth generation has only a low degree of "social competence." It shows how the members of the "caring community" cooperate in order to satisfy the needs of the infirm parents. Thereby the confrontation between the fifth and fourth generations in the family takes place quite independently of the third generation. The third generation of the Schumann family is not free from familial demands, but these demands stem rather from responsibility for the children than from the support of the parents.

V. Outlook

The two "patterns" of intergenerational contact presented do not claim any general validity. They are based on a small sample and intended to be viewed as a pilot study. In the study we tried to develop and apply categories which would help us to differentiate the intergenerational contact in a five-generation family. Our aim was to provide insight into the methods and manner through which we have tried to codify the intrafamilial relationships in five-generation families.

Footnotes

1 The author would like to thank Frau Professor Lehr and the Kuratorium Deutsche Altershilfe (KDA) for their generous support in this work.
2 All names have been changed.

Diagram 1: The Exchange of Help and Support Between the Fifth Generation (Frau Bader) and the Fourth Generation (Frau Eschenbach, Frau Dücker, Frau Siemers, Frau Bertrand) in the Bader Family

Exchange Between	Degree	Giving-Receiving Relation	Areas of Exchange	Areas in which (a) the Fifth Generation; (b) the Fourth Generation; (c) Both the Fifth and the Fourth Generations are in a **Giving Position**
Frau Bader and Frau Eschenbach	high	balanced	emotional area economical area health	emotional area (both generations) economical area (fifth generation) health (fourth generation)
Frau Bader and Frau Dücker	high	balanced	emotional area economical area household management	emotional area (both generations) economical area (fifth generation) household management (both generations)
Frau Bader and Frau Siemers	medium	balanced	emotional area economical area	emotional area (both generations) economical area (fifth generation)
Frau Bader and Frau Bertrand	very high	the fifth generation is clearly in the giv-ing position	emotional area economical area health household management	emotional area (fifth generation) economical area (fifth generation) health (fifth generation) household management (fifth generation)

Diagram 2: "Topics" Around which the Conflict in the Relationship Between the Members of the Fourth Generation and their Mother are Centered (the Elsässer Family)

	Members of the Fourth Generation		
	Frau Sebastian	Frau Heinrich	Frau Kayser*
The members of the fourth generation describe the relationship between themselves and their mother as: – completely free of conflict – not free of conflict – conflict in small amounts – conflict in medium amounts – strong conflict	conflict in small amounts	conflict in medium amounts	strong conflict
The conflict is centered around the following "topics" (hierarchically given):			
1	the solution of her own aging problems has been aggravated by the successful aging of her mother	the solution of her own aging problems has been aggravated by the successful aging of her mother	her "autonomy" is threatened by the strong family-focussed life of her mother
2	–	the dominating role of her mother within the family	she perceives her mother's care for the family as an intrusion into her own life
3	–	–	the dominating role of her mother within the family

* She stays with her mother in a three-generation household.

Diagram 3: Predominance, Tendency, and Aspects of "Topics" According to Analysis of Tape Transcript of Conversations with Herr and Frau Eschenbach

	Frau Eschenbach	Herr Eschenbach
Topic 1		
predominance of the theme	personal biography	profession
	high	very high
aspects of the theme	(1) review of past life (2) anticipation of future life	(1) opportunities the profession offers (2) anticipation of his retirement
tendency of the theme	both "demanding" and "rewarding"	both "demanding" and "rewarding"
Topic 2		
predominance of the theme	profession	family
	high	medium
aspects of the theme	(1) profession as an opportunity to gain "autonomy" within the family (2) occupational enjoyment	(1) education of his children (2) concern with the married child (3) role of grandfather
tendency of the theme	"rewarding"	both "demanding" and "rewarding"
Topic 3		
predominance of the theme	family	personal biography
	medium	medium
aspects of the theme	concern with the married child	future
tendency of the theme	"demanding"	"demanding"
Topic 4		
predominance of the theme	—	friends
		medium
aspects of the theme	—	(1) joint activities (2) feelings of being integrated
tendency of the theme	—	"rewarding"

The Role of Women in the Family Generation Context

Ursula Lehr

1. The Family — a Dynamic Process of Lifelong Interaction of All Family Members

Family policy as well as research in developmental psychology in most countries is directed only to two-generation families: to parents and their infants. Political measures and support systems for the family (from maternal leave to tax reduction) seem to neglect later stages in the family life cycle and seem to neglect the older generations. Also the Governmental Reports on the Situation of the Family ("Familienbericht") in our country are discussing only problems of the young family, especially problems of mother-child care. The important role of the father in the family, his influence on child development which is shown by empirical research during the last decade (see Lamb [ed.], 1976; 1977; Kotelchuk, 1976; Parke & O'Leary, 1976; Lehr [1974], 1980a; Fthenakis et al., 1982) seems not to be perceived.

Findings from empirical research confirm:
1. that not only the mother influences the development of the child; fathers are parents, too;
2. that not only parents are socializing their children, but children are socializing their parents, too;
3. that the processes of mutual socialization are not restricted to the beginning of family life; parents and children influence each other during the whole life-span. (We can report on some recent examples — see Kruse in this volume and Lehr, Schneider, & Kruse, 1983[1] — that 90-year-old great-great-grandmothers are socializing their daughters, who are great-grandmothers and vice versa.)

The family — consisting of father, mother, and (dependent) children — is very often regarded as a static entity rather than a dynamic process of changing role expectancies of all family members. It is necessary to regard the family as a dynamic process of lifelong interaction: development and changes of one family member cause the development and changes of all the other family members (Lehr, 1982b). Only such a view of developmental processes in family will be able to include the older generations in an adequate way.

The static family role model (young parents with their young child) produces specific role expectancies, especially related to the mother, who has to be present for the children all the time, who has to perform the role of the housewife, and who has to cultivate the emotional sphere. We find a glorification of the mother role; family relationship, family-role-specific interactions between children, parents, grandparents, and great-grandparents are very often seen as a special task only for women. This can be shown by analyses of schoolbooks, of adolescent books, of novels published in German magazines, also women in advertisement have the same

125

traits, they are characterized as dependent and restricted in their interests only to family and homes, no extrafamilial roles are mentioned; women in the labor force seem not to be a reality (see Lehr, 1982f; 1983). The family role expectancies concerning the father, grandfather, and son are less specific: He has to give the family name to his offspring, he has to provide the financial support and he has to concentrate on his job without being disturbed by family affairs (see Parsons, 1956).

These family role expectancies are based on

1. the hypothesis of inborn, hereditary sex-specific traits and abilities;

But: This basis of the general family role expectancies has been invalidated by recent research on sex role typing. Many studies have shown that sex differences in traits, personality variables, and achievement are socialized and not innate (see Lehr, 1969; 1972b; 1978; Maccoby, 1963; 1966; Maccoby & Jacklin, 1974; Bierhoff-Alfermann, 1977);

2. the theorem of lifelong adverse effects of mother-child separation (even for a few hours a day);

But: The emphasis on continuous closed contacts between mother and child as suggested by Freud, Spitz, Bowlby and other psycho-analytical therapists does not get support from modern research (see Lehr, 1974; 1980; Hoffman, 1979; Rutter, 1971; 1972; Schaffer, 1977; 1978; 1980). Some studies point to the danger of an exclusive mother-child relationship (Schaffer, 1977; 1980; Schmidt-Kolmer, 1980) and to the very important role of the father and of peers for child development even in the first and second year of life (Lamb [ed.], 1976; Fthenakis et al., 1982);

3. and on the focus of science as well as family policy on the two-generation family, consisting of parents and the little child(ren).

But: This static family model has to be changed into a dynamic model of the family in which the older generations are included. Many studies (Rosenmayr & Rosenmayr, 1978; Shanas & Sussman, 1977; Bengtson, 1979; Bengtson & Cutler, 1976; Marshall & Bengtson, 1983; Tews [1971], 1974; Lehr, 1981a; 1982b) brought a general agreement that harmonious family relationships are correlated to psychophysical well-being in old age. Furthermore, there is a general agreement that the interaction within the families does not decrease with increasing age. But we also found that the quantity of intergenerational contacts need not have a positive correlation with the perceived quality of those family role activities. We also found that an exclusive family centeredness of middle-aged women has to be seen as a risk for psychophysical well-being in old age (Maas & Kuypers, 1974; Fooken, 1980; 1981; Lehr, 1982b, c).

From all these findings it should be stressed *firstly*, that discussion on family roles should not focus on the mother and the baby, but also include the modifications of the mother role which becomes necessary with the ongoing development of the child and which becomes essential with the empty-nest situation and widowhood. *Secondly*, it is necessary to define the family role expectations not only related to the women (or to the female family members), but also to the men (and the male family members). *Thirdly*, it is essential to comprehend the family as a dynamic process of lifelong interaction, in which grandparenthood and great-grandparenthood have to be included.

2. Role Expectations of the Woman as Mother, Grandmother, Great-Grandmother, and Daughter

In the middle of the fifties when we started with our life-span developmental research (Thomae & Lehr, 1958; Lehr & Thomae, 1965; Lehr, 1961; 1969), we analyzed 120 biographies of women, 20 to 60 years of age. 35 to 40 percent of all statements regarding their attitudes toward the future (wishes, hopes, fears) were related to intergenerational relationship. 20 to 22 percent of the statements referred to conflict and stress situations in the interaction with their own children, and about 15 to 18 percent to stress situations with their own parents. Especially in the women group 40 to 50 years of age we found a "crises accumulation"; women of this age group very often were confronted with the role of the mother, mother-in-law, or even grandmother on the one hand, and with the role of the daughter or daughter-in-law of aged parents, who needed help and care, on the other hand.

3. Intergenerational Family Conflicts

A further analysis of our biographical archives which included the life histories of 185 men and 141 women under the aspect of perceived conflict and stress provided a sample of 13,316 situations of conflict which could be classified into 12 different areas of life (such as school, occupation, conflicts with parents, spouse, children, etc.).

Women reported generally more perceived conflict and stress situations and especially more intergenerational family conflicts than men who more often referred to conflicts related to occupational situation, to leisure time, or to conflicts aroused by historical-political events. A proportion of 25.5 percent of all conflicts reported by women was related to their interactions with their parents (16.9%) or with children (8.6%) compared to 18.1 percent intergenerational conflicts in men (12.9% related to parents, 5.2% to children). Especially it should be emphasized that life histories of men and women up to the sixth decade pointed to more conflicts with their own parents than with their own children (see Table 1).

In early adulthood there is no difference in the percentage of conflicts with parents (men 19.1%, women 20.6%). With increasing age there is a consistent trend toward a greater decrease in the numbers of reported stress in the interaction with parents in men compared to women whereas reported conflict and stress related to their own children increase in women with increasing age.

From data like this it can be concluded that the situation of middle-aged women regarding family roles is more likely to be exposed to conflict and stress than that of men. Another conclusion to be drawn from our data refers to a greater interrelationship of these intergenerational conflicts of women with other variables like occupation, personal interests, nonfamilial social contacts, subjective health compared to the men group. In this group the experience of the occupational situation or that regarding leisure time apparently is not influenced by intergenerational conflicts. Furthermore, we found that women more than men attributed maladjustment and failure of children to themselves and felt responsibility for these failures.

127

4. The Need for a More Differentiated View of Family Intergenerational Contacts

"The family is the natural environment for the aged" and "intensive family inter-generational contacts are correlated with successful aging" are statements very common in public opinion.

Many studies like the Bonn Longitudinal Study (Thomae, 1976; 1983; Lehr, 1972; 1981a; 1982a, c, d) brought a general agreement, that harmonious family interactions (which are not identical with frequent family contacts!) have a close relationship to psychophysical well-being in old age; but "intimacy with distance" is the formula, which defines the optimal lifestyle of most of the aged persons in our country, but not living in multi-generational households (Tartler, 1961; Tews [1971], 1974; Rosenmayr & Rosenmayr, 1978; Shanas & Sussman, 1977; Bengtson & Cutler, 1976; Lehr & Thomae [1968], 1977). There is a trend − at least among politicians − *to promote three or more generation households* as a measure which is supposed to solve most of the problems of the aged, including those of the disabled and infirm older persons.

Many empirical studies (see Lehr & Thomae [1968], 1977) confirm: The need for increased family contacts with children is expressed more frequently in those aged
− who have some problems in the spouse role (especially in women) or who have lost their partners (widowhood) ($p < 0.035$);
− who have a poorer health and are physically dependent ($p < 0.007$);
− who have economic strains ($p < 0.065$);
− who have a lack of extrafamilial participation ($p < 0.001$);
− who have restricted interests and a lower degree of mental activity ($p < 0.03$), lower IQ ($p < 0.005$), and a lower score in the "feeling of being needed" ($p < 0.008$);
− women who were living their whole life only for their family and their children and who did not find any other meaningful sense in their life ($p < 0.002$).

Focusing attention on the children is very often related to a negative perception of age or to life situations which are defined by deprivations and stress. One should regard this kind of extreme family centeredness in old age neither as normal nor ideal.

The competent aged who are able to live an independent life (without greater health problems and economic restrictions) and who perceive their (daily) life as stimulating and rewarding, persons who have a great range of interests, did not have the need for a more intensive parent-child interaction. There we did not find the wish for increasing intrafamilial social role activity, but we found a higher degree of satisfaction in intergenerational relationship, a higher degree of cooperation and less conflict situations in these relationships.

The same is true for the child-parent relationship: The need for increased family contacts with the old parents is also given mainly in problem situations of the (grown-up) children (like health or economic problems, divorce of daughter or son, or need for help in the household or child/grandchild-rearing).

5. The Need to Stress the Aspect of Quality and not that of Quantity

Our data on the Bonn Longitudinal Study of Aging (Thomae, 1976), gives evidence concerning the intrafamilial and the extrafamilial social role behavior of subjects over 60 or 70; within 12 to 15 years there is consistency as well as different kinds of change which should be conceptualized as role-specific, personality-specific (Lehr & Rudinger, 1970; Lehr, 1981a), situation-specific — and last but not least: sex-role-specific — rather than merely age-specific.

An increasing role activity in the mother and grandmother role correlated with decreasing satisfaction in these intergenerational relationships. This is not true for the father and grandfather role. A decreasing role activity in the mother and grandmother role correlated with increasing positive mood or morale, increasing activity, and increasing extrafamilial social participation. Generally, we found this extrafamilial social participation more correlated to psychophysical well-being in old age than intrafamilial participation, especially in the women group. According to the analyses of Fooken (1981; 1982), we have to state that single women (never married or widowed for a long time) have a more successful aging process than married women; married women had a higher degree of family intergenerational relationships corresponding with a lower degree of extrafamilial intergenerational relationships. Within the married women group we found during the 12 to 15 years a higher degree of restriction of their life space and decreasing scores of activity, satisfaction, and future time perspective.

Other studies of our department are related to the "empty-nest reaction" (Lehr, 1980b; 1981b; Mudrich, 1978). Very often the situation of the last child's leaving the home is experienced as very stressful especially by the mother. This is true especially for child-centered mothers, for those mothers who had very traditional concepts regarding their female role. According to our study the negative reactions to the empty-nest situation (which very often correlates to a perception of decreased health and to an increase of depressive reactions) are observed more frequently in family-centered women, who did not develop any other interests, involvements, or extrafamilial social participation during their lives. — These mothers believed that now their life has lost all meaning and they showed a very negative attitude toward their own aging. — However, women who had worked outside of their homes or who were involved in other extrafamilial roles perceived the departure of the child(ren) as an extension or expansion of their life space, which was reinforced by an extended and far-reaching future time perspective. They also perceived themselves as more healthy and had a more positive attitude toward their own aging.

It should be mentioned, too, that the relationship between "family-centered mothers" and their children shows decreasing interactions after child's leaving and an increase in conflict and stress situations. In the case of less family-centered mothers these intrafamilial contacts developed more positively and were perceived as more stimulating and less stressful by mother and child. In these cases familial intergenerational interaction is seen as a source of mutual enrichment and stimulation, which were promoted by extrafamilial social contacts and interests of parents as well as of adult children.

Any exclusive family-centeredness of the women has to be regarded as a risk for psychophysical well-being in old age. According to findings of the historian Imhof (1981), 200 to 300 years ago women died before their youngest child matured. Today, more than a third of their life expectancy is left when the last child leaves the home. In former times a togetherness of husband and wife without children was not existent. Today this kind of family structure is given for 27 percent of the whole life-span of the average woman — and another 11 percent of the whole life-span she has to spend as a widow. From this point of view family-centeredness in our time must be seen more as a risk than as a guarantee for quality of life!

6. Family-Centeredness — a Guarantee or a Danger for the Quality of Life of the Aged?

Summarizing the data of the last lap of the Bonn Longitudinal Study of Aging (sponsor: Volkswagenwerk Foundation) we can state that those women born between 1890 and 1905 who showed less activity in the role of mother and grandmother at the first measurement point (1965) survived up to 1980 in a state of physical and psychological well-being. Those with more such activity did not survive at all or were disabled or chronically ill in 1980. Long-lived women lived more often in one-person households than short-lived women whereas long-lived men more often lived in more-persons households than short-lived men. Survivors in the women group received higher scores in the intelligence tests, had a greater range of interests, more social contacts outside the family, and were less active in homemakers activities. In 1965 these kinds of activities were already more developed in the short-lived women group on the one hand, in the long-lived men group on the other hand.

Apparently there are sex-specific correlates of longevity which can be defined for women as well as for men by a prevalence of non-traditional sex roles. According to this finding an increase in the activities in family- and home-centered roles are to be recommended for men whereas a decrease in such activities improve the chances for well-being of women in old age.

7. The Role of Women in the Family Generation Context: Consequences for Family Policy and a Policy for the Aged

From this point of view we might say that quality of life in old age for most women (and men?) is dependent rather on moderate intrafamilial intergenerational interaction (with high quality) than on intensive intrafamilial interaction (with low quality); life quality in old age is dependent also on extrafamilial social participation. A high degree of family-centeredness of women (as suggested by traditional role expectations) causes adjustment problems in old age. (We also can state that extreme job-centeredness of men causes adjustment problems for them in old age: very often it makes him helpless and dependent on homemakers-help.)

What is needed is a family policy which looks at all members of the family from a lifelong perspective, which encourages women in young adulthood toward extrafamilial orientation and which encourages men in more intrafamilial orientation. It seems to be inexcusable to assign all family responsibilities — the care for children,

130

older parents, and grandparents — only to women and to suggest "family care" as the optimal and most economic way of caring for the dependent and frail elderly. This modern trend of our family policy can very easily be attributed to the increasing population of the very old, the "graying world," the economic crises, and to the belief, family care would be the cheapest way of solving the problems of long-term care.

While it is true that families caring for an aged person and keeping him out of nursing homes should be supported by societies, it is problematic, to praise this kind of family care as the only and best solution. The emphasis on the role of the family for the aged goes back to suggestions of many developing countries, which report on a very happy and satisfactory situation of the aged, who are integrated into their families. But, according to several experts (see Schade & Apt, 1983), these images of the aged in some developing countries are only expressions of wishful thinking. A real quality of life of the aged (in these countries the 40- to 50-year-olds belong to this group) very often is not guaranteed due to poverty and the migration of the younger generation from rural to urban areas. Furthermore it seems to be problematic to transfer experiences from one country to another.

Caring for a dependent and frail parent or grandparent may be valuable and helpful for all family members, and this may contribute to an increase of intergenerational understanding and enrich the experience of the younger generation — but it cannot be doubted that the same situation may lead to many problems within the family, especially for the women:
1) It may lead to the separation of the adolescent children from their caring parents and to conflicts in the relationship between husband and wife.
2) "Family care" is almost exclusively identical with "daughter care" ("daughter-in-law care" or "granddaughter care") assigning the responsibilities for the dependent person to women. This can result in adverse effects in the personality development of these women in multi-generational families and can sometimes cause negative self-geroprophylaxis. Based on the hypothesis that women are naturally destined for caring and nurturing, society assigns to them an additional burden, which makes it more difficult for them to adjust to aging and makes them more dependent. This aspect has to be stressed especially as there are some indications that the aging daughter has to take over the care of parents at an age in which she would have the last chance to rejoin the labor force or to take over extrafamilial roles in social or political organizations, church, community, etc. These extrafamilial roles would extend her own life space and would offer her the stimulation necessary for her mental development and psychophysical well-being in old age. Research has shown that "family-centered" women deteriorate earlier and achieve a lower degree of quality of life (see Maas & Kuypers, 1974; Fooken, 1980; 1981; Lehr, 1982b, d).
3) Demographic data show a growing number of single elderly persons who do not have children.
4) The decrease in the number of children means that the care for dependent old parents cannot be shared by several siblings or by several daughters and granddaughters.
5) More and more women are working; this does not allow for intensive care of a dependent family member.

6)   There are some indications also that some elderly people, especially those who face the grandparent role in their forties or fifties, are not too enthusiastic about living in a three-generation household.

7)   Finally, consider the increased number of four- and five-generation families. I wonder if in these cases it is expected that the great-grandmother (fourth generation) will take care of the great-great-grandmother (fifth generation).

This paper has tried to show the role of women in intergenerational context. So far empirical research findings exist only in regard of two- or three-generation families. But it seems to be one of the most important tasks for the near future to study the role of women in four- and five-generation families (see Kruse in this book; Lehr, Kruse, & Schneider, 1983)[2]. It seems to make a big difference if a woman becomes a grandmother at 35 or 65 and a great-grandmother at 56 or 90 years of age. The youngest great-great-grandmother of our sample of 340 five-generation families is 78 years of age, the oldest one 106. A first analysis of our data of 195 five-generation families shows that only 20 persons (about 10%) of the fifth generation are living in homes for the aged and only 2.5 percent in nursing homes; 87.5 percent are living in private households. From this last group 29 percent are living alone in one-person households; 50 percent with their daughter, 6 percent with their son (and daughter-in-law), 9 percent with their grandchildren, and 6 percent together with other relatives.

The role of the women within the great-grandparent generation seems to be extremely stressful. The role of women in the intergenerational context of multi-generational families seems to be also a very difficult one, means a restriction of their life space and reinforces very often the traditional role expectancies with an overestimation and glorification of family roles for women. But we should avoid generalizations reading too far. We know that interindividual variability grows with increasing age and with the differentiation of the life situation — also in the women group!

Table 1: Percentage of Conflicts in Four Age Groups of Men and Women
Concerning Parents and Children

Conflicts with	Men Decade					Women Decade				
	Total	3	4	5	6	Total	3	4	5	6
Parents	12.9	19.1	13.7	10.6	11.0	16.9	20.6	15.7	16.4	16.1
Children	5.2	1.6	3.7	5.5	8.0	8.6	2.6	5.5	8.8	15.6

Footnotes

1 Lehr, Schneider, & Kruse: Remarks at the International Symposium on Intergenerational Relationships, February 21–24, 1983 in Berlin.
2 See Footnote 1.

The Societal Context of Women's Role in Family Relationships and Responsibilities

Carol Hagemann-White

I. The Historical Shift from Material to Psychological Gender Difference

A brief contrast of pre-modern with modern industrialized societies suggests that the quality and meaning of separate spheres of action of women and men have changed. Both shared culture and gender-discontinuous culture were earlier closely interwoven with shared or separate material tasks. Even where anthropological analysis may show that the distribution of material tasks follows from the cultural construction of separate gender identities, this is not self-conscious; the division of labor is attributed to natural or supernatural prescriptions and given. Indeed it could be argued that this is a central function of the cultural construction of gender, to remove some differences and inequalities from the realm of that which has been, and can be decided upon, which is at our disposal.

Over the 18th and 19th centuries in Europe, contradictory tendencies emerged. The ideological salience of separateness of the sexes increased, while at the same time their separation was being undermined. For example, males were claiming new decision-making power over birthing, nursing, child-raising, even while these were being ideologized as innate capabilities of all (true) women (Oakley, 1976; Rich, 1976). Pestalozzi's idealization of the mother exemplifies this unconscious contradiction, which can be found in male-authored expert advice for mothers until today. It is by virtue of her sex and her physical birth tie to the child that the mother knows – prior to reasoning or education – how to meet her child's needs, yet it is the male authority who is able to recognize when her instincts are "right." This expert literature has not ceased to rail at the majority of birth-giving women whose "instincts" fail to guide them on the right path.

In regard to work the paradox is reversed: women move into men's spheres while their presence is denied. With industrialization there is a rapid neutralization of gender differences, and women increasingly do the same as men. The "sameness" appears in the transformation of gender-allocated handcrafts into factory production which may employ, for various reasons, one or the other gender; it appears in women's substantial or sole contribution of earnings through wage labor to the support of self and/or family; and finally, many domains of what became male jobs were increasingly associated with indispensable female assistants. One can view the job of secretary, after it had become "feminized," as paradigmatic: ostensibly an entirely different job from that of her boss, the work involves close acquaintance with and often discrete substitution for most aspects of the man's job. At the same time a sex-segregated labor market was evolving which was no longer predicated primarily on de facto differences in skills. And the historically new ideology arose that women normally do not work.

133

These examples aim to illustrate my broader thesis on the societal context of gender difference within which women's roles should be seen: the cultural construction of difference between women and men in modern European and American society seems to contradict, even compensate for the real dissolution of gender separation. Another description of this process would be to call it the "psychologizing" of the gender distinction. Sex identity is not equivalent to a given participation in the material reproduction of society (as in the case of an obligatory or chosen identity as a tiller of the fields, a grower of yams, a warrior); instead, this participation is seen as following from and required by sex identity, which itself consists of inner personality characteristics, feminity, or masculinity. We can see this new, psychological character of gender as part of a broader process of the psychologization of human subjectivity. By this I mean an experience of, and discourse on subjectivity such that "psychology" becomes thinkable. Each individual is now perceived as having a highly differentiated consciousness accessible only to oneself, with an infinite variety of possible feelings, attitudes, and thoughts to be cultivated and reflected on. Within this stream of consciousness there is a constant sequence of events and facts which can be discovered and explored, just as the strange continents and peoples and the inner structure of physical and biological nature can be explored, mapped, and nailed down. The prerequisite for the very conception of a science of psychology is a societal development by virtue of which people had begun to feel and see themselves as having such "worlds of inner space" (cf. Gehlen, 1949).

In contrast to the traditional ascription of feelings (such as grief, affection, loyalty) to given social situations, ascriptions which made these feelings obligatory on any person in the situation, we see the emergence of the concept of authenticity, grounded in the ever-present specter of possible dissimulation. In this context, relationships and understandings gradually cease to be the unreflected, "natural" concomitant of a common activity or a given community. Not that relationships were ever unproblematic or without ambivalence; David Gaunt[1] and Hilde Rosenmayr (see her contribution in this volume) both point to the function of folk tales in balancing and diverting the tension of such frequent ambivalence. What is new is that relationships, and in our century even communication, become conscious productions, as do personalities. There is, for example, an increasing literature on how to work at creating a good marriage, how to plan one's actions and reactions to produce a well-behaved or a non-neurotic, an intelligent or a liberated child. Currently, this attitude is expanding to include sexual pleasure, which is no longer assumed to erupt on its own or to be a gift of persons or circumstances, but something to be hygienically planned for and consciously worked at.

There are various names and conceptual approaches for this overall process; it can be looked at in the framework of civilization theory or of the social psychology of the technological era or of late or post-capitalism. Here, I am interested in its consequences for what we are familiar with as women's family and family-related roles. For this purpose it is important to see that the process does not apply to the intimate sphere only. Conscious work, much of it intellectual and emotional, also becomes necessary for the coordination of, and the actual effectivity of services which in their earlier forms would have needed no such mediation. Let us take, for example, illness. Today, sick persons not only have to solve organizational and transportation problems of access to a medical practitioner; they also have to do the psychological work of presenting complaints in a medicalized form which allows for — and in fact prestructures — a "diagnosis." Lack of information and skills for such self-presentation is apt to lead to inadequate diagnosis and treatment; it often devolves upon mothers (or wives!) to articulate the complaints of family members. The sick role dispenses a person from obligations, requires bed rest, avoiding exertion, etc., thus implicitly prescribing that a caretaking person be present to make this possible.

As Laura Balbo (1982) points out, the modern welfare state involves institutions both in the free-enterprise and in the public sector which guarantee a minimum quality of life, thus in a sense substituting for *Gemeinschaft* or direct personal solidarity in the community. It is in the nature of these institutions to presuppose a substantial amount of "consumer work" before the services can ever actually reach clients. For example, there is much psychological work necessary to present oneself successfully as a welfare claimant: mere neediness or poverty (states which would have been socially self-evident in earlier times) is not enough, and may even be irrelevant. Balbo discusses the different levels on which this "consumer work" presupposed in the welfare state makes up — along with or including housework in the better-known sense — the core of women's work at home and often in the labor market. It is not infrequently expected from, and volunteered by, women in typically female occupations. To be female is to be qualified for, and obligated to do the psychological and consumer work necessary to produce — out of economic and technological anarchy — a cohering society. It is to be responsible for the viability of relationships and personalities and for the effectiveness of services, regardless of their provider. Yet the relationships, the personalities, and the services pertain to both genders, as does the concept and experience of human subjectivity as accessible to and requiring psychological work. There is no immediately evident reason why the competence for relational, emotional, and organization work should be gender-specific, and in fact, wherever it is professionalized, men participate in it and usually dominate the instructional and directing positions. In the second part of this paper, the thesis will be presented that the gender-specification of this work as female is disfunctional in important respects.

II. Dysfunctionality of the Gender Division of Family Responsibilities and Roles

The modern maternal role of women is historically unique and in many ways disfunctional (Rossi, 1964). It evolved rather by default than as the expression of social consensus on the appropriate care of children. In the bourgeois family one can trace a gradual contraction of the large household with servants and relatives and then the gradual substitution of domestic technology for servants (Bock & Duden, 1977). In the working class, to the degree that wage labor became the primary or exclusive source of subsistence, arrangements for child care (once capitalist factory organization had excluded them from their parents' workplace) were varied and haphazard, drawing on neighbors and relatives not in the factory or resulting in part in neglect. Bourgeois social reformers persistently redefined the working-class problem as being that of wage labor of the mother/wife. For exam-

135

ple, H. Mehner, an early social researcher with a great commitment to precise detail, presented in 1887 a careful description of a working-class family's daily life. In a postscript he maintains that the woman's wage labor is uneconomical. Her own comparison between her low factory wage and the possibilities of seasonal work with the children (gathering camomile for sale) is translated by Mehner to mean regret that she cannot be at home doing housework (Mehner in: Rosenbaum, 1974, 330 f.). Parallel to the propagation of the family ideal by social reformers were the efforts of working-class men to improve wages by restricting female competition. The "nuclear family" can be seen as the point of convergence between the contraction of the middle-class family and the construction of a working-class family. Their normative nucleus was the isolated mother with sole responsibility for integrating children into the community from which she was cut off.

Such a sketch of family history is, of course, a ruthless oversimplification whose sole purpose is to remind us of the *residual* nature of the home as space, the mother as caretaker for children. In similar ways, the care of the sick, care of the aged, and even the spousal role of women emerged by default. As a consequence of the destruction of all the support networks, all of the community and consensus upon which the distribution of responsibilities formerly rested, the small family and within it the woman remained to catch up the slack. It is not because our culture conceived of and defined marriage as involving a woman's participation in her husband's job that this has become widespread. On the contrary, the older European-American culture saw marriage as the alliance of two differing but complementary work capacities; and the later cultural construct overlaying this was that of love and the happy home. Yet against the rapacity of employers' demands, passing some of the pressure on to the wife was, if nothing else, the path of least resistance, and the diffuse concept of marriage "for good or ill" justifies defining auxiliary duties of a man's job as those of his wife. Still, even now this notion is not explicit in the culture. Women believe they are marrying a person, perhaps a secure provider, and it is with a shock that they realize they have married a job (Finch, 1983). In the same way, the realization that a woman has married her husband's parents and may have to live with them and care for them in old age is likely to contradict the cultural concept of marriage as an emotional-sexual alliance of the young (love), oriented towards founding a new (and better) family. Indeed, in an era of prolonged adolescence, love tends to be experienced as a common bond against the parents, legitimizing the attenuation of bonds and responsibilities and even compensating for the mistakes, and injustices that the spouse is perceived as having suffered from the parents. Wives of men who drink or are violent are often told that the husband has to work out his aggressions against his mother in his relationship with her.

Institutions which emerge by default tend to be haphazard in meeting essential needs as well as being highly resented, since the obligations they impose are not well integrated with the cultural constructions with which individuals enter into them. Although an overall view of social institutions may conclude that women's family roles are "functional" in that real social needs are not met elsewhere and converge here, we should be cautious about assuming that they do, in fact, function. The places and people upon which older members of society, for example, become dependent for care do not, by virtue of that fact, always become care-giving places and people.

Before considering more closely the actual quality of women's family work, let me recur to the theme of psychologization of the gender difference. I hypothesize some relationship between the emergence of family roles for women by default and the development of a highly ideologized psychological gender difference without a discernible or plausible material basis. The two developments parallel each other and only seem to make sense together. For example, the emergence and persistence of a sex-segregated wage labor market cannot be adequately explained either by the persistence of traditional gender-differentiated qualifications, or by the profit maximization of capitalists. There is something to be said for both factors, but countervailing examples exist as well. At best, analogies can be drawn between the products of branches of production that employ women (such as textiles, food), and women's housework, but these analogies tend to be forced. In any case, the actual skills employed by mechanized factory work are very different from those of crafts and of home production. Of course, capitalist employers maximize profit, but there are countless examples where profits could be increased by employing or training women with lower wage aspirations for traditional "male" jobs, and yet this is resisted.

The sex segregation of the labor market makes sense when we see it as a means of defining women as temporary/auxiliary wage earners who are — not an industrial, but a home labor reserve. Women are socially defined as in readiness to be drawn back into, or even fully absorbed by the roles that, having emerged by default, make unpredictable and unforeseen demands. Labor market segregation prevents women and men from ever actually experiencing how materially identical their respective capabilities and achievements are, thus supporting the cultural construction of inherent, psychological differentness. And this ideological construct is the strongest bond which ties specifically to the woman the unpredictable and unforeseen demands of intergenerational relationships, consumer work, and spousal needs. When a child is sick, a parent or grandparent needs to be taken in, or the load of uncompleted housework and consumer work begins to pile up intolerably, some mechanism is needed to define who is obligated to do something about the situation — if necessary, at the cost of her/his job. The cultural construction of marriage and the family does not, in itself, solve this problem, because there is no basic cultural consensus that all of these demands ought to be delegated to the family at all — they merely come home to roost. (There is, for example, a fairly widespread consensus that inclusion of aged parents in the child's marriage/family of procreation is undesirable for all concerned.) It is the cultural construct of psychological gender differences that solves the problem of allocation. *If* a problem of this kind devolves upon the family, however resented this may be, it is clear that the woman is the *person* whose job it is to deal with it, because *femininity makes her alone competent* to do so adequately.

Given the effective functioning of allocation of rights and duties through the "gender difference," I submit that the psychologizing of the gender distinction is no mere ideological delusion but a very real historical and societal process. Women and men have become so different that — despite the lack of visible or empirically demonstrable differences in what they can do or do do — the sexes scarcely speak the same language. This profound communication gap of societal dimensions may make women reluctant to delegate genuine responsibilities in intergenerational relationships or even in housework to men. It can be nearly impossible to generate a sense of confidence about how someone of the opposite sex will handle critical situations. (The same factor may aggravate men's reluctance to concede positions of power to women.) Even when they say the same words, one is in doubt about what they mean, and most certainly about what they would do in a crisis. Thus although it is clear that, as Lehr points out in her contribution to this volume and I will elaborate in other respects, the assignment of all family responsibilities only to women is unjustified and detrimental, we need to understand the ways in which the construction of the gender distinction makes women accept such one-sided responsibility before we can design effective policies for change.

At the same time, there is much evidence that women resent their sole responsibility for "family work." Indeed, on many levels it is true that emotional work and servicing are what women do, and they can be seen as the glue that holds a fragmented *Gesellschaft* together. But glue is not without its drawbacks: it is often of doubtful quality, failing under strain while being nonethelesss overly sticky, stubbornly binding together just the parts that ought to have been allowed to separate; and its use can lead to dependency and damage. These aspects, too, may apply to women's relationship work.

Feminist research in recent years has emphasized the importance of women's work in the family and has raised our awareness of the many ways in which women are quietly and as a matter of course making (or trying to make) humane living possible even in the most impossible conditions, with inadequate resources, and against the indifference and even contempt of husbands and children. (Oakley, 1974; Prokop, 1976; Wolf-Graaf, 1981). That is important, and it is vital that women's work become visible, articulate, and recognized. Nonetheless, the first rumblings of new discontent were heard from women doing exactly this work as housewives (Friedan, 1963), and with good cause. My own research with women in a battered women's shelter (Hagemann-White et al., 1981) which included follow-up interviews up to two years after the shelter stay, has led me to question the quality of the "glue" constituted by women's emotional work. On the basis of the reports that women give of the history of their relationship to a batterer, we cannot help but be impressed by the extensive, persistent, and often imaginative efforts that women make to create or maintain relationships even when everything is working against them. But we also cannot help but see that the woman's efforts to understand and help her husband were self-defeating, producing little valid or useful insight. Before a woman arrives in a shelter she has usually worked for years to save her marriage (or cohabitation), for the sake of her own self-image, out of despair, trying to salvage an "intact family" for the children, and even not infrequently out of a sense of responsibility to his parents. What she has really done, above all, is to postpone her own actual coping while absolving him from responsibility – for if it is her duty and potential to create a viable relationship by empathy and sacrifice, then when he is destructive, she has failed: she can determine to try harder rather than to blame him.

It is commonplace in much feminist literature that women, as the oppressed, understand men better than men women. Over time, I have become distrustful of all the unhappy childhoods that women attributed to their batterers, just as I had begun to doubt the repeated descriptions of superhuman physical power that I often heard. It became clear to me that the women had been piecing together mosaics of the man's past out of his sparse anecdotes or those of his relatives, elaborating them in fantasy so as to yield an interpretation of *his* behavior that would make sense in *her* terms. Yet we know that women, growing up in similar or even more disadvantaged circumstances than such men, very seldom become criminally violent (Rausch, 1979; Jones, 1980). Whatever the reasons for this, one must at the least conclude that empathy of this kind — constructing one's own explanation out of what one knows or guesses of the other's past, without the cooperation of the other in any undertaking of self-reflection — is highly unlikely to enable a woman to understand a violent man. These efforts seemed to have, instead, a specific meaning, defining the batterer as the original victim who needs her help with his unacknowledged emotional problems. Thus, reluctance to admit to victimization (which would be, after all, humiliating) and fantasies of herself as rescuer enable a woman to endure the situation by removing the responsibility for the violence from the batterer. Of course, this is congruent with social pressure to preserve a marriage and not to subject children to divorce (and frequently, as a consequence, poverty). Yet we could observe in the shelter, and indeed the women were often clearly aware of this, that preserving the marriage had harmed the children more than it had helped them. All in all, the emotional work, the glue that the woman exuded over years, was destructive in every respect. Interestingly, it was in the mid-life phase, from age 30 to age 50, that women could most often make full use of what the shelter offered them: not only safe space but the chance to reconsider their self-image as family women, as rescuers and gluers-together, as mothers and as dutiful daughters and as wives, and to begin to think of what they owed themselves. It was almost exclusively within this age group that women were accessible to follow-up interviews which reactualized the shelter experience and with it that of being battered.

III. Diverging Structures of Moral Development and Converging Responsibilities in Intergenerational Relationships

In the final part of this paper I would like to suggest some thoughts on the nature of that psychological gender difference which makes communication and mutual, constructive empathy so difficult. On the basis of a recently completed expertise on gender socialization (Hagemann-White, 1982), I can only underline Ursula Lehr's remark that the widespread notions about behavior and character differences between the sexes are contradicted by the weight of the empirical evidence. Yet we see that a gender distinction (which goes far beyond the differences that may exist in bodily constitution) is experienced as real and takes on an effective social function in the allocation of responsibilities.

Drawing on the work of Carol Gilligan (1979), I would suggest that the historical and societal process of the psychologization of gender difference has resulted in profoundly differing structure and sequence in the development of moral responsibility in women and in men. This is directly relevant to the subject "Intergenerational Relationships" for given the absence (or scarcity) of culturally well-integrated institutions based on social consensus, the practical accomplishment of intergenerational relationships centers on issues of moral judgment: of responsibility, rights, and ethical obligations. If indeed the "inner differentness" of the sexes is the allocative mechanism for relationship work, then it makes sense to expect the societal production of such differentness to be located in divergent structuring of moral development.

Gilligan has pointed out that life cycle theorists in general, and theorists of moral development in particular, have based their theories on an exclusively male empirical population. Most of them have noted at some point that women do not "fit" their constructs. Freud at least gave some melancholy attention to explaining the "moral deficiency" of women; Erikson cheerfully acquiesced to traditional norms, assuming that young women simply do not need an identity of their own but should derive it from the men they marry; Piaget and Kohlberg alternately were puzzled by, or ignored the failure of girls to confirm their developmental generalizations (or more precisely: the failure of their generalizations to comprehend the development of girls).

Strongly influenced by Piaget, Kohlberg's work has focused narrowly on studying the sequential logic of the emergence of moral judgments and values in male children (Kohlberg, 1974). His publications have been primarily based on data from a longitudinal study in which moral dilemmas were presented to older children and adolescents, and their suggested resolutions of these dilemmas were studied at three-year intervals. On the basis of his data from boys, Kohlberg has categorized different kinds of moral reasoning and conflict resolution into six stages of moral development, which he claims emerge in a fixed sequence, each stage being more complex and (implicitly or explicitly) morally superior to the previous one. To emphasize the last point, Kohlberg has drawn on exemplary public figures: Eichmann is employed as an example of retarded moral development (stages 1 and 2), figures such as Gandhi illustrate stage 6.

Gilligan has followed Kohlberg in her methodology for studying empirically the moral development of girls and women. In concluding, however, that the logic of moral reasoning and the sequence of moral development in women differs from that which Kohlberg describes for men, she undercuts the assumption that there is one and only one mode of moral progress and the notion of universally valid moral values. By no means does she draw the conclusion of moral relativism, however. In contrast, her interviews with women and the data she cites on women's moral reasoning leads her to highlight the element of relativism in Kohlberg's conception as being specifically male. She points out that he discounts types of highly complex moral reasoning typical for women by equating them with naive conformism.

"Regarding all constructions of responsibility as evidence of a conventional moral understanding, Kohlberg defines the highest stages of moral development as deriving from a reflective understanding of human rights" (Gilligan, 1979, 442).

This rights conception (stages 5 and 6) "is geared to arriving at an objectively fair or just resolution to the moral dilemmas to which 'all rational men can agree'" (ibid., 444); a central concern is non-interference — that is, each individual may do as he pleases as long as this does not interfere with someone else's rights. Gilligan's interviews show by contrast that reflective women tend to regard this kind of moral attitude as immature. Moral maturity involves, for women, the realization that human interdependence and mutual responsibility for others *and* self aways exist.

"The problem becomes one of limiting responsibilities without abandoning moral concern," and its resolution lies in the recognition that others have responsibility for themselves (Gilligan, 1979, 444).

Gilligan's description, which could only be summarized here, corresponds closely to my own observation of the way in which women deal with, and grow through moral dilemmas involved in social change through the women's movement. Both increased personal growth through emancipation, and increased moral responsibility for others are involved in projects such as abortion counselling, rape hot lines, and battered women's shelters. The dilemmas and their resolution as debated and experienced among women correspond well to Gilligan's views. I would guess, on the other hand, that Kohlberg's analysis of the highest stages of moral development correspond closely to his observation of involvement and conflict between men. When we are thinking about intergenerational relationships in the family, however, we are no longer dealing with "homosocial" worlds (Lipman-Blumen, 1976). We have to ask ourselves, then, to picture the marriage of a stage 5 (Gilligan) woman with a stage 5 (Kohlberg) man. How do they communicate, decide on, and allocate responsibilities in moral issues?

To illustrate the problem, let me only suggest some not infrequent examples involving issues on which a morality of equal rights/non-interference might take a very different stance from a morality of responsibility/contextual mode of judgment. Let us imagine, for example, that a third or fourth child wants special lessons or a longer, more expensive education for vocational goals than that which could be afforded for the older siblings. Or consider the decision when several surviving adult children are confronted with aging parents who need home care, and when both the conditions for taking the parents in and the willingness to do so differ. When decisions of this kind devolve upon a family, they may require negotiation between persons who — by virtue of gender-specific experiences — are more than likely to think and talk at cross-purposes because their entire experience of moral maturing is incommensurable. The exercise of sheer power (perhaps legitimated by traditional sex role prescriptions), withdrawal of one partner from both decision-making and consequent responsibilities, or an unending chain of misunderstandings and resentments may be the result.

Indeed, we are probably seeing a progressive disintegration of the homosocial worlds of women and to some extent those of men. Within such homosocial worlds moral decisions could be worked out either within the male (Kohlberg) or within the female (Gilligan) mode. Furthermore, the development of moral responsibility and moral consciousness is interactional and continues beyond adolescence; the family of procreation may already be, and probably needs to be an important context within which this occurs. That makes the difference in modes even more problematic. I would suggest that it is difficult or impossible for women to resolve the dilemma of moral concern versus responsibility for oneself if they have to do this in primary interaction with persons for whom this dilemma does not exist; this would be the case with men who predicate their decisions either on legitimate male dominance over the female or on an individual rights conception of non-interference.

The disparity between women's and men's moral development, in conjunction with the dominantly heterosexual and heterosocial interactional context (as opposed to female support networks of the past!) within which women deal with intergenerational relationships, may help explain the inadequate quality and often negative effects of the "glue" constituted by women's emotional work. To mobilize, fall back on, or even idealize women's work and family caring as a way of even temporarily humanizing life would aggravate these problems rather than leading to solutions.

Footnote

1 Gaunt, David: The Multigenerational Family during Socio-Economic Transition, paper presented at the International Symposium on Intergenerational Relationships, February 21–24, 1983 in Berlin.

Mothers as Scapegoats
Patterns of Judging Intergenerational Relationships

Marianne Meinhold

1. Introduction

The utilization and application of knowledge resulting from social science has not yet been adequately investigated (Drerup & Terhart, 1979). Obviously, the application procedure and outcome is influenced by variables which intrinsically go beyond the reaches of science itself. Many of the theories devised and the findings observed will be soon forgotten; other concepts will be shaped and simplified; only a few elements of knowledge brought about might gain a higher degree of popularity. One of the most striking manifestations of an oversimplified psychological concept is the conviction that the child-rearing practices a person experiences in early childhood will determine his further life almost totally.

As with many simplified concepts, this concept also embodies some truth and plausibility; therefore, it is not intended to advocate abandonment of this idea, but to show how the concept "works" and what can be done to instill an awareness of other events and conditions relevant to the life course of a person.

This article looks at the question of how social workers and students of social work process information, particularly when performing professional tasks, if and how they use concepts of social science for problem solving. The tasks to be performed consist of a set of decisions to be made, including judgements about families, as we work together with family welfare services and infant services. The predominant interpretation patterns are described and the factors which promote and stabilize them are discussed.

An additional question deals with alternate intervention strategies to find out how social workers change their interpretation patterns on families when performing different interventions.

Finally, some suggestions are devised on how to consider the context of the sampling process when collecting data on intergenerational relationships.

2. Project I: Interpretation Patterns

The interpretation patterns are identified by observing and evaluating group discussions (four to eight members) in the context of a supervision procedure described earlier (Meinhold, 1982). The group members are used to thinking aloud.

In many areas of social work there is a lack of "well-defined" problems. The problems to be solved are ambiguous; usually the solutions expected are neither unequivocally "right" or "wrong," nor are they solutions at all, but seem to be the lesser of two evils. As these tasks require a person to have the ability to compare and relate different perceptions and to integrate conflicting views, one criterion by which the quality of decision-making is evaluated is its complexity (see Schroder et al., 1967; Hunt, 1978). Other criteria refer to the question of how far the decision-maker is able to anticipate the consequences of his decision.

Some typical attributes of the predominant problem-solving strategies are:
- When solving a practical problem the problem solver is in fact using different scientific concepts, but these concepts seem to be selected and combined at random. The rules and plans controlling the selection and combination represent common-sense-belief-systems, rather than scientific knowledge. The crucial point does not refer to the non-scientific combination of scientifically sounding labels — in fact there are not many rules available which might be suited to control the selection and application of knowledge for practical purposes (Mulkay, 1980) — but to the point that the problem solver is not *aware* of his prejudices, attitudes, and subjective experiences influencing the information processing.
- The patterns of defining and explaining problems are very simple; that is, regardless of the problem's complexity, attention is only directed at one or two aspects of the problem.
- Many aspects possibly relevant to the problem are ignored except those aspects which can be taken as problems of character.

Beyond the particular tasks of the different welfare institutions the social workers consistently aim at changing the client's personality. Whatever the client's reason may be for visiting the institution: if he has to handle an ejectment or his child staying away from school or shoplifting or being cut off by the electricity company or some obscurities in his health insurance — the social worker will look for the core of the problem which can be perceived by psychologizing interpretation patterns (Florecke & Herriger, 1982; Gutenberger & Spran-Kuhlen, 1980).

Even though the client is not presumed to have caused the problem all along the line, the social worker's interventions mainly lay stress on the client's personal traits and behavior.

There are several simplifications of the problem perception resulting from psychologizing interpretation patterns:
- Psychologizing interpretation patterns mainly refer to interpersonal relationships. As many clients of the welfare institutions are women, and as these women become clients because they are women and because they have to function in a family, the interpretation patterns refer to intrafamilial relationships concerning women living as mothers, daughters, or grandmothers in real families, but also concerning relationships to former family members, for example, mothers who have already died or moved away and are held responsible for the problems.
- Another simplification can be observed when social workers justify therapy-oriented interventions: the quality of the mother-child interaction is taken to depend mainly on the personal traits of the family members, particularly of the mother. Therefore, the interventions first aim at changing the attitudes and child-rearing practices of the mothers, mainly without considering the strains in the environmental situations of those mothers, even though these strains are known to cause a lot of intrafamilial conflicts (Peel, 1980).

Psychologizing interpretation patterns are propagated and used in many areas of our social reality — not only in social work. These interpretation patterns become very valid for middle-class families. Middle-class mothers especially tend to accept the responsibility for nearly every developmental outcome of their children; they feel guilty if their children fail in school or if they become drug addicts and view themselves as the cause of the problem (see Gross, 1978; Ender-Dragässer, 1981). On the other hand, lower-class families — especially low-income people, who become the clients of social work — do not care much about psychologizing interpretation patterns. Their needs and aspirations for change primarily lay on improving their material situation concerning housing, budgeting, and work (Liffman, 1978). Therefore, they often fail to understand what the social worker expects them to do.

There are several presumptions offered to answer the question of what is promoting and stabilizing the interpretation patterns described:

a) *The historical background of social work*, especially concerning the development of methods in social work from the beginning of this century: In the beginning it seemed to be necessary to devise some decision criteria for identifying worthy poor people and differentiating them from unworthy ones. And this "diagnostic instrument" had to be more efficient and valid than the test of the workhouse. This kind of psychodiagnostic procedure devised at that time has to be regarded as real progress compared to the practices before (Müller, 1982). Later in the thirties, the diagnostic instrument became refined by psychoanalytical terms and concepts. The social worker-client relationship was seen to be the most efficient instrument for changing the client, analogous to the psychotherapist-client relationship. Today social work is often defined as "relationship work." Obviously, the mystification of the "relationship" also results from the fact that social work at first was a female profession.
From the beginning the social workers' demands to become acknowledged as a profession were closely connected with the development of therapy-oriented techniques for social diagnosis and counselling.

b) *The long established organizations of social work*, especially the administrative rules regulating the social work in the public welfare services: In the public welfare services nearly 60 percent of the work consists of administrative activities; these "official" tasks mainly provide the documentation and control of social problems. Beside the official tasks the social worker chooses so-called "inofficial" tasks according to his professional identity. The inofficial tasks are directed at improving the client's circumstances — and this often amounts to changing the client's lifestyle.
As long as the social worker takes into account the administrative rules, no one will prevent him from performing his inofficial tasks. But all his good intentions have to be translated into a language fitting the bureaucratic rules. The administrative tradition of filing systems urges the social worker to consider social problems as single cases which can be perceived by psychologizing interpretation patterns. On the other hand, the social workers often forget that the institutional framework might destroy or deform the effects intended by therapy-oriented interventions. Outside the context of the therapeutic setting, a communication breakdown is experienced by both sides.
Additionally, the public services suffer from a lack of effective support programs. When the social worker realizes that he has not got any material relief, nor jobs, nor

accommodation to offer the client, he might tend to offer the client a "helping relationship."

c) In the seventies *the growing market for psychotherapeutic knowledge* was also justified by a forecast concerning social work: A decline in need for financial support was expected and an increasing need for psychological counselling. Such forecasts have proven to be wrong. Nevertheless, the market is expanding due to a high degree of unemployment for "helping professions." This urges social workers to acquire therapeutic competences and improve their work opportunities.

d) The preference for further therapeutic education results from both the market just mentioned and also from some *subcultural aspirations and problem-solving strategies*. When applying therapeutic knowledge, the social worker hopes to combine his needs for self-actualization with his professional tasks. Furthermore, lots of therapeutic strategies consist in talking – and talking seems to be a proven problem-solving strategy in this subcultural milieu. When the social worker encounters a real client requiring help, he gets the feeling that his professional need "for helping other people" will be satisfied, rather than that he is trying to improve infrastructural conditions.

e) Finally, there are several *patterns of learning theories in social sciences* that provoke narrow-minded perception styles. The students regard poor theoretical concepts or single experimental results as the whole reality; concerning socialization, they tend to overestimate the long-term outcome of early mother-child interaction instead of observing the houses, places, and communities where children grow up. This might possibly have to do with the theoretical concepts available in that area, too. Even though there are some socio-ecological concepts available (Bronfenbrenner, 1976), it is rare for them to be incorporated into the argument on mother-child interaction.

3. Project II: Comparison of Different Interventions

Beside the *person-directed*, therapy-oriented intervention mentioned above, there are so-called *"situation-directed"* interventions in social work. In alleged contrast the situational model claims that the lifestyles of the clients are often responses to the circumstances of poverty, to a lack of resources, and a lack of competences in benefiting from the resources available (Liffman, 1978). Additionally, the clients often know little about their welfare rights and the appropriate procedure for exercising these bureaucratic rights, because they fail to understand the bureaucratic schedules. The situation-directed interventions consist of a set of different services, providing alleviation from a family's distress, and also providing changes in the client's neighborhood. A context will be constructed within which the development of the client may be more favorably encompassed. This context could be partially designed and constructed by the client, but it is up to the client, if and how he will benefit from the change.

One prior condition of situation-directed working is to gather information on the environment, on the services available, and to bring about contacts between different groups.

The different meanings and effects of the two interventions can be experienced when working with families. The differences observed are based on long-term (generally up to 12 months) family work with 60 families recommended by the welfare services:

- The person-directed intervention is often described in the term "family help." The family helper has to support the parents, that is, the mothers and grandmothers in their educational work. One of his main tasks is to protect the children from being placed in an institution.

Family help does not amount automatically to a therapy-oriented approach, but as these interventions are highly estimated, many family helpers define the core of their work as talking with the mothers about child-rearing practices. Family help is seen by some families to be a proof of their own failure. The families often resist the family help, but sometimes fruitlessly when their children are threatened by being placed in a home. Other families expect the family helpers to give practical aid; in these cases the family helper feels exploited and tries to shift from practical help to counselling.

- As an alternative to family help we established a service called "Baby Sitter Emergency Service." We know that many cases of child negligence and even of child maltreatment result from the fact that single mothers are under many constraints, and even a simple intention like visiting a doctor sometimes seems to be an unsolvable problem to them.

The concept of the baby sitter service is based on three assumptions:

i) the "non-problem-approach" (Benn, 1978), that is, not waiting for some kind of crisis, with all its negative connotations of personal failure, but finding the point of intervention before the problems develop;

ii) the approach aims at meeting the client without a particular professional purpose to the contact; that is, the contact is not defined and limited by the social worker's professional purpose but by the family's own needs;

iii) we have no right to impose our diagnostic perceptions and goals on the families; that is, we do not claim to change the intrafamilial relationships, nor do we interfere with the "inner life" of the mothers if not asked to do so.

The service is free. In the initial stage of our project the baby sitters are advanced students of social work, because there are some incentives for them to be a baby sitter: Living in a subcultural milieu, many students have little access to concrete information on their clients, their value patterns, and competences which are closely associated with their life conditions. Working as a baby sitter for the same family provides the opportunity to learn about the family with no need to change the mothers. As the protective structure of social work has to be given up, it is intended to make the families become independent of the welfare services. Therefore, we have to establish resources, for example, in this case, to create a network of mutual help in the neighborhood and to encourage the families to use existing community facilities.

The first results from this type of work are quite encouraging. The families understand and accept the service immediately. The reality of the families perceived by the baby sitters is very different from the family's reality as documented in the files of social work. The families represent themselves to the baby sitters as more competent than they are when meeting a social worker. The social worker is not able to acknowledge some competences of the families, because these competences do not fit the administrative expectations (see example). There are several social competences in particular to be observed: "social competences" in a sense of inducing other people in the family and the neighborhood to give help. Furthermore, the families are very competent in organizing time schedules — we did not expect that. Since the service was established five months ago, the families observed every fixed time or cancelled a fixed date on time, even if a family had not got a telephone at home and the mother was not used to reading and writing. Incidentally, one reason for cancelling a fixed date was the temporary return of a father or a mother's friend.

Example:
One year ago, I was consulted by a social worker from an infant welfare service. She described the situation of a boy called Tom who was 10 months old at that time:

Tom's mother was just married — not to Tom's father — and she did not take care of Tom. Tom lived with his mother's sister who was unemployed, just divorced, and she wanted to take care of Tom.

The first problem was that Tom's mother did not function as a mother, and the mother's sister was not officially supposed to be a foster mother for Tom. Therefore, she did not receive maintenance for Tom.

The social worker helpfully aimed at arranging an official foster contract. Tom's mother promised to sign the document required. Everything was prepared, but Tom's mother did not observe the fixed time for signing the document. The social worker rearranged everything and tried to get financial support for the mother's sister without a formal acquiescence of the mother. The mother's sister agreed with that proposal, but when she had to come to sign the document, she did not come.

When being visited by the social worker, the mother's sister said she was not sure about taking care of Tom any longer, because she had been offered a part-time job in a large kitchen. The social worker felt a little alarmed and pressed by her colleagues: Would Tom be cared for sufficiently by this unreliable family? When visiting the mother's sister again, the social worker realized that Tom had been given away to his grandmother who lived in another district where another social worker was responsible for him.

It would take time for the social worker in the other department to be informed and be able to act.

In the meantime, Tom had been returned to his mother's sister and we had established the baby sitter service. Tom's aunt, who had got a part-time kitchen job, asked if she could get a baby sitter once or twice a week.

After several days, the baby sitter discovered a well-organized network of people all taking care of Tom when necessary.

This network consisted of:
— the mother's brother (living in the same house as the mother's sister),
— a female neighbor in the same house,
— the grandmother living 10 kilometers away,
— the grandmother's second husband,
— the mother's 15-year-old stepsister (living at the grandmother's),
— the sister of the mother's husband.

Usually, the social workers in the public services do not know much about such networks of mutual help as we observed in several cases; for example, Tom's aunt

148

was afraid of being forced to reveal her circumstances to the social worker when applying for a foster contract. She had good reasons for being "unreliable" and moving Tom away for a short time.

The baby sitter mentioned other advantages of the service:

— They learn a lot about the family's reality which is tremendously different from the social worker's reality. And they cease to interpret the client's dissimilarity as an illness.
— Therefore, they feel no need to prove themselves as "personality changers."
— They feel accepted by the mothers or grandmothers as a real support, but also as a person to be talked to.
— They describe the mothers not as multi-deficit people (as often used in social work), but as admirable women, who successfully solve problems which are almost insoluble.

4. Focusing on the Context of the Sampling Process

Reviewing our work — both as family helpers and as baby sitters — we doubt whether the use and interpretation of "extracontextual" data about families is suitable for acquiring meaningful knowledge about the families' reality. There are some proposals concerning the definition and evaluation of "context" (Bronfenbrenner, 1976; Eirmbter, 1982) which consider the socio-ecological conditions, sometimes including the context of the sampling process. While working with families, we tried to identify several conditions that influence the interviewer-interviewee interaction. As already reported, the social worker is impeded by the institutional framework of the welfare services from clearly apprehending several competences of the clients. Additionally, this data is often used to justify some material gratifications for the families. Owing to a lack of funds in the welfare departments, some social workers tend to declare a family member to be emotionally or mentally "disabled." Therefore, the data collected by the social worker and documented in the files is not a valid source of information about the families. On the other hand, we also view data collected by "neutral" researchers a little sceptically, for example, when the data is gained through questionnaires, single interviews, and observations. We observed how our images on a family and the corresponding facts dramatically changed in the course of time. This did not result from a family giving erroneous information, but from the tremendous discrepancy between our perception and interpretation patterns and those of a family. Therefore, our questions had been "falsely" interpreted by the families as well as that we had misconstrued the answers[1]. As we continuously work with a family during a period of time lasting nearly 12 months, we get closer to a family's language habits. The context of our sampling process — a setting of mutual "giving" and "taking"[2] — seems to be peculiarly appropriate for receiving data relevant to a family's reality. Beyond an approximation of the interpretation patterns and an increase in understanding each other, the family provides the opportunity to contrast "subjective" events reported by different family members with the "objective" facts observed by the baby sitters. We observed, for example, that certain events and facts were perceived and

149

reported by all family members in a similar way, even though the facts were objectively quite different or they were ignored by a family and taken as nonrelevant.

Example:
We worked with a family consisting of the great-grandmother, her daughter (the grandmother), and her great-grandson, a ten-year-old boy. Our initial task was to support the boy's homework, because he had been absent from school for a long period. All family members unanimously reported that the great-grandmother *was running* the family. At first, we agreed with this "image" of the great-grandmother. She had brought up her three children. Her daughter (the grandmother) had become the mother of a daughter (now the mother of the boy living on her own), and when the grandmother could not handle the feeding problems of her daughter, this infant was brought up by the great-grandmother, too. Similarly, some 20 years later the son of that daughter (the boy we worked with) was brought up by the great-grandmother as well. Everyone claimed consistently that the grandmother had no competence concerning care (except for her dog), decisions about family affairs, or even keeping house for the family. Later, we discovered that this "incompetent" grandmother did a lot of competent work for the family: she did all the shopping, partly the cooking; she sometimes oversaw the boy's homework and paid attention to his state of health. Three times she cancelled fixed appointments with us, without informing the great-grandmother.

We never found out whether she had internalized the self-concept of being incompetent, or if she was consciously fulfilling the expectations of other family members.

According to our findings, we regard it useful to investigate three different types of data on families:
— *"subjective" data*, information given by family members. This data reveals how the facts and events are differently or unanimously experienced, perceived, and communicated by the family members.
— *"objective" data*, data observed by the family helpers or baby sitters. This data refers to the interaction between the family members (e.g., their "supporting" and "influencing" activities) but also to a family member's handling of present environmental circumstances. This data completes the subjective data, for example, by disclosing events occurring but being neglected or regarded as nonrelevant by a family.
— *"situations"*: The observers have to describe as many situations as possible about what is happening in a family. The descriptions have to be very concrete, referring to the *behavior* of the family members and the observers. There are several reasons to collect "situations." First, the situations described display the context of interaction between family members and observers. Secondly, the observers learn about their own perception patterns when being obliged to interpret the situations reported during group discussions and to try alternate interpretations. Finally, the situations described might be suitable for further analyses, for example, process analysis.

Our work aims at new interventions for family work, and also at experiencing the family's reality. The results expected are not considered to be general or to confirm the presumptuous idea that there is a sound body of knowledge about *"the"* low-income family.

It is intended instead:

— to instill an awareness of *differences*, differences between the families observed as well as differences between the observer's and the family's reality;

— to enable the students and social workers to perceive nonsalient information, to generate conflicting views, and to tolerate or even utilize the complexity of life.

Footnotes

1 Several examples of such an absurd communication are reported by Schneider (1977).

2 We offer the families a useful service, but on the other hand, the families know that they also do the students a favor, because the students running the service at this stage are obliged to gather experience on children in families. The families are assured that no informaion is passed on to the welfare services.

Chapter III: Distance and Alienation of Different Life Worlds ("Lebenswelten")

The title of this chapter does not refer directly to the generation context. Instead, it characterizes a certain relationship among the age groups which will have become apparent to anyone who observes the manner in which they currently coexist in everyday life. Despite empirical findings to the contrary, the impression one gains is of distance, alienation, and membership in mutually exclusive life worlds ("Lebenswelten"); and it is strengthened by public discussions which persistently and with unremitting energy concentrate on divergencies among and conflicts between the age groups.

By using the term life worlds ("Lebenswelten"), A. Schütz already indicates that his focus will be on the experiential space or horizon potentially or actually available to the individual in everyday life. In dynamic Western societies its limits are demarcated by rapid social and technological change. Some of the consequences of this process on the *individual* level have already been pointed out by Dreitzel. In societies characterized by rapid social change, the demands made upon the individual continually alter; their nature is contradictory, requiring the individual to be flexible and stable at one and the same time (Meyer, 1982; Casch, 1979). Likewise, traditional contexts of meaning and knowledge are losing their cohesion at an ever increasing rate (Kade, 1983). In this regard Buchhofer/Friedrichs and Lüdtke speak of a permanent cultural change and acceleration of demands for information and knowledge (1970, 305). This compels the younger age groups to adapt quickly to innovations for which the "cultural memory" (Mitscherlich, 1957), that is, the older generations as vehicles of cultural values, have no answers. The intensity of collective experiences also increases during periods of rapid social transformation, and the more profound this transformation is, the larger the gap becomes between the generations and their forms of consciousness.

On the *social* level, change thus implies a sectorial differentiation of society, its segregation into age-homogeneous groups each of which has its own realm of experiences. This process extends even to spatial and social-spatial life realities (cf. Matthes, 1978).

The process has its parallels in all the different phases of social development. During the modernization and development of bourgeois society the process first manifested itself as a progressive differentiation between age groups. As development went on, differentiation began to take the form of association ("Vergesellschaftung"), until today the stage has been reached of a segregation of age groups accompanied by the formation of age-specific life worlds ("Lebenswelten") and realms of experience.

Segregation can be seen as a direct consequence of the association ("Vergesellschaftung") process, in the course of which the different age groups grew apart and began to live their everyday lives in relative isolation (cf. Preuss-Lausitz et al., 1983 and Attias-Donfut, this chapter). Scientific research helped to define their respective living conditions as specific, and research itself was also subject to fundamental changes in the course of these developments. It expanded tremendously, growing ever more specialized and distinguishing ever finer subdisciplines (e.g., youth and old age sociology). The form this process took in youth sociology, how youth

153

and/or various adolescent subcultures became a subject for research, and how science, as a consequence of its existence, contributes to the creation of certain youth phenomena — this is the subject of D. Hebdige's contribution to the present chapter.

A glance at the diverse cultures and experiential worlds of the age groups (e.g., the young's discos and bars, subcultural movements like the Teds, Mods, Punks, etc. and the senior citizens' culture and old age homes of the elderly) underscores the impression of effective separation and alienation tendencies. Advertising, marketing, and the manufacture of age-specific consumer goods (from toys and textiles to furniture, food, hobby and sporting goods, music, etc.) encourage these tendencies and contribute to a consolidation of age-specific worlds of experience. And this consolidation in turn implies the formation of age-specific spaces (Matthes, 1978), as, for example, children's playgrounds, which find their counterparts in youth centers for adolescents and leisure centers for the elderly. Due to the relatively monofunctional specialization of these spaces (Preuss-Lausitz et al., 1983) they reinforce the tendency towards age-specific segregation. Thus the conditions are created for such phenomena as speechlessness and estrangement in the interaction between age and generational groups — as Knopf describes in this chapter — especially in view of the fact that increasingly age-homogeneous worlds develop under conditions of an "epochal change of values" (Ingelhart, 1980), which leads to the coexistence and concurrence of diverse age-group value systems.

Admittedly, it is not clear whether this situation must necessarily be accompanied by conflicts between age groups, or whether the causes of existing social conflict are less generation-specific than of a social nature. Anne Foner and Walter Hollstein discuss these questions here.

The problem of age-group alienation outlined above has traditionally been a subject of the political sciences and of youth sociology (cf. Editors' Introduction). Here, it forms the focus of investigations on age-dependent attitudes and orientations and the conflicts these give rise to (e.g., Jennings & Niemi, 1981; Agnello, 1973; Foner, 1983; Riley et al., 1972, etc.), as well as entering into analyses which attempt to pinpoint characteristics of today's youth by asking "What makes these young people different from other 'generations' of adolescents in the past?" (e.g., Allerbeck & Rosenmayr, 1971; Jaide, 1961; Neidthardt, 1967, etc.). Contributions of this kind concern themselves primarily with a *single* age group, relating it to other age groups only from specific points of view. Common to all of these authors is their search for causes of generational and age-group divergencies in social inequalities. Their interest may focus on the significance of these divergencies for social changes and discontinuities and cultural transformation processes (e.g., Hollstein, this chapter). Other authors are more concerned with the factor of social inequality, as is the case with Anne Foner and Claudine Attias-Donfut. Both adhere to the structuralist-functionalist models which predominate in generation research, concentrating either on the relevance of age groups (cohorts) and old age for continuity and change in society (Foner) or on old age considered in relation to social stratum, the production sphere and their social implications (Attias-Donfut).

One of our aims in discussing the topic of intergenerational relationships under the heading, "Distance and Alienation of Life Worlds ('Lebenswelten')," is to bring in other research approaches which might be productively incorporated in generation studies. One key approach is subculture research — represented here by Dick Hebdige — which employs both structuralist models and hermeneutic, interpretive methods (Brake, 1981; Clarke et al., 1981; Diederichsen et al., 1983). Moreover, issues are being discussed in subcultural research which are central for generation research because they shed light on a number of aspects of the relevance of generation as actuality for cultural and social change. Among these issues are the reality of different subcultures and subgroups; the role of age-homogeneous (and sometimes age-heterogeneous) subgroups in social and cultural change; and the function of these groups as points of cultural orientation (Brake, 1981), as creative potential (Krause et al., 1980), as escape from or alternative to social reality (Brake, 1981), or as social pressure groups (Friebel et al., 1979; Zinnecker, 1981, etc.).

The question is still open, however, as to the relevance of subgroups and subcultures to generation membership. Do they represent diverse streams within a generational unit which "live through a common experience in different ways" (Mannheim, 1964)? Or are we confronted here with phenomena that cut across the generation as actuality? This question is prompted especially by age-heterogeneous subcultures such as those which have lately entered the public eye in the New Social Movement, for example, some feminist groups and homosexual and disabled persons' groups.

Phenomenological socialization research likewise devotes itself to questions which can provide impulses for generation studies, for example, questions concerning entelechy formation, the significance of youth as a formative phase influencing the life course, and also as regards the relevance of generation-specific experiences for the course of life (which Mannheim treats as a problem of experience layering — *Erlebnisschichtung*; cf. next chapter). This last-named problem points directly to *life course research*, which can help answer questions as to constancy and/or variability of values and political orientations, questions which have long been treated and discussed in the context of political science but which the research of life course and biography (Elder & Rockwell, 1978; Bertaux, 1982; Kohli, 1978) may well turn up promising answers for.

A completely different approach to the subject characterizes "ethno science" and also ethnomethodology. In the context of our present topic, this tradition seems particularly well suited to elucidating the basic question as to what relevance generation membership and old age have in everyday life (cf. e.g., the study by Atkinson, 1980), and how both come to be constituted as social facts at all (e.g., Langehennig, 1983).

Like the first chapter, the present one also obviously has the character of a programmatic outline. Under the leitmotif of "Distance and Alienation of Different Life Worlds ('Lebenswelten')" it should therefore be read as a program listing those current directions and research traditions which might help advance generation research.

The first contribution returns to the point of departure of this chapter. Claudine Attias-Donfut discusses the conditions which lead to age-differentiation, investigating the institutionalization of retirement culture in France. She shares the structuralist point of view, attempting, as she says, "to link structural and temporal dimensions, i.e., to clarify that it is the social structure which produces the stages of life." Accordingly, she gives special attention to the social function performed by the formation of age-homogeneous worlds. After outlining the relevant theoretical background she shows how the elderly are marginalized as a result of changes in the production sector, increasing division of labor, and the establishment of the social security system. Attias-Donfut illustrates the development, parallel to these structural processes, of "senior citizens' culture" (leisure and education measures) including age-specific worlds (homes and retirement centers). She also shows how the definition of this life stage undergoes a change when seen from the perspective of the entire life course.

The problem of age-group and generation conflicts is the focus of the following two papers. Though of course conflict represents only *one* possible type of inter-generational relationship, actual developments insure that it remains a center of interest both for general and scholarly discussion.

Anne Foner looks at the problem from a structural, functionalist perspective, arguing from the background of the age-stratification concept. She sees potential for age group conflicts — unlike, for example, Dreitzel or Hebdige, this volume — in social inequalities conditioned by the particular type of age-stratification in modern societies (i.e., inequalities in access to power, prestige, material resources, etc.). Other authors also recognize the possibility that age conflicts may increase with unequal distribution of material resources (cf. Marshall, next chapter). Despite existing conflict potential, however, Foner points out that open age-group conflicts are seldom identifiable. She emphasizes the effectiveness of conflict-reducing mechanisms, which she derives from the cohort flow model. According to that model, the members of older cohorts, based on their own earlier experience, practice indulgence with youth who are in process of gaining access to social gratifications. Conversely, the members of younger cohorts, anticipating their opportunity to obtain such resources, practice patience with their elders. Foner explains this mechanism by means of the social security system now developing in the United States.

Walter Hollstein conducts an analysis of age-specific movements. He classifies the various alternative tendencies and movements since the 1950s and describes their development. As the criterion for his classification, Hollstein takes the manner in which discontinuities in social development were recognized, discussed and/or raised to social and political goals by the various movements — an approach that is quite common in youth sociology (cf. Editors' Introduction). Bums, Hippies, Yippies, Beatniks, citizens' initiatives, basis groups and squatters — different as they are, all refused to accept the social *status quo* of the time and the values that underlay it. What distinguishes these groups is the scope of their alternative models for a better world. Hollstein doubts whether the most recent of these trends, the New Social Movement, can be characterized as an age-specific (youth) movement. Its age-heterogeneous composition alone speaks against such a view. Hollstein sees the New Social Movement as a logical continuation of previous alternative streams. He outlines a processual model of counter-cultural movements (cf. also Hollstein, 1981) which illustrates the way in which the various movements succeeded each other. All of them share the character of *social* movements; and Hollstein concludes that only those which aim not only at age-group oriented goals but advance *social* goals can be said to possess lasting potential for political change. He warns against succumbing to a myth — wishing to identify age or generational conflicts where in reality general social conflicts are involved.

Berger too thinks that generational or age conflicts are pseudo-conflicts which resolve themselves in the course of social development (cf. Berger, next chapter). In his view, they have the function of helping the younger age groups collect experiences in the struggle for social power. Thus Berger places the transformation potential of age and generational conflicts not so much in the political as in the cultural sphere, a view that in the German tradition is shared by many generation theoreticians, not lastly by Karl Mannheim.

How the process of cultural transformation takes place, and what role subcultures play in it vis-à-vis the mainstream culture — this is the subject of Hebdige's investigations (e.g., Hebdige, 1976; 1983, and this chapter). Like many other youth sociologists, Hebdige traces the formation of youth cultures back to structural conditions, or more precisely, to insoluble structural contradictions which are particularly exacerbated by rapid social change. Yet unlike the counter-cultural, alternative movements analyzed by Hollstein, adolescent subcultures do not generally advance social or political aims. Their protest and resistance take the form of fashion, a unique style meant to shock. Like Dreitzel, Hebdige suggests that youth subcultures be seen as a symbol of the collapse of traditional forms of meaning and as a symbol of resistance — symbolism which has recourse to the hermeneutic interpretation of the meaning of style.

On the level of style, Hebdige feels youth subcultures should be understood as a reaction and resistance to, and negation of, mainstream culture. On the other hand, they play the role of a cultural avant-garde: each subculture's specific style is rapidly co-opted by society, and through mass marketing their vanguard symbols become integral parts of general culture. This process may indeed involve conflict, which the media generally interpret as generation-conflict; however, it never fundamentally questions social developments. This is corroborated as well by investigations into the (sub)cultures of the elderly (Langehennig, 1983).

In his contribution to this chapter, Hebdige is concerned to elucidate a more inclusive problem, the production of youth phenomena, or, as he phrases it, "the construction of troublesome adolescence" by society and science. Hebdige gives an overview of youth research tradition and shows how changes in the social status of adolescents associated with general social transformation, bring in their wake changes in the paradigms with which researchers attempt to explain the problems of adolescence. In this contribution, too, special weight is placed on an analysis of subcultural trends.

Detlef Knopf leads us to a concrete problem that besets the interrelationships among the age groups. He asks whether and how the gap between age groups can be overcome through interaction in special contexts and through educational measures. Knopf devotes his discussion particularly to interaction between the elderly and the young, those age groups whose marginalization in age-specific worlds has proceeded farthest. Due to their segregation, opportunities have become more limited to gain insight into the life world of the other group, particularly since both elderly and adolescent groups bear strong subcultural traits. A consequence of this mutual estrangement of different life worlds is that opportunities for judgement and interpretation are minimized and the potential of activity-

157

structuring measures to maintain interaction between these age groups increasingly reduced (Schaeffer, 1981). Against this background, Knopf describes the difficulties involved in the interaction between these age groups and shows what efforts are demanded of interaction partners if they are to master the extremely sensitive dynamics of such encounters.

Aging and Generation: Social Structure and Cultural Dynamics

Claudine Attias-Donfut

Marked changes have occurred in the field of the elderly in France during the past two decades. The process of institutionalization has been accentuated in relation to the setting-up and development of a policy on aging, and has contributed to the production of new social and cultural practices of the retired. The evolution of the behavior of the way of life of the retired and the analysis of these lead to the question of their specific aspects compared with other age groups and to the question of the sociological interpretations which can be given to them.

It is first necessary to clarify the terms which will be used to characterize the phenomenon of aging and of generations. To do this, we shall outline the dimensions to which they refer, taking into account the various studies which were already conducted in this domain and which will be helpful in this respect.

It then becomes possible to outline an analysis which attempts to understand the significance of some cultural trends which can be observed at the present time among the elderly in France.

Trends in Research on Generations

During the past ten years, gerontologists have become aware of the limitations of the theories in the field of the elderly and have questioned the parameters on which they are based. They have turned towards studies on the cycle of life and the process of aging, thus meeting theories emerging from other issues such as youth, the family, and social changes. This trend is more noticeable among researchers outside France — Baltes et al. (1980), Foner (1978), Hareven (1978), Neugarten (1968), Riley (1972), Rosenmayr (1979) to name but a few — than among French researchers who have only recently taken up this trend. But it is strongly emphasized in the report on gerontological research prepared for the National Conference of the Retired and the Elderly (Attias-Donfut & Guillemard, 1983).

Authors differ in their concept of generations, cohorts, age groups, which often results in radically different levels of analysis. By distinguishing two main approaches, a summary classification can be attempted. The first one is concerned with the historical process and with social change. The second one is concerned with social structure, age being at once the principle and the product of social structure. A third and more recent approach tries to link the social structure with individual and social changes.

1. Generations and History

At the beginning of the 20th century, the reflections on generations were a product of political and social change. They were mainly directed towards the study of changes which affected society as a whole, taking the question of generations as a special means of defining and understanding change.

Carl Shorske (1978) established a link between the cultural movement which took place in Vienna at the beginning of the 20th century and the emergence of "jungen" in Austria. The young identified with German nationalism, opposing the Liberals who were Austrian nationalists. The opposition between generations coincided with cultural and political opposition.

Lewis S. Feuer (1978) introduces the generation factor into the analysis of scientific movements. The biography of great inventors invariably reveals the revolutionary character of their feelings and shows that this type of impulse is linked to their belonging to a generation which is in revolt against the preceding one. This state of mind is conducive to the search for new facts and systems which challenge traditional concepts. Einstein was one of those young men searching for liberty, ideas, revolutions, which helps us understand why relativity was discovered by Einstein and not by Poincare who had at his disposal all the intellectual, social, and material means to do so (S. Moscovici, 1978).

Albert Thibaudet's history of French literature (1936) is not based on the concept of "the era" and "empires" which correspond to some analyses of literary thought which are explanatory, didactic, and organized. Instead, he opts for a concept "coinciding closely with unforseeable changes and life expectancy which allow reality and the product of human activity to be better adapted to the ordinary dimensions of human life; it is order by generation." In his history of French literature, Albert Thibaudet does not write of opposition between generations or literary revolutions, but of the link between generations and history, between the literary expression of certain individuals and historical and cultural events, and literary milieu. Literary history is constructed through men socially belonging to a given period, having a specific age, living in their own environment, and practicing their own literary genre. It is as much a literary history as a study of generations.

In all the stimulating studies on generations which date back to the beginning of the century, the historic dimension is predominant. Across the succession of generations it is the progress of civilization which is followed. However, the duration of individual lives is not included in these analyses, not even in the most well-known and most profound essay of the period: "The Problem of Generations" (Mannheim, 1972).

In his analysis of the formation of generations, of their succession, of the incessant transmission between them, Mannheim does not speak of advance in age, nor of the changes which occur in the course of life. He does, however, in writing about the constitution of a generation, underline the importance of first impressions, which are a result of the influence of the environment during childhood and adolescence.

L. Rosenmayr (1976) criticized the fact that Mannheim limited the possibilities of environmental influences to the first phase of an individual's existence. He questions this theory by stating that the process of development and cultural change continues through subsequent phases of life. The dominant theory of Mannheim's time was not conducive to the idea that profound changes could take place beyond adolescence.

Rosenmayr's criticism is, in our view, relevant: everything experienced throughout the course of existence can contribute to build up one's "view of the world," according to Mannheim's terms. The process of adapting is continuous. Systems of thought are in a constant state of revision and reconstruction. Past and present serve constantly as mutual references and, as such, modify one another. There are, of course, periods of greater receptiveness, just as there are experiences of greater importance which leave deep impressions, such as war. In Mannheim's work, what is worth noting is that "Experiences are not accumulated in the course of lifetime through a process of summation or agglomeration but are 'dialectically' articulated ..." (1972, 298). This idea opens the way for research which allows historic and social experiences to be better integrated into the course of existence.

2. Generations and Social Structure

This second approach is the more widely developed. Anthropologists were the first to concentrate on the social divisions of age (Balandier, 1974; Eisenstadt, 1956; Lowie, 1964; Mead, 1970). Their work made possible comparative studies which emphasize the social variation of age. In this way it was established that stages of life such as childhood, adolescence, and middle age are a result of social organization, which can also be observed in primate societies (Rosenmayr, 1983a).

Georges Balandier (1974) states that the separation of generations (father/son, older/younger confrontations) is one of the first characteristics of the social order which clearly associates facts of nature and facts of culture, just as in the relationship between the sexes; age and sex being the basis of dominance. Various studies on organization by age have been carried out in Africa, because of the originality of association by age which is prevalent there (Paulme, 1971; Thomas, 1983). Modern society, in contrast, does not provide such clear-cut divisions. Some contemporary researchers are even doubtful of the relevance of age in the structure of complex societies (Balandier, 1974; Neugarten, 1979c). Studies on the cycle of life still stick implicitly or explicitly to the model of social structure described by the anthropologists.

As a result, the temporal perspective has paradoxically been relegated to second place in studies on social aging which attempt to reintroduce old age into the life course defined as the succession of socially limited stages.

On the contrary, dynamic psychology has been centered on the very mechanisms of the development of the individual. The emphasis was put on the changes in the early stages of life (Erikson, 1966) and on the changes throughout all the phases of life (Birren & Schaie, 1972; L'Ecuyer, 1978) without, however, making the link between individual and social history.

Sociological and psychosociological studies carried out on life cycles presented in terms of social behavior, of roles and status particular to a given phase of life have their starting point in an investigation of social behavior, which is specific to one age compared to another, as enforced by the structure of each society. However, it is necessary to distinguish two aspects in the temporal perspective: on the one hand, the unity of existence (i.e., the determination of successive stages), on the other hand, the anchoring of individual histories in social history.

The first aspect has been given more attention than the second. For instance, Lowenthal's (1975) life cycle research analyzes the relationship between different stages.

There is another investigation which does not deal with the specificity of groups of individuals who make up the elderly population, but with their specification, that is to say, with the social mechanisms which give rise to this specificity. The creation of new categories such as "Le 3ème Age" (Lenoir, 1979) or "Les pré-retraités" (Gaullier, 1982) refers to elements of social and economic policy.

Whether they be extended in space to comparative analysis (ethnography) or in time (history of old age, history of youth) centered on populations or on social processes, on micro or macro social level, all these studies share a common element: they all consider age and social divisions by age from the point of view of structural analysis.

Temporal processes, as such, are seldom taken into account. Consequently, this type of approach does not then allow the understanding of historic determination of behavior and values. Nor does it contribute to the understanding of the existential relationship the individual holds with his own culture, his achievements, and his history.

Individual social history is often treated and is even considered, in some studies, as a disturbing element in the observation of the processes of advancing age.

Essentially research geared towards the effects particular to age have disclosed three factors governing these effects: the time of birth which determines the cohort, age, and the period under observation. The researchers conclude that it is necessary to dissociate the three by different complex methods of observation, formulating hypotheses which isolate the effect of each factor (Baltes, 1968; Buss, 1973; Riley et al., 1972; Schaie, 1965). Until now, it has not been possible to validate these hypotheses, as it has been impossible to isolate the three factors. An approach which does not attempt to isolate the three factors, but on the contrary, tries to analyze how they are tied up together, seems more realistic and more productive.

Any life-span consists of different experiences and of events unique to the individual which cannot be generalized. What can be generalized is the analysis of the processes by which the temporal linkage between an individual and the history he lives determines his particular evolution.

The course of existence, with its successive ages of life cannot be abstracted from the actual duration which is anchored in social history and membership of the cohort. It seems futile to attempt to identify aging as an intrinsic phenomenon, since it is the product of the continuous interaction between individual and social factors.

3. Approach by the History of Life

The third approach, whose objective is to study life history, is even more susceptible to the introduction of the temporal dimension in the cycle of life. Biographical methods, which were used to a great extent in early sociological studies, then abandoned after the Second World War in favor of quantitative methods are at the present time becoming popular again (Bertaux, 1980; 1981).

These methods which were utilized to "read a society through its biography," to revalue the relationship between sociology and history are part of a fundamental epistemological investigation in the social sciences (Balandier, 1983). They are not specific to the field of aging and the elderly, but researchers in biography often carry out their research by interviewing the elderly who can provide more extensive data (Bertaux-Wiame, 1981; Lalive D'Epinay, 1981).

In addition, if the synthesized data of histories of life rather than analytical data of formalized sociology are taken into consideration, then it becomes necessary to reintroduce the temporal sequence into social analysis (Ferrarotti, 1983). Whence the resurge in interest for the courses of life, aging, and old age.

But if biographical research is the bearer of the future, its actual stage of development indicates that caution is necessary: epistemological obstacles still have to be overcome. The use of retrospective interviews and oral histories is full of dangers; subjectivity, studies of cases with limited scope or of an illustrative nature ...

The unreliable nature of memory in reminiscences of the past has been underlined by Elder (1981) who avoids this difficulty by using longitudinal methods of study in his research which has become a classic "Children of the Great Depression" (Elder, 1974). He brings the historic dimension into the study of the cycle of life by looking for the differential influence of the crisis of 1929 on the lives of families, according to the way in which they were economically affected by the crisis. His main question is centered on the influence of social change on life cycle changes but he also looks for their effect on mentality and the relationship between social structure and personality. These latter points are of particular interest. For the marks of time on the course of life indisputably affect social position, status, family, the accumulation of social and cultural resources, as well as an area which has not yet been studied to a great extent, that of personality structure, mentality, and cognitive structures. It is probably at the cognitive and emotional levels that an individual is most deeply marked by historical time, filtered by the consciousness he acquires of its historicity.

It is in these paths of research that a better understanding can be gained, among other things, of everything involving participation in a culture, which brings values and interest into the picture (Dumazedier, 1974), cultural and intellectual products which come from the world of thinking. The specificity of successive generations can be deepened in this way, as a result of the interaction of social structure and history.

As a result of this brief overview it is possible to clarify the use of the terms generations, cohorts, stages of life.

What is involved is not so much a definition of the concepts but the distinguishing of the phenomena which can be observed according to the point of view taken and the level of the social reality under study. This is the more necessary since we deal here with a topic which involves the extremely difficult notion of time.

Distinguished here are three principle levels in interaction, from the micro to the macro-social level[1].

1. *Cohort* refers to both the time of birth (chronological age) and the duration of the social history lived. It is a complex concept which is related to forms of interaction (action and retroaction) between the individual system and the social system by which individuals and social groups are autoproduced throughout time.

The cohort is always situated in a unique way in space and in time and is indicative of the impossibility of dissociating aging and individual history. Individual history offers, in this perspective, a particular version of certain aspects of social history reinterpreted individually.

2. *The stages of life* making up the life cycle are limited and regulated by society through specific institutions (school, work, retirement, associations, social services ...) as well as by systems of roles and expectations which orient the behavior of corresponding age groups varying according to class position.

Patterns of life cycles signify the regulation of social relationships by function of age, and vary according to social class. The cycle of life constitutes the formal framework of the course of existence, but it relies more on social structure than on historic and social change.

3. *Generations*: Without entering into a debate on the definition of terms (Marshall, 1983), we will assume here that generation is related to the macro-social level. According to Mannheim's definition, generation is interpreted from the point of view of social change. It may or may not be identified through its manifestations in the different fields of social, artistic, cultural, scientific, or political life.

Generations depart from the cohort by a shift in the level of analysis from the micro to the macro-social. They are, in fact, identified by their visible facets from the societal angle. This can be a political or cultural event such as May '68 in France (we refer frequently to the "generation of 68" or the "68ers"). Or it can be a demographic phenomenon which affects the structure and the economy of society: the baby boom or a drop in the birth rate. Generation provides a form of social identity, contrary to the membership of a cohort which does not always imply similarity between members, nor their social recognition in collective facts. Belonging to a generation means, on the contrary, that the individual recognizes himself in that by which the generation is defined.

This recognition applies, of course, only to a part of each generation. According to Mannheim's theories, which this definition refers to, generations do not necessarily attain social identification; intervals between generations are variable and depend on the context of social change.

Largely, the main element in identifying a generation is in the "entelechy" as referred to by Mannheim, quoting Pinder, that is to say the element by which it attains social visibility and participates as a generation to produce the history of which it is a product.

Cultural Trends Within the Elderly Population in France

Having dealt with the levels of analysis, it is now possible to speak of the evolution of cultural trends within the elderly population in France, by specifying the perspectives which are being adopted here. The analysis presented takes a structural approach: a definition of the social framework of the behavior of old people and an understanding of how it is produced by the social system is attempted here. The significance which can be attributed to the associative trends of the retired will be discussed within this framework. But this approach does not take into account the cultural content nor the meaning of what can be observed in terms of behavior. Interests, values, and ideas can only be understood and interpreted in a dialectic articulation between the social context and the individual, between the past, the present, and the future, that is to say, in the cohort and generation perspective[2].

Old Age as a Life Stage

Old age as a life stage has been produced mainly by the evolution of the world of labor on the one hand and the evolution of social welfare systems in industrialized societies on the other. Old age has been connected with institutionalization in various ways. This evolution, however, has produced contradictory forces which are expressed in the social relationships of the aged and in practices mainly oriented towards the area of leisure.

Let us begin with a brief reminder of the main changes in aging during these last two decades in France:

1. We observe changes in the definition of old age. Both the demographic and the social evolution have contributed to increase the so-called aged population which is defined by their working life coming to an end. Unemployment and reduction of work time have resulted in the progressive lowering of retirement age. The rate of professional activity has been reduced even in the period preceding retirement.

Workers aged between 50 and 60 have great difficulty either in finding new employment or in receiving professional training, but opportunities are available for them to stop working before retirement age and still receive payment. They are no longer workers and are still not yet retired in the full sense. The situation is an effect of the economic crisis and of the way in which our policymakers try to solve it. On the other hand, we observe an increase in the absolute and relative number of the very old due to the improvement of living standards and of the health of the aged. Thus the age span for the "non-active" group (the retired and the aged) has been enlarged from both directions, with earlier retirement and longer life expectancy. As a consequence of this we find more and more heterogeneous age groups among old people.

2. The standard of living and way of life of the retired have been greatly improved. Up to the 1960s the aged in France were characterized by extreme poverty. But this has been changed drastically. Insufficient income, though still prevalent, due to heavy social inequalities, is no longer the most pressing problem, as the minimum living standard is now insured by the social security system.

Social inequalities among the aged are deeper than those which are observed among active adults. We found a larger income scale among the retired than among the over 50 still at work (Attias-Donfut & Gognalons-Nicolet, 1980). An explanation has to be found not only in the effects of their social professional status but also in the effects of the social welfare system. Particularly in France, the great complexity of pension systems, developed directly by labor unions, are in them-

165

selves unequal. Thus the respective position for the different social categories are redistributed after retirement. Adverse effects which deepen the inequalities are a particular result of this. The balance sheet, comparing on the one hand the contributions paid into the pension system by different socio-professional categories and on the other hand respective allowances, shows that the poorest are paying for the richest. But these effects are partially corrected by supplementary benefits given to the lowest pension categories (Attias-Donfut, 1983). Subsequently the image of aging has been profoundly changed. The image of active old people has replaced that of poor old people. The term "3ème Age" which was popular during the 1970s is now being abandoned due to its segregational and ideological connotations (Guillemard, 1980).

Aging is a new professional field (Lenoir, 1978). Institutionalization in connection to aging is spreading. On the one hand, centralized public and private organizations which manage pensions and social welfare and on the other hand, facilities, services, and special housing are run by an increasing number of professionals. For example, during the last 15 years in France, 60,000 home helper posts have been created.

The aged are becoming a special category of client for health professionals, for social workers, for recreational organizers, and also for the market as consumers. The emergence of a number of professionals specialized in aging contributes to the production of the aged as a new social category.

Wishing to protect their own field and to make it more valuable, professionals are contributing on the one hand to promote the improvement of social policy for the aged, and on the other hand, to increase the specificity of the aged as a social category in its own right.

They are setting in motion various contradictory images of the aged of today; for example, they contribute to the medicalization of the aging and to the medicalization of death reinforcing the image of dependency for the very old.

A recent study of the medicalization of old age homes shows that pressure for obtaining finances to pay medical staff in homes comes from the directors and not from the residents. This pressure is supported by an argument in which the very old are readily classified as ill or dependent. The rise in availability of medical staff results in a rise in request for assistance and brings with it an increased risk of dependence (Attias-Donfut & Rozenkier, 1983).

The image of dependency requiring increased help brings another kind of alienation to the aged and is improving the status of professionals in aging more than helping the aged themselves. It also increases the cost to society. A new market geared towards the elderly is also being developed as can be seen most clearly in the field of tourism and vacations. As the retired can travel at any time of the year they are offered many opportunities during the low season in order, of course, to increase the profit earning capacity of the tourist industry. In this way separation between the ages is accentuated in both leisure time and leisure space.

These different factors have contributed to the emergence of forms of sociability particular to the retired and elderly. The most evident of these can be seen in the new associative trends.

Associative Trends Among the Retired

We can observe new associative trends among the aged. In France there were 2,000 clubs for the aged in 1972 and now there are nearly 15,000; about a quarter of the aged regularly visit an old age club or an association. Sixty "third age universities" have been created in the last 10 years. Several kinds of associations and federations of associations have emerged.

One interpretation of these movements has been the manifestation of the natural tendency of the elderly "to interact with each other increasingly as they grow older and hence to develop a subculture" (Rose, 1965).

The validity of the foregoing hypothesis depends on the meaning given to "subculture." If it is understood in the restricted "elitist" sense of the term implying the existence of the original cultural creation of a group, then, without any shadow of doubt, there is no subculture of the old. If it is understood in a wider sense of everyday culture (Poujol & Labourie, 1979) expressed in social representation, models of relationships and behavior then it can be said that any community or institution is susceptible to set in motion elements which constitute more or less a subculture. In this respect, associations and communities of the old also develop their own models and representations.

But "subcultures" developed in this way are varied and also limited to the institutions which have produced them and are not relevant outside the institution. It is therefore risky to apply this idea to the elderly population in general and to generalize the phenomena which are particular to institutional life.

It therefore seems that the theoretical interest in the interpretation of the associative movement of the retired in terms of a subculture is of limited value. This interpretation can however fill an ideological function by bringing a theoretical justification to the process of institutionalization and professionalization of old age, consequently reinforcing these processes.

Also, rather than speaking of a subculture in this respect, it would be preferable to try to understand the dynamics of this movement in the social context which defines the elderly today.

The first results of an enquiry in progress[3] show a great diversity among clubs and associations. They are scarcely comparable to one another. But they all offer recreation more or less combined with cultural, educational, or social activities. Associative trends can be classified in three categories according to the criteria of the age and the social level of their members.

Firstly, clubs are attended generally by the oldest age group, women in a great majority, belonging to the lower classes. They are mainly oriented towards recreational activities with a low level of active social participation.

Secondly, the "Third Age Universities," attended by different ages and both sexes belonging to the middle and upper classes, offer leisure activities together with cultural activities.

Thirdly, a new trend consists of associations set up to defend the interests of the elderly. Some seem to emerge among the pre-retired population, some are attended by the retired. Some include a number of clubs and other associations. The new French government is giving funds to each geographical district ("département") to create committees of associations for the aged, to be consulted in the

167

gerontological plans for each respective district. Associative trends, beginning as a spontaneous regrouping of the elderly are encouraged by public policy. The birth of this movement preceded policy measures. The model used by planners was based on various local initiatives which were then given a wider range, thus contributing to a new development.

Its social roots can be looked for in the social position of the retired in society today. Clubs for the elderly are, in effect, the emanation of an age group and represent a coming-together based on the affinity of age.

The generalization of retirement on the criterion of age at all social levels brings with it, within the older generation, the sharing of a kind of exclusion from economic, social, and cultural power. Distance from the sphere of production brought about through retirement and the new position in the family, brought about through age, compete to distend the links the individual has with the poles of social life.

The old and the retired are located in a "zone of incertitude" beyond established frameworks. The cohorts of the retired will become progressively more conscious of this "social void" and will work out a specific way of dealing with the situation they are experiencing. As far as the social body is concerned, it will do its best to integrate them, as much through institutions already in existence as through the setting up of institutions for that specific purpose.

The associative movement of the retired is located at the meeting point of two forces. On the one hand, that which underlies this new social layer in its attempt to define and re-appropriate itself, by function of a specificity and a system of values which would be particular to it. On the other hand, that of society attempting to control this new layer and to integrate it without however attempting a fundamental modification of its way of functioning.

The retired progressively perceive and express their needs and demands. This may conflict with the reply the social system is likely to give to these demands especially because of the dominant values and relationships between the forces which make up the social system. The associative movement of the elderly will not be exempt from ambiguity, as it is simultaneously the expression of an identity which offers an alternative project to the present social structure and an instrument of social cohesion whose objective is to maintain this very structure (Attias-Donfut & Rozenkier, 1979). This dual dimension — structure of social experiment and/or social reproduction — is found elsewhere in the different forms of the associative movement.

But associative trends among the retired cannot be looked upon as social movements, according to the definition of Touraine (1973), which would imply some kind of active contestation. One exception could be made perhaps regarding the forthcoming unionist movement among the retired. But we do not yet have the materialization of that contestation.

Are associations able to really offer channels of expression for the aged? Do they make it easier for the elderly to participate in the management of their own concerns which could go as far as cooperation in the policy of aging? In this case associations would participate in the institutionalization of aging by giving individuals the chance to become active, together with professionals and with administrators, in shaping up policy for the elderly. Associative trends do not seem to represent social movements oriented towards collective action, but rather they seem to represent the beginning of a more stable form of social organization regulating the period of retirement.

The analyses and hypotheses which have just been proposed have tried to connect certain trends observed among the elderly to the social context which has produced them.

The reflections on the different levels of analysis presented in the first part of this paper have been geared to a clarification of the perspective taken (that of the social structure which produces the stages of life) and to a description of its scope and its limitations, compared to other main perspectives.

It is appropriate to conclude by underlining the necessity of proceeding with this analysis in greater depth through the perspective of cohorts and generations, by which the structural and the temporal dimensions are linked together.

Footnotes

1   The psychophysiological process at the individual level has scarcely been touched upon in this paper. It is only referred to here as a reminder.
2   This analysis is presently being carried out from data obtained in the framework of a longitudinal study of the transition to retirement which we are working on in collaboration with the French National Foundation of Gerontology.
3   This enquiry is conducted among a sample of 4,000 old age associations and clubs by Attias-Donfut & Rozenkier.

The Issues of Age Conflict in Political Life

Anne Foner

It is more than a decade since youth protests reached their peak in the United States and several Western European countries. Although the potential for age conflicts is inherent in the structure and dynamics of age stratification systems, youthful upheavals like those of the 1960s and early 1970s have emerged only from time to time. And like the student protests of the 1960s and 1970s, they are generally short lived. In considering why militant, open age conflicts break out only sporadically, in the face of the great potential for such conflict, I suggested in an earlier paper (Foner, 1974) that counterbalancing the forces producing age conflicts are powerful conflict reducing mechanisms that mute or avert sharp age struggles. However, I argued that these mechanisms are not equally effective in all situations. Much depends on the issues dominating public discourse. The conflict reducing mechanisms are less effective when ideal issues, such as those concerning war and peace, justice, and the rights of all people, divide the public along age lines than when material issues, those concerning how the economic benefits of a society are distributed, emerge.

In the light of a decade's developments, how does this thesis hold up? It is a particularly propitious time to reexamine this hypothesis for, unlike the period in which it was first put forward, serious economic problems confront the world today and the prime issues in political life in many countries are now material issues. The situation in the United States provides a test case because some of the material issues before the public are clearly age-related.

In "revisiting" the theme of the earlier paper, I shall first review briefly the general argument put forward a decade ago and then consider both the potential for age conflict and the effectiveness of conflict reducing mechanisms around an age-related material issue confronting the United States in the early 1980s.

The Potential for Age Conflicts in Political Life

In all societies there is a potential for age conflicts because of age inequalities. That is, there is a potential conflict of interest between the "have-nots" who want a greater share of the material benefits, power, and prestige in the society and the "haves" who want to protect their advantages. In rapidly changing societies clashes among age strata are likely to emerge also because of the dynamic processes related to age. On the one hand, given a changing political climate, new cohorts are particularly sensitive to the political events at the time they enter political life and are likely to espouse new, sometimes radically new, ideas. On the other hand, older cohorts, whose life experiences have been different from those of the younger cohorts, while changing some of their views as they age in line with societal trends, are apt to resist sweeping changes in political orientations, or do not change sufficiently to bring their views in line with those of younger cohorts (see Glenn, 1980 for a recent review of studies on this point).

Age differences do not inevitably break out into sharp political clashes, however, for three reasons:

(1) The existence of age heterogeneous groups serves to strengthen bonds among people of different ages and provides opportunities for people of different ages to influence each other, thus blunting sharp age cleavages that might otherwise arise.

(2) The existence of multiple forms of social stratification means that other identities – class, sex, ethnic identities, for example – often take precedence over age identities and allegiance to age peers.

(3) The aging process operates to mute conflict in several ways. People tend to orient themselves to the next older age stratum, anticipating the roles they will soon fill and assimilating some of the attitudes considered appropriate for these future roles.

In addition, the inevitability of aging frequently takes the edge off resentment among the young about their inferior status. The young are willing to wait their turn for the social benefits of the society, *if* they believe that their current disadvantages are only temporary and that they will get their share not too far into the future.

Taking off from Weber's (Gerth & Mills, 1946) remarks about shifts in the significance of class and status concerns in public life, I argued that age-related conflict reducing mechanisms are relatively ineffective when ideal issues are to the fore. Many ideal issues such as moral issues and issues of style that do divide age strata are so general that the issues crop up and divide age strata in institutions throughout the society. Thus membership in age heterogeneous groups does not operate to mute age conflicts. Where the issues concern war and peace, anticipatory socialization for future roles, especially among the young, takes second place to concern about whether they will have a future at all and what the shape of their future will be. Indeed, there is a sense of urgency that such issues be resolved immediately. In addition, since many ideal issues do not involve the welfare of one age stratum alone, hope for future improvement for themselves is not likely to dampen the propensity of the younger age strata to openly challenge existing arrangements. They are fighting for the rights of all people. Finally, when the young push for changes, their relative powerlessness, on the one hand, and the open resistance of older age strata to change, on the other, heighten age conflicts.

In contrast, I proposed that conflict reducing mechanisms are more effective when material issues are at the center of political life, primarily because these issues activate class interests which take priority over age-based interests. Further, material issues, unlike many ideal issues that require all or nothing solutions, lend themselves to quid pro quo arrangements among age strata.

So much for the broad outlines of the argument, which appear to be consistent with the events during the youth revolts of the 1960s and 1970s when struggles over ideal issues dominated the political scene in many countries. Let us turn now to the current situation in the United States where key issues before the public concern the economy.

171

Age Conflicts and Material Issues

Many economic issues like those involving inflation and unemployment are not directly age-related. In the past at least, they have been of equal concern to all age strata and have not produced clear divisions by age on how the issues should be resolved. However, one issue that has been prominent in public life in the United States in the early 1980s does appear to be age-related: the question of economic support of the elderly. To an outside observer there appear to be conflicting objective interests of the several age strata in the way this problem is solved. Indeed, a repeated theme in the media has been that a war between young and old threatens to erupt over this question. Yet, so far at least, sharp age conflicts have not emerged. Exploring why this is so helps to specify just how conflict reducing mechanisms operate.

The Dilemma of Social Security in the United States

In the United States the question of support for older people centers on financing the Social Security System and its pension program. First, then, a few words about the dilemma of the United States Social Security program and then I shall go on to discuss the factors I think have deflected conflict between younger and older adults over the issue.

The Social Security program is the largest segment in the United States social welfare system and it is financed on a pay-as-you-go basis. That is, taxes from workers who are currently employed and their employers finance the current benefits of retirees and their dependents. Unlike several European countries, the old age pension program does not receive contributions from general revenues. The financial squeeze the system faces now is due in large part to a long period of inflation and to rising unemployment over a period of years. Since benefits are indexed to inflation, benefit levels have been rising. At the same time, contributions to the Social Security Fund have, been curtailed because of the increasing numbers of unemployed who, with their former employers, no longer contribute to the fund.

At the time this paper was written, legislation was soon to be enacted that would shore up the system — at least for the short term. Here it is of interest to analyze the types of solutions that were being considered and their likely effect on the various age strata. Most proposals for the immediate solution to the financial squeeze that were considered would result either in an added burden on the working-age population through higher payroll taxes *or* a reduction in the benefits of the older, retired population. Such a reduction could be accomplished in several ways: taxation of benefits or part of benefits, delayed retirement, or changes in the way benefit levels are calculated. We might expect, then, that there would have been outcries from people of working age against higher taxes and, on their part, protests from the retired population against direct or indirect reductions in benefits.

Organizations representing the old did lobby against most proposals that would lower benefit levels in some way; but a militant movement aiming to mobilize the old around this issue did not materialize. Such a movement seems unlikely to develop in the near future now that at least the short term problems of financing the

Social Security System appear to have been resolved. Perhaps more surprising is that not only did a concomitant movement among the working-age population not arise, but that the working-age population appears to have been willing to bear an extra tax burden to guarantee the solvency of the system. A mid-1981 survey is but one example of this reaction among people under age 65. Fifty-one percent of those 18–24, 45 percent among those 25–39, 48 percent among those 40–54, and 54 percent among those 55–64 said they supported raising Social Security taxes if this were necessary to provide an adequate income for older people (Harris, 1981). Even higher proportions of the under 65 adults said they were opposed to reducing benefits; and a solid majority opposed raising the retirement age. These reactions are especially noteworthy since this survey and earlier surveys indicate that about three-fourths of the respondents understand that the Social Security taxes they pay today are "used to pay Social Security benefits for retired people today" rather than being "set aside for their own future retirement" (Harris, 1979, 93; Harris, 1981, 118). The correct response was highest (more than 80 percent) among those still in the labor force and who were still paying into the system.

Factors Promoting Consensus Among Age Strata on Social Security

That the older, retired population supports measures that will guarantee adequate pensions is to be expected. What has to be explained is why younger adults also support such measures and why old people were not up in arms over the issue.

Membership in age-heterogeneous groups. One important reason for the willingness of people under 65 to support a public program for the old is that the alternative for many would be private support for the old in their own families. This would constitute an economic as well as social burden for many middle-aged adults – and some would simply not be able to manage. In addition, the Social Security program has enabled older people to maintain independent living quarters, an independence both the old and their offspring value. Not only the old, then, but the middle aged support policies that help free the middle aged from the social and economic burden of taking care of the old.

In working organizations too, people of working age stand to gain from continued public support of old age pensions. Much research in the United States has shown that people's willingness to retire is affected by their income prospects (Foner & Schwab, 1981). Thus, as long as Social Security provides a solid base of income for retirees, the incentive to retire early or at least not to remain working after age 65 is maintained. And this means job openings and promotion opportunities for workers under 65 or, in a period of unemployment, holding on to a job.

The more general point here is that membership in age-heterogeneous groups like the family and work organizations has meant that people of working age derive indirect benefits from a program designed for the old.

The inevitability of aging. Another factor undergirding widespread support for Social Security is related to the aging process. By shoring up the system, younger and middle-aged adults hope to guarantee that they will have the same benefits the old now have when they themselves get old. The point here is that the inevitability of aging provides people of working age with a stake in keeping the system healthy.

The age strata involved. A third aspect of this issue is that the age strata most deeply affected by the problems of Social Security financing are the ones especially likely to be subject to conflict reducing mechanisms. Sharp, open age conflicts in the advanced societies (and even in less complex, undifferentiated societies) are typically initiated by youth. The young, as many have suggested, are particularly likely to be open to new political views. In addition, they are relatively disadvantaged economically and kept in dependent, subordinate status. Not being well integrated into the full range of roles in the society, they have less to lose by challenging the system and engaging in risky protests. Student youth, especially in the United States, are relatively insulated from the influences of older people. Many of them live and study in age-homogeneous environments where they can build solidarity with age peers and are relatively impervious to contacts with older people with opposing views.

But note that the age strata most likely to be involved in conflicts over financing Social Security are not the young, but the middle aged, on the one hand, and the old, on the other. I have already suggested that the middle aged have little motivation to oppose the old on this issue. Further, unlike student youth, they are not isolated from the influence of older strata. Independent living of older people has not meant that ties between the old and their middle-aged offspring have been cut off (Bengtson, 1983). Rather, according to Hess & Waring (1978), the character of intergenerational relations has changed — these relations are on a voluntary rather than on an obligatory basis which was often characteristic of the past. These intergenerational contacts strengthen the middle-aged people's awareness of and sympathy to the needs of the old. And their bonds to the old that have been built up over many years help curb any inclination the middle aged might have to participate in political activity that could hurt the old.

What about the old themselves? Why has a militant movement among the old not emerged around this issue? In part, because significant cuts in benefits among the currently retired have been forestalled so far through conventional political processes — primarily lobbying by organizations of and for the old[1]. These lobbying efforts have been successful — in part at least — because legislators are aware that the old constitute a formidable voting bloc united around this issue. Let me again note the contrast with conditions which triggered the youth revolts. I have spoken of value differences betweeen the young and older strata. I did not sufficiently emphasize age inequalities and the relative powerlessness of youth. Young people resorted to demonstrations and other nonconventional political actions because they did not have access to established political mechanisms and because older people in power resisted demands for change. Some of the violent actions among youth were precipitated by the repressive (and sometimes violent) exercise of power by state and university authorities. In contrast, as a group, the old in the United States are not so powerless. They now have well established organizations with access to the means of power. And they have allies in younger strata.

Conflict or cooperation among age strata? Still another point concerns the character of interstrata relations. Following Marx's conception of class consciousness, we tend to think of within-stratum consciousness and solidarity as linked to recognition of the opposing interests of other strata and eventual conflict between these strata. The emergence of an organized movement within age strata need not, however, lead to such conflict. Solidarity and organization within a stratum can be directed either to cooperation or conflict with other strata. The Townsend Movement of the 1930s, a militant movement of old people in the United States, organized to push for the establishment of a pension program for the old, is a case in point. The essence, if not the specifics of its program, was backed by groups of the non-aged. In the early 1980s the line-up of organized groups in the United States supporting policies that would raise revenues to pay for Social Security rather than reduce benefits included not only the major organizations representing the old, but labor unions and religious and social organizations. A coalition of groups representing people of all ages was thus formed to "Save Our Security," as their slogan stated.

Social Security financing as a class issue. My last point concerns cross-cutting class interests. The supposed crisis over Social Security brought to light emergent class differences over future policies. For example, opposing the coalition organized to buttress the Social Security System were such groups as the National Association of Manufacturers and the Chamber of Commerce of the United States — representing business interests wishing to restrain the growth of the pension system. Another straw in the wind is suggested by survey data which show that the higher the person's income, the less likely he or she was to support raising Social Security taxes as a means of financing pensions (Harris, 1981). Thus the issue, like other material issues, appears to have developed more as a class-based than as an age-based issue.

To sum up, conflict reducing mechanisms have been effective in minimizing age conflicts over what would seem to be opposing material interests of the old and those under 65 in the United States. These mechanisms have weakened the motivation of the middle aged and younger adult strata to oppose policies supported by the old, even if this would be at some immediate financial cost to themselves. And the issues have activated class interests which cut across the age strata. The particular issue and the operation of these conflict reducing mechanisms are almost a text-book case. However, it is just one case. Old age pension systems in many countries are facing financial strains; and there are potential conflicts between age strata over jobs (Kohli, 1982). Moreover, perhaps dissatisfactions over material issues will find expression in non-political conflicts, as in youth subcultures which challenge established values (see Hebdige, 1983 in this contribution). Clearly what are needed are studies of other issues, in different societies, involving different strata to test the cogency of the general hypothesis examined here.

Footnote

1 The "solution" to the financial problems of the Social Security System embodied in the 1983 legislation entails relatively little additional cost to the currently retired — taxation of part of the benefits of retirees who have relatively high incomes and some changes in timing of benefit increases. Other parts of the program entail an increase in payroll taxes of workers and their employers and raising the age of eligibility for full retirement benefits for people who will retire in the first part of the next century. That a compromise could be worked out in which all age strata gave up something is an example of how material issues are subject to *quid pro quo* arrangements.

The Alternative Movement

Walter Hollstein

Development and Assessment

My subject is the development and evaluation of alternative lifestyles from the *fifties* onwards. In relation to the topic of this book it means: in what way does the alternative movement represent a new consciousness of generations and which new ideas, lifestyles, and values are incorporated in the alternative movement in opposition to the older generation.

My material is based on 16 years of occupation with those marginal groups and also on practical experience in manifold projects of the alternative movement.

Youth Protest and Conformity

The reality of the "alternative movement" entered the German speaking area only a few years ago and gained political relevance even later. Particularly in the United States and Great Britain, but also in Holland, Sweden, Denmark, and France the term has represented the cultural and political reality of "wanting to live differently" from the fifties onwards.

The representatives of this new movement have been and are to a large extent young. Although the percentage of young people in the alternative movement — according to evidence and research — has decreased, it still averages 55 percent.

Within the social context the relativity of that alternative movement becomes evident. All empirical studies available prove that within the German speaking area youth protest represents a minority attitude compared to conformity. Only 10 percent of the young people are representatives or sympathizers of alternative lifestyles.

The Binding Element

Groups as different as Beats and Beatniks, Gammler, Capelloni, Provos, Hippies, Diggers, Yippies, Kabouters up to the alternative projects of today and — in a more limited sense — the student movement, women's groups, community projects, and ecological groups are theoretically united in the term "alternative movement." In reality, they are connected under the historic aim of criticism of our time and the wish for something better. There is a threefold line which has linked all these groups from the fifties to the eighties:

1. The refusal of the given situation: All groups criticize a loss of sense in our

176

society. The balance which makes human life bearable is missing in the relationship between man and nature, society and technology, individual and collective, body and soul, social roles and self-fulfillment, competition and pleasure, man and woman, age and youth.

Individual and society exist to a large extent in extremes as can be exemplified by the macabre context of affluence in the first world and starvation in the third world and in extreme situations as, for example, the apocalyptic potentiality of mankind being able to extinguish itself by nuclear warfare.

2. New values and ways of behavior: All groups emphasize the ideological crisis and the decay of values. The aims in life publically appraised such as property, consumption, money, and status cannot motivate people into achievement any longer. The one-sided emphasis of such material values have left man hollow. Hungry for money, man is said to have lost his faculty for happiness, peace, harmony, and autonomy. From its very start, the alternative movement has been concerned with the revaluation of our value system.

3. Establishing new lifestyles: The development of the alternative movement has always been accompanied by the attempt of establishing communal housing, workshops, and places of production and to create communal leisure time activities and consciousness raising activities.

The aim has always been to create a frame materially and institutionally independent of the official society and thus free of social pressures and dangers of reintegration. In this counterculture a unity of life and work is attempted which has been for many decades so painfully torn apart in the official society.

A Phase Model of the Alternative Movement

A look back in history shows a phasic pattern in the wide area of alternative movements, which recurs with a recognizable regularity: the people who think and feel differently than officially prescribed norms, behavior patterns, and ideals, form a group through discussion and discourse. The group's first coherence arises from the common rejection of the reigning socio-cultural conditions; indignation, annoyance, anger, disgust, irritation, hate, and repulsion are the initial basis of solidarity among members of the group.

These feelings are accompanied by retreat from official society. After the period of criticism of traditional norms, carried out, or at least, felt, a second phase begins in which the dominating factor is the effort to radically break away from the society whose corruptness has been unveiled. The members of the group retreat from their material and normative obligations to the official world, and found a countermilieu. This countermilieu consists, in the beginning, of a loosely woven network of relationships, meeting places, and apartments. Furthermore, in the retreat phase, the emotion-charged criticism of the status quo is replaced by a more and more systematized confrontation with official society; a theoretical relational system develops upon which group members can found their rejection of existing social structures as well as their own new perspectives. This process of reflection has a twofold effect: by the invigoration of its individual and collective ideals, desires, plans, and utopias taking concrete form, the group secures itself internally and externally.

This reflective introspection, with the effects mentioned, already sets tendencies in motion toward the third phase, the return from self-imposed exile. Those leading alternative lives, have been strengthened, individually and in the workings of groups, by the period of reflection; they have reached a level of autonomy and self-assurance which makes it possible for them to approach existing conditions relatively in control.

Furthermore, their analysis of the socio-cultural status quo has enabled the group members to clearly identify and knowingly accept their social position as outsiders. Thus, the period of reflection has clarified a further aspect of the relationship of the members of the group to established society: it is now clear that an institutional and a personal psychological stabilization of the alternative lifestyle can only be possible if the lasting restraints and oppressions, pressures, power, and decisive structures of general society are changed. This offensive attitude comes from the historically correct understanding that opposition in the form of an island or a sect cannot survive over a longer period in conditions inimical to it, but rather, that it becomes successively absorbed and emptied of its contents.

Social commitment on the part of the group members follows this recognition. In this fourth phase, ways of communicating the group's criticism and its example of a new lifestyle to wider circles are conceived and carried out. The group opens up in order to demonstrate its aims and to make an impact on the outside with its discussion of those aims.

This development has consequences, in several respects. Aside from bringing the group "out of the ghetto" and causing it to have to deal with the general population, the group members' opening-up process confronts the reigning social system. The efforts of the alternatives to cause socio-cultural change encounter the resistance of established interests; conflicts between forces stubbornly hanging-on and of reform necessarily arise. Therefore, the group's one-dimensional concentration on spreading its new way of life among other interested groups of people is no longer enough, and it also has to give itself to the parallel effort against the holders of power, on the levels of public relations work, political fighting, wooing sympathizers, finding material support, and often in court. This fifth phase determines the decided politicalization of the group.

The fight with the various powers of the system, which the group has now taken on, but rarely wanted, leads it to a sixth phase of consolidation. Next to the effect of solidarization, which the growing pressure from outside has on the group, it is now also forced to secure and defend its material basis. The group must build the infrastructure of its way of life − all the more in situations where the powers do not stop at measures like open repression, persecution, and "Berufsverbot."

Under the constantly rising pressure from outside, the group has to look for greater security: legally (e.g., in structures of society), financially (through credit), politically (by making alliances), and professionally (taking jobs). Should this often most difficult step in the development of alternative movements succeed, the group is conceptually and materially secure.

In a seventh phase, this course is usually combined with the radicalization of the group members; the opposition to the existing system becomes even more relentless.

This is also to be noticed, socio-historically, in the development of the alternative movement; *as a whole* the consolidation of individual groups and projects in the late sixties was a deciding factor that in the seventies, women's, men's, ecological, regional, grass-roots, peace, and citizens' groups were able to voice their *particular* concerns.

Shortening the above, we can distinguish five phases in the history of the alternative movement:
1. Rejection
2. Return
3. Politicalization
4. Consolidation
5. Diversification

We can assign the following movements to the above phases as follows:
to 1: the American Beats and Beatniks, the German Gammler, the Italian Capelloni;
to 2: the Dutch Provos, the Hippies;
to 3: the student movement, the Yippies in the U.S., and the Kabouters in Holland;
to 4: the Diggers in the U.S. and England, the Underground;
to 5: the grass-roots movements, the alternative projects, the autonomous movements (e.g., squatters).

The New Characteristics of the Alternative Movement

In contrast to the progressive protest and opposition movements of earlier times, the continuing search for alternative lifestyles since the Beat Generation form a *caesura*, in that it can claim completely new characteristics of structure and being.

Let us summarize the most important here:
1. The movement's starting point is not some defined theory, as is the case with the socialists and communists, but also with anarchists and in the violence groups (RAF; the 2nd of June movement; the Red Brigade). The concrete life experiences, feelings, and desires of the alternative movement are much closer to it than any abstract theoretical structure. Its point of departure is vital, existential protest.
2. As opposed to earlier progressive social movements, the alternative groups also do not concentrate on the exact working out of a theory of revolution, or even on the description of those social forms and human relationships which should come into being after existing conditions have been changed. Actual practice is more important to them than beautiful ideals. Jerry Rubin explained: "Here and now, when we act, we must bring about the signs of that world towards which we are working: beauty, love, and openness."

Instead of distributing pamphlets or trying to win support for their aims and ideas with clever papers as the student movement did, the alternative groups prefer to advertise themselves with tangible practice. The visible, livable example of healthy eating, competitive working conditions done away with, solidarity in togetherness, equal pay and equal distribution, sensible provisions for energy and the like, seem more convincing to them than any intellectual speeches or papers. Thus, even outsiders to the groups could find out, experimentally, what an alternative lifestyle means, and lose their fears of the unknown experiment in the face of the concrete example.

3. Resistance to the existing social system is not supposed to take place in the traditional parties and the established political organizations anymore. It is supposed to be restructured. The alternative groups have developed an arsenal of possibilities and strategies for bringing politics out of the hardened organizations and into the street, and making politics every citizen's affair.

4. In their social and organizational criticism, the alternative groups object not only to capitalism, but just as much to socialism. The "Eisbrecher," the Zurich movement's paper, notes in a good example: "Capitalism and socialism are destined for downfall. Both follow a purely material aim, and degrade the individual to a creature of work and consumption. Both are governed by a small circle of influential men; whether by way of capital, which amasses more and more in the hands of a few, or by way of the Politbureau, which only consists of a narrow circle of the powerful." Since their beginnings the alternative groups instead of this have called for people to become aware of their own compulsions, fears, and limits, something they have to do for themselves before a freer society can come about. "No one else can make you change!" sang George Harrison of the Beatles as a *Leitmotiv* of the movement.

5. Already very early, the alternative groups with their demand for immediate change could be distinguished from the traditional left, which was willing to wait. They don't want to be pacified with far-off revolutions and a classless society in the distant future; they want to organize their current and only life in a new way. For that purpose they created the counter-cultural structures of their own workshops, stores, and other workplaces, their communes, living collectives, media, theaters, schools, etc. In these counterinstitutions they try to come closer to their goal of a new individual.

Protest and Social Change

The appeal which the alternative movement makes to the potential for change in people and in society is founded on anthropological and sociological recognitions, on the basis of which there can be no doubt that human beings are not immutable: that they change in time and society. On another level, in a more collective sense, the same is true as well for everything pertaining to society. What is social, is life and development, and therefore by definition *social change*. The sociological theory of conflict, especially, has built on this; according to that theory, society lives off the tension between what is and what should be. A social system that can no longer be challenged ritualizes itself and loses all power for creative innovation.

Alternative Successes and Ambivalences

In the preceding (theoretical) context we could establish that the alternative movement has undeniably succeeded in bringing world views and counterimages to light in its work, which are clearly antithetical to our present life: self-realization, interest in working, creativity, and social justice. Many projects and experiments of the alternative movement have in this way shown a considerable portion of the population, in a concrete way, what a meaningful life can really be today, and how it is to be realized. This concrete example is ambivalent. Let us sum up with the following theses:

— The alternative movement has the historical value of experimenting with new forms of living and working and thereby of at least demonstrating alternatives to stiffened social structures.

— The alternative movement gave early warning about problems which were taken up only 10 or 20 years later by the bourgeois public. Examples of this are the debates about alienation in industrial (capitalist and socialist) society, the question of the humanization of the work world, the energy problem, industrial growth, the disruption and protection of the environment.

— The alternative movement expresses itself in practical ways; in this sense it takes on the character of a model for others.

— The alternative movement has created forms of living and of communication which *in part* point the way for the future.
This is especially true with respect to the dissolution of the nuclear family, the combination of work and living spheres, new forms of cooperation in the workplace, the giving up of consumer values to turn to a new simplicity, the emphasis on the importance of body language, the accentuation of nonprofessional creativity, etc.

— The alternative movement, as a practical criticism of state-monopolized capitalism as well as of really existing socialism, illustrates the meaning of freedom, diversity of opinion, individuality, imagination, grass-roots organization, etc.

— The alternative movement has no future when it expresses itself in certain forms which try to live as parasites of the wastes of industrial society (such as Gammler and Punks).

— The alternative movement takes on the nature of a sect when fixated on isolated problems, like nourishment, sexuality, art, therapy, and the like. Total concentration on particular questions forces the alternative movement into the cut-off position of ridiculed outsiders.

— The alternative movement will fail where it interprets self-liberation as an ego trip, and ignores the social conditioning factor of compulsion and (collective) liberation.

— The alternative movement maneuvers its members into freaked-out dead ends when it separates existence, self-discovery, creativity, and love from the concrete spheres of life in our time.

— The alternative movement can only be an effective example when it dialectically combines individual and societal liberation, instead of bringing individual separate worlds into existence (like country communes and sects).

Alternation and Alternatives

The ambivalences of the alternative movement mentioned here point to moments of failure, which also — and above all — indicate personal fates. Seen with hindsight, it was only a minority which was able to live up to the demand of building alternative lifestyles, developing new living forms and actually making them stable. The majority, especially of the young, in the alternative "Scene" which had abandoned traditional society to look for the new and the completely different, soon found itself facing the ruin of its hopes. This majority was not able, either psychologically or in terms of material organization, to deal with the challenges which are posed by the creation of counter-cultural living spheres in a hostile environment. The young people who were frustrated in this way mostly tried, after their disappointment, to compensate with the subculture of the pop scene, of drugs, and of star cults. Escapism is the deciding and the linking point of this drifting youth, which no longer hopes for a transformation of social reality through its own efforts, but rather from some exterior "medium."

The desire for a different lifestyle (an alternative) becomes a desire for variety (alternation).

This shows that *disintegration* in social practice can have two meanings: It can be realized as a beginning point for the solution of collective (social) problems, and it can be realized as a flight from social contradictions. The decision about the way to one goal or the other always has to be taken if "wanting to be different" means developing and stabilizing concrete socio-political counterspheres to the existing society.

This means the step from *subculture* to *counterculture*: Subcultures come about when the status and the role of individuals are not defined well enough. These individuals come together in formal groups which develop their own value and behavior systems. Most of all it is the status and the role of the generation which is on the verge of adulthood which is left undefined by industrial societies: young people are predisposed to found subcultures. The difference between the subculture and the dominating culture is not considered to be fundamental. The dominant culture mediates indeed the subculture, as shown by the way teen and teen-subcultures express themselves in their own fashion, music, and peculiar habits of speech *without* attacking established society. The subculture, therefore, is only an *accidental dissension from the dominant culture*, which manifests itself in a limited time period by way of its particular behavioral patterns, values, and group relationships. The *counterculture*, meanwhile, expresses itself in decided opposition to the established system of society, and attempts the restructuring of its social space.

Youth Movement or Social Movement

The preceding is already an indication that the question of whether contemporary protest is a youth movement or a social movement can, of course, be answered, but not with the unambiguity of the yes or no one might have liked. It is certain that the alternative movement as a social movement is authentically new; compared with earlier social movements in the *progressive* spectrum of history, it stems from totally new problems (the potential extermination of human beings, the destruction of nature, the society of wasteful consumption, etc.) and addresses problems new to humanity (meaningless lives, loss of moral orientation, relationship crises, boredom, etc.). It has to find answers that neither the classical bourgeois theoretical systems nor those of Marxism can deliver. In addition, the emphasis in the answers to the questions posed above has changed since the sixties. Fifteen years ago the protest movement (pupils, apprentices, partly university students) became a youth movement because it articulated *primarily* problems in the area of reproduction: questions of family, education, leisure, and sexuality which mostly affected the young. Today it is undeniable that problems affecting the entire population are in the foreground: the danger of war, ecological crisis, unemployment, alternatives to the industrial society, etc. and less, those concerned with the specific socialization problems of youth. In that respect, what once was more a youth movement has now clearly changed into a social movement.

Nevertheless, this does not stop the youth movement, at times, from surfacing through the social movement. This happens in two ways:

1. The alternative movement is used by many young people as a catalyst for their unsolved problems at home and in school; these young people often drop out of the social movement again after they have successfully solved their problems.

2. Free space which youth formerly had available, and could use for finding their identity, is constantly shrinking as the capitalist society, acting on the principle of maximized profits, takes over more and more areas of young people's lives (fashion, music, discos, etc.) to impose its structure on them. The alternative movement, however, supplies shelter in which young people are relatively free from outside pressures.

The unquestionable fact that opponents of war, peace demonstrators, anti-nukes, ecologists, squatters, unemployment action groups, and alternative projects fall under the category of the *social movement* does not exclude us from establishing that the above can be used as vehicles for problems specific to youth.

Conclusions

This means for our subject altogether:

1. Alternative groups from the fifties to the present day have represented a minority within generations and cohorts.

2. Alternative groups are to be understood as social movements *within* certain young generations; they do not express the unity or spirit of a generation, but — on the contrary a new and opposite lifestyle.

3. Thus alternative groups are not a characteristic expression of their generation, but are so far an atypical avant-garde.

4. Alternative groupings and related marginal groups must be theoretically conceived as countercultures in a frame of sociology of conflict and of social change.

Framing the Youth 'Problem': The Construction of Troublesome Adolescence

Dick Hebdige

"Youth," "generation," "subculture," "conflict": These terms cannot be read as transparent and univocal, pointing at all times and in all places toward immutable referents. Nor is it necessarily fruitful to forcibly detach them from their everyday usages and to fix them within arbitrary schemata which can then be ennobled through the mystical incantation of the word 'Science.' The significance of these terms is historically and geographically variable and contingent. They cannot simply be *willed* into science.

These observations seem pertinent in an International Symposium where national differences in research traditions, in languages, in lines of enquiry are clear in every utterance; where we learn, if nothing else, that knowledge is generated under circumstances which are, in the final analysis, *local*. And if we concede that these categories are historically constructed, then we must also acknowledge the need, at some point, to deconstruct them. For the facts we habitually invoke do not speak for themselves. Part of our task must be a critical and reflexive interrogation of the categories themselves which attempts to trace how, when, and to what extent the 'facts' we miraculously 'find' have already been spoken for; how, when, and to what extent the 'things' we miraculously think have already been thought for us ...

I should like to use this opportunity to review some of the debates within British sociology concerning the significance and sources of generationally-based conflict with special reference to youth subcultures; and to trace the historical construction of youth as a privileged focus for concern and surveillance both within the social sciences and outside in the broader streams of cultural commentary. Clearly, the issues raised by such a broad historical survey can scarcely be adequately treated in a paper of this length. The overview will be somewhat schematic and any concluding remarks are likely to remain pitched at the level of suggestion and assertion. On the other hand, the concentration on a purely British context may seem overly restricted and parochial. A ludicrous admission, then, that what follows is both too general and too particular. I can see no way of refuting either charge. Perhaps one of the more paradoxical functions of international conferences is to expose the curiously narrow dimensions of the academic discourses and debates which we professionally inhabit and all too often (all too rashly) claim a spurious 'adequacy' for.

Industrialization: The Victims and the Culprits

The definition of the potentially delinquent juvenile crowd as a particular urban problem can be traced back, in Britain at least to the beginnings of the Sunday School movement — an attempt on the part of the Church to extend its moderating influence downwards in terms both of social class and biological age. Haphazard urbanization, child factory labor, and the physical and cultural separation of the classes into two separate 'Nations' were together held responsible for creating a new social problem: the unsupervised, heathen working class juvenile who appears in contemporary novels, journalism, and early Parliamentary reports as a symptom of the industrial city which is itself typically presented in this literature as a monstrous and unnatural place.

During the mid 19th century, when intrepid social explorers began to venture into the "unknown continents," the "jungles," and the "Africa's" of Manchester and the slums of East London, special attention was drawn to the wretched mental and physical condition of the young nomads and street urchins. The most celebrated 'sighting' of a working class youth subculture in this period occurs in Henry Mayhew's *London Labour and the London Poor* (1851) in a section devoted to the quasi-criminal costermongers who were visibly marked off from their peers and parents by their flamboyant style of dress, their argot and anti-authoritarian value system. However, the specter of the undersocialized, hence uncontrollable juvenile delinquent was by no means confined to the rudimentary ethnographies produced by men like Mayhew. It can be found haunting the pages of Mary Carpenter's (1853) influential submissions to the mid-century Parliamentary committees set up to advise on educational and punitive policy-committees which produced recommendations which were to lead in turn to the institutionalization in the form of Ragged, Industrial, and Borstal schools[1] of the Victorian distinction between the 'rough' and 'respectable' classes, the 'deserving,' and 'undeserving' poor. That same specter, reified yet personalized in the fashionable photographic images of 'quaint' ragamuffins and scowling street Arabs and in the literary portraits of urchins presented by novelists like Charles Dickens, Arthur Morrison, and Clarence Rook adorned the libraries and the library walls of the new socially concerned cultured middle classes.

Both photographs and written portraits of low-life types combined pity and fear in a manner redolent of a mid 19th century bourgeois structure of feeling. The urchin described by Charles Dickens in *Oliver Twist* in the disreputable person of the Artful Dodger is an indeterminate figure whose demeanor, at once ridiculous and menacing, confounds precise classification. As a "young man old before his time," the Dodger is both a humorous type and a threatening paradox:

"He was a snub nosed, flat browed, common faced boy enough; and as dirty a juvenile as one would wish to see; but he had about him all the airs and manners of a man. He was short for his age: with rather bow legs, and little sharp, ugly eyes. His hat was stuck on the top of his head so lightly that it threatened to fall off at every moment ... He wore a man's coat, which reached nearly to his heels. He had turned the cuffs back, halfway up his arms, to get his hands out of his sleeves ... He was altogether as roystering and swaggering a city gent as ever stood 4 feet 6 or something less in his bluchers ..."

This vignette, packed with physical detail, imbued with a kind of rapacious specularity, is entirely typical of its period. It bears the traces of a scientific 'episteme,' uniting figures as apparently dissimilar as Darwin and Lombroso, which dictates the strength and direction of an obsessively developed taxonomic drive. For the collection of a mass of detailed observations of urban street life was ultimately motivated by larger forces than the observers themselves were prepared or able to admit. Their testimony formed the documentary basis for legislative action, for the formation of charitable bodies and the mobilization of public opinion through newspaper articles on the plight of the "wandering tribes" of Britain's industrial cities. In these ways, the social explorers, philanthropists, novelists, journalists, and documentary photographers helped to direct the growing moral impetus towards the education, reform, and 'civilization' of the working-class masses — an impetus which was itself underwritten by a generalized concern with the problems involved in disciplining and monitoring the shifting urban population. This concern with cataloguing and collating information on the 'new race of men' which industrialism was seen to have engendered, found technological support in innovations like photography.

As John Tagg (1981) has indicated, photography supplanted earlier systems of classification (e.g., Bertillon's 'anthropometric' method) employed by the police and by charitable bodies like Doctor Barnado's Homes for Destitute and Working Lads, an organization which amassed for surveillance and advertising purposes some 55,000 portraits of the juveniles committed to its care. Inscribed in photography and photographic practice from its very inception, there were these official documentary uses, this potential for surveillance, by no means neutral, representing rather a particular point of view, particular interests, embodying a desire and a will to know the alien-in-our-midst the other: the victim and the culprit.

As the century wore on, the penetration of the working-class milieu, particularly of lower working-class youth subcultures, was given added impetus through the introduction, firstly, of a state-sponsored national school system in 1870 and then, at the turn of the century, of organizations like the Boys' Brigade and the Boy Scouts which were run on more or less military lines, were modelled on the upper class English public school and were steeped in the ideologies of imperialism, nationalism, and wholesome outdoor fun. Elsewhere, as Murdock & McCron (1976) have noted, youth began to be identified, in the writings of Stanley Hall (1904), Jane Addams (1909), & Ortega y Gasset (1931) with cultural and national resurgence and renewal, with the idealistic refusal of materialism and the 'spiritual' transcendence of narrow class interests. Although the success of these movements and tendencies in reshaping the cultural responses of working class youth remained strictly limited, the articulation of ideologies of generational identity and consciousness have had far reaching effects on the ways in which the category 'youth' has been deployed both within social scientific discourse and in popular journalism, advertising, and informed cultural commentary. Mannheim's more sophisticated typology based upon a recognition that "within each generation there can exist a number of differentiated, antagonistic generation-units" (Mannheim, 1952) tended, at least in Britain, to have relatively little influence in comparison with the more quotable proclamations made by pundits like Abrams (1959) that "generational differences are now replacing class differences as the primary source of social conflicts in our society" (Abrams, 1959).

The American Inheritance: The Juvenile Delinquent

However, it was in the late twenties that the category 'youth' emerged in sociology in a form which is recognizably current and the responsibility for that construction is generally attributed to the American tradition of ethnographic research, particularly to the work produced under the directorship of Robert Park et al. (1967) at the Chicago School for Social Ecology. Park and his colleagues at the University of Chicago were concerned with developing a broadly-based theory of the social ecology of city life. The high incidence of juvenile crime in inner city areas and the significance of peer-group bonding in distinctive juvenile gangs was explained by these writers through organic metaphors — the metaphors of social pathology, urban disequilibrium, the breakdown of the organic balance of city life. This tradition — qualitative, issue-oriented, and rooted in investigative journalism — was largely responsible for establishing the equation by now familiar in the sociology of youth, between adolescence as a social and psychological 'problem' of particular intensity and the juvenile offender as the victim of material, cultural, psychological, or moral deprivation. These two enduring images — the more general one of youth as a painful transitional period (an image which was given a much clearer *local* focus after Margaret Mead (1925) narrated the much smoother passage to maturity engineered for adolescent in more primitive societies); the more particular one of violent youth, of the delinquent as the product of a deprived urban environment were fixed within British sociology largely through the work of the Chicago school and of those American researchers who, throughout the fifties and sixties, continued to publish 'appreciative' studies of marginal groups based on the Chicago model.

It was this tradition which produced or secured the frames of reference which then got fixed on to the study of youth-in-general and which defined what was going to be deemed significant and worth studying in the area — the link between deprivation and juvenile crime, an interest in the distinctive forms of juvenile bonding: youth culture, the gang, the subculture. Throughout the fourties, fifties, and early sixties, most of the major debates on youth within British and American sociology can be traced back to that initial cluster of concerns and fall more or less within those original parameters. It may be fruitful to pursue the contours of those debates in a little more detail. The contribution of Cohen (1955) to the field of youth studies is generally considered seminal. Employing qualitative methods, Cohen set out to counter the structural-functionalists' stress on an absolute consensus of social norms and values. Arguing against this imaginary consensus he indicated the extent to which the delinquent teenage gang evolves its own standards and routines in reaction to the dominant value system encountered in institutional contexts — especially the school — contexts which the teenagers themselves experience as hostile and alien. He proposed a pattern of 'reaction-formation' whereby disaffected underachievers invert the dominant middle-class ethos with its positive valuation of personal ambition, academic achievement, deferral of gratification, and respect for property so that the gang offers a collective solution in which "the delinquent's conduct is right by the standards of the (gang)culture precisely because it is wrong by the norms of the parent culture" (Cohen, 1955).

A similar emphasis on the negative effects of generational segregation during schooling informed the work of Coleman (1961) who saw countercultural identities

187

based for the boys on athleticism, for the girls on the cult of personality and appearance developing in reaction to the formal values of the education system (Brake, 1980).

These explanations of the sources of subcultural values were then challenged by Miller (1958) who questioned the autonomy of youth culture and peer-group experience implicit in Cohen's thesis and the school-based work, and suggested that the focal concerns of juvenile offenders — the pursuit of risk, instant gratification, fatalism, and the cultivation of abrasive humor — are merely exaggerated extensions of those more dispersed values, attitudes, and dispositions which characterize the culture of the slum. Cloward & Ohlin (1960), adapting Merton's model of anomie (1938), sought to explain lower working-class juvenile delinquency by invoking the disjunction between legitimate and illegitimate means and ends. Far from being intrinsically opposed to consensual norms, the gang was presented here as pursuing goals which are socially sanctioned, for example, success, material wealth, pleasure, self esteem, etc. However, in this formulation, restricted access to material and vocational opportunities was cited as the catalyst which forces adolescents from ghetto environments to resort to illegitimate expedients which have nonetheless been assimilated into the parent culture as localized norms.

All these exchanges can be seen in part as permutations on the themes introduced by the Chicago School. Even the shift in the work of people like Matza (1961; 1969) and Young (1972) away from the particularity of urban ghetto life to a consideration of just how widespread those apparently forbidden subcultural values are in the wider society still share a structure of interests inherited from Chicago, namely an interest in the deviant, the delinquent, the rule-breaker. Just as the earlier researchers into subculture regarded juvenile crime as a symptom of more general problems — urban decay, poverty, anomie, etc. — so Matza and Young used the instance of youthful deviance to highlight wider contradictions in industrialized Western societies (e.g., between the regime of work and the fetishization of leisure; between the Protestant work ethic and the so-called "subterranean values" of mainstream society).

These debates were circulated in Britain during the fifties and early sixties when youth studies began to figure more prominently on the sociological agenda. American explanations of adolescent behavior were imported along with the new 'Americanized' youth culture and the accompanying mythologies of a dangerous yet fun-filled adolescence which were used to promote the appeal of commodities aimed at the new youth market. The experience of postwar British youth had undergone significant qualitative changes with the extension in 1944 of compulsory secondary education, to the age of 15, with military conscription (abolished in 1962) and with relative affluence and full employment. It was calculated that during the fifties, the spending power of those adolescents joining the workforce had effectively doubled (Abrams, 1959; Brake, 1980; Clarke et al., 1976; Hebdige, 1981a). Eventually, of course, a new range of commodities and commercial leisure facilities sprang up to absorb the surplus cash which for the first time, working-class youth was calculated to have at its disposal to spend on itself and to provide a space within which youth could construct its own immaculate identities untouched by the soiled and compromised imaginaries of the parent culture. By the mid sixties, youth culture had become largely a matter of commodity selection, of emphatically stated taste preferences: Mod not Rocker, Rocker not Ted, etc. Image had begun to serve for the members of the groups themselves as a means of marking boundaries, of articulating identity and difference. The regulation of body posture, styles, and looks had become anxious and obsessive. There was even a distinctive Mod way of standing:

"Feet had to be right. If you put your hands in your pocket, you never pulled the jacket up so it was wrinkled. You'd have the top button done up and the jacket would be pulled back behind the arm so that you didn't ruin the line. You'd only ever put one hand in your pocket if you were wearing a jacket ..." (Barnes, 1980).

The circuit of voyeurism closes here: Youth, subject to the multiple surveillances mounted by a range of authorities and interested parties — the police, teachers, the family, social scientists, journalists, advertisers, etc. — has come, at last, into its own (gaze); holds itself in high regard. Fractions of youth now aspire to the flatness and the stillness of a photograph. They are completed only through the admiring glances of a stranger ...

At the same time, throughout the fifties and sixties, 'youth' continued to function symbolically as an index to either cultural decline or regeneration depending on the inclinations of those moral entrepreneurs who were intent on measuring the social effects of the postwar Reconstruction. The spectacular subcultures of the 'submerged tenth' of lumpen youth whose tastes were most clearly conditioned by exposure to American musical and sartorial styles were singled out for what seems in retrospect an inordinate amount of attention (see, e.g., Hoggart, 1958; Fybel, 1963; and, for a critique Hebdige, 1981a). The old specter of a mutinous sub-race of "helots ... and ploughboys" was resurrected though the image now had some distinctly modern accessories: the Artful Dodger now wore sideburns. The discourses which were invoked to explain and interpret the new patterns of teenage consumption in Britain tended to be drawn from studies of juvenile delinquency, youth culture, and the 'youth problem' evolved originally in the United States. To take just one example, Downes (1966) in his influential study of delinquent boys in London's East End, applied categories derived directly from Cloward and Ohlin's work (1960) on deviance and opportunity.

Other kinds of literature, more closely and actively aligned with the emergence of the youth market, also helped to structure the field of youth studies in this period. The market researcher, Abrams (1959), served in his work to consolidate the notion later developed by Musgrove (1968) of youth-as-a-class — youth as a new historical subject — whilst MacInnes' (1959) popular novel, *Absolute Beginners*, helped to establish the stereotype of the teenage consumer as a narcissist, culturally and aesthetically isolated from adults, dedicated to self-image and the pursuit of pleasure.

Style and 'Magical Resolution'

The influence on British youth studies of the American school of deviance — particularly of the Chicago inheritance — are clear even in the work produced in the 1970s at the Birmingham Centre for Contemporary Cultural Studies (e.g., Hall et al., 1976) and the Leicester Centre for Mass Communications Research (e.g., Mungham & Pearson, 1976). However, before attempting to assess the possible ef-

189

fects of American paradigms on the structure of concerns elaborated in this more recent work, it is first necessary to summarize the major themes which might be said to characterize the Birmingham and Leicester contributions. First, this research, whilst remaining fully committed to a conflict model of social relations, sought to broaden the sphere of the 'political' to incorporate forms of ideological and cultural struggle not tied directly to the realm of production. From this perspective, even those spectacular subcultures of the young whose 'resistance' is most clearly and easily contained because it is articulated in and through consumption rituals begins to take on some subversive significance — as attempts at winning some kind of breathing space outside the existing cultural parameters. More specifically, subcultures could then be interpreted as collective responses on the part of youth to the dominant value system, as forms through which certain sections of youth oppose or negotiate the dominant definitions of their own subordination.

To take one example, the various subcultures associated with disaffected black adolescents in Britain — the 'Rude Boys' of the sixties, the 'Hustlers,' Rasta-oriented youth — were seen by some researchers (e.g., Hebdige, 1976; 1979; Hall et al., 1978) as oblique forms of opposition to dominant white definitions of how one should behave if one is black and at the bottom of the hierarchy. All these cultures play with and play on the contradictory mythologies of black ethnicity (black pride, 'primitivism,' West Indian culture, patois, the 'roots'). Hustling — making a living by 'scuffling' on the borders of legality — can then be interpreted as both a "resistance through rituals," a rejection of the meagre options offered to black youth (i.e., menial work or unemployment benefit) and a realistic response to — a negotiation of — the fact of increasing unemployment, what Hall et al. (1978) call "wagelessness and the relegation of young blacks to the position of deskilled labor." Hustling is, then, a *cultural* response in the fullest sense of the term — at once symbolic and material, expressive and expedient, concerned simultaneously with making sense and making money. It is a response to a verifiable set of social *facts* — the fact that, for instance, West Indians and Britons of West Indian descent are twice as likely as white Britons to be designated educationally subnormal at school, the fact that between 1974 and 1977, whereas unemployment for British youth in general went up by some 120 percent, for non-white youth it increased by 350 percent. These more or less deviant subcultural options can thus be seen to represent a kind of survival with style, a survival through style. They can be interpreted as bids for dignity, attempts at retaining 'grace under pressure.'

The approach recommended in the Birmingham and Leicester research begins by stressing the *particularity* of the subcultural response, analyzing the *distinctive* combinations of dress, dance, music, language, and gesture adopted by *specific* subcultures and referring these back both to particular material conditions of existence and to the particular ideological configurations (here I've suggested the idea of 'blackness') which are being handled, negotiated, or subverted in style. Contrary to the image projected in the mass media of subcultural groups as arbitrary and normless (as 'nature' rather than 'culture'), the work produced in Birmingham and Leicester went on to stress, perhaps excessively, the coherence of subcultural forms. For instance, Willis (1978) suggested that it is precisely through the symbolic 'fit' between subjective experience, the use of halucogenic drugs, 'acid rock,' and an alternative value system that Hippies made sense of the world. Hall et al. (1976) argued that the various items which comprise subcultural style are carefully chosen to communicate the desired qualities, to give concrete expression to the lived experience of the group. The Skinhead style: a 'bricolage' of severely cropped hair, industrial boots, workman's jeans, Reggae and Oi music, racial, territorial, and sexual chauvinism — formed a deliberately constructed expressive unity through which the desired qualities: 'hardness, masculinity, and working classness' could be advertised. According to Clarke (1976a), it was through these symbolic means that the Skinheads sought to nostalgically recover the cohesiveness of the pre-war working-class community — a community eroded by technological transformations of the work process, by the changing status and composition of the industrial proletariat, by slum clearance and relative prosperity. This approach extended the suggestive thesis put forward by Phil Cohen (1972) that working-class youth under specific historical conditions (i.e., conditions of 'rupture,' when stability and continuity is threatened) seek a "magical resolution" of the conflicts and contradictions faced by the whole community. This magical resolution, according to Cohen (followed by Clarke, 1976b; Hebdige, 1979; Brake, 1980) is achieved through the construction of a style which symbolically resolves or crystallizes experienced contradictions by literally tying everything up in a unique homology of dress, ritual, and value system. Whilst this thesis clearly shares some common ground with Mannheim's position (1952) and effectively reinstates social class as a significant variable in the formation of youth subcultures, any simple idea of corporate class identity is attenuated through the definitions of subculture as a *symbolic* response to the *imagined* conditions of existence. Further research (e.g., Hall et al., 1978; Hebdige, 1979; 1981a, b) has stressed the literally *mediated* nature of the subcultural response. Here, ideological themes prioritized and disseminated by the mass media are seen to be reworked into the fabric of subcultural style but in a disfigured or parodied form (e.g., the moral panic surrounding 'Americanization' and juvenile delinquency with the fifties Teddy Boys; the panic concerning black involvement in street crime both in black British youth culture in the seventies and the Skinhead 'revival'; economic or sexual 'crisis' in Punk, etc.).

However, despite the innovative nature of much of this work, the persistence of (often unacknowledged) strands from earlier American research led to a series of important omissions and a further truncation of what was defined as 'significant' adolescent behavior. First, the focus on deviance has tended to distract attention away from less dramatic forms of group association amongst youth. (The less visibly announced cultural forms of the 'respectable' majority have, for instance, been badly neglected.) The continuing interest in working-class street cultures (the gang, etc.) has also helped in recent British sociology to marginalize the more articulate, educated, and politically organized counterculture of disaffected middle-class youth (though it could be argued that the alternative movement in Britain has succeeded in producing its own prodigious rhetoric, its own (albeit limited) auto-critique). Finally, and most importantly, as Frith (1978), Brake (1980), McRobbie et al. (1976; 1981) have pointed out, the emphasis on spectacular transgressions of public order has served to negate the experience of adolescent girls by focusing attention on those dramatic street cultures from which girls — especially working-class girls — are conventionally excluded or within which they are tolerated but consigned to a minor role.

The second emphasis carried over from the Chicago work involves a preference for qualitative methodologies (particularly 'participant observation') and the consequent stress on the unifying rituals, meanings, and values of the various subcultures at the expense of more concerted attempts at situating adolescent experience within a broader macro-structural framework. The third inheritance from Chicago involves the commitment to *reading* subcultural rituals and values as symptomatic or expressive of larger cultural themes and conflicts. In the Chicago work, juvenile deviance was assumed to have its ultimate significance in relation to the 'classical' sociological concerns: anomie, social disequilibrium, etc.; whereas in the Birmingham research, the terms of the discrepancy between the appearance and underlying reality of subcultural signification was transmuted into the Marxian dichotomy between phenomenal forms and real relations. More recently in subcultural studies, this same opposition has been converted into variants of the structuralist polarity between parole and langue, between subcultural performance and the generative system(s) of difference which are seen to structure and determine that performance. One of the consequences of this tendency to read youth cultures as signs of something else is a failure to acknowledge the specificity of the cultural and institutional spaces within which youth culture operates. For instance, it is only recently that there has been any really concerted attempt at understanding precisely *how* youth culture functions in practical terms; how and to what extent adolescents are defined and serviced by the industries which set out to 'farm' them: the rock and pop music industries, the fashion business, the popular music press, TV programs, and films pitched at the youth market, etc. (see, e.g., Frith, 1976; Grossberg, 1982; Chambers, 1982). Despite these timely correctives, it is nonetheless true that much of the work on youth subcultures completed in recent years has been limited in scope because of this tendency to 'refer up' to superordinate questions, the importance of which is sociologically and/or politically self-evident and taken for granted (e.g., class or racial or gender conflict (Hebdige, 1981b)). Youth continues to be constituted as an object of study through a set of contractual relations between researcher and researched — relations which are either functionalist, philanthropic, or just plain voyeuristic in origin.

Power, Discourse, and the Body: A Possible Alternative

If genuinely fresh initiatives are to be taken in the field of youth studies, it would seem expedient to break this set of inherited relations in order to develop forms of knowledge which, whilst dispensing with some of the 'authority' conventionally claimed for academic research, may be more commensurate with and adequate to the (sub)cultural strategies and responses themselves. At the same time, the subcultural paradigm can no longer be regarded as exhaustive. At a time when the State is becoming increasingly involved in the mobilization, direction, and training of the growing sector of school-leavers who face long-term unemployment, the need to expand critical research on youth beyond what Young (1970) has called "the zoo of deviance," becomes a matter of more than academic concern. According to the Youth Task Group Report compiled by the Manpower Services Commission in April 1982, of the 508,000 16-year-olds who will be entering the British labor market in 1983, some 297,000 (59%) are likely to remain unemployed for the foreseeable future, and the plethora of hastily launched government-sponsored training schemes aimed at prolonging education and giving adolescents work experience (e.g., the Youth Opportunity Programme (YOP); the Unified Vocational Preparation Programme (UVP); the Training for Skills Programme, etc.) indicates a level of concern with the threat to social order posed by under-educated adolescents which has not been seen in Britain since the early Victorian period[2]. Since the riots in Britain's inner cities in July 1981, the increasingly powerful Law and Order lobby has prioritized working-class youth – irrespective of race – as a particularly acute and urgent social problem.

The work of Michel Foucault (1979) may provide an exemplary model on both counts offering a more flexible (and more suggestive) framework for understanding, on the one hand, youth subculture, and, on the other, these broader shifts in the 'official' conceptualization and attempted containment of troublesome youth. Foucault's insistence, first, on the productivity of discursive categories in defining social phenomena and influencing social policy and, secondly, on the primacy of local historical circumstances in generating particular strategies of power and resistance, particular patterns of dominance and subordination seems especially pertinent.

I can only outline possible lines of enquiry here. First, in relation to subculture, by building on Foucault's perception of the complicity between power and pleasure it may be possible to construct a less fractured account of subcultural style, one which refuses to privilege ideology (spirit) over sensation (body) and which attempts instead to reconcile what are conventionally regarded as the negative and affirmative effects of subcultural affiliation. A 'micro-politics' of the adolescent body would begin by recognizing that youth culture centers precisely on the conscious deployment of physical presence, on appearance, posture, dress; in the case of the more extreme subcultures, on the conversion of powerlessness into the power to discomfit. In other words, it would start at the most obvious level: the level of the obvious. For – obviously – its teenagers possess little else, they at least 'possess themselves.' They 'own' their own bodies. They 'play' their bodies as tokens of an individuality which is also a paradox (each body identical – endowed with the same features – yet unique – each feature, each person, instantly distinguishable). If power can be exercised nowhere else, it can at least be exercised here. The body is available as object and metaphor. It can be decorated and enhanced like a cherished object (as in Mod and neo-romantic options). It can be cut up and 'cooked' like a piece of meat (as in Punk, Biker, and some post-Punk styles). Self-mutilation is just the darker side of narcissism. In both cases, the body becomes the base-line: the place where the buck stops. It becomes the seat and symptom of personhood. Decorated/mutilated, it becomes the sole, conspicuous guarantor of personal 'authenticity.' To take just one example, for a British teenager to wear a Mohican hairstyle or facial tattoos in the current ideological and economic climate is a political act in miniature, a gesture of refusal. Such gestures invoke not only parental disapproval. They also draw the attention of the authorities. And in a recession, when employers can afford to pick and choose, they amount to a public disavowal of the will to queue for work; a determination to throw the Self away before the Others do it for you.

193

If such a corporal poetics seems fanciful and/or pretentious, it should nonetheless be possible, given the genealogy I have attempted in this paper, to situate youth subculture and subcultural style in the context of broader patterns of surveillance and social control. For the 'resistance' encoded in subcultural ritual cannot be usefully considered in isolation from the various forms of interest — punitive, vicarious, exploitative — which simultaneously surround it and seek to (re)define it. The obsessive curiousity of adults, far from defusing or incorporating subcultural resistance might be said, in the final analysis, to actively *constitute* it. For the subcultural milieu, as I hope I have indicated, has been constructed *underneath* the authorized discourses, *in the face* of the multiple disciplines of the family, the school, and the workplace. And subculture forms up in the space between surveillance and the evasion of surveillance. It translates the fact of being under scrutiny into the pleasure of being watched. Its outrageous displays are also a kind of concealment: a hiding in the light.

The subcultural response is, then, neither simply affirmation nor refusal, neither 'commercial exploitation' nor 'genuine revolt.' It is neither simply resistance against some external order nor straight forward conformity with the parent culture. It is both a declaration of independence, of otherness, of alien intent, an assertion of cohort identity, a refusal of anonymity, of subordinate status. It is an *in*subordination. And at the same time, it is also a confirmation of the fact of powerlessness, a celebration of impotence. In Willis' words, it is a "... rescue and a confirmation of the direct, the human, and the social *and* a giving up — at any conscious level — of claims to control the underworkings of these things ..." (Willis, 1977).

Subcultures are both a play for attention and a refusal, once attention has been granted, to be read according to the book. Youth subcultures are posited on a ground that shifts uneasily between 'politics' and 'pleasure.' They function both as a marketing category for the rock and fashion industries and as a site for the development of strategies of resistance which are simultaneously 'collective' and 'subjective.' Foucault (1979) conveys this ambiguity (or circularity) in a formulation which is, finally, more concise (and more profound) than I could manage:

"The pleasure that comes from exercising a power that questions, observes, watches, spies, searches out, palpates, brings to light; and, on the other hand, the pleasure that is aroused at having to evade, flee, mislead or travesty this power ... Capture and seduction, confrontation, and mutual reinforcement; parents and children, adult and adolescent, teacher and pupils ... all have played this game continually since the nineteenth century. These appeals, these evasions, these circular incitements have traced around sexes and bodies not closed frontiers, but perpetual spirals of power and pleasure ..." (Foucault, 1979).

For the rest (for the silent majority of 'troublesome youth' who do not present themselves as members of distinguishable subcultures), we can also follow Foucault (1979), poring over the documentary evidence, tracing discursive continuities, breaks, re-emergences:

"The child ... must be placed in a *family*. Faith in those around him being once thoroughly established, he will soon yield his own will in ready submission to those who are working for his good; it will thus gradually become subdued and trained, and he will work with them in his reformation and training, trusting, where he cannot perceive the reason of the measures they adopt to correct or eradicate the evil in him. This, it is apprehended, is the fundamental principle of all true reformatory action with the young, ..." (Carpenter, 1853).

"... Work Programme schemes are designed to improve young people's capabilities in basic social skills and to focus their interests and aptitudes in a positive way to help them find and retain a job ..." (Manpower Services Commission, 1982).

Needless to say, the continuities between these two statements are remarkable: remarkably depressing ...

Footnotes

1 Ragged schools, established in the mid 19th century originally by the philanthropist, Mary Carpenter, were designed to provide a sanctuary from the streets for neglected urchins. The industrial schools were designed (rather like the current YOP schemes (Youth Opportunity Programme)) to inculcate rudimentary skills and factory time-discipline. The Borstals were reserved for the hardened young recidivists (Pinchbeck & Hewitt, 1981).
2 Manpower Services Commission (1982): Youth Task Group Report (Great Britain).
   This report gives some indication of the current level of governmental commitment to sponsored training schemes. According to the document, the YOP scheme (Youth Opportunity Programme – established in 1978 –) trains some 55,000 youths annually whilst UVP (Vocational Preparation Programme – established in 1976 –) caters to some 6,000 adolescents and the TSP (Training for Skills Programme) 35,000. Other interesting statistics are included: Employers are to receive a grant of £2,000 for accepting new juvenile recruits who are paid £15 for working on average a 40-hour-week. Between 1975 and 1982, unemployment in Britain amongst those under 18 years of age went up by 500 percent and it is further estimated that 57 percent of all 16-year-olds and 48 percent of all 17-year-olds on the labor market are likely to be unemployed in September 1984.

195

Young and Old in Adult Education – On the Dynamics and Process Character of Intergenerational Encounters

Detlef Knopf

This contribution deals with a special type of intergenerational encounter-seminars in adult education designed to encourage intergenerational dialogue, to get the generations talking to one another. Entering first into the context in which these seminars take place, a context that structures the participants' activities and encounters in a certain way, I will describe and analyze a few of the key exchanges and experiences that typically take place at the "interface" between the generations. Finally, I will explore the question of how far the insights, gained within this frame of reference, can be considered relevant beyond it. My remarks are based on the results of participatory observation of several seminars in adult and senior citizens' education, on experiences gained through preparatory and follow-up work for and leadership of these seminars, and on evaluations of observation reports, transcripts of the conversations, discussions with smaller groups of participants of the same age, and interviews with individual participants.

In the Federal Republic of Germany, adult education has long served as an intermediary between various groups in society. It is hoped that talks and discussions, exchange of information in an atmosphere of conviviality, would yield mutual tolerance and understanding and hence integration or even "harmony" among these diverse groups. Adult educators have offered their services as interpreters and go-betweens, and less often as representatives or advocates, to certain social groups whose interests and viewpoints were either unknown or seemed unacceptable to other relevant groups. While training in the family and in school has traditionally concentrated on making society's demands and expectations known and clear to young people, adult education has frequently had to perform the task of reporting back to the adult world on the results of this socialization process: how young people as a whole view their responsibilities to themselves and to society. Particularly when problems arose (though since the discovery of the midlife and other crises among older people, youth has had no monopoly on problems) adult educators saw themselves called on to explain vicariously "what had gone wrong with young people nowadays." During the late sixties there were no end of seminars with titles like "What do the students really want?"

The most recent juvenile unrest at the start of the 1980s, soon found their commentators and explainers of course, but this time demands were raised to combine diagnosis with therapy: a proposed "dialogue with youth" was expected to fulfill both functions. It was expected on the one hand to provide answers to such concerned questions as, "What motivates these young people?" and "Are they still willing to be integrated into society at all?" On the other hand, the ensuing dialogue was expected to show young people that the adult world was worthy of consideration and maybe even of joining some day. In any case, the new dialogue had soon taken on the proportions of a wave. It found its critics (e.g., Roos, 1982; Deutsches Jugendinstitut, 1982) and in the meantime, in its officially sponsored form − TV discussions with leading political figures, ritual question and answer sessions held during party conventions, etc. − it seems to have ebbed considerably.

Nevertheless, after initial hesitation, adult educators again took up the traditional challenge to encourage dialogue among the age groups. In 1978, a program was issued by the adult colleges (Volkshochschulen) that contained these words: "Forms of communication must be developed which strengthen the self-confidence of every age group and which at the same time broaden mutual knowledge and respect for their different basic experiences." The appeal made here, in other words, was to go beyond vicarious interpretation and to offer opportunities for direct contact and interaction among the generations.

The youth debate was not the only source of impulses towards putting this program into practice. In adult education work for old people, the number of attempts has been increasing of late to break down the homogeneity of the groups by arranging contacts with other age groups, usually teenagers and school age children. In the field of political education, a recently awakened interest in biography and life experience is evident, as can be seen from a willingness on the part of those who lived through key phases of recent German history to pass on their experiences to younger participants. And, stimulated by the women's movement, seminars are now being offered on mother-daughter relationships, discussion meetings open to all concerned. Finally, in our seminars in adult and family education, we often have members of three age groups gathered around the same table. What all these examples point to is a recent tendency in adult education to increasingly and consciously provide opportunities for intergenerational contact.

No theoretical models − or even relatively consistent conceptions − have yet been developed for intergenerationally oriented educational work. Unlike "multigenerational family therapy," for instance (Sperling et al., 1982), educational efforts of this kind cannot fall back on any systematically collated or theoretically organized experiences, but must proceed more or less on the common sense assumption that talking to one another is a positive thing. Of course no educator can be satisfied to leave it at that: something of educational value must also come of his efforts. Tietgens, who in 1982 sifted the much-acclaimed Shell study *Jugend 81* for its relevance to adult education, has suggested to his colleagues in the field that a good subject for discussion between the generations might be that of status passages, for example the process of separation from the family that young people go through, or the process of integration that takes place when they change reference groups (Tietgens, 1982, 52). To adults he prescribes the task of representing "social reality" vis-à-vis youth, of setting up what he calls "a resistance characteristic of reality which is required if young adults are to develop independence" (55).

Even if one does not share Tietgens' specific educational impetus, one has to admit that it is a characteristic of the pedagogic frame of reference that learning be intended − that interpersonal contact be supplemented by some material or subject to be learned. This, of course, is why educational encounters are arranged in a certain way and given a didactically meaningful form. In the case of the seminars we have investigated, this subject is usually the intergenerational relation itself − and

197

this holds true, depending on the educational intention, both of the here-and-now of intergenerational encounters and of the there-and-then of the relations between age groups in everyday life. The subject of intergenerational relations, and of individual and collective experience of alienation between generations, can further be broken down into a horizontal perspective (e.g.: What does my own relationship to other generations look like here and now?) and a vertical one (e.g.: How did I gradually become alienated from members of other generations? What is the history of my alienation and what social factors played a role in it?).

For the success of the learning experience, however, the here-and-now of the given seminar situation is extremely important, since when people report on events in their lives which decisively shaped their dealings with other generations, or even if they choose to keep their silence, they do so in the face and within the context of a certain group situation. How they perceive this group situation is determined to a great extent by patterns of experience and opinion shaped by their biographies and which underlie their present situation in life. It cannot be assumed that these patterns are age-specific – although this is indeed an assumption that members of groups other than the persons in question do tend to make.

It is in the nature of such meetings, of course, that participants are identified as more or less typical representatives of their generations and must deal with this classification on the part of others. On the one hand, no one who participates in a seminar with a title like "Discussion between the Generations" can completely avoid being typified. He will expect to be confronted by images of his generation that members of other generations have formed, and he will be held responsible for any attempt on his part to exempt himself from such categorization. On the other hand, however, he has an opportunity to set up an alternate image of "his" generation and to show its validity, for example, by telling stories and relating appropriate experiences. This process is complicated by the fact, however, that such stories do not necessarily speak for themselves – in extreme cases they can even be cited by other age groups as exceptions that prove the rule, as evidence that their stereotyped image is, after all, correct.

It quite regularly turns out in these seminars that the majority of the participants attempt to reach some kind of compromise, particularly when mutual images are negatively colored. I have observed over and over again, for instance, that older people will retain their negative image of "modern day youth" while absolving from their verdict those young people actually present as remarkable exceptions. If the younger participants accept this view, they in turn are compelled in fairness to drop some of the "charges" they have against the older participants or at least to moderate them. The common denominator reached is then usually expressed in words like, "You can't generalize; you have to see people as individuals."

Following these possibly quite practical rules may, however, lead to a collusion – a secret and unadmitted agreement to be mutually deceived. The peculiar form of group dynamics which then develops is felt especially by those participants who either resisted the compromise or who infringe upon it after the fact, if only inadvertently. They are then treated as representatives of that "adversary" of the intergenerational dialogue who, existing somewhere outside the group in question, at all times and everywhere insists, for example, that "all teenagers are basically the same." Often one gains the impression that the participants actually assume that this adversary has gained control of large sectors of their own age group. From here it is not far to the attempt to explain the estrangement of the generations in terms of individual guilt.

Yet pressure is exerted not only on "representatives" of the external "adversary" within such groups. In a certain sense one can say that during intergenerational encounters, an age-group specific social control is in force. Younger participants, for example, might consider the behavior of a certain young woman, behavior which she herself feels to be polite, to be too respectful or even servile, and force her into a marginal position because of it. Among older persons too, infringements of a behavioral code, however defined, vis-à-vis the young can occur which bring down upon the heads of their perpetrators the violent criticism of their peers. Among such infringements are counted, apparently, any attempt to flatter younger participants at the expense of age-group peers, or, what is not a rare occurrence, to try to convince them during breaks or after the official session that one certainly does not belong to those prejudiced, ossified oldsters they meet in the seminars. Such "changes of sides" are strategies that amount to difficult challenges to the younger participants. Generally these maneuvers on the part of individual older people irritate and discomfort their younger counterparts and cause them to search for appropriate ways to withdraw from contact.

The happenings outlined here are examples of interactional tasks which the participants find quite difficult to solve. It should be remembered that most of the people who join these seminars have almost no lasting or even comparatively regular communicative or interactional relationships to members of other generations in their daily lives. The fact that conversation reverts spontaneously again and again to the fleeting but often dramatic confrontations with younger or older people in buses, on subways, or out shopping, shows clearly how unusual for all concerned was a concentrated interaction, not motivated by external goals, with age groups other than their own. The seminar participants were "strangers" to one another in very much the sense that Alfred Schütz described an adult who "would like to be accepted or at least tolerated by the group he approached" (Schütz, 1972, 53).

In the present case, we are dealing with an attempt on the part of those concerned to find acceptance as an interesting and if possible even valued conversation partner. This involves, for both older and younger participants, trying to achieve a careful equilibrium between a behavior that, in Goffman's words, is "respectful" and is self-respecting enough and not leading to a loss of face. If someone wishes to express his respect for another person, there are (again according to Goffman) in general two types of behavior: first, avoidance rituals which signal to the receiver that the actor wishes to retain distance and does not intend to penetrate into his "private sphere"; and second, presentational rituals, friendly gestures which express esteem and recognition (Goffman, 1971). A relationship of tension, not always easy to keep in equilibrium, exists between these two behavioral extremes, since it is both possible to express "too much" detachment and, in a presentational mode, to become more involved in the relationship than one intended.

The participants' difficulties in finding behavioral patterns that met these criteria became evident in the insecurity, disorientation and anxiety they either showed at the time or admitted later to having felt. Very roughly speaking, the phases that most of the seminar groups went through in solving such and related problems, can be outlined as follows:

(a) Insecurity during first approaches; exchange of stereotyped phrases and clichés; difficulty in finding the "right" forms of address;

(b) Exchange of stories about encounters with members of other age groups, stories that seem cast in an unchanging mold and which are not clearly addressed to those present but as if into a vacuum;

(c) Withdrawal of the participants, as a rule into their respective age groups, the older ones usually feeling aggravated, helpless, and sometimes disgruntled but not openly admitting it, the younger experiencing aggravation, anger, or feelings of insufficiency which likewise are aired only "behind the scenes" of the seminar;

(d) Conflict and debate, including attempts to express at least some of the judgments and experiences that up to now had been suppressed;

(e) Rapprochement, growing intensity of contact; sometimes mutual avowal of good feelings, bad feelings, or disappointments; members of the group begin to look for common interests and subjects which the whole group can discuss.

The groups do not always pass through these phases one after the other, but may have relapses or be – in some respects – quite advanced, whilst "lagging behind" in others. Further differences arise out of the specific composition of the groups, their internal structure, and tasks set or proposed externally.

Experience shows that the greatest problems arise in the transition from phase (c) to (d). The fact that the adults demonstrate behavior expectations or judgments, or implicitly remonstrate with their younger discussion partners by means of stories, without explicitly clarifying or admitting them, without, indeed, perceiving them (as such) to a certain extent, seems to be a normal phenomena which renders communication more difficult. It is not easy for the group leader and the other participants to elaborate these implicit explanations and demands addressed to the communication partners, since they need not necessarily be congruent with those interests and needs of which the older adults are more or less conscious. It is possible to observe situations in which the younger participants receive "messages" made unintentionally by adults who are not even aware of making them. More than anything else, the non-verbal aspects of communication, and in certain cases the differing meanings of specific idioms and assertions to both young and old participants, can lead to considerable difficulties in communication. A further problem is due to younger group members not infrequently picking out things – on the basis of already existing "expectation-expectations" – which they have been hearing from adults "since the day they were born."

However, in the stories of the older participants it is generally possible to recognize that they are neither being told for the first time, nor in response to an encounter taking place in the present: One young member disrespectfully described them as "records played at every opportunity." The stories certainly abound in clichés and stereotypes about "the youth of today" even if those speaking combine their own experiences with those of others.

It is of minor importance for the interaction process whether such narrative descriptions or experiences with the young generation do justice to the subject matter or not. The reactions of the younger members vary between diffuse feelings of guilt and anger – or fury; however, there are hardly any behavior patterns available to them which have been tested and "proven" in interaction enabling them to express their emotions. Thus the consequence is usually the withdrawal referred to as phase (c) which, in most of the seminars observed, had proven to be a decisive "transitional stage" to more intense contact (in conflicts) or into a dead end from which it is difficult to escape. In order to successfully break through this predicament, the participants must be able to respond to the contributions of the others not only by justifying and defending themselves, making accusations or "anti-thetical" stories but also by expressing the emotions and irritation which had previously been held back in some suitable manner. It is essential that the participants are able to have this experience and that the communication partners now present are really the ones meant and being spoken to. It can often be seen that the opinions, discussion contributions, anecdotes, etc. exchanged up to this point also at least functioned as a reproduction of relationships to members of other generations which are unfinished and still not fulfilled.

The task of the seminar leader is to clarify to the participants the connections between the unsatisfying and unsatisfactory intergenerational relationship which occurs in the stories, and the manner in which these problems are communicated in the here-and-now of the seminar situation. Especial attention must be paid to the difficulties and "disturbances" in the process of communication. However, the seminar leader must cautiously aim at conceptualizing these "disturbances" and the frustrations which arise along with them, without thereby turning them into a completely frustrating event. Experience shows that one main danger is that the meta-communicative analysis of the problem of the dialogue deteriorates into all-round accusations of guilt or self-incrimination accompanied by reproaches which psychologize the problem or involve inadmissable generalizations. It may be decisive for the seminar leader to refrain from participating in such fights and instead confront the participants with an attitude of complete acceptance and esteem. Sometimes it is quite simply necessary to "cover over" arising conflicts which might hinder the analysis of more important matters and seminar problems. Thus the eruption of conflicts, or rather their working through — referred to as phase (d) is in no way to be confused with a naive "conflict oriented pedagogy."

However, the success of the seminar depends, to a great extent, on whether the group and the seminar leader succeed in confronting the arising difficulties.

A decisive factor in overcoming interactional difficulties and creating deeper contact has proven to be the ability to face up to, if not completely surmount, the following "blocks":

— More or less unconscious projections or assumptions, which, as closer analysis showed, usually resulted from latent unresolved conflicts in earlier intergenerational relations in the family, in school, or at work;
— A more or less unconscious insistance on conflict-free "harmony" and "understanding";
— An overcompensating readiness to adapt and an overhasty "liking for young people" on the part of older or a "liking for old people" or maintenance of a too respectful distance on the part of younger participants;
— Extreme reserve and inconsiderate or contact-shy behavior, which tends to be interpreted as domineering.

A special problem is presented by unquestioningly held opinions on the part of young people to the effect that older persons must be met either with conventional respect or even quasi-therapeutic care. These attitudes often seemed to me to express variants of common, negative stereotypes, such as that older people are extremely touchy and easily angered and thus must be treated protectively. This stereotype naturally conflicted violently with young people's image of themselves as being "authentic" and "straightforward." Particularly those "interaction-sensitive" young persons, as Tietgens has called them, who frequently (and often enough correctly) hear undertones of accusation, implicit degradation, or other insinuations in what older people say, often had a hard time remaining relaxed.

The dynamics of encounter described above are not equally apparent throughout all the phases of encounter. They can be derived not so much from what the group talks about as from observing closely *how* certain subjects are introduced, taken up, illustrated by gestures, etc. If he concentrates his attention on this aspect, the discussion leader is in a position, at least in principle, to intervene more flexibly in each respective phase of the process. Generally speaking, it is important to give the group members sufficient time to become conscious of the intentions that underlie their actions or behavior, and to become aware of the possibly unintentional consequences of such behavior. On the other hand, every participant must be given the opportunity to achieve a degree of self-confidence sufficient to insure that any refusal he makes to face such confrontations will be accepted. Obviously, ways which go beyond the strictly regulating forms of adult educational discussion as now practiced must be executed forms that are devoted primarily to checking the validity of claims made in conversation. Such breakthroughs with more sociability of atmosphere, as an opposite of mainly guided interactions and traditional conversation-oriented procedures have proven very helpful.

The experiences I have gained in seminars under my supervision have shown that there are great difficulties involved in transforming socio-structurally solidified segregation and overcoming the alienation among age groups in interactional situations. Moral appeals clearly complicate matters rather than alleviating them. I tend to believe that what is required is to provide more, and more varied opportunities for contact, particularly of a sociable kind. In West Germany particularly, the relationship between the generations is still overshadowed by the great strains to which it was subjected during and after the last war (Stierlin, 1982). In this regard intergenerational encounters here always include an element of mourning — guilt, disappointment, and resignation that have still to be worked out. Yet there is a path to each other that leads through sadness, and it can be found.

Chapter IV: The Generation Concept and Tendencies in Research

A number of conceptions designed to elucidate the relationships and the differences between contemporaneous and successive generations have crystallized out of the scientific discussion over the past century. Among the most important of these models is that advanced by Karl Mannheim on the formation and succession of generations and their "new manner of access" to sociocultural change. According to Mannheim, the collective determining condition for a generation is what he calls the "lot," or location, of its birth cohort, a concept which bears similarities to that of class membership. However, for him the lot of a birth cohort does not involve necessarily the formation of a generation as an "actuality" or a generation "unit" which possesses a generation consciousness. A generation as an actuality does not arise simply from its members belonging to the same chronological age group, but rather develops through its members' active participation in certain historical events. Even within this "actuality," a generation unit develops only if a group of individuals consciously participates in a commonly felt experience. Generation lot or location is determined by the natural condition of generational succession, in a way similar to the location of individuals in social classes due to socio-economic conditions. The continual appearance and disappearance of those who are the conveyers of the culture; the fact that human beings participate only in a certain limited slice of history; and the necessity of passing down the accumulated products and knowledge of a society, constitute, according to Mannheim (1968, 292[1]), the prerequisites for the existence of different generations.

In the introduction to this volume "Intergenerational Relationships: Approaches in Theory and Research," references were made to the various theoretical and empirical approaches concerned to elucidate problems of demarcation and duration of generations, the significance of the individual life-time concept for research on development and change of societies, the question concerning the mechanisms of these processes, and efforts to explain the periodic occurrence of innovative tendencies in society. Various perspectives and applications of the subject in different sociological disciplines, and within each discipline, were also discussed in the introduction. Mention was made of a certain narrowing down of Mannheim's perspective which is evident in many studies, particularly those which investigate problems experienced by selected age groups in their relations to others: these problems may be explained in terms of the social position of an age group within society but not in terms of a fundamentally different access to the dynamics of social change. On the other hand, neither the dynamics of social change, nor the duration of societies, nor the rapidity of their transformation, can be explained solely in terms of the biological reproduction of generations.

Hence it was maintained in the introduction that there are fewer problems involved with the use of the term "generation" in the case of lineage generation as it is employed in family research. There, however, other problems arise, particularly when it is a matter of differentiating between biological and sociohistorical ramifications of the term. The same can be said of the frequently ambiguous use of the term "generation" in sociological or developmental psychological research on socialization. Here, the conceptual ambiguity comes in at that point where the lineage generation is in a sense considered as equivalent to the sociohistorical generation.

Studies of the relations between children, parents, grandparents, etc. who belong to different age groups and, due to their position in the life course, assume different roles and positions within the family, does not require *per se* the use of a sociohistorical generation concept. Only when certain data are considered in light of historical and social development do children, parents, grandparents, etc. represent social characters who can be associated with different historical times. Hence in the interest of a more precise definition of the generation concept employed in family research, Kertzer (1983), following Elder's proposal (1978c; 1979), suggested that the term "generation cohort" be adopted, in which "individuals of a certain limited birth cohort are taken as the focus . . ." (p. 143). Troll (1970) already pointed out that the use of the generation concept was lacking precision. Kertzer lists four different meanings which have been attached to the term generation: (1) generation as a principle of kinship descent; (2) as a cohort; (3) as a life stage; and (4) generation as a historical period (p. 126). We shall go into two of these usages below.

Both the concept of *age stratification* and the sociological term *cohort* are frequently used in place of the generation concept. In classifying data by age group (Buchhofer, 1970, 300) and by birth cohort, the concept of generation as defined by Mannheim tends to be neglected. The subject of structural-functional analyses of age stratification is the continual process of aging which the members of a society undergo, and their relation to social structures and interrelationships among age groups. In other words, the age stratification concept focusses on the structural aspect of social change. Studies of this type concentrate on changes in age-graded roles and positions within the social system, on the social status of old age, and on "changes in the people as they grow up and grow old" (Riley, 1978, p. 40 and introduction, this volume).

When demarcated age groups are labelled generations, this concept involves a relational classification of the social functions of age-homogeneous and age-heterogeneous groups rather than an indication of the perspective different age groups take towards social change. In the age stratification concept, it is assumed implicitly that opposition among age groups — particularly between the young and the old — arises as a consequence of that "new manner of access" to a society's culture. Rarely is the assumption sufficiently tested whether conflicts among age groups actually do have their basis in changing structures, or whether these conflicts might more justifiably be attributed to social mechanisms other than those of age or a particular phase in the life course (cf. Chapter III, this volume).

The sociological concept of *cohorts* resulted from dissatisfaction with cross-sectional analyses (Cain, 1964; Ryder, 1965; Pfeil, 1967). First, cohort is a statistical concept which defines a certain number of individuals on the basis of their sociohistorical location (year of birth, shared experience of a certain historical event, or entry into some institution — school, army, prison, university, or business). In this sense, the cohort concept is an empirical instrument to organize data. By empirically combining different birth cohorts — according to the historic period of their birth or historical events that transpired during their life courses — clusters evincing common sociohistorical characteristics may emerge. However, while the members of a generation form a conscious association of individuals into a social group, for members of a cohort no contact is assumed. The sociological concept of cohorts has a structural dimension and a comparative dynamic one. The structural dimension refs to the historical entry of a cohort into society and therefore determines the life course of that cohort as an ascriptive characteristic, such as numerical size of birth cohort or its social composition. The comparative dynamic dimension of this concept refers to the uniqueness of each cohort's access to social resources. This access generates a specific, historical macrobiography which distinguishes that cohort from every other cohort (Children of the Great Depression, of World War II, of Affluence, of Crisis).

Still the differences between a cohort and Mannheim's concept of a generation are obvious. Common age or membership in a birth cohort are but one precondition for the formation of a generation unit possessing a generation consciousness. The concepts neither explain the sense of shared life experience in its historical uniqueness that characterizes members of a generation, nor do they explain the emergence of generation consciousness or the structure of the generation as actuality.

"The great complexity of the generation approach (namely) the interaction of historical, cultural and local factors, while reducing the sameness of same-age people to the modest role of one aspect among many others, on the other hand establishes it as one of the fundamental factors of historical dynamics" (Pfeil, 1967, 656).

Marshall in his contribution takes the conceptual divergencies among age group, cohort, and generation as the point of departure. He then attempts to find out what these concepts have in common and how they may be distinguished from each other. Moreover, he discusses possible applications to empirical research.

But conceptual and terminological clarification, as attempted by Marshall, are seldom taken notice of in the subdisciplines concerned with generation phenomena (cf. also Kertzer, 1983). Conceptual ambiguity is far from being eliminated. On the contrary, the terms generation, age group, and cohort are frequently used synonymously, for instance in demographic research. In youth sociology, by contrast, the term generation is generally used to describe particular, selected age groups. In research on social stratification and social mobility the generation concept refers to reproduction, that is, to the natural succession of lineage (Duncan et al., 1972; Duncan, 1966; Sewell & Hauser, 1972; Featherman & Carter, 1976; Mayer, 1975; Müller, 1978). Here, there has been a shift in emphasis away from intergenerational mobility processes and towards selected cohorts. This shift has been intended to systematically eliminate sources of error that arise out of cohort scattering in the lineage generations, rather than to clarify the generation concept. In the political sciences, "generation" is employed when what is really meant would have to be called "cohort" (Jennings & Niemi, etc., cf. introduction, this volume). Reference to Mannheim is almost ubiquitous, but it tends to serve only a legitimating function.

The model of generational succession developed by Mannheim is also meant to explain historical and social change. In this perspective, Mannheim emphasizes the qualities characterizing and differentiating specific generations.

This perspective, which had long been characteristic of the German-language tradition in generation research, has largely vanished from the current discussion, empiricist approaches neglecting the qualitative aspects of the generation model having won the day. Structural-functional concepts elucidate social change against the background of structural inequalities and social disparities. Berger, who feels indebted to Mannheim's conception, sets off in his contribution the qualitative aspects of the generation model against a restricted, empiricist approach, by showing that the periodic occurrence of youth cultures does not possess the scope of the social change initiated by generational succession.

Obviously, the frequent recourse to Mannheim's generation model can be explained by the fact that one line of his argument is particularly appealing and deceptively concise: his remarks on the formative phase in the life course, specifically the phase of youth. A one-sided reception of his view, however, has narrowed down the investigators' field of vision: rather than taking into account the continual succession of generations, they tend to focus their attention solely on the respective "young generation" (cf. the introduction and Chapter III). Indeed certain aspects of social change can be elucidated in this manner (Hollstein & Berger, this volume), but sociohistorical change in all its complexity cannot.

What has been hardly digested at all are Mannheim's thoughts on the *relation* between various generation-formative entelechies that are constitutive of a generation and of a "Zeitgeist," entelechies which arise in areas as different as religion, philosophy, literature, science, and politics. As a rule these various streams cannot be derived from one another, but they can be compared and collated (Berger, 1960). They are certainly not discrete entelechies whose interrelation is of an "arbitrary nature," as Pinder has assumed. Nor do they represent "new" entelechies which are superadded in a quasi unprecedented way, to existing tradition: their *dynamic relationship with tradition, the tension between old and new entelechies*, is expressed by the formula of the "contemporaneity (Ungleichzeitigkeit) of the coetaneous (Gleichzeitigen)" (Marías, 1970, 114).

"We may conclude from this: generation units are no mere constructs, since they have their own entelechies; but these entelechies cannot be grasped in and for themselves: they must be viewed within the wider framework of the trend entelechies. It follows, furthermore, that it is quite impossible either to delimit or to count intellectual generations (generation units) except as articulations of certain overall trends. The trend entelechy is prior to the generation entelechy, and the latter can only become effective and distinguishable within the former – but this does not mean to say that every one of the conflicting trends at a given point of time will necessarily cause new generation entelechies to arise" (Mannheim, 1968, 315).

A concept of intergenerational relationships which on the one hand, is unambiguous and, on the other can be applied empirically, has yet to emerge. More effort will have to be devoted to terminological and conceptual clarification of the generation concept, in order to exhaust its possibilities without overexhausting the concept. Obviously, this will be necessary above all in those subdisciplines whose object of study is the problem of intergenerational relationships.

Footnote

1 The following editions from the complete works of Karl Mannheim were used in preparing this chapter: Mannheim, K.: "Das Problem der Generationen." In: Kölner Vierteljahresschrift für Soziologie 7 (1928), 2, 157–185 and 3, 309–330; Mannheim, K.: "Das Problem der Generationen," reprinted in: Mannheim, K., Wissenssoziologie. Auswahl aus dem Werk, ed. and introduction by Kurt H. Wolff (Berlin & Neuwied: Luchterhand 1964), 509–565; Mannheim, K.: "The Problem of Generations." In: Mannheim, K., Essays on the Sociology of Knowledge, ed. Paul Kecskemeti (London: Routledge & Kegan Paul 1968, 4th ed.), 276–321.

Tendencies in Generational Research: From the Generation to the Cohort and Back to the Generation[1]

Victor W. Marshall (copyright Victor W. Marshall, 1983)

This paper calls for conceptual clarity, rigor, and complexity in an area of inquiry which is indicated by the following terms: cohort, generation, age grade, age stratum, age group, generation group. In contemporary scholarship in the sociology of age relations these terms are unclear and ill-defined and, consequently, often used interchangeably. Attempts have been made to expunge the term "generation" from the social science vocabulary, except in the sociology of the family and kinship studies (Glenn, 1977; Kertzer, in press; Ryder, 1965). This paper presents an argument that cohort and generation be precisely defined and that both terms, as well as other, accompanying concepts, be retained for sociological analysis.

In addition to conceptual blurring of the cohort and generation terms, similar ambiguity is found in the interchangeable use of the terms cohort and age group (e.g., Easterlin, 1980; Elder, 1974). A similar argument will be made that these terms be kept conceptually distinct in the sociological analysis of age relations.

Cohorts of individuals, generations, and generation groups may be viewed as passing through a life course demarcated by age grades or age strata (Riley, 1971; 1973; 1976b). It is therefore necessary to be precise about age grading and stratification concepts.

The central thrust of this paper is a call for a return to the conceptualization of Mannheim about generations, and for a parallel conceptualization concerning age groups. Difficulties with Mannheim's framework will be discussed, but these difficulties are not viewed as insurmountable. Nor are they serious enough to warrant abondoning his approach. The generations concept is required because of limitations of the cohort concept. These limitations are particularly evident when attempting to develop either a political sociology of age and generation based groups or an analysis of the cultural distinctiveness of generations. The discussion will touch on such well-known theoretical areas of the sociology of aging as age stratification theory, the aging subculture/minority group thesis, and the argument that we are approaching an era of "age irrelevance."

This paper is one of a series of attempts I have made to sort out the many meanings of generation and the set of related concepts which describe the different facets of age relations (Bengtson, Cutler, Mangen, & Marshall, 1982; Bengston, Cutler, Mangen, & Marshall, in press; Marshall, 1981a, b; Tindale & Marshall, 1980). It differs from other attempts in excluding, for purposes of brevity, consideration of generations in the lineage sense and in emphasizing the distinction between age groups and generations.

The Concept of Cohort

There are many lay usages of the term cohort. I have to emphasize that point because the fact that there are also many lay usages of the term generation is taken, mistakenly, as a reason to abandon its usage in social science. The original meaning of the term is "one of the 10 divisions in an ancient Roman legion, numbering from 300 to 600 men"; but it can also mean "any group of warriors," "a group or company," or "a companion or associate" (Random House Dictionary of the English Language). In the social sciences the term is also used in many ways. Norval Glenn, in his book, *Cohort Analysis* (1977, 8) defines cohort as "... those people within a geographically or otherwise delineated population who experienced the same significant life event within a given period of time." Depending on what is meant by "significant life event," this definition can be treated as quite broad and could, for example, be applied to distinguish all those workers in a formal organization who experienced the sacking of the first vice-president from those who were hired after that sacking or who had left the organization before it happened. This is a possible and legitimate use of the cohort concept, but it is not the usage commonly intended by social scientists. As Glenn points out, while the boundaries of a cohort are arbitrarily delineated, and while cohorts may be defined in terms of any number of different events, the term cohort most often deals with a birth cohort, and should be taken as such unless accompanied by a specific modifier (Bengtson, Cutler, Mangen, & Marshall, in press).

I want, in fact, to argue that we continue to use the term cohort to refer to birth cohorts defined arbitrarily, that is, in terms of methodological convenience. Maddox & Wiley (1976, 16) have cautioned analysts to recognize the atheoretical nature of the cohort concept defined in this manner, as Glenn, Ryder (1965), and most demographers define it:

"The decision of investigators to define a cohort in terms of a single year or some longer period appears to be based primarily on practical rather than theoretical grounds. Cohorts differentiated by year of birth are conventional in the construction of life tables. Cohorts differentiated by five-year age spans are conventional in social scientific research in which census data are used."

The cohort concept, then, is not a theoretical concept but a methodological one. *It is a way to organize data.* I do not mean that the notion of cohort is completely unrelated to theory; the concept has theoretical implications. The most important of these is that defining a collection of people in terms of their cohort instead of in terms of their age points to a historical, rather than a maturational interest in them. That is, even though age is fully determined by birth cohort, and vice versa, when one speaks of cohort, one is led to think in terms of the historical period of birth and the historical circumstances experienced by the cohort. This is not a necessary connotation of either term, but, at least in usage in the English language, the connotations and implicit meanings of the two concepts, age and cohort, are quite different. There are, then, implicit, theoretical notions involved here, but the explicit use of the concept of cohort is methodological, as a way to organize data; and that, I submit, is the only usage to be recommended.

Arraying Cohort Data to Define or Describe Generations

Think for a moment in terms of single-year birth cohorts as objects which can be collected together into clusters of adjacent cohorts. Think of an ideal data-set in which we had a great deal of information about a large number of individuals, whose year of birth was known. It would then be possible to examine the data to see if a set of adjacent birth cohorts could be collected together in such a way that they shared some social characteristic not shared by other birth cohorts. An example would be vulnerability to being drafted for military service when both the nation's state of war or peace and its rules governing conscription varied over time (see, e.g., Hogan, 1981, 46–50; Winsborough, 1978; Elder, 1974, 159). It is necessary to dispense with any notion of equal-intervalled birth cohorts here. In some cases you might want to collect three adjacent single-year birth cohorts together and claim (on the basis of data, of course) that this set differed in some important way from other cohorts. In other cases, you might find that five, or seven, or seventeen adjacent single-year birth cohorts could, empirically, be clustered in terms of similarity on some social characteristic.

If we could do that, we would be using the *methodology* of cohort analysis to describe a patterning in the social world — and that is a major objective of the sociologist. We would be extremely surprised if such an analysis produced clusters of equal numbers of single-year cohorts.

It seems useful to me to have a term to describe such cohorts or clusters of cohorts which differentiates them from the single-year birth cohort, or similar cohorts defined arbitrarily for methodological purposes, such as the five-year or the ten-year cohort. A different term is called for because these clusters are defined by some social reality (such as draft laws, in the example above) and not just by the methodological procedure of arraying data by birth year (this point is persuasively argued by Rosow, 1978). The term to use for *non-arbitrary* clusters of single-year birth cohorts which can be shown to be *qualitatively* different on some social variable is "generation."

Norval Glenn (1977, 8), who does not like the term "generation," in fact makes the distinction between generation and cohort quite explicitly:

"The term *generation* is sometimes used synonymously with birth cohort, or it may refer to a birth cohort with 'natural' rather than arbitrary boundaries. In the latter sense, it consists of a birth cohort (or of adjacent birth cohorts) internally homogeneous in some important respect and distinctly different from persons born earlier or later."

My argument is that, if there indeed are birth cohorts with "natural" rather than arbitrary boundaries, then we need a conceptual framework which can handle this social reality.

In fact, there are never "natural" boundaries, but only theory-relevant boundaries; but that is a problem which I will deal with later. At this point, my argument calls for an acceptance of the position that, at least some of the time, it is possible to group single-year birth cohorts in a non-arbitrary way, to call such grouping a "generation," and to distinguish this categorization from the arbitrary array of birth cohorts by regular intervals. The very purpose of describing generations is to point to qualitative differences on some theory-related variables.

Difference and Relationship

Why make this distinction? Because we should never use one term to define two different things. Scientists value parsimony and elegance. We find it counter-productive to find in use two or more terms which mean the same thing. If two terms are closely related, we want to be very sure they have sufficiently distinct referents to justify the added weight in our conceptual and terminological baggage. At the same time, though, we value precision, and do not have much tolerance for words with multiple meanings or a situation in which multiple referents must share the same sign. In general, most of us would agree with Hempel on this point (1965, 141):

"Science aims at knowledge that is *objective* in the sense of being intersubjectively certifiable ... This requires that the terms used in formulating scientific statements have clearly specified meanings and be understood in the same sense by all those who use them."

This argument might sound trivial if not for an additional point. This is that the term generation also carries with it the possibility of dealing with the *relationship* between different socially real groups. This possibility is not readily available when describing cohorts. In short, cohorts describe quantitative or incremental differences, but *generations describe qualitative differences and also social units capable of relating to each other.*

Let me expand a little on the point of differentiation. The differences between a generation and a cohort is analogous to the difference between an array of color words, such as the color wheel or color chart, and the specification of colors by the wave-length (the example is adapted from Kaplan, 1964, 174). Another analogy comes from the measurement of temperature. It is possible to take an incremental approach to the description of temperature, using the Celsius or Fahrenheit scales and treating temperature as a continuous variable. However, on those scales there are critical points at which an additional increment leads to a qualitative, and not just a quantitative change: there is the freezing point and the boiling point. Using the generation concept is analogous to using the broad categories rather than Celsius or Fahrenheit scales. Each approach has its advantages, its strengths, and weaknesses for different purposes.

To take a last analogy from sociology, the difference between a generational approach and a cohort approach is like that between using Marxist social class categories and using the indices of occupational prestige so common in status attainment research in North American "social stratification" research. It is a class versus stratification approach, seeking to directly identify qualitatively different social groups, rather than to describe quantitative differences in some lineal view of reality.

Let us now consider not difference, but relationship. It may be possible, but it is not easy, to talk concretely about the *relationship* between a member of the upper-upper class and of the middle-middle class, on a nine-category social class scale even though this terminology is somewhat useful for talking about differences. It is even more difficult to talk about concrete relationships between persons scoring, for example, 86 on the North-Hatt occupational prestige scale, and those scoring 58. The difficulty in trying to envision studying meaningful social relationships this way – even though the scale scores might be useful in describing differences – suggests the superiority of formulating one's relationship to the economic structure in class terms which delineate concrete social groups[2]. I am suggesting that this applies, by analogy, to the distinction between cohort and generation.

To summarize my argument so far: We need a way to organize data for certain sociological purposes that have to do with age relations and generational relations. The notion of cohort provides a nice methodological technique for doing this. We then want to be able to talk about more than just degrees of difference, but to talk about qualitative differences, and therefore a terminology should be used which clearly tells a reader whether we are dealing with incremental (cohort) or qualitative (generational) differences. Moreover, by providing a way to characterize social groupings which are treated for theoretical purposes as real, the concept of generation also allows us to talk about the relationship between two or more socially real groups or generations.

Generations: Conceptual Distinctions

In his essay, "The Problem of the Intelligentsia ...," Mannheim (1956, 106 f.) begins with the general notion of "social location":

"Social location is a general term of reference to the continuing exposure of individuals to like influences or to the same opportunities, inducements, and restrictions. A common social habitat does not necessarily create like interests ... The term 'location' may even be widened to include such phenomena as generations and age groups. *Class Position*, on the other hand, does imply a certain affinity of interests within a diversified society which selectively allocates power and distributes differential prerogatives and economic opportunities ... Now we may speak of a *class* if individuals act uniformly in accordance with their like interests and like position in the productive process. A *conscious class*, on the other hand, is constituted by the tendency of its members to act collectively in accordance with a conscious evaluation of their class position in relation to all other strata of society.

Class position, class, and conscious class constitute three levels of differentiation. Their personnel need not, and usually do not, coincide."

This brief passage contains the essence of Mannheim's conceptual framework for the analysis of generational phenomena. The analogy to generation and cohort would make cohort location, such as that of a single-year birth cohort, analogous to social location. In many instances, members of a set of adjacent single-year cohorts would share interests, thereby constituting a generation. Finally, there is the possibility that any generation, or some subset of it (or generational grouping) might recognize these common interests, becoming a conscious generation (an "actual" generation) or conscious generational grouping.

A generation does not always become conscious (Mannheim, 1952, 303). Also, not all members of a generation will come to share the same consciousness. To deal with this fact, Mannheim defines the "generation unit." As an example, he noted that German youth from about 1800 onwards tended to move into two opposing directions, one more rationalistic and liberal, the other more conservative. "Can we speak, in this case, of the same actual generation?" Yes, we can, in that these represented "... two *polar forms* of the intellectual and social response to an historical stimulus experienced by all in common." The groups "... belong to the same actual generation but form separate 'generation units' within it" (Mannheim, 1952, 304).

Generation unit, then, refers to "those groups within the same actual generation which work up the material of their common experience in different specific ways ..." (Mannheim, 1952, 304). It becomes a sociological task to describe the social construction of generational consciousness (see, e.g., L. Jones, 1982, on the "baby boom" generation; Howard Becker, 1946, on "Hitler Youth" and C. Levitt, 1979, and R. Flacks, 1967 on "Sixties Radicals").

The concrete group which articulates the ideology of a generation need not even be within the generational location itself, as in the case of the "detached intellectual," or what Mannheim calls, the "forerunner" (1952, 308). This is an important point to consider with respect to the social construction of age and generation groups in a politics of aging. *The meaning of a generation or of an age group may be constructed in diverse ways.* The media, governmental agencies, and interest groups who may or may not share in generation or age-group location, can contribute to such construction (see, e.g., Berger, 1959; Lauter & Bengtson, 1974; Estes, 1978; Guillemard, 1979; Heer, 1974; Jones, 1980).

Age Groups and Age Strata

Birth cohort is by direct implication a perfect predictor of age. If data are organized by single-year birth cohorts, it is quite easy to convert them to data organized by age distinctions, which we may call single-year *age strata.* Again, it becomes possible to empirically investigate whether or not adjacent clusters of people in age strata can be qualitatively differentiated from those in other age strata as measured on some variable. The age-stratification systems of various societies do this in different ways through socially recognized age grades such as childhood, youth, adulthood, old age, etc. However, this clustering can be based on criteria other than social definitions. We can inquire, for example, about the ability to organize data on income, marital status, civil status, eligibility for military service, educational attainment, or virtually anything according to clusters of single-year strata.

It is of course possible to organize these data on the basis of single-year age strata, and this is what we commonly do. And it is usually easier as well. However, the examples I gave do point to qualitative breaking points, which for some theoretical purposes will be better suited to analysis.

Age strata, as Matilda Riley noted when defining the age-stratification perspective (1971; 1976b), are properties of social structure. Cohorts pass through age strata, and, of course, generations also pass through clusters of age strata. *Let us call clusters of age strata "age groups,"* to emphasize their qualitative differentiation from one another. Just as generations or social classes might be seen as relating to or interacting with one another, we can inquire as to the *relationship* between age groups. I distinguished between the ability to differentiate quantitatively and the ability to characterize qualitative differences and then treat sociologically real group relationships in the case of generations. It should be obvious that the argument is identical to that given above for the distinction between cohort and generation.

Now, if these distinctions are accepted, then the following should also be accepted:

(1) Knowing year of birth and knowing time elapsed since birth provides evidence for entertaining three distinct possible causes, correlates, or determinates of social behavior: age (as maturation), cohort, and age stratum, when considered in incremental or quantitative terms.

(2) If attention focuses on qualitative distinctions, then age group and generation become the relevant explanatory alternatives to age (as maturation).

(3) The three locators of the individual may compete with one another or they may interact with or complement one another as explanations for behavior.

Thus, if one finds person A different from person B as measured against some sociological criterion, one is left with the further question of assessing whether this difference is due to age, as maturation, to generation, or to age group (Rosow, 1978). Making the conceptual distinctions does not solve the analytical problem, but, on the other hand, failure to make them disguises the problem and is therefore misleading. Analytical problems are one type of difficulty which fails to disappear when ignored.

Generational Conflict and Age-Group Conflict

I turn now to the question of conflict between people, or collections of people, who differ in age. Conflict is only one form of social relationship, but it is of much interest to social gerontologists interested in public policy. Some of these claim that differences based on age are disappearing as we move to an "age irrelevant society" (Neugarten, 1970). Others see increased tensions and conflict between age groups over the allocation of scarce resources across the life-span (Tindale, 1980a, b; Tindale & Marshall, 1980). Others who focus on the life course of specific cohorts or generations in relation to economic opportunities (Easterlin, 1980; Jones, 1980) raise implications for conflicting interests of different generations or age groups.

Not all single-year birth cohorts will experience profound historical and social events in the same way (Rosow, 1978)[3]. A difference of a year or two, for example, may mean being too old or too young to serve in the armed forces during a major war; or it may mean entering the labor force during a boom period or a period of economic recession or depression. Wars and economic swings are usually thought of as "watershed" events (Cain, Jr., 1967), but, as Ryder points out (1965), "... such vivid experiences are unnecessary to the argument. Cohorts can also be pulled apart gradually by the slow grind of evolutionary change." When a set of adjacent single-year birth cohorts is pulled away from earlier and later cohorts in this manner, the qualitative differentiation that emerges between them should be recognized by the term generation.

It is convenient to address these differences in two analytically and concretely distinct areas: life chances (or life experiences) and consciousness. A generation can be a socially real group in terms of structured life chances; sociologically it would be analogous to a "class in itself" in being distinct from other generations. The extent to which such structuring of life experience leads to differences in consciousness or ideology is a distinct, though of course, important question (Rosow, 1978). Generation members *may* respond to their "shared fate" by developing a consciousness of kind, just as can happen when a "class in itself" becomes a "class for itself."

213

Generational consciousness developed early in life, for example, due to the shared military experience of a large proportion of cohort members from a small set of adjacent cohorts, might be expected to persist to some extent throughout life. One can then talk about a conscious generation passing through the life course.

At some point generational consciousness may be modified (Rosenmayr, 1982a, 30 f.) or come in conflict with age-based consciousness, as when the veteran becomes the pensioner or as the 1960s anti-war political activist enters the age grade or age stratum of middle age (see, e.g., Levitt's 1979 analysis of the "New Left" in Germany, Canada, and the United States).

If one then finds evidence of conflict between persons of different ages, is this conflict age group based, generation based, or maturation based? (Here I leave out of consideration the possibility that it is generation-based in the sense of lineage.)

Authors such as Cain (1964) and Foner, & Kertzer (1978) have described conflict between age groups as highly prevalent in societies with highly developed age groups or a clearly demarcated age stratification system. However, in the industrialized, relatively modernized societies there appears to be little evidence of overt conflict based on age groupings or generational factors (or, for that matter, on lineage generational factors, the "generational gap" being largely a media creation. See Bengtson, 1971). A conflict perspective is nonetheless called for because it brings attention to overt conflict as well as social processes and mechanisms which contain or diminish the expression of overt conflict despite objectively different interests of groups based on age or generation (see Bengtson, Cutler, Mangen, & Marshall, in press; Marshall, 1981). In other words, it is just as important to explain why conflict is so low as it would be to explain why it might be so high (Bengtson, Cutler, Mangen, & Marshall, in press; Marshall, 1981b).

The process of cohort flow (as movement of cohort members over time through the age-stratification system is called by stratification theorists) can itself reduce the potential for conflict between age strata (Foner, 1974). A cohort may change its age-strata affiliation or location, as it moves on to the next older age stratum, before having had time to develop a conscious recognition of collective interests distinct from other age grades. The cohort does not then become a conscious age group. Age-group conflict may also be obviated because members of cohorts who are now in the older age strata, having passed through the earlier levels of the age-stratification system, may develop a tolerance for the vicissitudes of youth. At the same time, the young can themselves look forward to advancing to the older age strata of their society. Surely willingness of young people to support social security programs for the older age strata is increased by their desires to establish or preserve benefits which they will themselves one day enjoy.

While the process of cohort flow (or, in the analysis I recommend, generational flow) through the age stratification system can serve to mitigate age-group conflict, the timing of that flow can, as Foner & Kertzer have shown (1978), itself become a basis for conflict. Progression through the age-stratification system is normally associated with increasing access to power and rewards, except for transitions to the oldest age strata, such as, in our society, through retirement. As a result, cohorts entering the higher age strata may seek to delay their transition, while younger cohorts may seek to accelerate the timing of such transitions. A current example is the increased efforts to encourage early retirement so as to open job vacancies for the young, coupled with resistance to compulsory retirement by those nearest to retirement ages (Tindale, 1980a, b). Flexibility in the age-stratification systems of the advanced post-industrial societies, such as advanced school promotion, gradeless schools, or flexible retirement, reduces the potential for age-group based conflict by obscuring the boundaries between age groups.

Age-group conflict should be conceptually and analytically distinguished from generational conflict. It is based on structured relationships between more or less concrete groups in the age-stratification system. The "more or less" in this statement refers to the empirical question of the extent to which people, as they pass through the age-stratification system, identify with age groups. For example, if people develop a shared consciousness of kind on the basis of age-structured social inequality ("gray power" or "never trust anyone over thirty"), this is a consciousness that is assumed and lost because of the inexorable movement of cohorts through the age-grade system.

Generational consciousness, however, should it arise, is something which can be assumed to persist, with modifications due to maturation, the accumulation of experience, changing age-group interests, social class location, and the interaction of all these factors. As an analytical strategy, it would be unwise to search for generational conflict without recognizing the intersection of other structural bases of conflict; and the same advice applies to any analytical interest in age-group consciousness. Indeed, the intersection of age and class with generational experiences perhaps suggests the most important research areas.

The Problem of Boundaries

A major reason for social scientists to be reluctant to use the concept of generation has been their sense that the concept is imprecise. Methodologically, this leads to the question of how to define a generation. We noted earlier Ryder's point that cohorts can be pulled apart from one another in ways more subtle than responses to cataclysmic events such as wars and depressions. Yet where does the "baby boom generation" begin and end? At what point, with what birth cohorts do we begin and end the demarcation of a generation? How do we decide that a difference in the life experiences of adjacent birth cohort groupings is qualitative and not merely quantitative? These are difficult questions for which no easy answers are possible (Rosow, 1978). But we should nonetheless seek the answers because we do know that there are qualitative differences between generations. We know that the baby boom did face a qualitatively different opportunity structure in the labor force. We know, that the "children of the depression" did have qualitatively different experiences in an atmosphere of poverty and low fertility rates, etc.

Identical problems occur in the delineation of age groups and in the currently very high interest in description of the "life course" for analysis. How do we identify the meaningful age distinctions and exactly where to place the boundaries? Is the distinction between youth and adulthood marked by the end of schooling? By marriage? By citizenship rights, voting, military service, and the like? By parenthood? Is the "old age" group set off from younger age groups by labor force participation criteria? By health? By eligibility for state-supported old age income security?

215

In either case, whether demarcating boundaries of generations or of age groups, the answer is likely to be different depending on the theoretical interests of the investigator. If one is interested in the qualitative structuring of life experiences by one's place in the flow of generations by one's place in the age-stratification system, qualitative differentiation may occur at different points in different spheres. Thus arises problems akin to "periodization" for historians, who will analytically break up the flow of history according to different dates depending on whether they are doing constitutional, social, military, or some other form of history. And yet do we deny the analytic usefulness of periodization?

The essence of Mannheim's concept of generation and generation units lies in the intermingling of birth-cohort categories and historical experiences, and this intermingling is unlikely to be characterized by tremendous precision. Mannheim recognized the problem of establishing exact generational boundaries and cautioned against developing "... a sort of sociology of chronological tables" (Mannheim, 1952, 311). Similarly, Ortega y Gasset warned:

"History has need of a peculiar exactitude, historical exactitude, which is not in any sense mathematical ... the concept of age is not the stuff of mathematics, but of life. Age is not, in point of origin, a date ..." (Ortega y Gasset, 1962, 46).

When members of a generation, or of an age group, become conscious of their positional similarities of interests and articulate them, the social scientist can call upon the definitions of generational members or age-group members themselves to define such boundaries. When people talk of a "lost generation," "baby boom generation," or when they talk of "senior citizens," or warn, "never trust anyone over thirty," or when they describe a "Pepsi generation," they are pointing to something with some reality — at least in a language-game sense. In such cases, our analytic constructs can be "constructs of the second degree, namely, constructs of the constructs made by the actors on the social scene ..." (Schutz, 1967, 6). And while the "Pepsi generation" may really refer, in sociological parlance, to not a generation but an age group, it is equally the case that, when President Franklin D. Roosevelt, in his speech of June 27, 1936 accepting the renomination for the U.S. Presidency, said "A generation of Americans has a rendezvous with destiny," he referred to a generation and not a cohort. And his prediction was certainly confirmed well as various generations experienced in vastly different ways the impact of World War II.

These examples point to something else as well. Generational experiences or age-group experiences need not be based on active conflict. The interests of coexistent generations or age groups may be different but complementary or unrecognized. Much of the "stuff" of generations appears to signify identity-marking tastes and fashions, be they in patterns of dress, musical taste, or recreational activities (e.g., Nash, 1970). In such cases of generational or age-group identity-marking, a sense of "other" is required, but tolerance, even celebration of difference, can characterize the relationship between the different groups[4].

The Mannheimian legacy, however, gave us the tools to address generational phenomena and, by extension, age-group phenomena, even when there is little evidence of consciousness. Just as it is important to investigate the factors which lead, or which inhibit, a "class in itself" to become a "class for itself," so too we ought to investigate the conditions which foster or impede generational consciousness or age-group consciousness. One of the persistent sociological problems of age groups and age relations is precisely to seek an understanding of why there is so little overt conflict (and probably in fact little covert conflict) between age groups and between generations.

Another set of problems, and one about which much research interest had developed, refers to the ways in which the fate of one generation is structured by the fate of another. Richard Easterlin's work on the importance of relative generational size raises important questions here (and answers few of them) (Easterlin, 1968; 1978; 1980). And this work does not explicitly include analyses of generational consciousness. Similarly, Waring's (1976) discussion of the societal effects of "disordered cohort flow," which also gives emphasis to the different relative sizes of cohorts, treats cohorts in terms of generational location without raising issues concerning generational consciousness or "actual generations."

Conclusion

A complex collection of concepts is required to distinguish methodological approaches (which organize data) from a variety of social phenomena which constitute relations between people or groups of people who happen to differ in age. Failure to distinguish conceptually and terminologically between cohort and generation and age stratum and age group will serve to blur or obfuscate phenomena of longstanding sociological interest. Many of the needed conceptual distinctions are to be found in the work of Mannheim. Our concepts should allow for analyses of concrete, socially real differences between generations or age groups, as well as relationships between such groups. Generational and age-group interpretations of many aspects of social life and consciousness may complement or conflict with one another. The difficulties in defining the boundaries of generations and age groups should not deter us from the attempt to examine their importance.

Footnotes

1 My work on this paper has been supported by grant number 6606–1568–48 from Health and Welfare Canada through its National Health Research Development Program, and through grant number 492–79–0075–R1 from the Social Sciences and Humanities Research Council of Canada to Byron Spencer, Frank Denton, and myself. Some of the material is adapted from a paper presented to the 1981 meetings of the Canadian Sociology and Anthropology Association and appears as well in V. Bengtson, N. Cutler, D. Mangen, & V. Marshall, "Aging, Generation, and Inter-generational Relations," forthcoming in E. Shanas & R. Binstock (Eds.), Handbook of Aging and the Social Sciences, Revised Edition, New York: Van Nostrand Reinhold, in press. This version has benefited greatly from discussion at the Symposium on Intergenerational Relationships. I am particularly grateful to Vern Bengtson and Joe Tindale, with whom I have been pursuing conceptual clarity on these issues for some years, for their detailed, helpful critique of an earlier draft.

2   There are of course superior occupational prestige scales, but as my intention was not to debate their merits, I drew on the first important such scale, described by North & Hatt in 1947. My interpretation has been influenced in a general way by Ossowski's contrast between dichotomic conceptions of class structure and "synthetic gradation," although my use is somewhat different. See Ossowski, *Class Structure in the Social Consciousness* (1963). As I discuss below, Mannheim explicitly conceptualized generations along class lines in his essay, "The Problem of the Intelligentsia" (1956).

3   That is to say, generational effects are to be distinguished from "period" effects, which are environmental, social, or historical events which effect all cohorts more or less equally. See Blanchard & Wachs, 1977; Palmore, 1978.

4   I am grateful to Hilde von Balluseck for emphasizing this to me in reaction to the earlier version of this paper. James Dowd (forthcoming) has begun a provocative examination of age group and generational based "otherness," drawing on the sociological concept of "the stranger."

The Resonance of the Generation Concept

Bennett M. Berger

I want to use this essay as a means of commenting (1) on the significance of the unusually wide variety of the contributions in this book, and (2) on the generation concept itself. Although I have strong doubts about the empirical usefulness of the concept of generations, I continue to think that its theoretical significance is considerable, and I will attempt to make that plain by using the sociology of knowledge to analyze why the generations concept has been increasing in theoretical importance since the beginning of this century.

I have been writing on generations in general and generations of youth in particular for more than 20 years (Berger, 1960). Therefore it might well be inferred that I have a vested interest in the vitality of the concept. Yet the persistent diffuseness and elusiveness of the concept of generation are indicated not only by the painstaking care many of us have had to devote to specifying what we mean by the term, but also by the variety of the contributions in this book. A clearly defined concept probably could not comprehend so wide a variety — which ranges from macro-theoretical consideration of issues in the sociology of culture as Mannheim conceived it (Dreitzel), to a careful historical study of household composition and authority (Held), to studies of the problematic character of youth culture (Hebdige) to surveys of three-, four-, and even five-generation families (Bengtson, Hagestad, Kruse), to studies of the aged, including a historical study of attitudes toward the aged (Knopf, Kondratowitz), to family studies emphasizing the role of women (Lehr, Hagemann-White), to a demographer's consideration of some of the difficulties involved in specifying the empirical content of age-related concepts (Mackensen), to (last but surely far from least) Victor Marshall's formal effort to utilize Mannheim's understanding of generations by attempting careful definitions which theoretically distinguish terms like generation, cohort, age-group, age-stratum, conscious-generation, and a number of related terms in order to achieve the kind of conceptual clarity that can then be empirically deployed.

It may seem ironic that, after a culturally ambitious paper like Peter Dreitzel's on generational conflict, and after Marshall's learned and admirable attempt to clarify usage, that the clearest actual use of the generation idea was in some of the contributions concerned primarily with family research, the papers least self-consciously concerned with conceptual problematics. Focusing on the family had the clear merit of operationalizing the idea of generations in terms of the relations of kinship units. If the clarity is ironic, it is ironic because the clarity was achieved without great theoretical stretching or other conceptual discomfort: by simply using the definition of generation found in the most commonly used dictionaries, that is, generation as primarily membership in a kin unit, positioned vis-à-vis descendents and antecedents.

This should not be a surprise. Since the early fieldwork of anthropologists, kinship studies have been the kinds of research settings that lent themselves most readily to conceptual clarity. In functionalist studies of family and kinship, for example, the otherwise elusive concept of integration may be most clearly exemplified; the same is true of the idea of a social *system*: The boundaries that seem clearest in kinship relations become more elusive when attempts are made to apply the concept in larger and more complex social units. But even the relative clarity of the generation concept in family settings may begin to slip away in advanced industrial societies where, for example, high divorce rates lead to large numbers of second and third marriages, and to fathers who have two "generations" of children, thus confounding the clarity of the generation idea and generational "position" even in family settings.

The leap from the culture of families to the culture of cohorts is still more complex. For research purposes, families have the merit (and the troubles) of being real interacting groups. Cohorts and age-strata, however, are statistical categories, not real groups, and one of the many merits of Marshall's contribution is to clarify the fact that cohorts only become generations (in the classic Mannheimian sense) when intersections of biography and history lead to empirical clusterings of behavior by those of roughly the same age on a number of important variables. Those clusterings suggest the probability of real interaction, and that probable interaction suggests the sources of a common culture. Nevertheless, age-phenomena never appear in isolation. They are always confounded by the variables that eternally puzzle sociologists — class, religion, ethnicity, gender, education — and these variables, of course, are likely to weaken the imputed solidarity of cohorts even when it can be shown that by virtue of a common birthdate they have been subjected to common formative influences from the massive social facts of a given era. Even in some of the excellent family studies in this book, it is clear that the structure of a generational position is affected not only by kinship but by property relations, by authority, by residence, and other variables that affect family relations.

It is, in part, for reasons like these that Marshall's efforts to clarify "generation" and related terms are so important. Those efforts are designed to enable us to move from definitional criteria set on "arbitrary" methodological grounds to criteria set on theoretical or naturalistic grounds. On the whole, I think, his efforts at clarity are successful. But Talcott Parsons (himself no paragon of lucidity) once said in ironic behalf of obscurity that to be clear these days is to be found out[1]. The empirical usefulness of Marshall's clarity depends on the facts it enables us to find — particularly facts which qualitatively distinguish one cohort from another, and hence to warrant designating them as distinct "generations." When applied to some empirical subject matter, Marshall's conceptual clarity could, at best, conceivably enable us to discover "generations of ..." students, soldiers, mental patients, politicians, or any other group the age-structure of whose behavior was studied. But Mannheim's notion of "generation-as-actuality" (to say nothing of his idea of "conscious generation") would still be elusive in these empirical terms unless we were able to find high levels of intercorrelated cohort behavior on a large number of variables whose connections were sufficiently palpable to justify the theoretical imputation of a common culture to a historically located age group. My guess is that they will not be easy to find, at least not a lot of the time; in any case they have not in fact been frequently found. But the question is an empirical one, and the burden of proof or persuasion is on the investigator.

In a sense, the conceptual problem of clarifying the concept of generation is not unlike the problems in the evolution of the concept of culture itself. From its ancient usage in Latin, down toward the end of the 18th century, the word "culture" consistently conveyed the idea of "tending" or "cultivating" (from crops and herds to manners and sensibilities). Near the end of the 18th century the German historian Herder, in a Romantic effort to oppose the ethnocentrism of Europeans who regarded their own modes of spiritual cultivation as the acme of human civilization, spoke (for probably the first time) of other "cultures" — that is, of peoples as "having" a culture. Herder thus introduced a new usage which took almost another hundred years to be fully institutionalized in the vocabulary of anthropology through Edward Tylor's influential text, *Primitive Culture* (1870)[2].

The change in the usage of the word "culture" was from a noun of process (the culture — or cultivation — of ...) to an independent substantive noun (Balinese culture, primitive culture, German culture, etc.). Similarly, there is a parallel difference, subtle yet important, between "generation" as a noun of process indicating the ways in which the historical location of a cohort may predispose it (by virtue of its shared occupancy of a specific intersection of biography and history) toward common behavior patterns, and "generation" as an independent substantive noun which characterizes *an* age group as sharing or "having" a culture by virtue of that common historical location. The difference is a difference between seeing historically located cohorts (a statistical category) as being "influenced" by their "age" (both their chronological age and their "age" in the sense of era) *to some extent* (the extent being variable, depending on the influence of other powerful factors), and seeing the intersections of biography and history as sufficiently hegemonic to impute *decisive* cultural influence to it. In another sense, it is a difference between the empirical or nominalistic tradition of variable probability, and the "realistic" tradition of reification.

It should, then, be clear from the above that I remain skeptical about the potential of the concept of generations to empirically reveal fresh and important dimensions of social structure or culture. But as a sociologist of ideas I could not fail to be impressed by the persisting (and even increasing) *resonance* of the idea of generations in contemporary cultural discourse. And in light of what I take to be its doubtful empirical status, the resonance of the concept itself invites sociological analysis. One promising beginning for such analysis is to note the ways in which the generation concept has been utilized, the groups and issues to which it has been applied — and not applied. Until very recently, for example, discussions of generations proceeded as if women were not a part of them. But note that with the large increase in the number of female scholars in recent decades, the prominence of women in the discussions of generations has increased — surely. Again, until recently, most of the theoretical work on generations has focused on "younger" generations: youth culture, student movements, and the like — although in recent years the best empirical work has probably been on the "older" generation — on the "aged," the "senior citizens," and those other designations of the elderly that enable "us" (i.e., the middle-aged or the no-longer-young) to cultivate our welfare attitudes toward them.

It seems unlikely that the predominant focus in generation studies either on the young or the old is entirely inadvertent. Studies are usually funded for more or less practical purposes, and both the young and the old are actually or potentially problematic populations. Most of the old are poor and female, and many of them are widowed and alone. Large proportions of them are, consequently, a burden and a problem for the community. The young become a problem when significant numbers of them assert claims or behave in ways that the dominant community may be reluctant to honor or respect or tolerate, particularly when the young are politically rebellious or culturally recalcitrant or otherwise behave in ways inappropriate to the age-graded culture which is assigned to them.

In either case, both groups, the young and the old, are largely *dependent*, relatively powerless populations who are vulnerable to efforts by dominant middle-aged sectors of the community to conceive and characterize them in such a way that the problematic features of their status become accessible to treatment or correction or other forms of social control. Note, however, that variables other than age have a strong effect on the vulnerability of members of these groups. There are wealthy and powerful members of the community who are over 65 years of age, and who, strictly speaking, belong to the statistical category of the "aged," but who are not likely to be characterized or treated in terms of the patronizing category of "senior citizen." I might have several suggestions, for example, regarding how Ronald Reagan, 71, might spend his declining years more wholesomely. But he, and others like him would not permit it because their wealth and power are sufficient to insulate them from the welfare designs of others. That, of course, is what wealth and power are about: maintaining sufficient autonomy to prevent others from altering the conditions of one's life — indeed to enable one to alter the conditions of other people's lives. In multi-racial Brazil, it is said that "money whitens." In industrial societies money and power make the aged younger.

But even where money and power are absent, the increasing health and longevity of Western populations are making it more difficult to characterize the aged population homogeneously. At least two studies of the aged in this book, for example, found it necessary to distinguish in their samples between the "decrepit" aged and those who are still relatively hale and hearty, and (above all) competent (Attias-Donfut in this book). Indeed, to speak of the hearty and competent "aged" seems almost like a contradiction in terms, so accustomed have we become to thinking of the "aged" as basically a welfare category: a concept whose major function it is to enable agencies of social control legitimately to adopt patronizing attitudes toward them.

Similarly, when a generational focus is on youth, relatively little attention is typically paid to working-class youth or lower-middle class youth (Dick Hebdige's work is exceptional in this respect), except, perhaps, when they form gangs or otherwise engage in structured forms of delinquency — and even in these cases the conceptual focus is usually less on generations than it is on "deviance" or "subcultures." But generations of youth (males mostly) which are distinctive enough to warrant labeling (i.e., the lost generation, the beat generation, the "hippie" generation, etc.) are, strictly speaking in Mannheimian terms, not generations but generation-units: relatively elite, well-educated groups from the upper-middle class or higher whose "unitary" character may be fleeting or transitory and which, even when it is not, is sometimes as much a result of the self-fulfilling character of the publicity it attracts as it is an expression of a common culture actually shared.

I have said enough in these pages so far to indicate (1) that there is relatively little evidence to suggest that the historical location of cohorts by itself induces important and significant empirical clusterings of behavior and attitude sufficient to warrant designating such cohorts as generations, and (2) that the generation concept is, nevertheless, profound because, like other constructed realities ("cultural" phenomena exist to the extent that it is believed they exist), it "frames" and legitimates the dominant attitudes and modes of social control toward the age groups so conceived. In this sense, the major significance of generation-rhetoric is mythic or ideological.

Saying this, however, in no way denies that specific, historically located cohorts may face special, even unique conditions or problems which predispose them toward common responses. Kohli is probably correct in saying that the generational approach to problems is more relevant on the European continent — particularly Germany — where sharp breaks in cultural and social continuity have been more common than in the United States (Kohli, 1978, 33 ff.). But even where, for example, a severe economic depression impacts most sharply on a cohort just entering the labor force for the first time, it does not necessarily produce real generational conflict between a unified (by their economic problems) younger generation and an older generation unified (by its economic security) against it. For one thing, all but the most severe kinds of economic crises affect those just entering the labor force *differentially*; many, even majorities, do find work, and that is likely to be one, among other factors which fracture cohort solidarity into "units." Moreover, a severe depression is a crisis not just for those entering the labor force; it is a crisis for the whole society which is thus threatened by political destabilization. Economic crises, then, are likely to produce political conflicts *within* a middle-aged (or older) ruling class over means of solving the crisis, thus creating the conditions for the alliance of the young with those sectors of the older population who favor solutions which, by serving the legitimate economic interests of the young, can contribute to defusing the political crisis. But it is also significant that the very framing of an economic crisis in terms of generational relations has the ideological function of distracting attention from its class basis.

My skepticism, then, about the generation idea goes to the root of its most common usage in the sociology of culture — although not in demography or survey research, where the generation concept is seldom used in that sense. In the sociology of culture a generation is usually understood as a cohort whose members, by virtue of their historical location, undergo certain common experiences at a formative stage of their lives which decisively affect their attitudes, mentalities, and sensibilities, which eventually leave their mark on the culture of an era as the "spirit of the age," or *Zeitgeist*. Moreover, the generation idea usually also assumes that generations so shaped carry their distinctive psychology through time, as the course of their lives moves them through the various age-strata from vigorous youth to aged decrepitude.

I have been trying to convey the view that not only is there relatively little evidence to sustain this conception of generations, but that the conception itself is replete with doubtful assumptions that should make one wonder how and why the generation idea achieved the plausibility and the resonance it did. That an age group has a common temporal (or historical) location and is thus exposed to the "same" set of objective events does not mean that those events will be *experienced* in the same way. In addition, for most generation theorists, the "formative stage" is usually conceived as late adolescence and early adulthood. Orthodox Freudians would surely not agree, given their emphasis on the importance of early childhood experience for subsequent psychological development. Moreover, one's very exposure to objective events (to say nothing of one's experience of them) is affected not only by a person's temporal location but by his or her structural (class, religion, ethnicity, education, etc.) location as well. Mannheim's notion of "generation-unit," therefore, is, I think, far more important than his concept of generations.

It seems to me that a sociology of knowledge approach to the idea of generations is the most promising one for understanding its development and its increasing *chic* over the past 60 or 70 years. I have no doubt that the generation idea has been successful enough to induce certain groups to *think* of themselves as a generation (Mannheim's "conscious generation"), and that some generation-units to some extent experience a common *Lebenswelt* (or what I would prefer to call a subculture). But I think also that these subjective experiences are less a function of a common temporal location (i.e., birthdate) than of social structures which may induce a *sense* of generational solidarity when they *concentrate* large *numbers* of age-homogeneous people in relatively restricted places and thus encourage dense *interaction* and *communication* among them.

Karl Marx himself saw the conditions for the development of working-class consciousness in the numbers, concentration, and communication of the proletariat in restricted places called factories — although even that, however plausible, is empirically questionable. Similarly, the concentration of large numbers of the young in places called schools, and the concentration (as well as the increasing numbers) of the "aged" in places called retirement communities or old-age homes or senior citizen centers can promote dense interaction and communication among them (their dispersion into age-heterogeneous groups would not), and thus induce the development of subcultures and a common sense of generational identity. It plausibly follows that the age group, say, from 35 to 65 years old are seldom thought of in "generational" terms precisely because they are far less structurally concentrated.

I am suggesting, then, that generational consciousness has less to do with one's placement in a birth cohort than with the social structures into which persons are channeled by virtue of the age-grading imperatives of macro-political and economic development. Those structures are historically variable, and they have changed radically in Western countries since the introduction of industrialization, the consequent urbanization of populations, and the spread of democracy (more literally the spread of entitlement rights to broader sectors of the population). Specifically, since the late 19th century, the gradual exclusion of youth and the aged from the labor force, and the gradual spread and lengthening of compulsory education for the former (as well as the lengthening life of the latter) create some of the conditions which facilitate the development of subcultures with, perhaps, common sorts of grievances. (Urbanization and the unification of school districts and the expansion of universities have created large schools with thousands, sometimes tens of thousands of students which enable these grievances to be quickly communicated among them.) But the result is not one subculture or *Lebenswelt*, but pluralities of them, which continue to reflect the impact of powerful factors other than age. It is perhaps the most commonplace feature of research in American high schools and universities to note the pluralities of subcultures to be found in them.

But not just any of these subcultures (and not at just any time) get characterized and mythicized as generations. I first became aware of this aspect of the problem of generations late in the 1950s, when there was much discussion in the United States of a so-called "Beat Generation." As a marginal "member" of that group or cohort in its prime location (the San Francisco Bay area) I was aware that the concept was in large part a creation of publicity – in sociological terms, a myth, and in both senses of that term: it was clear that "we" represented only a tiny minority of that cohort, and that it was hence simply inaccurate and misleading to characterize the cohort as a "Beat Generation"; but it was also a myth in the sense of a powerful cultural claim to manifest a *Zeitgeist*. That claim may have been made by a few literary figures (Jack Kerouac, Allen Ginsberg) in the small "beat" sector of the cohort. But given the small size of the sector (in Mannheim's terms a generation-unit – and a tiny one at that), the claim would have seemed absurd without the mass media who, for reasons perhaps best known to itself, decided to "take up" the "Beat" phenomenon and celebrate and/or deplore it in every town and hamlet of the nation.

That I was there, on the scene, observing – and even participating in – the creation of a myth made me profoundly skeptical of the idea of generational solidarity, and sensitive to the purposes of the gatekeepers of culture in their decisions about whether or not to select this or that political or cultural (usually cultural) ripple among young intellectuals and attempt to transform it into a generational wave. It also started me thinking about the meaning of the generation idea. If generations were an important political and cultural category, why is it that it had not been used as a major explanatory variable prior to the very late 19th century or the turn of the 20th? Is it true that it had not been so used? That's the kind of question that tests one's historical learnedness, and I make no great claims for my own. But my reading on the topic suggested that the idea of generation as an expression of cohort-solidarity was a relatively new historical phenomenon. The first references to it that I could find occur around the turn of the century and accelerate with the First World War (Hughes, 1958; Wohl, 1979).

Lewis Feuer's book on generational conflict surely makes clear that differences between the young and the old, and tensions between fathers and sons are as old as the oldest human writings. But that is not the same as invoking generations as a conscious political category – which requires a leap from the cultures of families to the culture of cohorts. Feuer assigns the origin of the contemporary use of the generation idea to the influence of Romanticism on the post-French revolutionary period of nationalist movements, for example, Mazzini's movement of "Young Italy," and comparable movements in other countries (Feuer, 1969). Moreover, it is possible to see the incipient development of the generation idea in the activities and rhetoric of the Russian intelligentsia from about the 1840s onward.

Conceptual origins are, of course, difficult to date precisely, not only because of the inevitable incompleteness of historical search, but also because of the subtleties of linguistic usage, particularly where it involves translation from one language to another. But the leap from the culture of families to the culture of cohorts (which is the core of the contemporary generation idea) is bridged by the idea of *subculture*, which is itself rooted in the selective interaction of a population which is relatively homogeneous on one or more variable (age, sex, religion, ethnicity, class, etc.), relatively insulated, and relatively concentrated. Moreover, however stable and viable subcultures are (ethnic subcultures tend to be the most viable because they often have a relatively full complement of mini-institutional structures undergirding them — religion, polity, economy, endogamy, etc.), they are always vulnerable to harassment or worse by dominant authorities, and hence require support, or at least passive toleration by authorities.

Now, I place the development of the contemporary idea of generations (i.e., cohort subcultures) across the divide of the 19th and 20th centuries not only because I have been unable to find its unambiguous usage earlier, but because the idea takes on plausibility and resonance in rough correlation with processes that appear to create some conditions for subcultural development. The unionization of labor gradually excludes the young from the labor market through anti-child labor legislation; compulsory education laws are passed; the length of minimal required education increases; schools are established and gradually consolidated; the idea of "adolescence" is popularized (Hall, 1904); by the late 1920s scholars are already talking about "youth cultures" as they had talked of "the generation of 1914" and the "generation of 1890" earlier.

If it is true that "a little education is a dangerous thing" (through its ability to de-provincialize and render broader sectors of the population articulate) and if it is true that "younger" generations (at least the ones so designated) are often characterized as in "revolt" against some (usually "bourgeois") status quo, does it seem odd that ruling authorities do not routinely crush such generational solidarities? Not if one understands that generational solidarity is usually the putative solidarity of an elite sector ("unit") of a cohort, and, short of an extreme Freudianism, there is relatively little visible basis in chronological age (surely far less than in ethnicity) to sustain a durable subculture or for the common expression of major political grievance by "youth" against a ruling "older generation." Thus, in a manner not unlike that in which the conceptualization of the "aged" serves social control functions, an asserted generational solidarity diverts the potentialities of real political conflict (which have their basis in such durable differences as wealth, status, ethnicity, religion, etc.) into a false and relatively innocuous pseudo-conflict which time itself naturally resolves[3]. Such diversion helps train young elites, gives them some experience in struggles over political power which, because they are elites, they would in any case probably inherit or otherwise come by naturally.

Hence, ruling authorities are frequently (although not always) tolerant even of "radical" younger generations — so long as the radicalism is primarily cultural rather than political — by which I mean when the demands for radical change are limited to things like manners, art, sexual behavior, mores, and "lifestyle" generally, rather than demands for radical change in the structure of political power or the distribution of wealth. Indeed, my impression is that *political* radicals of the Left seldom identify with "generations" (the 1960s were a major — and brief — exception) whereas *cultural* radicals (Right and Left) frequently do. There are some good reasons for this. The natural constituencies of political radicals are the op-

226

pressed classes; hence serious political radicals must aim at winning the allegiance of masses or majority coalitions of groups with deep and serious grievances, and that requires solidarities that *bridge* cohorts. Cultural radicals, on the other hand, are usually running off to the frontiers of experience – in art, sex, drugs, religion, the occult, "lifestyle," etc., leaving "the people" far behind. Moreover, the natural constituencies of young avant-garde or modernist innovators in art and lifestyle are certain sectors of the high bourgeoisie and lower levels of the aristocracy or upper classes, who buy their work, adopt their styles, and otherwise abet such swings in fashion.

To the extent that it is recognized that certain forms of modernist and avant-garde culture are not major threats to the political and economic interests of ruling classes, the cultural radicalism of the young can be tolerated by ruling groups, and cultural radicals can come to terms with them. Bismarckian and Wilhelmine Germany tolerated a lot of youthful cultural radicalism (Green, 1974), and even the Soviets did for a short while, and I think that the sharp and sudden decline of the New Left was accelerated by the realization that the counter*culture* of the young was going to be tolerated, perhaps even co-opted, whereas the radical political actions of the young were going to be suppressed. Still, I do not wish to overstate the hypothesis: The Greek Colonels and the military leaders of Chile's Right-wing coup were as hostile to cultural deviance as they were to socialism.

Nevertheless, the major point is that young cultural innovators (the groups most frequently labeled over nearly the past century as "generations") don't typically need a major transformation of the political and economic order to achieve their aims. More often than not, all they need are relatively restricted audiences, publics, ambiances, milieux, which are sufficiently insulated against the large community or functionally important to it (in the way, e.g., that "colorful" Latin Quarters of cosmopolitan cities bring tourist business to them, are defended by active merchants' associations, and are therefore at least tolerated, if not wholly respectable parts of their economies). I think, therefore, that the concept of generations will continue to have significant cultural resonance so long as it is relatively toothless politically, and dominant authorities will not seriously discourage generational identities.

Footnotes

1 Unfortunately, Parsons never made this remark in print. It was made at a party, after a talk he gave in Palo Alto, California.
2 See the account by Raymond Williams in *Keywords* (New York; Oxford University Press, 1976).
3 In putting the matter this way, I do not intend to write off culture as epiphenomenal nor generational identities as simply a kind of "false consciousness." Even relatively innocuous identifications can leave lasting impressions on sensibilities and have later unanticipated political consequences when conditions are ripe for them.

References

ABRAMS, M. 1959: The Teenage Consumer. London: Press Exchange.

ACOCK, A. & V. BENGTSON 1980: "Socialization and Attribution Processes: Actual Versus Perceived Similarity Among Parents and Youth." J Marr Fam 40 (3): 501–515.

ADAMS, B. N. 1967: "Interaction Theory and the Social Network." Sociom 30 (1): 64–78.

ADAMS, B. N. 1968: Kinship in an Urban Setting. Chicago, Ill.: Markham.

ADAMS, B. N. 1970: Isolation, Function and Beyond: American Kinship in the 1960's. J Marr Fam 32: 575–597.

ADDAMS, J. 1972: The Spirit of Youth and the City Streets. Chicago, Ill.: University of Illinois Press (originally published 1909).

AGNELLO, T. J. J. Jr. 1973: "Aging and the Sense of Political Powerlessness." Publ Op Q 37: 251–259.

AINSWORTH, M. D. S. 1973: "The Development of Infant-Mother Attachment." In: CADWELL, B. M. & H. N. RICCIUTI (eds.), Review of Child Development Research. Chicago, Ill.: University of Chicago Press 3, 1–94.

AINSWORTH, M. D. S., BLEHAR, M. C., WATERS, E., & S. N. Wall 1978: A Psychological Study of the Strange Situation. Hillsdale, N.J.: Erlbaum.

ALDOUS, J. 1978: Family Careers: Developmental Change in Families. New York: Wiley.

ALLERBECK, K. & L. ROSENMAYR 1971: Aufstand der Jugend? Neue Aspekte der Jugendsoziologie. München: Juventa.

ALPERT, J. L. & M. S. RICHARDSON 1980: "Parenting." In: POON, L. W. (ed.), Aging in the 1980s. Psychological Issues. Washington, D.C.: American Psychological Association, 441–454.

ANGRES, S. 1975: Integrational Relations and Value Congruence Between Young Adults and their Mothers. Chicago, Ill.: University of Chicago (unpublished doctoral dissertation).

ARIES, P. 1960: L'enfant et la vie familiale dans l'ancien régime. Paris: Librairie Plon.

ARIES, P. 1975: Geschichte der Kindheit. München and Wien: Hanser.

ARIES, P. 1979: "Phasen der Geschichte der Familie." In: PERREZ, M. (ed.), Krise der Kleinfamilie? Bern: Huber, 43–48.

ARIES, P. 1982: Geschichte des Todes. München: Deutscher Taschenbuchverlag.

ARIES, P. 1983: "The Origin and Development of the Segregation of Youth in Contemporary Western Societies." Abstract prepared for the International Symposium on Intergenerational Relationships, February 21–24, Berlin.

ATKINSON, M. A. 1980: "Some Practical Uses of 'A Natural Lifetime'." Human Studies 3: 33–46.

ATTIAS-DONFUT, C. 1983: "La vieillesse inégale." In: Communications. Vol. 37: Le Continent Gris. Paris: Seuil, 125–135.

ATTIAS-DONFUT, C. & M. COGNALONS-NICOLET 1980: "Après 50 ans, la redistribution des inégalités." Documents d'information et de gestion, Cagnes s/Mer: CNRO, 46–47

ATTIAS-DONFUT, C. & A. M. GUILLEMARD 1983: "Recherche. Le parcours des âges." Rapports des groupes de travail nationaux. Assises Nationales des Retraités et Personnes Agées. Paris: Secrétariat d'Etat chargé des personnes âgées, 105–147.

ATTIAS-DONFUT, C. & A. ROZENKIER 1979: "Vieillesse et identité collective." In: TAP, P. (ed.): Identité individuelle et personnalisation. Toulouse: Privat, 90–95.

ATTIAS-DONFUT, C. & A. ROZENKIER 1983: La médicalisation des logements-foyers. Paris (unpublished manuscript).

BABCHUK, N. 1978: "Aging and Primary Relations." Aging and Human Development 9: 137–151.

BADINTER, E. 1980: L'amour en plus. Paris: Flammarion.

BALANDIER, G. 1974: Antropo-logiques. Paris: Presses Universitaires de France (P.U.F.).

BALANDIER, G. 1983: "Préface." In: FERRAROTTI, F., Histoire et histoires de vie. Paris: Librairie des Méridiens, 1–9.

BALBO, L. 1982: "Statement for a Panel Discussion." In: Sektion Frauenforschung in den Sozialwissenschaften (ed.), Beiträge zur Frauenforschung am 21. Deutschen Soziologentag. München: 4–10.

BALTES, P. B. 1968: "Longitudinal and Cross-Sectional Sequences in the Study of Age and Generation Effects." Hum Dev 11: 145–171.

BALTES, P. B., REESE, H. W., & L. P. LIPSITT 1980: "Life-Span Developmental Psychology." Ann Rev Psych 31: 65–110.

BARNES, R. 1980: Mods. London: Eel Pie Publishing.

BECKER, H. 1946: German Youth: Bond or Free. London: Kegan Paul, Trench, Trubner and Co.

BECKER, W. 1975: "Jugendkriminalität und Resozialisierung. Einführungsvortrag." In: Deutsche Akademie für medizinische Fortbildung Kassel (ed.), Jugendkriminalität und Resozialisierung (Kongreßbericht 1974). Stuttgart: Enke, 8–15.

BENGTSON, V. L. 1971: "Inter-age Differences in Perception and the Generation Gap." Geront II (4, Part II): 85–89, 103–108.

BENGTSON, V. L. 1975: "Generation and Family Effects in Value Socialization." Am soc R 40: 358–371.

BENGTSON, V. L. 1979: "Research Perspectives on Intergenerational Interaction." In: RAGAN, P. K. (ed.), Aging Parents. Los Angeles, Calif.: University of Southern California Press, 37–57.

BENGTSON, V. L. 1983: "The Multi-Generational Family: Concepts and Results from Gerontological Research." Paper presented at the International Symposium on Intergenerational Relationships, February 21–24, Berlin.

BENGTSON, V. L. et al. 1983 (in press): "Aging Generations and Relations Between Age Groups." In: BINSTOCK, R. & E. SHANAS (eds.), Handbook of Aging and the Social Sciences. New York: Van Nostrand-Reinhold.

BENGTSON, V. L. & K. BLACK 1973: "Intergenerational Relations and Continuities in Socialization." In: BALTES, P. B. & K. SCHAIE (eds.), Life-Span Developmental Psychology: Personality and Socialization. New York: Academic Press, 207–234.

BENGTSON, V. L., BURTON, L., & D. MANGEN 1981: "Morale and Family Supports: Contrasts Among Blacks, Mexican-Americans, and Whites." Paper presented to the Symposium on Families Caring for Elders, Annual Meeting of the Gerontology Society of America, November 8–12, Toronto.

BENGTSON, V. L. & N. E. CUTLER 1976: "Generations and Intergenerational Relations." In: BINSTOCK, R. H. & E. SHANAS (eds.), Handbook of Aging and the Social Sciences. New York: Van Nostrand-Reinhold, 130–159.

BENGTSON, V. L. & J. A. KUYPERS 1971: "Generational Differences and the Developmental Stake." Aging and Human Development 2 (1): 249–260.

BENGTSON, V. L., MANUEL, R. C., & L. M. BURTON 1981: "Competence and Loss: Perspectives on the Sociology of Aging." In: DAVIS, R.H. (ed.), Aging: Prospects and Issues. Los Angeles, Calif.: The University of Southern California Press, 22–39.

BENGTSON, V. L., OLANDER, E., & A. HADDAD 1976: "The 'Generation Gap' and Aging Family Members: Toward a Conceptual Model." In: GUBRIUM, J. F. (ed.), Time, Roles and Self in Old Age. New York: Human Sciences Press, 237–263.

BENGTSON, V. L. & S. SCHRADER 1982: "Parent-child Relations." In: MANGEN, D. J. & W. A. PETERSON (eds.), Research Instruments in Social Gerontology. Vol. 2. Minneapolis, Minn.: University of Minnesota Press, 115–185.

BENGTSON, V. L. & E. de TERRE 1980: "Aging and Family Relations: A Decade Review." J Marr Fam 3 (2): 51–76.

BENGTSON, V. L. & J. TREAS 1980: "The Changing Family Context of Mental Health and Aging." In: BIRREN, J. E. & B. SLOANE (eds.), Handbook of Mental Health and Aging. Englewood Cliffs, N.J.: Prentice-Hall, 400–428.

BENN, C. 1978: The Family Centre Project. Progress Report 1972–1978, Melbourne: Brotherhood of Saint Laurance.

BENNETT, T. (ed.) 1981: Culture, Ideology, and Social Process. Batsford: Open University Press.

BERGER, B. M. 1960: "How Long is a Generation?" B J S 11: 557–568.

BERKNER, L. K. 1972: "The Stem Family and the Development Cycle of the Household: An Eighteen-Century Austrian Example." Am Hist Rev 77: 398–418.

BERKNER, L. K. 1975: "The Use and Misuse of Census Data for the Historical Analysis of Family Structure." Journal of Interdisciplinary History 5: 721–738.

BERTAUX, D. 1980: "L'approche biographique. Sa validité methodologique, ses potentialités." Cahiers Internationaux de sociologie. Histoires de vie et vie sociale (N° spécial). LXIX: 197–227.

BERTAUX, D. (ed.) 1981: Biography and Society. The Life History Approach in the Social Sciences. Beverly Hills, Calif.: Sage.

BERTAUX-WIAME, I. 1981: "Artisanal Bakers in France. How they Live and Why they Survive." In: BECHHOFER, F. & B. ELLIOTT (eds.), The Petit Bourgeoisie. Comparative Studies of an Uneasy Stratum. London: Macmillan.

BETTELHEIM, B. 1963: "The Problem of Generations." In: ERIKSON, E. H. (ed.), Youth: Change and Challenge. New York: Basic Books, 64–92.

BEVERS, A. M. 1982: Oudere mensen en hun kinderen. Nijmegen: Sociol. Instit.

231

BIERHOFF-ALFERMANN, D. 1977: Psychologie der Geschlechtsunterschiede. Köln: Kiepenheuer & Witsch.

BINSTOCK, R. H. 1983: "The Aged as Scapegoat." Geront 23 (2): 136–143.

BIRREN, J. E. & K. W. SCHAIE 1977: "Research on the Psychology of Aging: Principles and Experimentation." In: BIRREN, J. E. & K. W. SCHAIE (eds.), Handbook of the Psychology of Aging. New York: Van Nostrand-Reinhold, 3–38.

BLAKE, M. 1981: Soziologie der jugendlichen Subkulturen. Eine Einführung. Frankfurt a.M. and New York: Campus.

BLANCHARD, R. D., BUNKER, J. B., & M. WACHS 1977: "Distinguishing Aging, Period and Cohort Effects in Longitudinal Studies of Elderly Populations." Socio-Economic Planning Sciences 11 (3): 137–146.

BLAU, Z. S. 1973: Old Age in a Changing Society. New York: Franklin Watts.

BLENKNER, M. 1965: "Social Work and Family Relationships in Later Life with Some Thoughts on Filial Maturity." In: SHANAS, E. & G. STREIB (eds.), Social Structure and the Family. Englewood Cliffs, N.J.: Prentice-Hall, 46–59.

BLÜCHER, V. Graf 1966: Die Generation der Unbefangenen. Düsseldorf and Köln: Diederichs.

BOCK, G. & B. DUDEN 1977: "Arbeit als Liebe – Liebe als Arbeit." In: Frauen und Wissenschaft. Berlin: Courage, 118–199.

BOSZORMENYI-NAGY, I. 1975: "Dialektische Betrachtungen der Intergenerationen-Familientherapie." Ehe 12: 117–131.

BOSZORMENYI-NAGY, I. & J. L. FRAMO (eds.) 1975: Familientherapie – Theorie und Praxis. Opladen: Westdeutscher Verlag.

BOSZORMENYI-NAGY, I. & G. M. SPARK 1973: Invisible Loyalties: Reciprocity in Intergenerational Family Therapy. New York: Harper & Row.

BOURDIEU, P. B. & J.-C. Passeron 1971: Die Illusion der Chancengleichheit. Stuttgart: Klett.

BOWLBY, J. 1951: Maternal Care and Mental Health. (Monogr. 2) Genf: WHO.

BRAKE, M. 1980: The Sociology of Youth Culture and Youth Subcultures. London: Routledge and Kegan Paul.

BRAUNGART, R. G. 1974: "The Sociology of Generations and Student Politics: A Comparison of the Functionalist and Generational Unit Models." J Soc Iss 30: 31–54.

BRAUNGART, R. G. 1982: "Historical Generations and Youth Movements: A Theoretical Perspective." Paper presented at the World Congress of Sociology, August 16–21, Mexico City.

BRAUNGART, R. G. & M. M. BRAUNGART 1980: "Political Career Patterns of Radical Activists in the 1960s and 1970s: Some Historical Comparisons." Sociological Focus 13: 237–254.

BRIM, O. G. 1968: "Adult Socialization." In: Clausen, J. A. (ed.), Socialization and Society. Boston: Little, Brown & Co., 182–226.

BRODY, E. M. 1979: "Aged Parents and Aging Children." In: RAGAN, P. K. (ed.), Aging Parents. Los Angeles, Calif.: University of Southern California Press, 267–287.

BRODY, E. M. 1981: "Women in the Middle and Family Help to Older People." Geront 21 (5): 471–480.

BRONFENBRENNER, U. 1976: Ökologische Sozialisationsforschung. Stuttgart: Klett.

BRONFENBRENNER, U. 1978: "Ansätze zu einer experimentellen Ökologie menschlicher Entwicklung." In: OERTER, R. (ed.), Entwicklung als lebenslanger Prozeß. Hamburg: Hoffmann & Campe, 33–65.

BRONFENBRENNER, U. 1979: The Ecology of Human Development. Cambridge, Mass.: Harvard University Press.

BROWN, R. 1960: "Family Structure and Social Isolation of Older Persons." J Geront 15: 170–174.

BRUDER, J. 1982: "Interaktionsstile im Mehrgenerationshaushalt." In: RADEBOLD, H. & G. SCHLESINGER-KIPP (eds.), Familien- und paartherapeutische Hilfen bei älteren und alten Menschen. Göttingen: Vandenhoeck & Ruprecht, 76–83.

BRUDER, J., KLUSMANN, D., & I. LÜDERS 1981: "Umgangsformen mit dementiven Störungen in der Familie – Zwischenergebnisse eines laufenden Forschungsprojekts." Aktuelle Gerontologie 11: 156–159.

BRUNNER, R. 1975: "Schwerpunkte der Jugendkriminalität." In: Deutsche Akademie für medizinische Fortbildung Kassel (ed.), Jugendkriminalität und Resozialisierung (Kongreßbericht 1974). Stuttgart: Enke, 16–23.

BUCHHOFER, B., FRIEDRICHS, J., & H. LÜDKE 1970: "Alter, Generationsdynamik und soziale Differenzierung. Zur Revision des Generationsbegriffs als analytisches Konzept." Kölner Z S S 22: 300–334.

BULLENS, H. 1982: "Eltern-Kind-Konflikte im Jugendalter." In: OERTER, R. & L. MONTADA (eds.), Entwicklungspsychologie. Ein Lehrbuch. München, Wien, and Baltimore: Urban & Schwarzenberg, 743–768.

BURDACH, K. F. von 1837: Der Mensch nach den verschiedenen Seiten seiner Natur. Anthropologie für das gebildete Publicum. Stuttgart: P. Balzsche Buchhandlung (2nd ed.: 1847).

BUSS, A. R. 1973: "An Expression of Developmental Models that Separate Ontogenetic Changes and Cohort Differences." Psychological Bulletin 80: 466–479.

CAIN, L. D. Jr. 1964: "Life Course and Social Structure." In: FARIS, R. E. L. (ed.), Handbook of Modern Sociology. Chicago, Ill.: Rand McNally, 272–309.

CAIN, L. D. Jr. 1967: "Age Status and Generational Phenomena: The New Old People in Contemporary America." Geront 7: 83–92.

CANGUILHEM, G. 1974: Das Normale und das Pathologische. München: Hanser.

CANGUILHEM, G. 1979: Wissenschaftsgeschichte und Epistemologie. Frankfurt a.M.: Suhrkamp.

CAPLAN, G. 1974: Support Systems and Community Mental Health. Lectures on Concept Development. New York: Behavioral Publications.

CAREW, J. V. 1977: "Die Vorhersage der Intelligenz auf der Grundlage kindlicher Alltagserfahrungen." In: GROSSMANN, K. E. (ed.), Entwicklung der Lernfähigkeit in der sozialen Umwelt. München: Kindler, 108–144.

CAREW, J. V. 1980: "Experience and the Development of Intelligence in Young Children at Home and in Day Care." Monogr Soc Res Chld Devel 45: 6–7 (Serial No. 187).

CARLSSON, G. & K. KARLSSON 1970: "Age, Cohorts, and the Generation of Generations." Am soc R 35: 710–718.

CARPENTER, M. 1853: Juvenile Delinquents, their Condition and Treatment. London (publisher unknown).

CAVAN, R. S. & K. H. RANCK 1969: The Family and the Depression. A Study of One Hundred Chicago Families. New York: Books for Libraries Press Freeport (1st ed.: 1928).

CHAMBERS, I. 1982: Popular Culture and Popular Music. London: Macmillan.

CLARKE, J. 1976a: "The Skinheads and the Magical Recovery of Community." In: HALL, S. & T. JEFFERSON (eds.), Resistance Through Rituals. London: Hutchinson, 99–102.

CLARKE, J. 1976b: "Style." In: HALL, S. & T. JEFFERSON (eds.), Resistance Through Rituals. London: Hutchinson, 175–191.

CLARKE, J. et al. 1979: Jugendkultur als Widerstand. Milieus, Rituale, Provokationen. Frankfurt a.M.: Syndikat.

CLOWARD, R. & L. E. OHLIN 1960: Delinquency and Opportunity. Chicago, Ill.: Free Press.

COHEN, A. K. 1955: Delinquent Boys: The Culture of the Gang. Glencoe, Ill.: Free Press.

COHEN, P. 1972: "Subcultural Conflict and Working Class Community." In: Working Papers in Cultural Studies, 2, Spring. Birmingham, Ala.: University of Birmingham, Center for Contemporary Cultural Studies.

COLE, T. R. 1980: Past Meridian: Aging and the Northern Middle Class. Rochester, N.Y.: University of Rochester (doctoral dissertation).

COLEMAN, J. S. 1961: The Adolescent Society. New York: Free Press.

COLEMAN, J. S. 1970: "Interpretations of Adolescent Culture." In: ZUBIN, J. & A. M. FREEDMAN (eds.), The Psychopathology of Adolescence. New York: Grune & Stratton.

COLEMAN, P. G. C. 1974: Psychologische meetinstrumenten; vooronderzoek over de meting van variabelen met betrekking tot de verplaatsing van oudere mensen. Nijmegen: Geront. Centrum, 32.

CONNELL, R. 1972: "Political Socialization in the American Family: The Evidence Re-Examined." Publ Op Q 36: 321–333.

CONRAD, C. 1982: "Altwerden und Altsein in historischer Perspektive. Zur neueren Literatur." Zeitschrift für Sozialisationsforschung und Erziehungssoziologie 2 (1): 73–90.

COTTLE, T. J. 1967: Time's Children. Impression of Youth. Boston, Mass.: Little, Brown & Co.

CROSSMAN, L., LONDON, C. & C. BARRY 1981: "Older Women Caring for Disabled Spouses: A Model for Supportive Services." Geront 21 (5): 464–470.

CUMMING, E. & W. E. HENRY 1961: Growing Old: The Process of Disengagement. New York: Basic Books.

CYTRYNBAUM, S., BLUM, L., PATRICK, R. et al. 1980: "Midlife Development: A Personality and Social Systems Perspective." In: POON, L. W. (ed.), Aging in the 1980s. Psychological Issues. Washington, D.C.: American Psychological Association, 463–474.

CZAP, P. 1982: "The Perrenial Multiple Family Household, Mishino, Russia 1782–1858." Journal of Family History 7: 5–26.

DAHLIN, M. 1980: "Perspectives on the Family Life of the Elderly in 1900." Geront 20: 99–107.

DEUTSCHES JUGENDINSTITUT (ed.) 1982: Die neue Jugenddebatte. Was gespielt wird und um was es geht: Schauplätze und Hintergründe. München: Juventa.

DICKENS, C. 1838: Oliver Twist. London (republished by Penguin, London 1969).

DIEDERICHSEN, D., HEBDIGE, D. & D. O. MARX 1983: Schocker. Stile und Moden der Subkultur. Reinbek: Rowohlt.

DILTHEY, W. 1961[3]: "Über das Studium der Geschichte der Wissenschaften vom Menschen, der Gesellschaft und dem Staat." In: DILTHEY, W., Die geistige Welt. Einleitung in die Philosophie des Lebens. Erste Hälfte. Abhandlungen zur Grundlegung der Geisteswissenschaften. Stuttgart: B. G. Teubner; Göttingen: Vandenhoeck & Ruprecht, 31–73 (1st ed.: 1875).

DORN, H. F. 1959: "Mortality." In: HAUSER, P. M. & O. D. DUNCAN (eds.), The Study of Population. Chicago, Ill.: University of Chicago Press, 437–471.

DOUGLAS, M. 1973: Natural Symbols. London: Barrie/Jenkins (2nd ed.).

DOWD, J. J. 1983 (in press): "The Old Person as Stranger." In: MARSHALL, V. W. & A. HARRIS (eds.), Later Life: Social Psychological Issues. Norwood, N.J.: Ablex Publishing Co.

DOWNES, D. 1966: The Delinquent Solution. London: Routledge and Kegan Paul.

DREITZEL, H. P. 1981: "The Socialization of Nature – Western Attitudes toward Body and Emotions." In: HEELAS, P. & A. LOCK (eds.), Indigenious Psychologies. London: Academic Press.

DRERUP, H. & H. TERHORST 1979: "Wissensproduktion und Wissensanwendung im Bereich der Erziehungswissenschaft." Zeitschrift für Pädagogik 25: 377–394.

DUBY, G. 1981: "Zur Stellung der Frau innerhalb der Familie im Frankreich des 12. Jahrhunderts." In: MANNZMANN, A. (ed.), Geschichte der Familie oder Familiengeschichten? Zur Bedeutung von Alltags- oder Jedermannsgeschichte. Königstein/Ts.: Scriptor, 92–101.

DUMAZEDIER, J. 1974: Sociologie empirique du loisir. Paris: Seuil.

DUNCAN, O. D. 1966: "Methodological Issues in the Analysis of Social Mobility." In: SMELSER, N. J. & S. M. LIPSET (eds.), Social Structure and Mobility in Economic Development. Chicago, Ill.: Aldine, 51–97.

DUNCAN, O. D., FEATHERMAN, D. L., & B. DUNCAN 1972: Socioeconomic Background and Achievement. New York: Seminar Press.

DUNKEL-SCHETTER, C. & C. WORTMAN 1981: "Dilemmas of Social Support: Parallels Between Victimization and Aging." In: KIESLER, S., MORGAN, J., & V. OPPENHEIMER (eds.), Aging: Social Change. New York: Academic Press, 349–381.

DURKHEIM, E. 1893: De la division du travail social. Paris: Presses universitaires de France (7th ed.: 1960).

DURKHEIM, E. 1964: The Division of Labor in Society. New York: Free Press (1st ed.: 1893).

EASTERLIN, R. A. 1968: Population, Labor Force, and Long Swings in Economic Growth: The American Experience. New York: National Bureau of Economic Research (Columbia University Press).

EASTERLIN, R. A. 1978: "What Will 1984 be Like? Socioeconomic Implications of Recent Twists in Age Structure." Demography 15 (4): 397–432.

EASTERLIN, R. A. 1980: Birth and Fortune: The Impact of Numbers on Personal Welfare. New York: Basic Books.

EHMER, J. 1982: "Zur Stellung alter Menschen in Haushalt und Familie – Thesen auf der Grundlage von quantitativen Quellen aus europäischen Städten seit dem 17. Jahrhundert." In: KONRAD, H. (ed.), Der alte Mensch in der Geschichte. Wien: Verlag für Gesellschaftskritik, 62–103.

EHRMANN, W. 1976: Das Ausgedinge im 19. Jahrhundert im österreichischen Donauraum. Wien: Institut für Wirtschafts- und Sozialgeschichte (unpublished manuscript).

EIRMBTER, W. H. 1982: "Bildungsaspiration und sozialökologischer Kontext." In: VASKOVICS, L. A. (ed.), Umweltbedingungen familialer Sozialisation. Stuttgart: Enke, 237–254.

EISENSTADT, S. N. 1956: From Generation to Generation: Age Groups and the Social Structure. Glencoe, Ill.: Free Press.

EISENSTADT, S. N. 1978: Revolution and the Transformation of Societies. New York: Free Press.

ELDER, G. H. Jr. 1974: Children of the Great Depression. Chicago, Ill.: University of Chicago Press.

ELDER, G. H. Jr. 1975: "Age Differentiation and the Life Course." In: INKELES, A., COLEMAN, J., & N. SMELSER (eds.), Annual Review of Sociology. Vol. I. Palo Alto, Calif.: Annual Reviews, 165–190.

ELDER, G. H. Jr. 1978a: "Approaches to Social Change and the Family." Am J Soc 84: 1–38.

ELDER, G. H. Jr. 1978b: "Family History and the Life Course." In: HAREVEN, T. K. (ed.), Transitions. New York: Academic Press, 17–64.

ELDER, G. H. Jr. 1978c: "Approaches to Social Change and the Family." In: DEMOS, J. & A. BOOCOCK (eds.), Turning Points. Chicago, Ill.: University of Chicago Press, 1–38.

ELDER, G. H. Jr. 1979: "Historical Change in Life Patterns and Personality." In: BALTES, P. B. & O. G. BRIM, Jr. (eds.), Life Span Development and Behavior. New York: Academic Press, 118–162.

ELDER, G. H. Jr. 1981a: "History and the Life Course." In: BERTAUX, D. (ed.), Biography and Society. Beverly Hills, Calif.: Sage, 77–115.

ELDER, G. H. Jr. 1981b: "History and the Family: The Discovery of Complexity." J Marr Fam 43: 489–519.

ELDER, G. H. Jr. & J. K. LIKER 1982: "Hard Times in Women's Lives. Historical Influences Across Forty Years." Am J Soc 88 (2): 241–269.

ELDER, G. H. Jr. & R. C. ROCKWELL 1978: "Historische Zeit im Lebenslauf." In: KOHLI, M. (ed.), Soziologie des Lebenslaufs. Darmstadt and Neuwied: Luchterhand, 78–102.

ELIAS, N. 1978: The Civilizing Process. Vol. I: The History of Manners. New York: Urizon Press.

ELIAS, N. 1982a: The Civilizing Process. Vol. II: Power and Civility. New York: Urizon Press.

ELIAS, N. 1982b: Über die Einsamkeit der Sterbenden. Frankfurt a.M.: Suhrkamp.

236

ELIAS, N. 1983: "Über den Rückzug der Soziologen auf die Gegenwart." Kölner Z S S 35: 29–40.

ELKIND, D. 1980: "Egozentrismus in der Adoleszenz." In: DÖBERT, R., HABER-MAS, J., & G. NUNNER-WINKLER (eds.), Entwicklung des Ichs. Meisenheim: Hain, 170–178.

EMERSON, R. 1981: "On Last Resorts." Am J Soc 87 (1): 1–22.

ENDERS-DRAGÄSSER, U. 1981: Die Mütterdressur. Basel: Mond-Buch.

ERIKSON, E. H. 1966: Enfance et Société. Paris: Delachaux et Niestlé.

ERIKSON, E. H. 1968: Identity. Youth and Crisis. New York: Norton.

ESLER, A. 1971: Bombs, Beards and Barricades: 150 Years of Youth in Revolt. New York: Stein & Day.

ESLER, A. (ed.) 1974: The Youth Revolution. The Conflict of Generations in Modern History. Lexington, Mass.: D. C. Heath and Co.

ESTES, C. L. 1979: The Aging Enterprise. San Francisco, Calif.: Jossey-Bass.

FEATHERMAN, D. L. & T. M. Carter 1976: "Discontinuities in Schooling and the Socioeconomic Life Cycle." In: SEWELL, W. H., HAUSER, R. M.. & D. L. FEATHERMAN (eds.), Schooling and Achievement in American Society. New York: Academic Press, 133–160.

FENDRICH, J. M. 1974: "Activists Ten Years Later: A Test of Generational Unit Continuity." J Soc Iss 30: 95–118.

FENGLER, A. & N. GOODRICH 1979: "Wives of Elderly Disabled Men: The Hidden Patients." Geront 19 (2): 175–183.

FENGLER, A. & V. WOOD 1972: "The Generation Gap: An Analysis of Studies on Contemporary Issues." Geront 12: 124–128.

FERRAROTTI, F. 1983: Histoire et Histoires de vie. Paris: Librairie des Méridiens.

FEUER, L. S. 1969: The Conflict of Generations. New York: Basic Books.

FEUER, L. S. 1978: Einstein et le conflit des générations. Préface de Serge MOS-COVICI. Paris: Ed. Complexe.

FILIPP, S.-H. (ed.) 1981: Kritische Lebensereignisse. München, Wien, and Baltimore: Urban & Schwarzenberg.

FILIPP, S.-H. 1982: "Kritische Lebensereignisse als Brennpunkte einer angewand-ten Entwicklungspsychologie des mittleren und höheren Erwachsenenalters." In: OERTER, R. & L. MONTADA (eds.), Entwicklungspsychologie. München, Wien, and Baltimore: Urban & Schwarzenberg, 769–788.

FINCH, J. 1983: Married to the Job. London: Allen & Unwin.

FISCHER, D. H. 1977: "Growing Old: An Exchange." N Y R B: 47–48.

FISCHER, D. H. 1978: Growing Old in America. New York: Oxford University Press (2nd ed.).

FITZGERALD, M., McLENNAN, G., & J. PAWSON 1981: Crime and Society: Readings in History and Theory. London: Routledge and Kegan Paul.

FLACKS, R. 1967: "The Liberated Generation: An Exploration of the Roots of Student Protest." J Soc Iss 23 (1): 52–75.

FLACKS, R. 1971: Youth and Social Change. Chicago, Ill.: Rand McNally.

FLOERECKE, P. & N. HERRIGER 1982: "Prävention als sozialpädagogisches Pro-gramm." In: MÜLLER, S. et al. (eds.), Sozialarbeit als soziale Kommunalpolitik. Neue Praxis, Sonderheft 6: 43–56.

FONER, A. 1974: "Age Stratification and Age Conflict in Political Life." Am Soc R 39: 187–196.

FONER, A. 1976: "Age Stratification and Age Conflict in Political Life." In: ATCHLEY, R. C. & M. M. SELTZER (eds.), The Sociology of Aging: Selected Readings. Belmont, Calif.: Wadsworth, 191–205.

FONER, A. 1978: "Altersschichtung und Alterskonflikte im politischen Leben." In: KOHLI, M. (ed.), Soziologie des Lebenslaufs. Darmstadt and Neuwied: Luchterhand, 107–121.

FONER, A. & D. KERTZER 1978: "Transitions Over the Life Course: Lessons from Age-Set Societies." Am J Soc 83 (5): 1081–1104.

FONER, A. & K. SCHWAB 1981: Aging and Retirement. Monterey, Calif.: Brooks & Cole.

FOOKEN, I. 1980: Frauen im Alter – eine Analyse intra- und interindividueller Differenzen. Frankfurt a.M.: Lang.

FOOKEN, I. 1981: "Women in Old Age: The Need of a Differentiated View." Proc. XII. International Congress of Gerontology, July 12–17, Hamburg, Vol. II: 97.

FOUCAULT, M. 1971: Die Ordnung der Dinge. Eine Archäologie der Humanwissenschaften. Frankfurt a.M.: Suhrkamp.

FOUCAULT, M. 1973: Die Geburt der Klinik. Eine Archäologie des ärztlichen Blicks. München: Hanser.

FOUCAULT, M. 1979: The History of Sexuality. Vol. 1. London: Allen Lane.

FREUD, S. 1950: Collected Papers. Vol. V. London: Hogarth Press.

FRIEBEL, H. et al. (eds.) 1979: Selbstorganisierte Jugendgruppen zwischen Partykultur und politischer Partizipation am Beispiel von Jugendzentren und Fußball-Fanclub. Opladen: Westdeutscher Verlag.

FRIEDAN, B. 1963: The Feminine Mystique. New York: Norton.

FRITH, S. 1978: The Sociology of Rock. London: Constable.

FTHENAKIS, W. E., NIESEL, R., & H. R. Kunze: Ehescheidung. München: Urban & Schwarzenberg.

FYVEL, T. R. 1963: The Insecure Offenders. A Rebellious Youth in the Welfare State. London: Penguin.

GARMS-HOMOLOVÁ, V. 1982: "Gemeindepsychologische Perspektiven der Versorgung alter Menschen." In: JUNKERS, G., PETERMANN, F., RÖNNECKE, B. et al. (eds.), Anwendungsfelder der klinischen Psychologie und Psychotherapie in verschiedenen Lebensaltern. München: Steinbauer & Rau, 122–125.

GARMS-HOMOLOVÁ, V. 1983: "Einführung: Gesundheitslage und Versorgungsbedarf alter Menschen aus ökologischer Perspektive." In: BLUMENSTOCK, J. (ed.), Gesundheitslage alter Menschen – Epidemiologische Daten im Umweltvergleich. Berichte aus der Studie Ökologische Bedingungen der Gesundheitserhaltung alter Menschen in einer Großstadt. Berlin: Institut für soziale Medizin, Selbstverlag, 3–16.

GASSETT, J. O. y 1931: The Modern Theme. New York: Daniel (see also ORTEGA).

GAULLIER, X. 1982: "Economic Crisis and Old Age. Old Age Policies in France." Aging and Society 2: 165–182.

GAUNT, D. 1983: "The Property and Kin Relationship of Retired Farmers in Northern and Central Europe." In: WALL, R., ROBIN, J., & P. LASLETT (eds.), Family Forms in Historic Europe. Cambridge: Cambridge University Press, 249–280.

GEHLEN, A. 1949: Sozialpsychologische Probleme in der industriellen Gesellschaft. Tübingen: Mohr (revised 1957 as: Die Seele im technischen Zeitalter. Reinbek: Rowohlt).

GERGEN, K. J. & J. MORAWSKI 1980: "An Alternative Metatheory for Social Psychology." In: WHEELER, L. (ed.), Review of Personality and Social Psychology. Beverly Hills and London: Sage, 326–352.

GERTH, H. H. & C. W. MILLS 1946: From Max Weber: Essays in Sociology. New York: Oxford University Press.

GILLIGAN, C. 1979: "Woman's Place in Man's Life Cycle." Harv Ed R 49 (4): 431–446.

GILLIS, J. R. 1981: Youth and History. New York: Academic Press.

GLENN, N. D. 1974: "Aging and Conservatism." Annals 415: 176–186.

GLENN, N. D. 1977: Cohort Analysis. Beverly Hills and London: Sage.

GLENN, N. D. 1980: "Values, Attitudes, and Beliefs." In: BRIM, O. G. Jr. & J. KAGAN (eds.), Constancy and Change in Human Development. Cambridge, Mass.: Harvard University Press, 596–640.

GOFFMAN, E. 1971: Interaktionsrituale. Über Verhalten in direkter Kommunikation (Interaction Ritual). Frankfurt a.M.: Suhrkamp.

GOSLIN, D. (ed.) 1969: Handbook of Socialization Theory and Research. Chicago, Ill.: Rand McNally.

GROHMANN, H. 1980: Rentenversicherung und Bevölkerungsprognosen. Frankfurt a.M. and New York: Campus.

GROHMANN, H. 1981: "Wege zur Bewahrung der langfristigen Stabilität der Rentenversicherung im demographischen, ökonomischen und sozialen Wandel." Deutsche Rentenversicherung 5: 265–290.

GROSS, M. L. 1978: The Psychological Society. New York: Random House.

GROSSBERG, L. 1982: Some Observations on Rock 'n' Roll in American Culture. Chicago, Ill.: University of Illinois, Unit for Criticism and Interpretative Theory (unpublished manuscript).

GUILLEMARD, A. M. 1980: La vieillesse et l'Etat. Paris: Presses Universitaires de France (P.U.F.).

GUMBRECHT, H. U. 1981: "Sozialgeschichte als Geschichte der Verteilung und Evolution gesellschaftlicher Wissensvorräte." In: GUMBRECHT, H. U., REICHARDT, R., & T. SCHLEICH (eds.), Sozialgeschichte der Aufklärung in Frankreich. Vol. I. München: R. Oldenbourg, 37–51.

GUTENBERGER, B. & V. SPRAN-KUHLEN 1980: Erziehungshilfen. Materialien zum 5. Jugendbericht. München: Deutsches Jugendinstitut.

HAAN, N. 1977: Coping and Defending. Processes of Self-Environment Organization. New York: Academic Press.

HAGEMANN-WHITE, C. et al. 1981: Hilfen für mißhandelte Frauen. Stuttgart: Kohlhammer.

HAGEMANN-WHITE, C. 1982: Die Entwicklung des weiblichen Sozialcharakters (unpublished manuscript).

HAGESTAD, G. O. 1977: "Role Chance in Adulthood: The Transition to the Empty Nest." Chicago, Ill.: University of Chicago, Committee on Human Development (unpublished manuscript).

HAGESTAD, G. O. 1981: "Problems and Promises in the Social Psychology of Intergenerational Relations." In: FOGEL, R. et al. (eds.), Aging: Stability and Change in the Family. New York: Academic Press, 11–46.

HAGESTAD, G. O. 1982a: "Life-Phase Analysis." In: MANGEN, D. & W. PETERSON (eds.), Research Instruments in Gerontology. Vol. 1. Minneapolis, Minn.: University of Minnesota Press, 463–532.

HAGESTAD, G. O. 1982b: "Parent and Child: Generations in the Family." In: FIELD, T. et al. (eds.), Review of Human Development. New York: Wiley, 485–499.

HAGESTAD, G. O. & R. DIXON 1980: "Lineages as Units of Analysis: New Avenues for the Study of Individual and Family Careers." Paper presented at the NCFR Theory Construction and Research Methodology Workshop, Portland, Oregon.

HAGESTAD, G. O., SMYER, M. A., & K. L. STIERMAN 1983: "Parent-Child Relations in Adulthood: The Impact of Divorce in Middle Age." In: COHEN, R., WEISSMAN, S., & B. COHLER (eds.), Parenthood: Psychodynamic Perspectives. New York: Guildford Press.

HAJNAL, J. 1982: "Household Formation Patterns in Historical Perspective." Population and Development Review: 449–494.

HALL, G. S. 1904: Adolescence: Its Psychology and its Relations to Physiology, Anthropology, Sociology, Sex, Crime, Religion and Education. New York: Appleton.

HALL, S. et al. (eds.) 1978: Policing and Crisis — Mugging, the State and Law and Order. London: MacMillan.

HALL, S. & T. JEFFERSON (eds.) 1976: Resistance Through Rituals. London: Hutchinson.

HAMMEL, E. A. 1972: "The Zadruga as a Process." In: LASLETT, P. & R. WALL (eds.), Household and Family in Past Time. Cambridge: Cambridge University Press, 335–373.

HAREVEN, T. 1978: "Historical Changes in the Life Course and the Family: Policy Implications." In: YINGER, J. N. & S. J. CULTER (eds.), Major Issues. New York and London.

HARRIS, L. et al. 1979: American Attitudes toward Pensions and Retirement. New York: Johnson & Higgins.

HARRIS, L. et al. 1981: Aging in the Eighties: America in Transition. Washington, D.C.: National Council on the Aging (NCOA).

HAUSEN, K. 1976: "Die Polarisierung der 'Geschlechtscharaktere' — Eine Spiegelung der Dissoziation von Erwerbs- und Familienleben." In: CONZE, W. (ed.), Sozialgeschichte der Familie in der Neuzeit Europas. Stuttgart: Klett, 363–393.

HAUSER, P. M. & O. D. DUNCAN (eds.) 1959: The Study of Population. Chicago, Ill.: University of Chicago Press.

HAVIGHURST, R. J. 1972: Developmental Task and Education. New York: Davis McKay.

HEBDIGE, D. 1976: "Reggae, Rastas and Rudies." In: HALL, S. & T. JEFFERSON (eds.), Resistance Through Rituals. London: Hutchinson.

HEBDIGE, D. 1979: Subculture. The Meaning of Style. London: Methuen.

HEBDIGE, D. 1981a: "Towards a Cartography of Taste 1935–1962." In: BENNETT, T. et al. (eds.), Popular Culture: Past and Present. London: Croom-Helm.

HEBDIGE, D. 1981b: "Subculture: Image and Noise." In: DALE, R. et al. (eds.), Education and the State. Vol. 2: Politics, Patriarchy and Practice. London: Falmer Press, 87–95.

HEBDIGE, D. 1983: "The Subculture as Interaction Context and its Relevance to Generational Affiliation." Paper presented at the International Symposium on Intergenerational Relationships, February 21–24, Berlin.

HEBERLE, R. 1951: Social Movements. New York: Appleton-Century-Crofts.

HEER, F. 1974: Revolutions of Our Time: Challenge of Youth. London: Weidenfeld and Nicolson.

HELD, T. 1982: "Rural Retirement Arrangements in Seventeenth to Nineteenth-Century Austria: A Cross-Community Analysis." Journal of Family History 7: 227–254.

HEMPEL, C. G. 1965: Aspects of the Scientific Explanation and other Essays in the Philosophy of Science. New York: Free Press.

HENKE, A. 1841: Lehrbuch der Gerichtlichen Medizin. Leipzig and Erlangen: Dämmler (10th ed.).

HESS, B. B. & J. M. WARING 1978: "Parent and Child in Later Life: Rethinking the Relationship." In: LERNER, R. M. & G. B. SPANIER (eds.), Child Influences on Marital and Family Interaction: A Life-Span Perspective. New York: Academic Press, 241–273.

HILL, R. et al. 1970: Family Development in Three Generations. Cambridge, Mass.: Schenkman.

HIRSCHFIELD, I. S. & H. DENNIS 1979: "Perspectives." In: RAGAN, P. K. (ed.), Aging Parents. Los Angeles, Calif.: University of Southern California Press, 1–10.

HÖRL, J. 1983: Alter und Hilfe. Wien (unpublished doctoral dissertation).

HOERNING, E. M. 1983: "Historical and Biographical Time. The Effects of an Historical-Political Event on Generational Consciousness: The Case of the Berlin Wall." Paper presented at the 32nd Annual Meeting of The Society for the Study of Social Problems (SSSP), August 27–30, Detroit.

HOFFMAN, L. W. 1979: "Maternal Employment – A Review." Am Psychol 34: 859–865.

HOGAN, D. F. 1981: Transitions and Social Change: The Early Lives of American Men. New York: Academic Press.

HOGGART, R.: The Uses of Literacy. London: Penguin.

HOLLSTEIN, W. 1981: Die Gegengesellschaft. Alternative Lebensformen. Reinbek: Rowohlt.

HOLLSTEIN, W. 1983: Die gespaltene Generation. Jugendliche zwischen Aufbruch und Anpassung. Berlin and Bonn: J. H. W. Dietz Nachf.

HOMANS, G. 1950: The Human Group. New York: Harcourt, Brace & World.

HORNSTEIN, W. 1982: Unsere Jugend: Über Liebe, Arbeit, Politik. Weinheim: Beltz.

HOUSE, J. S. 1983: Work, Stress and Social Support. Philippines: Addison-Wesley.
HUBBARD, W. H. 1983: Familiengeschichte. Materialien zur deutschen Familie seit dem Ende des 18. Jahrhunderts. München: Beck.
HUBER, H. 1979: "Die Familie: Sozialanthropologische Sicht." In: PERREZ, M. (ed.), Krise der Kleinfamilie? Bern, Stuttgart, and Wien: Huber, 27–41.
HUDSON, R. B. & R. H. BINSTOCK 1976: "Political Systems and Aging." In: BINSTOCK, R. H. & E. SHANAS (eds.), Handbook of Aging and the Social Sciences. New York: Van Nostrand-Reinhold, 369–400.
HUNT, D. 1978: "Theorie und Forschung über konzeptuelle Niveaus als Wegweiser zur Erziehungspraxis." In: MANDL, H. & G. L. HUBER (eds.), Kognitive Komplexität. Göttingen: Hogrefe, 293–310.
HUNT, J. P. 1982: "Political Behavior, Political Alienation, and the Sociology of Generations." Sociological Focus 150: 93–106.
IMHOF, A. E. 1981: Die gewonnenen Jahre. Von der Zunahme unserer Lebensspanne seit dreihundert Jahren oder von der Notwendigkeit einer neuen Einstellung zu Leben und Sterben. München: Beck.
INGELHART, R. 1980: "Zusammenhang zwischen sozioökonomischen Bedingungen und individuellen Wertprioritäten." Kölner Z S S 32: 144–153.
JAEGER, H. 1977: "Generationen in der Geschichte. Überlegungen zu einer umstrittenen Konzeption." Geschichte und Gesellschaft 3 (4): 429–452.
JAIDE, W. 1961: Eine neue Generation? Eine Untersuchung über Werthaltungen und Leitbilder der Jugendlichen. München: Juventa.
JAIDE, W. 1970: Jugend und Demokratie. Politische Einstellungen der westdeutschen Jugend. München: Juventa.
JAIDE, W. 1978: Achtzehnjährige – zwischen Reaktion und Rebellion. Politische Einstellungen und Aktivitäten Jugendlicher in der Bundesrepublik. Opladen: Westdeutscher Verlag.
JENNINGS, M. K. & R. G. NIEMI 1974: The Political Character of Adolescence. Princeton, N.J.: Princeton University Press.
JENNINGS, M. K. & R. G. NIEMI 1975: "Continuity and Change in Political Orientations: A Longitudinal Study of Two Generations." American Political Science Review 69: 1316–1335.
JENNINGS, M. K. & R. G. NIEMI 1981: Generations and Politics. A Panel Study of Young Adults and their Parents. Princeton, N.J.: Princeton University Press.
JOHNSON, C. L. 1983: "Interdependence and Aging." In: SOKOLOVSKY, J. (ed.), Growing Old in Different Societies. Belmont, Calif.: Wadsworth, 92–103.
JONES, A. 1980: Women Who Kill. New York: Fawcett Columbine.
JONES, L. Y. 1980: Great Expectations: America and the Baby Boom Generation. New York: Ballantine Books.
KADE, S. 1983: Methoden des Fremdverstehens. Ein Zugang zu Theorie und Praxis des Fremdverstehens. Bad Heilbrunn: Klinkhardt.
KAHN, R. & T. ANTONUCCI 1981: "Convoys of Social Support: A Life Course Approach." In: KIESLER, S., MORGAN, J., & V. OPPENHEIMER (eds.), Aging: Social Change. New York: Academic Press, 383–405.
KALISH, R. & A. JOHNSON 1972: "Value Similarities and Differences in Three Generations of Women." J Marr Fam 34: 49–54.
KAPLAN, A. 1964: The Conduct of Inquiry. San Francisco, Calif.: Chandler.

KENISTON, K. 1968: Young Radicals. New York: Harcourt, Brace & World.

KERCKHOFF, A. C. 1966a: "Norm-Value Clusters and the Strain Toward Consistency Among Older Married Couples." In: SIMPSON, I. H. & J. McKINNEY (eds.), Social Aspects of Aging. Durham, N.C.: Duke University Press, 138–159.

KERCKHOFF, A. C. 1966b: "Husband-Wife Expectations and Reactions to Retirement." In: SIMPSON, I. H. & J. McKINNEY (eds.), Social Aspects of Aging. Durham, N.C.: Duke University Press, 160–172.

KERCKHOFF, A. C. 1966c: "Family Patterns and Morale in Retirement." In: SIMPSON, I. H. & J. McKINNEY (eds.), Social Aspects of Aging. Durham, N.C.: Duke University Press, 173–192.

KERTZER, D. I. 1977: "European Peasant Household Structure: Some Implications from a Nineteenth Century Italian Community." Journal of Family History: 333–349.

KERTZER, D. I. 1983: "Generation as a Sociological Problem." Annual Review of Sociology 9: 125–149.

KIEFFER, C. 1977: "New Depths in Intimacy." In: LIBBY, R. W. & R. N. WHITEHURST (eds.), Marriage and Alternatives: Exploring Intimate Relationships. Glenview, Ill.: Scott, Foresman and Co.

KIMMEL, D. C. 1974: Adulthood and Aging. New York: Wiley.

KNIPSCHEER, C. P. M. 1980: Oude mensen en hun sociale omgeving. Den Haag: VUGA.

KNIPSCHEER, K. & A. BEVERS 1981: "Older Parents and their Middle-Aged Children: Symmetry or Assymmetry in their Relationship." Paper presented at the XII. International Congress of Gerontology, July 12–17, Hamburg.

KOHLBERG, L. 1969: "Stufe und Sequenz: Sozialisation unter dem Aspekt der kognitiven Entwicklung." In: KOHLBERG, L. 1974 (ed.), Zur kognitiven Entwicklung des Kindes. Frankfurt a.M.: Suhrkamp, 7–255.

KOHLI, M. 1978: Soziologie des Lebenslaufs. Darmstadt and Neuwied: Luchterhand.

KOHLI, M. 1982: "Social Organization and Subjective Construction of the Life-Course." Paper presented at the International Conference on Life-Course Research on Human Development, September 16–21, Berlin.

KOHLI, M. 1983: Discussion, "Political Attitudes and Political Behavior in the Generational Context." International Symposium on Intergenerational Relationships, February 21–24, Berlin.

KOMAROVSKY, M. 1973: The Unemployed Man and his Family. New York: Octagon Book (1st ed.: 1940).

KOSELLECK, R. 1979: Vergangene Zukunft. Zur Semantik geschichtlicher Zeiten. Frankfurt a.M.: Suhrkamp.

KOTELCHUK, M. 1976: "The Infant's Relationship to Father." In: LAMB, M. E. (ed.), The Role of the Father in Child Development. New York: Wiley, 329–344.

KRAUSE, C., LEHMERT, D., & K. SCHERER 1980: Zwischen Revolution und Resignation. Alternativkultur, politische Grundströmungen und Hochschulaktivitäten in der Studentenschaft. Eine empirische Untersuchung über die politischen Einstellungen von Studenten. Bonn: Verlag Neue Gesellschaft.

KUYPERS, J. A. & V. L. BENGTSON 1973: "Social Breakdown and Competence, a Model of Normal Aging." Hum Dev 16 (2): 181–201.

LALIVE D'EPINAY, Ch. et al. 1981: "Popular Culture, Religion and Everyday Life." Soc Comp 17 (4): 405–424.

LAMB, M. E. (ed.) 1976: The Role of the Father in Child Development. New York: Wiley.

LAMB, M. E. 1977: "Father-Infant and Mother-Infant Interaction in the First Year of Life." Child Dev 48: 167–181.

LANGEHENNIG, M. 1983: "An die Perspektiven alter Menschen anknüpfen. Teilnehmende Beobachtung in einer Seniorenfreizeitstätte." In: Arbeitsgruppe Interpretative Alternsforschung, "Alltag in der Seniorenfreizeitstätte. Soziologische Untersuchungen zur Lebenswelt älterer Menschen." Berlin: Deutsches Zentrum für Altersfragen (DZA), 45–77.

LASLETT, P. 1965: The World We Have Lost. London: Methuen 1965.

LASLETT, P. 1977: Family Life and Illicit Love in Earlier Generations. Cambridge: Cambridge University Press.

LASLETT, P. & R. WALL (eds.) 1972: Household and Family in Past Time. Cambridge: Cambridge University Press.

LAUFER, R. & V. L. BENGTSON 1974: "Generations, Aging, and Social Stratification: On the Development of Generational Units." J Soc Iss 30 (3): 181–205.

L'ECUYER, R. 1978: Le concept de soi. Paris: Presses Universitaires de France (P.U.F.).

LEE, G. R. 1980: "Kinship in the Seventies. A Decade Review of Research and Theory." J Marr Fam 42: 923–934.

LEHR, U. 1961: "Veränderungen der Daseinsthematik der Frau im Erwachsenenalter." Vita Hum 4: 193–228.

LEHR, U. 1966: "Zur Problematik des Menschen im reiferen Erwachsenenalter — eine sozialpsychologische Interpretation der 'Wechseljahre'." Psych Neurol med Psychol 18 (2): 59–62.

LEHR, U. 1969: Die Frau im Beruf — eine entwicklungspsychologische Analyse der weiblichen Berufsrolle. Frankfurt a.M.: Athenäum.

LEHR, U. 1972a: Psychologie des Alterns. Heidelberg: Quelle & Meyer (4th ed.: 1979).

LEHR, U. 1972b: "Das Problem der Sozialisation geschlechtsspezifischer Verhaltensweisen." In: GRAUMANN, C. F. (ed.), Handbuch der Psychologie. Vol. II/2: Sozialpsychologie. Göttingen: Hogrefe, 886–954.

LEHR, U. 1973: Die Bedeutung der Familie im Sozialisationsprozeß. Unter besonderer Berücksichtigung psychologischer Aspekte familiärer Grenzsituationen. Stuttgart: Kohlhammer (Schriftenreihe des Bundesministers für Jugend, Familie und Gesundheit. 5).

LEHR, U. 1974: Die Rolle der Mutter in der Sozialisation des Kindes. Darmstadt: Steinkopff (2nd ed.: 1978).

LEHR, U. 1975: "Der ältere Mensch in der Familie." aktuelle gerontologie, 5: 539–550.

LEHR, U. 1978: "Stereotypie und Wandlung der Geschlechtsrollen." In: HEIGL-EVERS, A. (ed.), Lewin und die Folgen. Vol. VIII: Die Psychologie des 20. Jahrhunderts. Zürich: Kindler, 264–275.

LEHR, U. 1980a: "Die Rolle von Mutter und Vater in der frühen Sozialisation des Kindes." Therap Wo 30: 649–665.

LEHR, U. 1980b: "Alterszustand und Alternsprozesse – biographische Determinanten." Zeitschrift für Gerontologie 13: 442–457.

LEHR, U. 1981a: "Generations: Conflict and Cooperation: Consistency and Change in Family Role Activity." Paper presented at the International Congress of Gerontology, July 12–17, Hamburg, Vol. I: 155.

LEHR, U. 1981b: "Partnerschaft in Ehe, Familie und Beruf." In: PROSS, H., LEHR, U., & R. SÜSSMUTH (eds.), Emanzipation und Familie. Hannover: Niedersächsischer Landesverband für politische Bildung, 31–63.

LEHR, U. 1982a: "Hat die Großfamilie heute noch eine Chance?" Dt Arzt 18: 32–45.

LEHR, U. 1982b: Familie in der Krise? – Ein Plädoyer für mehr Partnerschaftlichkeit in Ehe, Familie und Beruf. München: Olzog.

LEHR, U. 1982c: "Depression und 'Lebensqualität' im Alter – Korrelate negativer und positiver Gestimmtheit." Zeitschrift für Gerontologie 15: 241–249.

LEHR, U. 1982d: "Subjektiver und objektiver Gesundheitszustand im Lichte von Längsschnittstudien." M M G 7: 242–248.

LEHR, U. 1982e: "Social-Psychological Correlates of Longevity." In: Annual Review of Gerontology and Geriatrics 3. New York: Springer, 102–114.

LEHR, U. 1982f: "Lebenssituation von Frauen in unserer Zeit." In: MOHR, G., RUMMEL, M., & D. RÜCKERT (eds.), Frauen – psychologische Beiträge zur Arbeits- und Lebenssituation. München: Urban & Schwarzenberg, 103–122.

LEHR, U. 1982g: "Permanence et changements des roles familiaux et de la satisfaction lors de la vieillesse." Gerontologie et société 21: 105–114.

LEHR, U. 1982h: "Patterns of Aging – Biographical Determinants." Paper delivered at the X. World Conference of Sociology, August 1982, Mexico City.

LEHR, U. 1982i: "The Elderly and the Family: Intrafamilial and Extrafamilial Social Participation." Paper presented at the International Congress on the Family and the Elderly in the Society, Milano.

LEHR, U. 1983: "Der ältere Mensch und die Familie." Archiv für Wissenschaft und Praxis der sozialen Arbeit 1: 15–25.

LEHR, U. & G. RUDINGER 1970: "Strukturen der sozialen Teilhabe im höheren Lebensalter." In: STÖRMER, A. (ed.), Geroprophylaxe, Infektions- und Herzkrankheiten, Rehabilitation und Sozialstatus im Alter. Darmstadt: Steinkopf, 81–88.

LEHR, U., SCHMITZ-SCHERZER, R., & E. ZIMMERMANN 1983: Sozialpsychologische Korrelate der Langlebigkeit. 2. Zwischenbericht an die VW-Stiftung. Bonn (unpublished manuscript).

LEHR, U. & H. THOMAE 1958: "Eine Längsschnittuntersuchung bei männlichen Angestellten." Vita Hum 1: 100–110.

LEHR, U. & H. THOMAE 1965: Konflikt, seelische Belastung und Lebensalter. Köln and Opladen: Westdeutsche Verlagsanstalt.

LEHR, U. & H. THOMAE 1968: "Die Stellung des älteren Menschen in der Familie." In: WURZBACHER, G. (ed.): Die Familie als Sozialisationsfaktor. Stuttgart: Enke 170–211 (2nd ed.: 1977).

LEHR, U. & J. ZERNER 1979: "Midlife-crisis — Psychomode oder Lebenswende." Bild der Wissenschaft 10: 194–206.

LENOIR, R. 1979: "L'invention du 3ème Age et la constitution du champ des agents de gestion de la vieillesse." Actes de la Recherche en Sciences Sociales 26/ 27: 57–82.

LEPENIES, W. 1976: Das Ende der Naturgeschichte. Wandel kultureller Selbstverständlichkeiten in den Wissenschaften des 18. und 19. Jahrhunderts. München: Hanser.

LEVITT, C. 1979: "The New Left, the New Class and Socialism (1)." Higher Education 8: 641–655.

LEVY, R. 1977: Der Lebenslauf als Statusbiographie. Stuttgart: Enke.

LIEBERMAN, G. L. 1978: "Children of the Elderly as Natural Helpers: Some Demographic Variables." In: GLIDEWELL, J. C. & M. A. LIEBERMAN (eds.), American Journal of Community Psychology. See: NEUGARTEN, B. L. 1979: "The Middle Generations." In: RAGAN, P. K. (ed.), Aging Parents. Los Angeles, Calif.: University of Southern California Press, 258–266.

LIFFMAN, M. 1978: Power for the Poor. Sidney: Allen and Unwin.

LIFTON, R. J. 1968: "Protean Man." Part Rev 35: 13–27.

LINDE, H. 1978: "MACKENROTH's Theorie der Generativen Strukturen aus heutiger Sicht." In: Ursachen des Bevölkerungsrückgangs. Stuttgart: Kohlhammer (Schriftenreihe des Bundesministers für Jugend, Familie und Gesundheit. 63), 31–41.

LIPMAN-BLUMEN, J. 1976: "Toward a Homosocial Theory of Sex Roles. An Explanation of the Sex Segregation of Social Institutions." Signs 1 (1): 15–32.

LIPSET, S. M. (ed.) 1967: Student Politics. New York: Basic Books.

LIPSET, S. M. 1976: Rebellion in the University. Chicago, Ill.: University of Chicago Press.

LIPSET, S. M. & P. G. ALTBACH (eds.) 1969: Student in Revolt. Boston, Mass.: Houghton-Mifflin.

LITWAK, E. 1960: "Reference Group Theory, Bureaucratic Career and Neighborhood Primary Group Cohesion." Sociom 23: 78–84.

LITWAK, E. 1965: "Extended Kin Relations in an Industrial Democratic Society." In: SHANAS, E. & G. F. STREIB (eds.), Social Structure and the Family: Generational Relations. Englewood Cliffs, N.J.: Prentice-Hall, 290–323.

LOEWENBERG, P. 1974: "A Psychohistorical Approach: The Nazi Generation." In: ESLER, A. (ed.), The Youth Revolution. Lexington, Mass.: Heath and Co., 82–105.

LOPATA, H. Z. 1979: Women as Widows: Support Systems. New York: Elsevier.

LOWENTHAL, M. F. & B. ROBINSON 1976: "Social Networks and Isolation." In: BINSTOCK, R. H. & E. SHANAS (eds.), Handbook of Aging and the Social Sciences. New York: Van Nostrand-Reinhold, 432–456.

LOWENTHAL, M. F., THURNHER, M., & D. CHIRIBOGA 1975: Four Stages of Life. San Francisco, Calif.: Jossey-Bass.

LOWENTHAL, M. F. 1975: "Psychological Variations Across the Adult Life Course: Frontiers for Research and Policy." Geront 15: 6–12.

LOWIE, R. 1964: Traité de sociologie primitive. Paris: Payot.

LOZIER, J. & R. ALTHOUSE 1974: "Special Enforcement of Behavior Toward Elders in an Appalachian Mountain Settlement." Geront 14: 69–80.

MAAS, S. & J. A. KUYPERS 1974: From Thirty to Seventy. San Francisco, Calif.: Jossey-Bass.

MACCOBY, E. E. 1963: "Women's Intellect." In: FARBER, N. & W. C. WILSON (eds.), The Potential of Women. New York: McGraw-Hill, 24–39.

MACCOBY, E. E. 1966: The Development of Sex-Differences. Stanford, Calif.: Stanford University Press.

MACCOBY, E. E. & C. N. JACKLIN 1974: The Psychology of Sex-Differences. Stanford, Calif.: Stanford University Press.

MacINNESS, C. 1959: Absolute Beginners. London: McGibbon & Kee.

MACKENROTH, G. 1953: Bevölkerungslehre. Berlin: Springer.

MACKENSEN, R. 1968: "Probleme der Weltbevölkerung." Allgemeines Statistisches Archiv 52: 1–26.

MADDOX, G. L. & J. WILEY 1976: "Scope, Concepts and Methods in the Study of Aging." In: BINSTOCK, R. H. & E. SHANAS (eds.), Handbook of Aging and the Social Sciences. New York: Van Nostrand-Reinhold, 3–34.

MANGEN, D. et al. 1982: "Conceptualizing Intergenerational Solidarity: Six Dimensions of Family Support Potential." Paper presented at the Annual Meeting of the Gerontological Society of America, November 15–18, Toronto.

MANNHEIM, K. 1952: "The Problem of Generations." In: KECSKEMETI, P. (ed.), Essays on the Sociology of Knowledge. London: Routledge and Kegan Paul (1st ed.: 1928).

MANNHEIM, K. 1956[2]: "The Problem of the Intelligentsia: An Inquiry into its Past and Present Role." In: MANHEIM, E. & P. KECSKEMETI (eds.), Essays on the Sociology of Culture. London: Routledge and Kegan Paul.

MANNHEIM, K. 1964[3]: "Das Problem der Generationen." In: WOLFF, K. H. (ed.), Mannheim: Wissenssoziologie. Auswahl aus dem Werk. Berlin and Neuwied: Luchterhand, 509–565 (1st ed.: 1928, in: Kölner Vierteljahreshefte für Soziologie 7 (2): 157–185 and (3): 309–330).

MANNHEIM, K. 1968[4]: "The Problem of Generations." In: KECSKEMETI, P. (ed.), Essays on the Sociology of Knowledge. London: Routledge and Kegan Paul, 276–321 (1st ed.: 1928).

MANNHEIM, K. 1972[5]: "The Problem of Generations." In: KECSKEMETI, P. (ed.), Essays on the Sociology of Knowledge. London: Routledge and Kegan Paul, 276–321 (1st ed.: 1928).

MANNZMANN, A. (ed.) 1981: Geschichte der Familie oder Familiengeschichten. Zur Bedeutung von Alltags- oder Jedermannsgeschichte. Königstein/Taunus: Scriptor.

MANPOWER SERVICES COMMISSION 1982: Youth Task Group Report. London: Manpower Services Commission.

MARIAS, J. 1967: Generations. A Historical Method. Alabama: University of Alabama Press.

MARIAS, J. 1970: Generations. A Historical Method. Alabama: University of Alabama Press.

MARSHALL, V. W. 1981a: "Generations and Cohorts: A Generation is a Cohort But a Cohort is Not Necessarily a Generation." QSEP Research Report No. 11, Program for Quantitative Studies in Economics and Population. Hamilton, Ontario: McMaster University.

MARSHALL, V. W. 1981b: "Societal Toleration of Aging: Sociological Theory and Social Responses to Population Aging." Proceedings, IX. International Conference of Social Gerontology, Paris, Vol. 1: Adaptability and Aging: 85–104.

MARSHALL, V. W. 1983: "Tendencies in Generational Research: From the Generation to the Cohort and Back to the Generation." Paper prepared for the International Symposium on Intergenerational Relationships, February 21–24, Berlin.

MARSHALL, V. W. & V. L. BENGTSON 1983: "Generations: Conflict and Cooperation." In: BERGENER, M. et al. (eds.), Gerontology in the Eighties. New York: Springer, 298–310.

MATTHES, J. 1978: "Wohnverhalten, Familienzyklus und Lebenslauf." In: KOHLI, M. (ed.), Soziologie des Lebenslaufs. Darmstadt and Neuwied: Luchterhand, 154–172.

MATZA, D. 1961: "Subterranean Traditions of Youth." Am Ac Pol Sci A 338: 102–118.

MATZA, D. 1969: Becoming Deviant. New York: Prentice-Hall.

MAYER, K. U. 1975: Ungleichheit und Mobilität im sozialen Bewußtsein. Untersuchungen zur Definition der Mobilitätssituation. Opladen: Westdeutscher Verlag.

MAYHEW, H. 1851: London Labour and London Poor. Vol. 1–4. London: Museum Library.

McROBBIE, A. 1981: "Settling Accounts with Subculture. A Feminist Critique." In: BENNETT, T. et al. (eds.), Popular Culture: Past and Present. London: Croom-Helm.

McROBBIE, A. & J. GARBER 1976: "Girls and Subcultures. An Exploration." In: HALL, S. & T. JEFFERSON (eds.), Resistance Through Rituals. London: Hutchinson, 209–222.

MEAD, M. 1952: Growing up in Samoa. London (republished by Penguin, London 1966).

MEAD, M. 1970: Culture and Commitment. A Study of the Generation Gap. Garden City, N.Y.: Natural History Press/Doubleday.

MEHNER, H. 1887: "Der Haushalt und die Lebenshaltung einer Leipziger Arbeiterfamilie." In: ROSENBAUM, H. 1978 (ed.), Seminar: Familie und Gesellschaftsstruktur. Frankfurt a.M.: Suhrkamp, 309–333.

MEINHOLD, M. 1982: "Kognitive Komplexität in sozialpädagogischen Ausbildungsgängen." In: HAGEMANN, W. et al. (eds.), Kognition und Moralität in politischen Lernprozessen. Opladen: Leske, 120–141.

MENDEL, G. 1972: Generationskrise (La crise de générations, 1969). Frankfurt a.M.: Suhrkamp.

MENNE, F. W. 1981: "Rekonstruktion der Familie. Kognitive Distanzierung angesichts der Verstrickung in Alltagsgeschichte(n)." In: MANNZMANN, A. (ed.), Geschichte der Familie oder Familiengeschichten? Zur Bedeutung von Alltags- oder Jedermannsgeschichte. Königstein/Ts.: Scriptor, 57–73.

MERTON, R. K. 1938: "Social Structure and Anomie." Am soc R 3 (5): 672–682.
MESSER, M. 1968: "Age Grouping and the Family Status of the Elderly." Soc Soc Res 3: 271–279.
MILLER, W. 1958: "Lower Class as a Generating Milieu of Gang Delinquency." J Soc Iss 14: 5–19.
MITSCHERLICH, A. 1957: "Jugend in der technischen Welt." Neue Deutsche Hefte 3: 396–405.
MITSCHERLICH, A. & M. MITSCHERLICH 1967: Die Unfähigkeit zu trauern. München: Piper.
MITTERAUER, M. 1976: "Auswirkungen von Urbanisierung und Frühindustrialisierung auf die Familienverfassung an Beispielen des österreichischen Raums." In: CONZE, W. (ed.), Sozialgeschichte der Familie der Neuzeit Europas. Stuttgart: Klett, 53–146.
MITTERAUER, M. 1981: "Zur Kritik von Familienideologien aus historischer Sicht." In: MANNZMANN, A. (ed.), Geschichte der Familie oder Familiengeschichten? Zur Bedeutung von Alltags- oder Jedermannsgeschichte. Königstein/Ts.: Scriptor, 42–56.
MITTERAUER, M. 1982: "Problemfelder der Sozialgeschichte des Alters." In: KONRAD, H. (ed.), Der alte Mensch in der Geschichte. Wien: Verlag für Gesellschaftskritik, 9–61.
MITTERAUER, M. 1983: Formen ländlicher Familienwirtschaft. Wien: Institut für Wirtschafts- und Sozialgeschichte (unpublished manuscript).
MITTERAUER, M. & A. KAGAN 1982: "Russian and Central European Family Structure: A Comparative View." Journal of Family History 7: 103–131.
MITTERAUER, M. & R. SIEDER 1977: Vom Patriarchat zur Partnerschaft. Zum Strukturwandel der Familie. München: Beck.
MITTERAUER, M. & R. SIEDER 1979: "The Developmental Process of Domestic Groups: Problems of Reconstruction and Possibilities of Interpretation." Journal of Family History 4: 257–284.
MITTERAUER, M. & R. SIEDER 1982: The European Family. Oxford: Basil Blackwell.
MONTADA, L. & M. SCHMITT 1982: "Systematik der angewandten Entwicklungspsychologie: Probleme der Praxis, Beiträge der Forschung." In: OERTER, R. & L. MONTADA (eds.), Entwicklungspsychologie. München, Wien, and Baltimore, 677–703.
MORGAN, L. A. 1981: "Aging in a Family Context." In: DAVIS, R. H. (ed.), Aging: Prospects and Issues. Los Angeles, Calif.: University of Southern California Press, 98–112.
MORIOKA, K. 1982: Life Course and Generational Relationships of the Middle Aged in Japan. Tokyo: Seijo University (unpublished manuscript).
MORRISON, A. 1896: A Child of the Jago. London: Museum Library.
MORRISON, A. 1902: The Hole in the Wall. London: Museum Library.
MOSCOVICI, S. 1972: "Society and Theory in Social Psychology." In: ISRAEL, J. & H. TAJFEL (eds.), The Context of Social Psychology: A Critical Assessment. New York: Academic Press, 65 ff.
MOSCOVICI, S. 1976: Social Influence and Social Change. London: Academic Press.

MOSCOVICI, S. 1978: Preface in "Einstein et le conflit des générations." Paris: Ed. Complexe.

MUDRICH, B. 1978: Der Wegzug des letzten Kindes aus dem Elternhaus im Erleben der Mutter. Bonn: Psychologisches Institut der Universität (unpublished M.A. thesis).

MÜLLER, W. 1978: "Der Lebenslauf von Geburtenkohorten." In: KOHLI, M. (ed.), Soziologie des Lebenslaufs. Berlin and Neuwied: Luchterhand, 54–77.

MÜLLER, W. 1982: Wie Helfen zum Beruf wurde. Weinheim: Beltz.

MULKAY, M. 1980: "Wissen und Nutzen. Implikationen für die Wissenssoziologie." Kölner Z S S, Sonderheft 22: Wissenssoziologie, 52–72.

MUNGHAM, G. & G. PEARSON 1976: Working Class Youth Cultures. London: Routledge and Kegan Paul.

MURDOCK, G. & R. McCRON 1976: "Consciousness of Class and Consciousness of Generation." In: HALL, S. & T. JEFFERSON (eds.), Resistance Through Rituals. London: Hutchinson, 192–207.

MUSGROVE, F. 1968: Youth and the Social Order. London: Routledge and Kegan Paul.

NAEGELE, G. 1983: "Abkehr vom Prinzip der Sozialstaatlichkeit? Anmerkungen zur Wiederentdeckung des Subsidiaritätsprinzips." Theorie und Praxis der Sozialarbeit 2: 42–53.

NASH, R. 1970: The Nervous Generation: American Thought, 1917–1930. Chicago, Ill.: Rand McNally.

NATIONAL COUNCIL ON AGING 1975: The Myth and Reality of Aging in America. Washington, D.C.: N. C. O. A.

NEIDHARDT, F. 1967: Die junge Generation. Opladen: Leske.

NETTING, R. M. 1979: "Household Dynamics in a Nineteenth Century Swiss Village." Journal of Family History 4: 39–58.

NEUGARTEN, B. L. 1968: Middle Age and Aging. Chicago, Ill.: University of Chicago Press.

NEUGARTEN, B. L. 1970: "The Old and the Young in Modern Societies." Am beh Scien 14 (1): 13–24.

NEUGARTEN, B. L. 1979a: "The Future and the Young-Old." Geront 15 (5, Part II): 4–9.

NEUGARTEN, B. L. 1979b: "The Middle Generations." In: RAGAN, P. K. (ed.), Aging Parents. Los Angeles, Calif.: University of Southern California Press, 258–266.

NEUGARTEN, B. L. 1979c: "Time, Age and the Life Cycle." Am J Psych 36: 887–894.

NEUGARTEN, B. L. & N. DATAN 1976: "Sociological Perspectives on the Life Cycle." In: ATCHLEY, R. C. & M. M. SELTZER (eds.), The Sociology of Aging: Selected Readings. Belmont, Calif.: Wadsworth, 4–22.

NEWMAN, S. 1976: Housing Adjustments of Older People: A Report from the Second Phase. Ann Arbor, Mich.: Institute for Social Research, University of Michigan.

NIE, N. H. et al. 1975: Statistical Package for the Social Sciences. New York: McGraw-Hill (2nd ed.).

NORTH, C. C. & P. K. Hatt 1947: "Jobs and Occupations: A Popular Evaluation." Public Opinion News 9: 3–13.

NYDEGGER, C. N. 1983: "Family Ties of the Aged in Cross-Cultural Perspective." Geront 23 (1): 26–32.

NYE, F. & W. RUSHING 1966: Toward Family Measurement Research. Proceedings of the Family Measurement Conference. Washington, D.C.: Department of Health, Education and Welfare.

OAKLEY, A. 1974: The Sociology of Housework. London: Martin Robertson.

OAKLEY, A. 1976: "Wisewoman and Medicine Man, Changes in the Management of Childbirth." In: MITCHELL, J. & A. OAKLEY (eds.), The Rights and Wrongs of Women. Harmondsworth: Penguin, 17–58.

OPPENHEIMER, V. K. 1981: "The Changing Nature of Life-Cycle Squeezes: Implications for the Socioeconomic Position of the Elderly." In: FOGEL, R. W. et al. (eds.), Aging: Stability and Change in the Family. New York: Academic Press, 47–81.

ORBACH, H. L. 1983: "Symposium: Aging, Families, and Family Relations: Behavioral and Social Science Perspectives on Our Knowledge, Our Myths, and Our Research." Geront 23 (1): 24–25.

ORTEGA y GASSET, J. 1962: Man and Crisis. New York: Norton (see also GASSET).

OSSOWSKI, S. 1963: Class Structure in the Social Consciousness. London: Routledge and Kegan Paul.

PALMORE, E. 1978: "When Can Age, Period, and Cohort be Separated?" Soc Forc 57 (1): 202–295.

PAPOUŠEK, H. & M. PAPOUŠEK 1979: "Lernen im ersten Lebensjahr." In: MONTADA, L. (ed.), Brennpunkte der Entwicklungspsychologie. Stuttgart: Kohlhammer, 194–212.

PARKE, R. D. & S. E. O'LEARY 1976: "Family Interaction in the Newborn Period." In: RIEGEL, K. F. & J. A. MEACHAM (eds.), The Developing Individual in a Changing World. Vol. II. Den Haag: Mouton, 653–663.

PARR, J. 1980: "The Interaction of Persons and Living Environments." In: POON, L. W. (ed.), Aging in the 1980s. Washington, D.C.: American Psychological Association, 393–406.

PARSONS, T. 1943: "The Kinship System of the Contemporary United States." In: PARSONS, T. (ed.), Essays in Sociological Theory. Glencoe, Ill.: Free Press, 177–196.

PARSONS, T. 1963: "Youth in the Context of American Society." In: ERIKSON, E. H. (ed.), Youth: Change and Challenge. New York: Basic Books, 93–119.

PARSONS, T. & R. F. BALES 1955: Family: Socialization and Interaction Process. New York: Free Press.

PARSONS, T. & N. J. SMELSER 1956: Economy and Society. Glencoe, Ill.: Free Press.

PAULME, D. 1971: Classes et associations d'âge en Afrique de l'Ouest. Paris: Plon.

PEARL, R. & L. J. REED 1920: "On the Rate of Growth of the Population of the United States since 1790 and its Mathematical Representation." In: Proceedings of the National Academy of Sciences 6.

PEEL, R. 1980: Die Wahrnehmung von Wohnzimmern und ihrer Bewohner. Heidelberg (unpublished dissertation).

PFEIL, E. 1967: "Der Kohortenansatz in der Soziologie. Ein Zugang zum Generationsproblem?" Kölner Z S S 19: 645–657.

PINCHBECK, I. & M. HEWITT 1981: "Vagrancy and Delinquency in an Urban Setting." In: FITZGERALD, M. et al. (eds.), Crime and Society: Readings in History and Theory. London: Routledge and Kegan Paul.

PLAKANS, A. 1975: "Seigneurial Authority and Peasant Family Life: The Baltic Area in the Eighteenth Century." Journal of Interdisciplinary History 5: 629–654.

PLASCHKE, J. 1983: Gesellschaftliche Sicherheit alter Menschen. Zustandsbeschreibung, Perspektiven und Alternativen. Frankfurt a.M.: Eigenverlag des Deutschen Vereins für öffentliche und private Fürsorge, Schrift 262.

POMIAN, K. 1979: "The Secular Evolution of the Concept of Cycles." Review 2 (4): 563–646.

POUJOL, G. & R. LABOURIE 1979: Les cultures populaires. Toulouse: Privat.

PREUSS-LAUSITZ, U., ZEIHER, H., & D. GEULEN 1983: "Was wir unter Sozialisationsgeschichte verstehen." In: PREUSS-LAUSITZ, U. et al.: Kriegskinder, Konsumkinder, Krisenkinder. Zur Sozialisationsgeschichte seit dem 2. Weltkrieg. Weinheim: Beltz, 11–28.

PROKOP, U. 1976: Weiblicher Lebenszusammenhang. Von der Beschränktheit der Strategien und der Unangemessenheit der Wünsche. Frankfurt a.M.: Suhrkamp.

RADEBOLD, H. & G. SCHLESINGER-KIPP (eds.) 1982: Familien- und Paartherapeutische Hilfen bei älteren und alten Menschen. Göttingen: Vandenhoeck & Ruprecht.

RAUH, H. 1976: "Entwicklung des Denkens." In: GRAUMANN, C. F., HECKHAUSEN, H., & H. RAUH (eds.), Pädagogische Psychologie. Teil II: Entwicklung und Motivation. Weinheim: Beltz, 141–201.

RAUSCH, K. 1979: "Geschlechtsspezifische Vorurteile gegenüber Frauen in Strafrechtswissenschaft und Justiz in der BRD." In: ECKERT, R. (ed.), Geschlechtsrollen und Arbeitsteilung. München: Beck, 97–123.

REBEL, H. 1978: "Peasant Stem Families in Early Modern Austria: Life Plans, Status Tactics, and the Grid of Inheritance." Social Science History 2: 255–291.

REULECKE, J. 1983 (in press): "Zur Entdeckung des Alters als eines sozialen Problems in der ersten Hälfte des 19. Jahrhunderts." In: CONRAD, C. & H.-J. von KONDRATOWITZ (eds.), Gerontologie und Sozialgeschichte. Wege zu einer historischen Betrachtung des Alters. (Beiträge zur Gerontologie und Altenarbeit, 48.) Berlin: Deutsches Zentrum für Altersfragen e.V., 413–423.

RICH, A. 1976: Of Woman Born. New York: Norton.

RICHTER, H. E. 1974: Lernziel Solidarität. Reinbek: Rowohlt.

RIEGEL, K. F. 1976: "The Dialectics of Human Development." Am Psychol 31: 689–700.

RILEY, M. W. 1971: "Social Gerontology and the Age Stratification of Society." Geront 11 (1): 79–87.

RILEY, M. W. 1973: "Aging and Cohort Succession: Interpretations and Misinterpretations." Publ Op Q 37 (1): 33–49.

RILEY, M. W. 1976a: "Social Gerontology and the Age Stratification of Society." In: ATCHLEY, R. C. & M. M. SELTZER (eds.), The Sociology of Aging: Selected Readings. Belmont, Calif.: Wadsworth, 22–37.

RILEY, M. W. 1976b: "Age Strata in Social Systems." In: BINSTOCK, R. H. & E. SHANAS (eds.), Handbook of Aging and the Social Sciences. New York: Van Nostrand-Reinhold, 189–217.

RILEY, M. W. 1978: "Aging, Social Change, and the Power of Ideas." Daed 107 (4): 1, 39–52.

RILEY, M. W. & A. FONER (eds.) 1968: Aging and Society. Vol. 1: An Inventory of Research Findings. New York: Sage.

RILEY, M. W., JOHNSON, M., & A. FONER (eds.) 1972: Aging and Society. Vol. 3: A Sociology of Age Stratification. New York: Sage.

ROBERTSON, J. F. 1975: "Interaction in Three Generation Families. Parents as Mediators: Toward a Theoretical Perspective." International Journal of Aging and Human Development 6: 103–108.

ROBINSON, B. & M. THURNHER 1979: "Taking Care of Aged Parents: A Family Cycle Transition." Geront 19 (6): 586–593.

ROOK, C. 1906: Hooligan Nights. London: Museum Library.

ROOS, P. 1982: Kaputte Gespräche. Wem nützt der Jugend-Dialog? Weinheim and Basel: Beltz.

ROSE, A. M. 1965: "The Subculture of the Aging: A Framework for Research in Social Gerontology." In: ROSE, A. M. & W. A. PETERSON (eds.), Older People and their Social World. Philadelphia, Pa.: Davis.

ROSENBAUM, H. 1974: Familie und Gesellschaftsstruktur. Frankfurt a.M.: Fischer.

ROSENBERG, G. 1970: The Worker Grows Old: Poverty and Isolation in the City. San Francisco, Calif.: Jossey-Bass.

ROSENMAYR, H. & L. ROSENMAYR 1978: "Die Familie." In: ROSENMAYR, L. & H. ROSENMAYR (eds.), Der alte Mensch in der Gesellschaft. Reinbek: Rowohlt, 176–230.

ROSENMAYR, L. 1973: "Family Relations of the Elderly. Recent Data and Some Critical Doubts." Zeitschrift für Gerontologie 6 (4): 272–283.

ROSENMAYR, L. 1976: "Schwerpunkte der Jugendsoziologie." In: KÖNIG, R. (ed.), Handbuch der empirischen Sozialforschung. Vol. 6: Jugend. Stuttgart: Enke.

ROSENMAYR, L. 1977: "The Family – a Source of Help for the Elderly?" In: SHANAS, E. & M. B. SUSSMAN (eds.), Family, Bureaucracy, and the Elderly. Durham, N.C.: Duke University Press, 132–157.

ROSENMAYR, L. 1978: "Elemente einer allgemeinen Alter(n)stheorie." In: ROSENMAYR, L. & H. ROSENMAYR (eds.), Der alte Mensch in der Gesellschaft. Reinbek: Rowohlt, 46–70.

ROSENMAYR, L. 1982a: "Biography and Identity." In: HAREVEN, T. K. & K. J. ADAMS (eds.), Aging and Life Course Transitions: An Interdisciplinary Perspective. New York and London: Guildford Press, 27–53.

ROSENMAYR, L. 1982b: "Changes in the Family – Changes in the Position of the Old." Introductory paper delivered at the X. International Conference of EURAG: 'Europe's Older Generation – Reality and Future,' June 1–5, Graz.

ROSENMAYR, L. 1983a: "Les étapes de la vie." Communications 37: Le Continent Gris. Paris: Seuil, 89–104.
ROSENMAYR, L. 1983b: Die späte Freiheit. Das Alter — ein Stück bewußt gelebten Lebens. Berlin: Severin & Siedler.
ROSENMAYR, L. & E. KÖCKEIS 1965: Umwelt und Familie alter Menschen. Neuwied and Berlin: Luchterhand.
ROSENMAYR, L. & H. ROSENMAYR 1978: Der alte Mensch in der Gesellschaft. Reinbek: Rowohlt.
ROSENTHAL, C., MARSHALL, V., & J. SYNGE 1981: "Maintaining Intergenerational Relations: Kinkeeping." Paper presented at the Annual Meeting of the Gerontological Society of America, November 15–18, Toronto.
ROSENTHAL, G. 1983: "The Nazi-Youth-Generation: Coming to Terms with Recent German History." Paper presented at the International Symposium on Intergenerational Relationships, February 21–24, Berlin.
ROSOW, I. 1967: Social Integration of the Aged. New York: Free Press.
ROSOW, I. 1978: "What is a Cohort and Why?" Hum Dev 21: 65–75.
ROSSI, A. 1964: "Equality Between the Sexes. An Immodest Proposal." Daed 93 (2): 607–652.
ROSSI, A. S. 1980: "Life-Span Theories and Women's Lives." In: SIGNS 6 (17): 4–32.
ROUSSEAU, J. J. 1755: "Quelle est l'origine de l'inégalité parmi les hommes et si elle est autorisée par l'Académie de Dijon." In: LAHURE, C. (ed.), Oeuvres complètes. Vol. 1. Paris: Hachette, 71–152 (1st ed.: 1856).
RUTTER, M. 1971: "Parent-Child Separation: Psychological Effects on the Children." J Child Psychol 12: 233–260.
RUTTER, M. 1972: Maternal Deprivation reassessed. London: Penguin.
RYDER, N. B. 1965: "The Cohort as a Concept in the Study of Social Change." Am soc R 30 (6): 843–861.
SCHADE, B. & N. A. APT 1983: "Aging in Developing Countries." In: BERGENER, M. et al. (eds.), Aging in the Eighties. New York: Springer, 383–390.
SCHAEFFER, D. 1981: "Stereotypes and Communication Between Members of Different Generations." Paper presented at the XII. International Congress of Gerontology, July 12–17, Hamburg.
SCHAFFER, H. R. 1977: Mothering. London: Fontana/Open Books.
SCHAFFER, H. R. 1978: Mütterliche Fürsorge in den ersten Lebensjahren. Stuttgart: Klett-Cotta.
SCHAFFER, H. R. 1980: "Early Development and Socialization." Proc. XXII. International Congress of Psychology, July 6–12, Leipzig.
SCHAIE, K. W. 1965: "A General Model for the Study of Developmental Problems." Psychological Bulletin 64: 92–107.
SCHELSKY, H. 1957: Die skeptische Generation. Düsseldorf and Köln: Diederichs.
SCHMID, J. 1976: Einführung in die Bevölkerungssoziologie. Reinbek: Rowohlt.
SCHMIDTBAUER, P. 1983: "The Changing Household: Austrian Household Structure from the Seventeenth to the Early Twentieth Century." In: WALL, R. (ed., with ROBIN, J. & P. LASLETT), Family Forms in Historic Europe. Cambridge: Cambridge University Press, 347–379.

SCHMIDT-KOLMER, E. 1980: "Die Sozialisation in Familie und Kinderkrippe in den ersten Lebensjahren." Proc. XXII. International Congress of Psychology, July 6–12, Leipzig, 242.

SCHNEIDER, J. 1977: Emanzipation und Familie. München: Deutsches Jugendinstitut.

SCHOFIELD, R. S. & E. A. WRIGLEY 1981: The Population History of England 1541–1871: A Reconstruction. London: Arnold.

SCHORR, A. 1960: Filial Responsibility in the Modern American Family. Washington, D.C.: Social Security Administration.

SCHORSKE, C. E. 1978: "Generational Tension and Cultural Change: Reflection on the Case of Vienna." Daed 107 (4): 111–122.

SCHRODER, H. M. et al. 1967: Human Information Processing. New York: Holt, Rinehart and Winston.

SCHRÖDINGER, E. 1958: Mind and Matter. Cambridge: Cambridge University Press.

SCHÜTZ, A. 1972: "Der Fremde. Ein sozialpsychologischer Versuch." In: SCHÜTZ, A.: Gesammelte Aufsätze 2. Studien zur soziologischen Theorie. The Hague: Nijhoff.

SCHÜTZ, A. 1982: Das Problem der Relevanz. Frankfurt a.M.: Suhrkamp.

SCHULZ, W. 1982: Familie und Lebensqualität im Rahmen der gesellschaftlichen Entwicklung. Wien: Institut für Soziologie der Universität.

SCHUTZ, A. 1967: "Common-Sense and Scientific Interpretation of Human Action." In: NATANSON, M. (ed.), Alfred Schutz, Collected Papers I: The Problem of Social Reality. The Hague: Nijhoff.

SEWELL, W. H. & R. M. HAUSER 1972: "Causes and Consequences of Higher Education: Models of the Status Attainment Process." American Journal of Agricultural Economics 54: 851–861.

SCHAIE, K. W. 1976: "Age Changes and Age Differences." In: ATCHLEY, R. C. & M. M. SELTZER (eds.), The Sociology of Aging: Selected Readings. Belmont, Calif.: Wadsworth, 52–59.

SHANAS, E. et al. 1968: Old People in Three Industrial Societies. London: Routledge and Kegan Paul; New York: Atherton Press.

SHANAS, E. 1973: "Family Kin-Networks and Aging in Cross-Cultural Perspective." J Marr Fam 35: 505–511.

SHANAS, E. 1978: A National Survey of the Aged. Final Report to the Administration on Aging. Washington, D.C.: Department of Health, Education and Welfare.

SHANAS, E. 1979a: "Social Myth as Hypothesis: The Case of the Family Relations of Old People." Geront 19 (1): 3–9.

SHANAS, E. 1979b: "The Family as a Social Support in Old Age." Geront 19: 169–174.

SHANAS, E. 1980: "Older People and Their Families: The New Pioneers." J Marr Fam 42: 9–15.

SHANAS, E. et al. 1968: Old People in Three Industrial Societies. New York: Atherton Press.

SHANAS, E. & P. M. HAUSER 1974: "Zero Population Growth and the Family of Older People." J Soc Iss 30: 79–82.

SHANAS, E. & M. B. SUSSMAN (eds.) 1977: Family, Bureaucracy, and the Elderly. Durham, N.C.: Duke University Press.

SHELL-STUDIE JUGEND '81 1983: Lebensentwürfe, Alltagskulturen, Zukunftsbilder. Opladen: Leske & Büdrich.

SIEDER, R. & M. MITTERAUER 1983: "The Reconstruction of the Family Life Course: Theoretical Problems and Empirical Results." In: WALL, R. et al. (eds.), Family Forms in Historic Europe (The Social Science Research Council). Cambridge: Cambridge University Press, 309–345.

SMITH, D. S. 1978: "Life Course, Norms, and the Family System of Older Americans in 1900." Journal of Family History 4: 285–298.

SMITH, D. S. 1981: "Historical Change in the Household Structure of the Elderly in Economically Developed Societies." In: MARCH, J. G. et al., Aging. Stability and Change in the Family. New York: Academic Press, 91–114.

SMITH, L. 1983: Meeting Filial Responsibility Demands in Middle Age. University Park, Pa.: Pennsylvania State University (unpublished M.A. thesis).

SORENSEN, A. B. 1975: "The Structure of Intragenerational Mobility." Am soc R 40: 456–471.

SPERLING, E. et al. 1982: Die Mehrgenerationen-Familientherapie. Göttingen: Verlag für Medizinische Psychologie im Verlag Vandenhoeck & Ruprecht.

SPITZ, R. 1945: "Hospitalism." In: EISSLER, R. et al. (eds.): The Psychoanalytic Study of the Child. Vol. 1. New York: International University Press, 53–74.

SPITZER, A. B. 1973: "The Historical Problem of Generations." Am Hist Rev 78: 1353–1385.

SPRANGER, E. 1926: Psychologie des Jugendalters. Leipzig: Quelle & Meyer.

STIERLIN, H. 1975: Eltern und Kinder im Prozeß der Ablösung. Frankfurt a.M.: Suhrkamp.

STIERLIN, H. 1982: "Der Dialog zwischen den Generationen über die Nazizeit." Familiendynamik 1: 31–48.

STONE, L. 1977a: "Walking over Grandma." NYRB 24: 10–16.

STONE, L. 1977b: "Reply." NYRB 24: 48–49.

STREIB, G. F. 1965: "Intergenerational Relations: Perspective of the Two Generations on the Older Parent." J Marr Fam 27: 469–476.

STREIB, G. F. 1976: "Social Stratification and Aging." In: BINSTOCK, R. H. & E. SHANAS (eds.), Handbook of Aging and the Social Sciences. New York: Van Nostrand-Reinhold, 160–185.

STREIB, G. F. & R. BECK 1980: "Older Families: A Decade Review." J Marr Fam 42 (4): 937–956.

STREIB, G. F. & M. H. PENNA 1982: "Anticipating Transitions: Possible Options in 'Family' Forms." Annals 464.

STROTZKA, H. 1983: Fairness, Verantwortung, Fantasie. Wien: Deuticke.

SUSSMAN, M. B. 1959: "The Isolated Nuclear Family: Fact or Fiction." Social Problems 6: 333–340.

SUSSMAN, M. B. 1965: "Relationships of Adult Children with their Parents in the United States." In: SHANAS, E. & G. F. STREIB (eds.), Social Structure and the Family: Generational Relations. Englewood Cliffs, N.J.: Prentice-Hall, 62–92.

SUSSMAN, M. B. & L. BURCHINAL 1962: "Kin Family Network: Unheralded Structure in Current Conceptualizations of Family Functioning." Marr Fam Liv 24: 231–240.

TAGG, J. 1981: "Power and Photography: A Means of Surveillance. The Photograph as Evidence of Law." In: BENNETT, T. et al. (eds.), Culture, Ideology, and Social Process. Batsford: Open University Press.

TARTLER, R. 1955: "Die soziale Gestalt der heutigen Jugend und das Generationsverhältnis in der Gegenwart." In: SCHELSKY, H. (ed.), Arbeiterjugend gestern und heute. Heidelberg: Quelle & Meyer.

TARTLER, R. 1961: Das Alter in der modernen Gesellschaft. Stuttgart: Enke.

TENBRUCK, F. (ed.) 1965: Jugend und Gesellschaft. Soziologische Perspektiven. Freiburg/Br.: Rombach.

TEWS, H. P. 1971: Soziologie des Alterns. Heidelberg: Quelle & Meyer (2nd ed.: 1974).

THIBAUDET, A. 1936: Histoire de la littérature française de 1789 à nos jours. Paris: Stock.

THOITS, P. A. 1982: "Conceptual, Methodological, and Theoretical Problems in Studying Social Support as a Buffer Against Life Stress." J Hlth Soc behav 23: 145–159.

THOMAE, H. 1951: Persönlichkeit – eine dynamische Interpretation. Bonn: Bouvier.

THOMAE, H. 1959: "Zur Entwicklungs- und Sozialpsychologie des alternden Menschen." In: THOMAE, H. & U. LEHR (eds.) 1968, Altern – Probleme und Tatsachen. Frankfurt a.M.: Akademische Verlagsanstalt, 1–17.

THOMAE, H. 1960: "Die Lebensproblematik des erwachsenen Menschen." In: THOMAE, H. (ed.) 1969, Vita Humana – Beiträge zu einer genetischen Anthropologie. Frankfurt a.M.: Athenäum, 238–244.

THOMAE, H. 1968: Das Individuum und seine Welt. Göttingen: Hogrefe.

THOMAE, H. (ed.) 1976: Patterns of Aging – Findings from the Bonn Longitudinal Study of Aging. Basel: Karger.

THOMAE, H. 1983: Altersstile und Alternsschicksale. Bern: Huber.

THOMAE, H. & U. LEHR 1958: "Eine Längsschnittuntersuchung bei 30–50jährigen Angestellten." Vita Hum 1: 100–109.

THOMAE, H. & U. LEHR 1984 (in press): "Conflict and Stress – Organizers of the Life Course?" In: SORENSEN, A. B., WEINERT, F. E., & L. R. SHERROD (eds.), Human Development: Interdisciplinary Perspectives.

THOMAS, L. V. 1983: "La vieillesse en Afrique Noire." In: Communications. Vol. 37: Le Continent Gris. Paris: Seuil, 69–88.

TIETGENS, H. 1982: Jugend-Kultur und Erwachsenenbildung. Einsichten aus der Shell-Studie 'Jugend '81: Lebensentwürfe, Alltagskulturen, Zukunftsbilder.' Frankfurt a.M.: Deutscher Volkshochschul-Verband. Pädagogische Arbeitsstelle. Arbeitspapier 94 – 7.82.

TINDALE, J. A. 1980a: Generational Conflict: Class and Cohort Relations Among Ontario Public Secondary School Teachers. Toronto: York University, Department of Sociology (doctoral dissertation).

257

TINDALE, J. A. 1980b: "The Intersection of Age and Class Interests in a Profession Facing External Pressure." Paper presented at the IX. Annual Scientific and Educational Meeting, Canadian Association of Gerontology, Saskatoon, Saskatchewan.

TINDALE, J. A. & V. W. MARSHALL 1980: "A Generational Conflict Perspective for Gerontology." In: MARSHALL, V. W. (ed.), Aging in Canada: Social Perspectives. Toronto: Fitzhenry and Whiteside, 43–50.

TOURAINE, A. 1973: Production de la Société. Paris: Seuil.

TREAS, J. 1977: "Family Support Systems for the Aged: Some Social and Demographic Considerations." Geront 17: 486–491.

TREAS, J. 1979: "Intergenerational Families and Social Change." In: RAGAN, P. K. (ed.), Aging Parents. Los Angeles, Calif.: University of Southern California Press, 58–67.

TRILLING, L. 1972: Sincerety and Authenticity. New York: Oxford University Press.

TROLL, L. E. 1971: "The Family of Later Life: A Decade Review." J Marr Fam 33: 263–290.

TROLL, L. E. 1975: Early and Middle Adulthood. Monterey, Calif.: Brooks & Cole.

TROLL, L. E. 1980: "Interpersonal Relations." In: POON, L. W. (ed.), Aging in the 1980s. Psychological Issues. Washington, D.C.: American Psychological Association, 435–440.

TROLL, L. E. & V. BENGTSON 1979: "Generations in the Family." In: BURR, W. et al. (eds.), Contemporary Theories about the Family. Vol. 1. New York: Free Press, 127–161.

TROLL, L. E., MILLER, S., & R. ATCHLEY 1979: Families in Later Life. Belmont, Calif.: Wadsworth.

UNGERN-STERNBERG, R. 1931: The Cause of the Decline in Birth-Rate within the European Sphere of Civilization. Cold Spring Harbor: Eugenics Research Association Monograph Series 4.

U. S. BUREAU OF THE CENSUS 1973: "Some Demographic Aspects of Aging in the United States." Current Population Reports, Series P-23, No. 43 (February). Washington, D.C.: Government Printing Office.

VERHULST, P. F. 1838: "Notice sur la loi que la population suit dans son accroissement." In: QUETELLET, A. (ed.), Correspondance mathématique et physique.

WACHTER, K. W. (with E. A. HAMMEL & P. LASLETT) 1978: Statistical Studies of Historical Social Structure. New York: Academic Press.

WARING, J. M. 1976: "Social Replenishment and Social Change: The Problem of Disordered Cohort Flow." In: FONER, A. (ed.), Age in Society. Beverly Hills and London: Sage.

WATZLAWICK, P. 1981: "Epilog." In: WATZLAWICK, P. (ed.), Die erfundene Wirklichkeit. München: Piper.

WEBER, M. 1972: Wirtschaft und Gesellschaft. Grundriß der verstehenden Soziologie. Tübingen: Mohr (5th ed., Studienausgabe).

WEINBERG, I. & K. N. WALKER 1969: "Student Politics and Political Systems: Toward a Typology." Am J Soc 75: 77–96.

WESTBY, D. L. & R. G. BRAUNGART 1966: "Class and Politics in the Family Backgrounds of Student Political Activists." Am soc R 31: 690–692.

WHEATON, R. 1975: "Family and Kinship in Western Europe: The Problem of the Joint Family Household." Journal of Interdisciplinary History 4: 601–628.

WHELPTON, P. K. 1954: Cohort Fertility. Princeton: Princeton University Press.

WHITE, B. L. 1970: Human Infants: Experience and Psychological Development. Englewood Cliffs, N.J.: Prentice-Hall.

WHITE, R. W. 1974: "Strategies of Adaptation." In: COELHO, G. V., HAMBURG, D. A., & E. B. MURPHY (eds.), Coping and Adaptation. New York: Wiley, 47–68.

WIEDER, D. L. & D. H. ZIMMERMAN 1974: "Generational Experience and the Development of Freak Culture." J Soc Iss 30: 137–162.

WILKENING, E., GURRERO, S., & S. GINSBERG 1972: "Distance and Intergenerational Ties of Farm Families." Sociol Q 13: 383–396.

WILLIS, P. 1977: Learning to Labour. London: Saxon House.

WILLIS, P. 1978: Profane Culture. London: Routledge and Kegan Paul.

WINSBOROUGH, H. H. 1978: "Statistical Histories of the Life Cycle of Birth Cohorts: The Transition from Schoolboy to Adult Male." In: TAEUBER, K. E., BUMPASS, L. L., & J. A. SWEET (eds.), Social Demography. New York: Academic Press, 231–259.

WOLF-GRAAF, A. 1981: Frauenarbeit im Abseits. München: Frauenoffensive.

WOOD, V. & J. F. ROBERTSON 1978: "Friendship and Kinship Interaction: Differential Effect on the Morale of the Elderly." J Marr Fam 40: 367–375.

YARROW, L. J. et al. 1979: "Conceptualization of Father Influences in the Infancy Period." In: LEWIS, M. & L. A. ROSENBLUM (eds.), The Child and its Family. New York: Plenum, 45–66.

YOUNG, J. 1970: "The Zookeepers of Deviance." Catalyst 5.

YOUNG, J. 1972: The Drugtakers. London: Paladin.

YOUNG, M. & P. WILLMOTT 1973: The Symmetrical Family. London: Routledge and Kegan Paul.

ZARIT, S., REEVER, K., & J. BACH-PETERSON 1980: "Relatives of the Impaired Elderly: Correlates of Feelings of Burden." Geront 20: 649–655.

ZIEHE, T. 1981: "Lebensgeschichte und politisches Bewußtsein." In: MAURER, F. (ed.), Lebensgeschichte und Identität. Beiträge zu einer biographischen Anthropologie. Frankfurt a.M.: Fischer TV.

ZIEHE, T. & H. STUBENRAUCH 1982: Plädoyer für ungewöhnliches Lernen – Ideen zur Jugendsituation. Reinbek: Rowohlt.

ZINNECKER, J. 1981: "Jugendliche Subkulturen. Ansichten einer künftigen Jugendforschung." Zeitschrift für Pädagogik 3: 421–440.

List of Contributors

ATTIAS-DONFUT, Claudine;
Head of the Center for Research of Caisse Nationale D'Assurance Vieillesse (Social Security for the Aged), Paris (France).

BENGTSON, Vern L.;
Director: Gerontology Research Institute, University of Southern California, Los Angeles, Calif. (USA).

BERGER, Bennett M.;
Professor of Sociology: University of California, San Diego, Calif. (USA).

DREITZEL, Hans Peter;
Professor of Sociology: Freie Universität Berlin (West).

FONER, Anne;
Professor of Sociology: Rutgers State University, New Brunswick, N.J. (USA).

GARMS-HOMOLOVÁ, Vjenka;
Assistant Professor: Institute for Social Medicine, Freie Universität Berlin (West).

HAGEMANN-WHITE, Carol;
University Instructor for Sociology: Freie Universität Berlin (West).

HAGESTAD, Gunhild O.;
Associate Professor: Pennsylvania State University, Pa. (USA).

HEBDIGE, Dick;
Senior Lecturer: West Midlands College of Higher Education (Great Britain).

HELD, Thomas;
Lecturer and Principal Investigator: Department of Sociology, Universität Zürich (Switzerland).

HOERNING, Erika M.;
Research Associate: Max-Planck-Institut für Bildungsforschung, Berlin (West).

HOLLSTEIN, Walter;
Professor of Sociology: Evangelische Fachhochschule für Sozialarbeit, Berlin (West).

KNIPSCHEER, Kees;
Senior Faculty Member: Department of Sociology, Catholic University of Nijmegen (The Netherlands).

KNOPF, Detlef;
Research Associate: Institute for Social Paedagogy and Adult Education, Freie Universität Berlin (West).

KONDRATOWITZ, Hans-Joachim von;
Research Associate: Deutsches Zentrum für Altersfragen, Berlin (West).

KRUSE, Andreas; Research Associate: Department of Developmental Psychology, Universität Bonn (West Germany).

LANDRY, Pierre H., Jr.;
Research Co-ordinator: Gerontology Research Institute, University of Southern California, Los Angeles, Calif. (USA).

LEHR, Ursula;
Professor of Psychology and Director of the Institute for Developmental Psychology, Universität Bonn (West Germany).

MACKENSEN, Rainer;
Professor of Sociology: Technische Universität Berlin (West).
MANGEN, David J.;
Vice-President: Over 45, Inc., Minneapolis, Minn. (USA).
MARSHALL, Victor W.;
Associate Professor: Department of Behavioural Science, University of Toronto (Canada).
MEINHOLD, Marianne;
Professor of Social Psychology: Evangelische Fachhochschule für Sozialarbeit, Berlin (West).
ROSENMAYR, Hilde;
Research Associate: Ludwig Boltzmann Institute for Social Gerontology and Life Course Research, Vienna (Austria).
SCHAEFFER, Doris;
Research Associate: Institute for Social Medicine, Freie Universität Berlin (West).

262